and his sage and benign influence can be found everywhere in this book. Chapter 5 deals with ideas for which he is famous, and which will endure.

My family, to whom I dedicate this book, has had a lot to put up with, not least my insistence that my last days must be as creative as possible. And that is only the culmination of years of no doubt excessive drive to produce new work, as full of new ideas as possible. Much to his mother's consternation and amusement my son Henrik (21) let years of my so-called 'philosopher attacks' at the dinner table get under his skin, and has shown some remarkable talent and skill already as an undergraduate philosophy student. My daughter Annika (16) is a musician above all but even she quite likes the idea of a 'philosopher attack' and shows signs of being able to give as good as she gets. The holdouts are my youngest Audra (10) and my wife Jenny. Audra tells me that she plans to become an historian, chef, yoga teacher, and novelist. She cultivates a studied impatience towards philosophy, whereas her mother prefers a studied indifference. Or maybe feigned indifference? A boy can dream. I love them all more than any words can convey.

John Gardner
Oxford, May 2019

A note about the book

With amazing strength of mind, John completed the manuscript himself not much more than a few weeks before he died in July 2019. Consequently there was no need for me to make any academic decisions about its content, a possibility he envisaged in his preface. I have merely assisted with the final stages of the book's production. There is perhaps a small consolation in knowing that John and his work, of which this book is an important part, will be remembered and discussed for a very long time to come.

Sandy Steel
Oxford, August 2019

ACKNOWLEDGEMENTS

Chapter 1, 'Torts and Other Wrongs', was first published in *Florida State University Law Review* 39 (2011), 43.

Chapter 2, Reprinted by kind permission from the Springer journal *Law and Philosophy*. John Gardner, 'What is Tort Law For? Part 1. The Place of Corrective Justice', *Law and Philosophy* 30 (2011), 1. © Springer 2010.

Chapter 3, 'What is Tort Law For? The Place of Distributive Justice', is reprinted with changes from John Oberdiek (ed), *Philosophical Foundations of Tort Law* (OUP 2014).

Chapter 4, 'Backwards and Forwards with Tort Law' was first published in Joseph Keim Campbell, Michael O'Rourke, and David Shier (eds), *Law and Social Justice* (MIT Press 2005). Reprinted by kind permission of MIT Press.

Chapter 5, 'Obligations and Outcomes in the Law of Torts', is reprinted with corrections from Peter Cane and John Gardner (eds), *Relating to Responsibility* (Hart Publishing 2001). Used by kind permission of Bloomsbury Publishing Plc.

Chapter 6, 'Some Rule-of-Law Anxieties about Strict Liability in Private Law' first appeared in Lisa Austin and Dennis Klimchuk (eds), *Private Law and the Rule of Law* (OUP 2014).

Chapter 7, 'The Negligence Standard: Political Not Metaphysical' was my Chorley Lecture at the London School of Economics and was published in *Modern Law Review* 80 (2017), 1.

Chapter 8, 'The Mysterious Case of the Reasonable Person' is reprinted from *University of Toronto Law Journal* 51 (2001), 273.

Chapter 9, 'The Many Faces of the Reasonable Person', is from *Law Quarterly Review* 131 (2015), 56.

Chapter 10, 'Public Interest and Public Policy in Private Law', appears here for the first time in print.

Chapter 11, 'Breach of Contract as a Special Case of Tort', appears here for the first time in print.

CONTENTS

1

TORTS AND OTHER WRONGS

I

It is hard to think of any contemporary writers who have done more than John Goldberg and Ben Zipursky to reassert and reinvigorate what might be called the classical interpretation of the common law of torts. I for one am greatly in their debt. They have taught me a great deal, not only about torts, but also about how to combine legal argument felicitously with philosophical insight and historical scholarship. Like them, and partly because of them, I believe that the classical interpretation is the correct one. Other familiar ways of explaining what is going on in the common law of torts, while often illuminating in their own ways, are parasitic. They rely on the classical interpretation, often surreptitiously, for their appeal or even their intelligibility.

Given their influence over my own thinking, it hardly comes as a surprise that I have few significant disagreements with Goldberg and Zipursky. I do think, however, that they tend to equivocate on an important point of law, in a way that puts them at odds with some writers with whom they would do better to make common cause. This charge of equivocation is one that I make only with grave misgivings. That is not only because Goldberg and Zipursky stand out, among theorists of tort law, for their detailed knowledge of and sustained interest in legal doctrine, which they usually go to great lengths to spell out clearly. It is also because I am not sure to which body of law, exactly, their treatment should be held answerable. They give the impression that they are writing about the tort law of the United States of America. But it is doubtful whether there is such a thing. There are at least 51 legal systems in the United States with tort jurisdictions. Even if a national tort law can be distilled from this *melée*, it might well be hard to work out what it says on the point of law I have in mind. US legal systems, unlike other common law legal

Torts and Other Wrongs. John Gardner, Oxford University Press (2019). © John Gardner
DOI: 10.1093/oso/9780198852940.003.0001

systems, tend to use jury trials for the bulk of their tort litigation. It may be that trial judges tend to pass the buck to the jury on the point in question, and appellate judges then stay clear of it, with the result that the legal position is indeterminate. In that case there is no point of law for Goldberg and Zipursky to report, equivocally or otherwise.

In what follows, I will focus my attention on the law of torts, not in the United States, but in some other major common law jurisdictions (England and Wales, Canada, Australia, and New Zealand) in which tort cases are normally adjudicated by judges sitting without juries. So far as I am aware, these legal systems are all determinate, and all agree, on the point of law in question. If tort law in the United States is not determinate, or is determinate but does not agree, then what I am calling Goldberg's and Zipursky's equivocation is really something else. It is really their testimony to a respect in which the law of the United States has parted company with the law in the rest of the common law world. The problem, an English lawyer might then teasingly say, is with American tort law rather than with the Goldberg and Zipursky rendition of it. If that turns out to be the right diagnosis, then it goes a long way to explain why (as Goldberg and Zipursky lament) 'academics [in America] have lost their feel for this basic legal category [viz. tort].'[1] For, as I hope to show, one cannot have a proper feel for the category until one takes to heart this point of law that has only faltering or grudging recognition in the Goldberg and Zipursky analysis.

II

Goldberg and Zipursky famously say that 'civil recourse' is a defining feature of the law of torts.[2] I could not agree more. To

[1] John C P Goldberg and Benjamin C Zipursky, 'Torts as Wrongs', *Texas Law Review* 88 (2010), 917 at 919. I am relying principally on this article as a conspectus of Goldberg's and Zipursky's views, since it is a recent restatement. They have openly changed their minds over time on a number of points, so trawling through their extensive *oeuvre* may sometimes lead one astray. Having said that, I will also refer in §v below to Zipursky's important sole-authored article 'Civil Recourse, Not Corrective Justice', *Georgetown Law Journal* 91 (2002), 695 which deepens the theoretical foundations.

[2] 'Torts as Wrongs', above note 1, e.g. at 946.

spell the claim out: There is no law of torts if there is no legal power for someone who holds herself to have been on the receiving end of a tort (a 'plaintiff') to summon the alleged tortfeasor (a 'defendant') before the courts, and to do so unilaterally (without the leave of any official), with a view to obtaining a court-imposed or court-approved remedy against that defendant. It is then for the defendant, not any official, to apply for the case to be struck out. Otherwise the case marches on to trial, and in the absence of any defence marches on at the sole instance of the plaintiff to judgment against the defendant, and to the award of a remedy against the defendant. This feature (or set of features) amply distinguishes the law of torts from the criminal law, and from most if not all of public law.[3] In criminal law, even where private prosecutions are possible, they can be taken over (and discontinued) by the prosecutorial authorities. In public law a cause of action is available, in general, only with leave of the court. The unilateral power of the plaintiff is limited to applying for leave of the court, which issues the writ (traditionally *certiorari, mandamus, prohibito*, or *habeas corpus*) on the application of (or '*ex parte*') the applicant. Public law and criminal law therefore lack the defining apparatus of civil recourse.

Yet there is nothing here to help us distinguish the law of torts from the rest of private law. Indeed civil recourse, as I have just

[3] Some statutory causes of action are *sui generis* and hard to classify as public or private, so I am hedging my bets with 'most if not all'. For example, the cause of action against public authorities under the Human Rights Act 1998 s7, is not a cause of action in tort, and 'damages' under s8 are not to be measured on tort-law principles: *R* v *Secretary of State for the Home Department ex parte Greenfield* [2005] UKHL 14, [2005] 1 WLR 673. 'The 1998 Act,' said Lord Bingham, 'is not a tort statute' (para 19). Nevertheless, there is civil recourse under the Act in the Goldberg-Zipursky sense. For similar examples and *dicta* see *Maharaj* v *Attorney-General of Trinidad and Tobago (No 2)* [1979] AC 385, 399; *Kearney* v *Minister of Justice* [1986] IR 116; *Simpson* v *Attorney-General* [1994] 3 NZLR 667; *Taunoa* v *Attorney General* [2007] NZSC 70, [2008] 1 NZLR 429. But compare *Crossman* v *R* (1984) 9 DLR (4th) 588, where a violation of a Canadian Charter right is classed and treated as a tort. Goldberg and Zipursky lead us to believe that the latter is also the Federal United States position ('Torts as Wrongs', above note 1, 939) although the leading case of *Bivens* v *Six Unknown Federal Narcotics Agents* 403 US 388 (1971) seems to me to point the other way. The Goldberg and Zipursky talk of 'constitutional torts' in this context may, of course, incorporate their own (I will suggest insufficiently discriminating) analysis of what a tort is.

explained it, is a defining feature of private law as a whole in the common law systems. It is equally a feature of the law of breach of contract, the law of unjust enrichment, and the law of equitable (including trustee) liability. What do Goldberg and Zipursky say to help us understand how the law of torts is different from these other departments of private law?

Here is one thing they say. They say that torts are wrongs, so that the tort plaintiff seeking recourse necessarily alleges (whether expressly or by implication) that she has been wronged by the defendant—that the tortfeasor has violated her rights—and that she is entitled to have a remedy against him on that very ground.[4] Again I could not agree more. Torts are legal wrongs, i.e. breaches of legal duty or obligation[5], and they are legal wrongs against particular people, i.e. they violate particular people's legal rights. But this feature (or set of features) still does not help to distinguish the law of torts from the law of breach of contract or from the law of equitable liability. It only helps to distinguish it from the law of unjust enrichment. Although a wrongdoer may be unjustly enriched by his wrong, a claim against him for unjust enrichment does not depend for its success on his having been a wrongdoer.[6] It is enough that, were he to keep his gains at the plaintiff's expense, *that* would be a wrong against the plaintiff. Or, to put the contrast differently, the law of unjust enrichment offers remedies for what would be wrongs if not remedied. Whereas the law of torts, like the law of breach of contract, offers remedies for what are already wrongs at the time of the remedy, and on the ground that this is what they are.

On this point, as Goldberg and Zipursky point out, many have abandoned the classical interpretation of the law of torts. Following in Holmes' footsteps they have said that the law of torts and the law of breach of contract are, in the respect just discussed, no different from the law of unjust enrichment. The nomenclature notwithstanding, it is not wrong to commit a tort or

[4] Goldberg and Zipursky, 'Torts as Wrongs', above note 1, e.g. 918.

[5] In this chapter I will mainly speak of 'duty' but I could equally have chosen 'obligation', which means exactly the same.

[6] For painstaking analysis, see Peter Birks, *Unjust Enrichment* (2nd ed, Oxford 2005), 11–38.

to breach a contract. The only wrong (if there is one) is not to pay the price when one does.[7] Goldberg and Zipursky will have none of this. They argue that the supposed counterexamples to the thesis that torts are wrongs are not counterexamples at all (the trespass in *Vincent* v *Lake Erie*, for example),[8] or, if they are, that they should be regarded as peripheral (the innominate tort in *Rylands* v *Fletcher*).[9] Here Goldberg and Zipursky stand shoulder to shoulder with those who have exposed for the mistake it is the Holmesian heresy (later an economistic orthodoxy) about breach of contract.[10] In the process they implicitly maintain the classical continuity between the law of torts and the law of breach of contract, and draw the classical contrast between these two areas of law and the law of unjust enrichment.

So Goldberg and Zipursky agree that the law of breach of contract and the law of torts share the twin defining features mentioned so far (civil recourse, and for wrongs). They presumably think, and they would be right to think, that torts and breaches of contract differ from each other in some other yet-to-be-identified respect. But they say nothing at all about what I have called equitable liability, at least some of which is liability for wrongdoing. A breach of trust, a breach of fiduciary duty as a company director or attorney or agent, a breach of confidence: all these are equitable wrongs for which there is undoubtedly civil recourse against the wrongdoer. Goldberg and Zipursky ignore these

[7] Oliver Wendell Holmes, 'The Path of the Law', *Harvard Law Review* 10 (1897), 457 at 462. I should mention that, although I repeat it here, the attribution of this view to Holmes himself is contested: Joseph M. Perillo, 'Misreading Oliver Wendell Holmes on Efficient Breach and Tortious Interference', *Fordham Law Review* 68 (2000), 1085.

[8] John C P Goldberg, Anthony J Sebok, and Benjamin C Zipursky, *Tort Law: Responsibilities and Redress* (2nd ed, New York 2008), at 783–90, discussing *Vincent* v *Lake Erie Transportation Co* 124 NW 221 (Minn. 1910). The discussion is cited approvingly in 'Torts as Wrongs', above note 1, at 953.

[9] 'Torts as Wrongs', above note 1, 951–2, discussing *Rylands* v *Fletcher* (1868) LR 3 HL 330. Personally, I would tend to class *Rylands* with *Vincent* as not a counter-example at all. See chapter 5 below for explanation.

[10] Particularly effective *exposés* of the Holmesian mistake in the breach-of-contract context are Ian R Macneil, 'Efficient Breaches of Contract: Circles in the Sky', *Virginia Law Review* 68 (1982), 947 (where a useful catalogue of economistic true-believers may be found), and Daniel Friedmann, 'The Efficient Breach Fallacy', *Journal of Legal Studies* 18 (1989), 1.

wrongs. Indeed they do not seem to leave any separate logical space for them. They quote the characterization of tort law found in Prosser and Keeton's classic textbook. Torts are 'civil wrong[s], other than breach[es] of contract, for which the court will provide a remedy'.[11] As part of their move away from the classical interpretation and towards the newfangled Holmesian alternative, Prosser and Keeton ended up rejecting this as a way of demarcating tort law, but Goldberg and Zipursky endorse it.[12] In the light of this endorsement, we may legitimately ask them: Where do equitable wrongs fit into the classification? They are clearly 'civil wrongs ... for which the court will provide a remedy'. Equally clearly, they are not breaches of contract. Trusts, non-trust fiduciary duties, and confidences may but need not be contractually created, and when they are contractually created, an action for breach of contract exists alongside, and does not replace, the action for breach of trust or breach of fiduciary duty or breach of confidence (as the case may be). So should these breaches, these wrongs, be regarded as torts? No. Let me explain why not.

III

[C]ompensation is an equitable monetary remedy which is available when the equitable remedies of restitution and account are not appropriate. By analogy with restitution, it attempts to restore to the plaintiff what has been lost as a result of the breach, i.e. the plaintiff's lost opportunity. The plaintiff's actual loss as a consequence of the breach is to be assessed with the full benefit of hindsight. Foreseeability is not a concern in assessing compensation, but it is essential that the losses made good are only those which, on a common sense view of causation, were caused by the breach.[13]

[11] 'Torts as Wrongs', above note 1, 920 citing W Page Keeton et al, *Prosser and Keeton on the Law of Torts* (5th ed, St Paul MN 1984), 2. 11

[12] 'Torts as Wrongs', above note 1, 920.

[13] *Canson Enterprises* v *Boughton* (1991) 85 DLR (4th) 129 at 163. Although McLachlin J was speaking for a concurring minority in *Canson*, the passage above was quoted and endorsed as 'good law' by Lord Browne-Wilkinson in his lead speech in *Target Holdings Ltd* v *Redferns* [1996] 1 AC 421, and also found favour at the highest level in (e.g.) *Cadbury Schweppes Inc* v *FBI Foods Ltd* (1999) 167 DLR

Let's temporarily bracket what McLachlin J says about causation and foreseeability. Our immediate concern is with the trio of remedies that she associates with breach of equitable duty. Allow me briefly (and crudely) to expand on her taxonomy.

(a) Restitution. As McLachlin J uses the term, restitution is the return of an asset *in specie*. It reunites one party with the very thing that she lost to the other party, thereby extinguishing—in one fell swoop—the one's loss of that thing and the other's gain of it. An everyday situation (usually arising out of an unhappy contractual transaction rather than breach of an equitable duty) is that of mutual restitution. You have the car; I have the $1000 you paid me for it. Mutual restitution involves your returning the car to me and my returning the $1000 to you. The abstractness and fungibility of money means, of course, that it usually makes little sense to ask whether the $1000 I returned to you is the same money that originally changed hands, as opposed to just the same *amount* of money. This fact has licensed a wider loosening of talk about restitution, so that the word is often used to refer to returns of assets no longer *in specie*. You passed the car to a third party in exchange for a painting; so now, instead of the car, can I please have the painting? A court will sometimes 'trace' my claim on the car through to the painting. The problem is that, as the onward transactions build up, my loss and your gain increasingly come apart. You exchanged a bad car for a good painting, so if I get the painting in place of the car, on the basis that you transferred my $1000-worth of car for it, I take a $2000 gain off your hands even though I only made a $1000 loss on the car. That is no longer restitution in the strict sense. In fact there can no longer be restitution in the strict sense unless your transaction with the third party is unwound as well. If you have to pay me your full $2000's worth of gain, as distinct from the $1000's worth of loss that I suffered, it is usually better to think of that as a different kind of remedy, to which we now turn.

(b) Account (of profits). A trustee has a duty to restore to the trust accounts any assets that have been displaced from them by his or

(4th) 577 para 93, and *Youyang Pty Ltd* v *Minter Ellison Morris Fletcher* (2003) 212 CLR 484 para 40.

her breach of trust. Often there can be restitution in the strict sense, because the trustee still has the asset. But a trustee also has a duty to surrender to the trust accounts any profits he or she made on a trust asset, whether or not it was made by a breach of trust. So if she swapped the trust's car for a painting for herself, she has to hand over the painting even though it is worth $2000, and the car was only worth $1000. And she has to hand over the extra $1000 even if she already sold the painting for $2000 and used $1000 of the proceeds to buy back the car and return it faithfully to the trust. Why? Because any profit on dealings with a trust asset is automatically impressed with the trust. Disgorgement of this profit, as already indicated, is not restitution in the strict sense.[14] It extinguishes a gain, but it does not necessarily extinguish a loss. Any off-accounts profit made by the trustee is repayable to the trust even if it would not have accrued to the trust but for the off-accounts dealing, i.e. even if the trust is no worse off than it would have been had the off-accounts dealing not occurred.[15] So there need be no loss involved except the notional ('accounting') loss that is constituted by the absence of the gain. That gain, *qua* gain, is what equity chases under the heading of 'account', as McLachlin J is using the term.

One short path leads off from here to equity's handling of unjust enrichment; the trustee, to repeat, need commit no wrong to incur the liability to disgorge a profit, and in that respect he or she is in the same position as someone unjustly enriched (e.g. by the mistake of another). But a different short path connects the disgorgement liability of the trustee to the equitable liability of confidants and non-trustee fiduciaries. True, one cannot literally extend beyond the trust context the idea that the profit

[14] Compare a restitutionary claim against the trustee for the market rental value of the car during the period when it was, so to speak, missing from the trust. The two remedies are compared by Sarah Worthington, 'Reconsidering Disgorgement for Wrongs', *Modern Law Review* 62 (1999), 218. In writing this section, Worthington's analysis has helped me more than any other. However Worthington's analysis in turn owes much to James Edelman's path-breaking *Gain-based Damages: Contract, Tort, Equity, and Intellectual Property* (Oxford 2002), where the restitution/disgorgement contrast takes pride of place.

[15] A good example is *Bishopsgate Investment Management Ltd* v *Maxwell (No 2)* [1994] 1 All ER 261.

on a trust asset is automatically impressed with the same trust. Information can be held in confidence, but profit cannot. So when equity chases the gain made from trading in confidential information, or from fiduciary double-dealing not involving any use of a trust asset, it does so, not on the footing that the gain on an asset automatically belongs to whomever the asset belongs to (there is no asset here[16]) but on the different footing that the gain is *ill-gotten*. There is a duty not to make unauthorized profits from these equitable relationships, and the remedy for its breach is disgorgement of the very profits made.[17] What we have here is disgorgement as a remedy for equitable wrongs.

(c) Compensation. What McLachlin J calls 'compensation' is the mirror image of the disgorgement remedy just described. The latter remedy aims to eliminate gains made by a wrongdoer even when he inflicted no losses; the former aims to eliminate losses inflicted by a wrongdoer, even when she made no gains. A tort lawyer might be tempted to say that what we are dealing with here are compensatory or reparative *damages*. But '[w]oe betide' the lawyer who speaks of 'damages for breach of trust' or 'damages for breach of fiduciary duty'.[18] McLachlin J offers one reason why these are solecisms. The rules for the assessment of equitable compensation, she says, differ from the rules for the assessment of reparative damages at common law. In equity, she says, '[f]oreseeability is not a concern in assessing compensation'. This

[16] For discussion, see P M North, 'Breach of Confidence: Is There a New Tort?', *Journal of the Society of Public Teachers of Law* 12 (1972), 149.

[17] On disgorgement for breach of confidence, see *Peter Pan Manufacturing Corp* v *Corsets Silhouette Ltd* [1963] 3 All ER 402; *Lac Minerals Ltd* v *International Corona Resources Ltd* [1989] 61 DLR (4th) 14. On disgorgement for breach of fiduciary duty, see *Furs Ltd* v *Tomkies* (1936) 54 CLR 583 at 592; *Regal (Hastings) Ltd* v *Gulliver* [1967] AC 134; *Gwembe Valley Development Co Ltd* v *Koshy* [2003] EWCA Civ 1478; *Glazier* v *Australian Men's Health (No 2)* [2001] NSWSC 6. Note that a trustee dealing in assets can be made liable on the ill-gotten gains theory too, for she too—indeed *par excellence*—is a fiduciary bound by the duty not to profit. For discussion of the relationship of these two bases of liability see Steven B Elliott and Charles Mitchell, 'Remedies for Dishonest Assistance', *Modern Law Review* 67 (2004), 16 at 31–2.

[18] Sir Peter Millett, 'Equity's Place in the Law of Commerce', *Law Quarterly Review* 114 (1998), 214 at 225.

claim is contentious,[19] and more generally the differences in respect of assessment between common law damages and equitable compensation are unsettled.[20] Less contention, however, attaches to another difference—also brought out by McLachlin J's remarks—between reparative damages in tort law and compensation for equitable wrongs.

According to McLachlin J, equity prefers restitution and/or disgorgement, and resorts to a reparative award only where these other remedies are 'not appropriate'. Or at any rate, equity prefers restitution, and resorts to reparation only '[b]y analogy with' restitution. Either way, reparation does not have pride of place as a remedy for equitable wrongs. In this respect the law of torts is different. Reparative awards against tortfeasors can be supplemented by the court and eschewed by the plaintiff. But still they have pride of place as a remedy for tortious wrongdoing. They are not the remedy of last resort that they are for equitable wrongdoing; they are the remedy of first resort in the law of torts. Why this difference in remedial primacy? Here is one natural explanation, which is the explanation that I favour. The main reason why the defendant has duties to the plaintiff in the law of torts is to protect the plaintiff from losses, and the main mode of recourse that a plaintiff has against the defendant in a tort case is therefore recourse in respect of his losses.[21] This contrasts with

[19] This was the key point on which McLachlin J's concurring minority in *Canson* differed from the majority. See also Lionel Smith, 'The Measurement of Compensation Claims Against Trustees and Fiduciaries' in Elise Bant and Matthew Harding (eds), *Exploring Private Law* (Cambridge 2010) where McLachlin J is taken to task (I think wrongly) for thinking that 'a common sense view of causation' can do without remoteness restrictions.

[20] See *Bristol & West Building Society* v *Mothew* [1998] Ch 1 at 17 and *Bank of New Zealand* v *New Zealand Guardian Trust Co Ltd* [1999] 1 NZLR 664 at 681 for the suggestion that different equitable wrongs go with different assessment rules, some more like the common law rules than others.

[21] The 'therefore' in this sentence is licensed by what I have elsewhere called 'the continuity thesis', according to which reasons for not having φd survive one's φing and are now reasons for taking remedial measures. See chapter 2 below for further elaboration. As I emphasize there, it would be better still if one's φing could have been prevented. Prevention is analytically better, *ceteris paribus*, than cure. So we should welcome anything that the courts can offer by way of tort-prevention (including injunctions, exemplary damages, etc.). What I am adding

the position in equity where the main reason for the defendant's duties is to secure that the defendant's dealings are conducted for the plaintiff's advantage, and not for the defendant's own. So the emphasis in equity is on the diversion of advantage—in the form of assets or profits—as opposed to the causation of loss, which is tort law's first concern.

This explanation of the difference between tort remedies and remedies for equitable wrongs may touch a nerve for Goldberg and Zipursky. They contrast those who 'have placed losses at the center of tort theory' with 'those who wish to retain a tort theory centered on wrongs'.[22] They are not sure, on the evidence of my writings, where I stand with respect to this supposed divide.[23] You can now see why. In my view, the divide is artificial. My view is that the wrongs of tort law (including those that are actionable without proof of loss) exist primarily in order to protect people from loss. This view, which calls for a lot of careful unpacking, is both wrong-centred and loss-centred. For present purposes, however, further unpacking is unnecessary. We are not concerned here with how to *explain* the different remedial priorities of the law of torts and the law of equitable wrongs. What concerns us here is simply that there *are* such different remedial priorities. Why does this concern us here? Because Goldberg and Zipursky call it into question. Since they say nothing at all about equitable wrongs, they obviously do not query the claims I just made about the primacy of gain-based remedies for equitable wrongs. But they do make it their business to query the claims I just made about torts. They do not exactly deny, but they certainly put up resistance to, the idea that there is a primary or pride-of-place remedy in the law of torts, and they resist, in particular, the idea that reparative damages are it.

in this paper is only that all of this tort-prevention rides opportunistically (and discretionarily) on the coat-tails of the civil recourse that tort law offers as of right to those who have already been wronged, which is a specifically reparative kind of recourse.

[22] 'Torts as Wrongs', above note 1, 920.

[23] Ibid, 928, citing a draft of what now appears as chapter 2 below.

IV

I say that Goldberg and Zipursky 'do not exactly deny' the primacy of reparative damages because they agree that '[a] longstanding principle of remedies for nonwillful wrongs sets make-whole [reparative damages] as the default remedy'.[24] This turns out, however, to be both a limited and a double-edged concession. First, 'default remedy' is too weak to capture the special place of reparative damages in the law of torts. Second, 'for nonwillful wrongs' already sets the scene for the introduction of a rival view. Those who think of the primacy of reparative damages as extending more widely are portrayed by Goldberg and Zipursky as falling into the trap of mistaking the law of negligence for the law for the whole law of torts.[25]

The rival view is not long in coming. Goldberg and Zipursky resist the idea that reparative damages have a more general remedial primacy in the law of torts by observing that diverse remedies, indeed bewilderingly diverse remedies, are commonly granted in tort cases.[26] These include injunctions and exemplary (Americans say 'punitive') damages as well as reparative damages. Although Goldberg and Zipursky do not mention them, we could also add gain-based damages to the list.[27] We could also amplify some of their points. For some torts—notably private nuisance and trespass to land—plaintiffs are very often less interested in obtaining an award of damages than they are in obtaining an injunction against continuation or repetition of the tort. Indeed, it is common for plaintiffs in nuisance and trespass to land cases not even to claim damages, or rather to claim damages only in *lieu* of an injunction should the court for some reason decline to issue the injunction sought. Should we conclude that private nuisance and trespass to land are not torts? Clearly not. So why, ask Goldberg and Zipursky, should we think that torts are characterized by the

[24] Ibid, 947.

[25] See also Zipursky, 'Civil Recourse, Not Corrective Justice', above note 1, 752.

[26] 'Torts as Wrongs', above note 1, 955.

[27] *Attorney-General* v *Blake (Jonathan Cape Ltd Third Party)* [2001] 1 AC 268, a contract case but one in which analogies to tort were suggested *obiter*.

primacy of reparation? Different torts, different scenarios, different remedial devices.

This argument proceeds from good observation of legal practice, but it misses the point. Even if almost all tort litigation ended in injunction, because plaintiffs did not seek damages, reparative damages would still be the common law's remedy of first resort in the sense that we are after. For this is the only remedy against a tortfeasor that the successful plaintiff enjoys *as of right*. Injunctions (an equitable remedy)[28] and damages in *lieu* of injunctions (originally a statutory equitable remedy[29]) are available only in the

[28] *Law Debenture Trust Corporation* v *Ural Caspian Oil Corporation Ltd* [1995] Ch 152 per Saville LJ at 172 (where the point was of the essence); *Attorney-General* v *Blake*, above note 25, per Lord Nicholls at 284–5; *Virgin Atlantic* v *Premium Aircraft* [2009] EWCA Civ 1513, [2010] FSR 15 at para 23; *Cardile* v *LED Builders Pty Ltd* (1999) 198 CLR 380 at 396; *Maggbury Pty Ltd* v *Hafele Aust Pty Ltd* [2001] HCA 70, (2001) 210 CLR 181 at para 76; *Roberts v Rodney District Council* [2001] 2 NZLR 402; *Delta Hotels Limited* v *Okabe Canada Investments Company Limited* [1992] ABCA 176 at para 10.

[29] Under the Chancery Amendment Act 1858, also known as Lord Cairns' Act. Held to have survived the repeal of the Act in *Leeds Industrial Co-operative Society Ltd* v *Slack* [1924] AC 851. You may ask how, other than in being discretionary, these damages in *lieu* of injunction differ from ordinary reparative damages that the successful plaintiff enjoys as of right. To see what differentiates them, think about cases in which the defendant's trespass, if allowed to continue, would amount to an expropriation of property (e.g. cases of trespass by building on a neighbour's land). In such cases injunctions are often granted on the basis that reparative damages would not be an adequate remedy, this being one of the established criteria for the discretionary issue of an injunction. People are free, say the courts, to decide not to alienate their property even if they would be amply compensated for doing so; that freedom is of the essence in distinguishing property rights from some other rights. But where a trespassory building is already in place the courts may be reluctant to order its demolition (which may strike them as too wasteful) and may instead award damages in *lieu* of the injunction. These are equitable damages and may sometimes be calculated on a disgorgement basis: *Wrotham Park Estate Co. Ltd* v *Parkside Homes Ltd* [1974] 1 WLR 798. Notice that this all begins from the thought that these expropriation-like cases are cases in which the primary reparative measure of tort damages is not enough, and that could not be true were reparative damages not the primary measure. This all holds equally true in the other common law jurisdictions to which the 1858 Act was exported: *Madden* v *Kedereski* [1983] 1 NSWLR 305; *Roberts v Rodney District Council* [2001] 2 NZLR 402 (describing the disgorgement measure as 'anomalous' in the tort context); *Semelhago* v *Paramadevan* [1996] 2 SCR 415.

discretion of the court. Likewise exemplary damages[30] and disgorgement of profits.[31] This is one way in which the law, in all the jurisdictions I am familiar with, distinguishes torts from equitable wrongs. Whether equitable wrongs attract any remedy as of right is debatable. Possibly, as McLachlin J hints, all equitable remedies (or all equitable remedies except for proprietary remedies against trustees) are discretionary, and possibly that includes even what McLachlin J casts as equity's 'default remedy', restitution of an asset *in specie*. But it is not a matter of any significant debate—it is 'trite law'—that torts do attract a particular remedy as of right, and that that remedy is an award of reparative damages.[32]

I say that this is not a matter of any significant debate without meaning to suggest that it attracts no sceptical reactions. Andrew Burrows, for example, notes the received wisdom that 'equitable remedies are discretionary, while common law remedies are not', but brushes the distinction aside as 'highly misleading':

> It surely cannot seriously be suggested that the law is less certain—that a judge has more discretion—in deciding whether specific performance [of a contract] should be ordered than in deciding, in relation to damages, whether a loss is too remote or whether an intervening cause has broken the chain of causation or whether the claimant has failed in its duty to mitigate its loss.[33]

[30] *Kuddus* v *Chief Constable of Leicestershire Constabulary* [2001] UKHL 29; *A* v *Bottrill* [2002] UKPC 44; *Couch* v *Attorney-General* [2010] NZSC 27; *Whiten* v *Pilot Insurance Co* [2002] 1 SCR 595.

[31] *Attorney-General* v *Blake*, above note 25, per Lord Nicholls at 284–5. It is arguable that *Blake* awards, available only where an injunction is denied, are better classified as damages in *lieu* of an injunction. Be that as it may, there has been little enthusiasm for the decision. Much (award-avoiding) emphasis has been placed on Lord Nicholls' remark that disgorgement awards for common law wrongs are 'exceptional'. See *Hospitality Group Pty Ltd* v *Australian Rugby Union Ltd* [2001] FCA 1040, (2001) 110 FCR 157; *Bank of America Canada* v *Mutual Trust Co* (2002) 211 DLR (4th) 385.

[32] Recent judicial remarks in which this is treated as a trite point not requiring citation of authority include *Anufrijeva* v *Southwark LBC* [2003] EWCA Civ 1406, [2004] QB 1124 paras 50, 56; *Majrowski* v *Guy's and St Thomas' NHS Trust* [2006] UKHL 34, [2007] 1 AC 224 paras 21–2 per Lord Nicholls, para 46 per Lord Hope; *Taunoa* v *Attorney General* [2007] NZSC 70, [2008] 1 NZLR 429 paras 252, 318; *Commonwealth* v *Mewett* [1997] HCA 29, (1997) 191 CLR 471 per Gummow and Kirby JJ.

[33] Andrew Burrows, 'We Do This at Common Law but That in Equity', *Oxford Journal of Legal Studies* 22 (2002), 1 at 2.

That's quite true, but again it misses the point. A right to reparative damages at common law is a right to some reparative damages. The job of the court is, *inter alia*, to determine what the amount is to be. The tort plaintiff claims unliquidated damages and the court liquidates them, i.e. crystallizes them into a money sum, which can then be recovered as a judgment debt. I would be the first to agree that in doing so the court exercises discretion about a range of matters bearing on the quantification of loss.[34] It even has some discretion about how to conceptualize 'loss' for these purposes. But it has no discretion about whether to exercise these discretions. It is legally bound to make a reparative award of some kind if one is sought by the successful plaintiff, because he or she has a right to such an award.[35] By contrast, the court is not legally bound to issue an injunction of any kind, or to order any kind of disgorgement of profits, or to award any kind of exemplary or punitive damages (even at common law).

How about restitution, a remedy known to common law as well as to equity? There are many important tort cases (mainly in conversion and trespass to land) in which damages have been awarded on an ostensibly restitutionary basis,[36] and occasionally the successful plaintiff is said to have a right to elect that basis of

[34] Why would I be the first? Because I am what they call a 'hard legal positivist' who thinks that when the law invites courts to judge the 'reasonableness' of something (or to use other evaluative criteria) it necessarily invites courts to step outside the law to complete their deliberations, except to the extent that the evaluative criteria have already been unpacked by law into non-evaluative ones. For more detail of this view, see my 'Justification under Authority', *Canadian Journal of Law and Jurisprudence* 23 (2010), 71.

[35] There is a general lesson here about rights, both legal and moral. As Joseph Raz says, '[a]ssertions of rights are typically intermediate conclusions in arguments from ultimate values to duties.... [T]he implications of a right ... and the duties it grounds, depend on additional premisses and these cannot in principle be wholly determined in advance.... Because of this rights can be ascribed a dynamic character. They are not merely the grounds of existing duties. With changing circumstances they can generate new duties.' Joseph Raz, *The Morality of Freedom* (Oxford 1986), 181 and 185–6.

[36] I am thinking of miscellaneous cases including *Livingstone* v *Rawyards Coal Co* (1880) LR 5 App Cas 25; *Carr-Saunders* v *Dick McNeil Associates Ltd* [1986] 1 WLR 922; *Inverugie Investments Ltd* v *Hackett* [1995] 1 WLR 713; *Costello* v *Chief Constable of Derbyshire* [2001] EWCA Civ 381, [2001] 1 WLR 1437; *Severn Trent Water Authority Ltd* v *Barnes* [2004] EWCA Civ 570.

award.[37] The proper interpretation of these cases is disputed. At least some of them, it is sometimes said, should be reclassified as discretionary disgorgement cases.[38] Or in at least some of them, it is said, the award, although genuinely restitutionary, should be understood as remedying an unjust enrichment which occurred in tandem with the commission of the tort, thus not as a tort remedy at all.[39] Or, it is said, there was indeed a restitutionary award for the tort itself in at least some of these cases, but it can be reanalysed, in one way or another, as reparative.[40]

Such a reanalysis would not be totally surprising since, as noted above, restitution *strictu sensu* annuls the defendant's gains and the plaintiff's losses in one fell swoop. Equity is more interested in chasing the defendant's gain; so in equity, restitution fades into disgorgement. The common law of torts, by contrast, is more interested in remedying the plaintiff's loss, and so tends to emphasize the loss side of the restitutionary equation. It is true that in property-use cases the courts sometimes have to go to considerable lengths to present what they tellingly[41] call 'restitutionary damages' as loss-rectifying, and in doing so they may even be forced to abandon ways of thinking about loss that are standard elsewhere in tort law, even resorting to fictions.[42]

[37] *United Australia Ltd* v *Barclay's Bank* [1941] AC 1.

[38] See *Attorney-General* v *Blake*, above note 25, at 284–5 per Lord Nicholls.

[39] See *Strand Electric Co* v *Brisford Entertainments* [1952] 2 QB 246 at 254–5 per Denning LJ; *Greenwood* v *Bennett* [1973] QB 195 at 202 per Lord Denning MR; *Kuwait Airways Co* v *Iraqi Airways Co (Nos 4 & 5)* [2002] 2 AC 883 paras 67 and 79 per Lord Nicholls.

[40] See *Stoke City Council* v *W & J Wass* [1988] 1 WLR 1406 at 1416; Law Reform Committee, *18th Report* (Cmnd 4774, London 1971), para 91.

[41] Harvey McGregor, 'Restitutionary Damages' in Peter Birks (ed), *Wrongs and Remedies in the Twenty-First Century* (Oxford 1996), 203: 'damages for damage'.

[42] For lively discussion (with rival proposals for sorting out the mess) see Edelman, *Gain-based Damages*, above note 14, at 114–36; Robert Stevens, *Torts and Rights* (Oxford 2007), 79–84. Stevens suggests that we should think of the damages in most such cases as 'substitutive', not reparative, a distinction that is also drawn by Edelman in 'Money Awards of the Cost of Performance', *Journal of Equity* 4 (2010), 122 using the terms 'substitutive compensation' and 'reparative compensation', and crediting the distinction to Steven Elliott. I regard Elliott's proposed 'substitution' measure of compensation, not as a rival to the reparative measure, but as just one among many possible reparative measures, the choice among which depends on the logic of 'next-best conformity' as sketched in my 'What is Tort Law For?', chapter 2. (On my view, in summary, substitution stands to reparation

That they do so is not a sign of cracks appearing in the doctrine of the primacy of reparation in the common law of torts. It is, on the contrary, testament to the power of that doctrine. The courts are under pressure to find a loss, however understood, to which they can attach a quantification, because reparative damages are the damages to which the successful plaintiff has a right.

Where a tort can be committed without causation of loss (e.g. trespass or libel) there is, of course, a possible scenario in which a plaintiff proves the tort but has no losses to recover, even by an unorthodox accounting of losses. Here the court is bound to award nominal damages. Goldberg and Zipursky regard this as another sign that reparative damages are not as special as they are made out to be.[43] But again it points the other way. The courts do not regard themselves as legally free to deny reparative damages to the plaintiff even when there is nothing to repair. The court can however express the point that there is nothing to repair by awarding a symbolic sum. Indeed the court can go further. It can award such a conspicuously trifling sum that it thereby expresses contempt for the plaintiff who was such a stickler for his rights that he insisted on upholding them expensively and painfully in court even when the defendant's violation of them caused him no loss. If the plaintiff had no right to damages, nominal and contemptuous damages would not be needed and would not carry the meanings that they do. The court could simply declare that a tort was committed and be done with it. And if the defendant's right to damages were not a right to reparative damages, how would we explain the fact that nominal (and contemptuous) damages are to be awarded only in cases in which the plaintiff proved no loss, i.e. had nothing relevant to repair? The explanation is that they are not just nominal damages but nominally reparative damages. In that way, the existence of nominal damages confirms rather than refutes the primacy of reparative damages as a remedy in the law of torts.

as terrier stands to dog. Reparation in turn stands to correction as dog stands to canine.)

[43] 'Torts as Wrongs', above note 1, 955.

V

In buttressing the Goldberg-Zipursky case against the primacy of reparative damages as a remedy in the law of torts, Zipursky (writing alone) is at great pains to deny that there is a legal duty on tortfeasors to pay reparative, or indeed any other, damages. 'Rather,' he says, 'the law imposes liability upon a tortfeasor.'[44] I am not sure what he means. Sometimes he seems to be saying that even after an award of reparative damages has been made by the court—even after the court has liquidated the plaintiff's unliquidated claim—there is no legal duty on the tortfeasor to pay those damages.[45] If that is what he means then he is helping himself to a false contrast between 'duty' and 'liability'. The primary liability of tortfeasors is none other than a liability to be placed under a duty by the court to pay a liquidated sum in reparative damages. Paying that sum is what the court orders the defendant to do, on pain of further recourse against him by the plaintiff in an action, now not for tort, but for recovery of an unpaid judgment debt.[46] That this action for recovery of a debt is an action for enforcement of a duty to pay can only be doubted by way of a further Holmesian heresy with which (I take it) Zipursky would not wish to be associated, according to which one has no legal duty to pay one's legally recognized debts.

Fortunately, however, Zipursky more often appears to mean something more limited and less Holmesian by his 'no legal duty to pay' thesis. He appears to mean only that the tortfeasor has no legal duty to pay any reparative damages *unless and until ordered to pay them by the court*.[47] I disagree, and with reason,[48] but happily the

[44] 'Civil Recourse, Not Corrective Justice', above note 1, 719, cited with apparent approval in Goldberg and Zipursky, 'Torts as Wrongs', above note 1, at 954.

[45] 'Civil Recourse, Not Corrective Justice', above note 1, 698: 'tort judgments represent liabilities, not duties to pay'.

[46] Which brings with it a new raft of remedies, such as attachment of earnings and seizure of assets.

[47] 'Civil Recourse, Not Corrective Justice', above note 1, 720: a tortfeasor does not have 'a freestanding legal obligation to pay independent of any action against her'.

[48] In England and Wales, statutory interest may (and in some circumstances must) be awarded on damages awards for the period between the cause of action arising and the award of damages by the court, on the basis that 'a judgment

disagreement is irrelevant here. Even if the tortfeasor lacks a legal duty to pay reparative damages before the court awards a liquidated sum in reparative damages against her, that does not alter the fact that the court has a legal duty to award a liquidated sum in reparative damages against her if the tort is proved. This legal duty exists because the successful plaintiff has a legal right to reparative (now taken to include nominally reparative) damages. The plaintiff's right grounds a legal duty on the court to impose a new legal duty on the tortfeasor, a legal duty that is also grounded (by the court, and by the law) in the plaintiff's right.

VI

Their resistance to the idea that reparative damages have a special primacy in the law of torts combines with their scattered remarks partly conceding the opposite to yield a pattern of equivocation in Goldberg and Zipursky's work. If I am right it is equivocation on a point of law on which (in the common law systems I am familiar with) no room for equivocation exists. This equivocation by Goldberg and Zipursky is patently connected—I am not sure whether as cause or as consequence—with their wish to keep their distance from what they call 'corrective justice' explanations of tort law. They regard a 'corrective justice' explanation as a rival to a 'civil recourse' explanation; they would rather set up in competition to than in league with those, such as Jules Coleman,[49] Ernest Weinrib,[50] Stephen

against the defendant means that he should have admitted the claim when it was made and have paid the appropriate sum as damages': Law Revision Committee, *Second Interim Report* (Cmd 4546, London 1934). This rationale was approved by the Court of Appeal in *Jefford* v *Gee* [1970] 2 QB 130 at 144 and associated with earlier (common law) *dicta* on the same point. On this view an award of tort damages places a retrospective legal duty on the defendant, a duty to have paid the award before it was awarded. Consider, in broad support of this view, McLachlin J's *dictum* in *Canson*, above note 13, that 'viewing the issue of compensation from the date of the breach [is] required at common law' (but not, she adds, in equity, which looks at losses instead from the date of the trial).

[49] See e.g. Jules Coleman, 'Tort Law and the Demands of Corrective Justice', *Indiana Law Review* 67 (1992), 349.

[50] See e.g. Ernest Weinrib, 'Understanding Tort Law', *Valparaiso Law Review* 23 (1989), 485.

Perry,[51] and Arthur Ripstein,[52] who emphasize the element of corrective justice in tort law. That seems to me to be a mistake—not a legal one but a philosophical one. It is a mistake because 'corrective justice' is an answer to a different question from 'civil recourse'. Once we know that the law of torts involves civil recourse, we naturally want to know what form the recourse takes. 'Corrective justice' tells us that it takes a primarily corrective form, that the law of torts attempts, through the recourse it gives, to put one or both of the parties to the proceedings into the same position that they would have been in had the wrong, the tort, not been committed. Compare that, if you like, with civil recourse that takes a primarily punitive form, attempting to impose loss on the defendant because of some wrong he did whether or not it thereby corrects any gain or any loss that came of the wrongdoing itself. There is no corrective justice in that. That is purely retributive justice. Possibly in some jurisdictions the retributive and the corrective are given equal pride of place in the award of damages in (what are still called) tort cases. But to go this way is to have 'lost [one's] feel for this basic legal category'.[53] Or so I have claimed in this paper.

So it is tempting to render what I have claimed in this paper in the following (more theoretically highfalutin) terms. To distinguish the law of torts adequately from other branches of law we need to combine the Goldberg and Zipursky 'civil recourse' theory of tort law with some kind of 'corrective justice' theory, such as Coleman's. This restatement of what I have said would give the right general impression, but it is in several respects misleading. For a start, everything I have said above about the law of torts applies equally (*mutatis mutandis*) to the law of breach of contract, so the manoeuvre of combining 'civil recourse' with 'corrective justice' would still not be adequate to distinguish the law of torts from the law of breach of contract. To do that, we would clearly need to add a further criterion on top of 'civil

[51] See e.g. Stephen Perry, 'The Moral Foundations of Tort Law', *Iowa Law Review* 77 (1992), 449.

[52] See e.g. Arthur Ripstein, 'As if It Had Never Happened', *William and Mary Law Review* 48 (2007), 1957.

[53] Zipursky may well agree. See his critical remarks on the culture of punitive damages in his 'Civil Recourse, Not Corrective Justice', above note 1, 751–2.

recourse' and 'corrective justice'. Otherwise we accidentally, and mistakenly, classify breach of contract as a tort.

More significantly, however, the combination of 'civil recourse' and 'corrective justice' doesn't distinguish tort law from the law of unjust enrichment or from the law of equitable wrongs. These departments of private law are equally about correcting things, about putting one or both of the parties to the proceedings into the same position that they would have been had something not gone amiss. They just have different things to correct, and different ways of correcting them. Corrective justice can be reparative but it can also be disgorgative (excuse the coinage) or restitutionary. So 'corrective justice' doesn't really help with the specific problem that has been the focus of this paper, namely that of how to isolate tort law from its various private law neighbours. By the time we get to *that* problem we are already in the neighbourhood of corrective justice. Two criteria we need to add to differentiate tort from two of its close neighbours in the neighbourhood (I have argued) are these: that the correction involved in tort law is the correction of wrongs (unlike in the law of unjust enrichment), and that it is correction that takes a primarily reparative form (unlike in the law of equitable wrongs). But all of this is corrective justice.

We could sum up the position that I have sketched in this paper by saying that the law of torts is a law of

(a) civil recourse
(b) for wrongs
(c) in which primarily corrective justice is attempted
(d) in a primarily reparative mode
(e) in response to claims for unliquidated sums
(f) where the duties breached are non-contractual.

Criterion (a) serves to distinguish the law of torts from criminal law and most if not all of public law. Within private law, criterion (b) keeps it apart from the law of unjust enrichment and some parts of the law of trustee liability. Criterion (c) makes the contrast between the law of torts and a conceivable branch of law in which there is, say, a primarily retributive aim to civil recourse. Criterion (d) keeps the law of torts distinct from the law of equitable wrongs. Criterion (e) is needed to draw the distinction—which I have only mentioned in passing—between the original proceedings to obtain an award of damages against the tortfeasor and subsequent proceedings for enforcement of the award as a judgment debt (a liquidated sum). More generally, criterion (e) means that proceedings for debt recovery are not tort proceedings. Finally, criterion (f) serves as a placeholder for some future explanation of why breach of contract is not a tort even though it meets all of the other conditions.[54]

Criteria (a), (b), and (f) are endorsed by Goldberg and Zipursky, whereas criteria (c), (d), and (e) are not. I suppose they may think that (e) is redundant on the basis that actions for debt already fall outside tort law thanks to criterion (b). I suggested at the end of section v that this is a mistaken thing to think; actions for debt, including actions for enforcement steps to be taken towards recovery of a judgment debt, are premissed on wrongful non-payment of the debt. More central to this paper, however, has been my argument that Goldberg and Zipursky's resistance to (d) involves them in equivocations about a settled legal doctrine, and that this is bound up with the philosophical error that Goldberg and Zipursky make in trying to distance themselves from (c). Tort law cannot be understood without understanding the primacy of the reparative, which entails the primacy of the corrective, in its remedial doctrines. The result of their omitting these criteria is that, in the work of Goldberg and Zipursky, the law of torts is incompletely differentiated from the rest of private law. It follows that the classical interpretation is incompletely, even though valiantly and insightfully, represented.

VII

You may think there is something decidedly vain, or academic in the pejorative sense, about the task of identifying the defining features of the law of torts, as my list (a) to (f) purports to do. If

[54] Although the details cannot be entertained here, my explanation would link the distinction between breach of contract and tort to the source of the obligations breached (do they or don't they have their source in a contract?), rather than to the remedies available for the breach.

true, this is bad news for Goldberg and Zipursky as well as for me. So let me end by explaining some of the project's importance.

First, it is important in the law. Legally, designating some wrong as a tort is a way of taking quite a significant body of doctrine off the shelf and applying it to that wrong. Not only do we import the right to reparative damages, with all of its implications; we also import, as McLachlin J suggests, various standard common law doctrines about causation, remoteness, quantification, mitigation of damage, exclusion and limitation of liability, and so on. It is a big question, in drafting legislation that creates new civil wrongs, and in interpreting such legislation, whether to make the new wrongs part of the law of torts (with all of these potential common law implications) or whether to make them freestanding.[55] You may say that if this is true then I should add various other defining features to my list (a) to (f) above. I should add criteria about causation, remoteness, quantification, mitigation, etc. But that doesn't follow. Not everything that is a legal implication of making something a tort is by that token a defining feature of the law of torts. There are some legal implications that could be present in one legal system but absent in another, although both have a law of torts. There are also some implications that could change over time without the law of torts being thereby abandoned or 'lost sight of'. That is important, because when legislation designates some wrong as a tort, one consequence is that the legal treatment of the wrong will tend to vary with future changes in the law of torts as a whole (i.e. changes in its standard common law doctrines). There would come a point, however, at which such future changes would destabilize the category, by removing defining features in such a way as to make the decision to designate something as a tort unintelligible to those who come afterwards. Perhaps that has happened in some jurisdictions in the United States? That would help to explain the otherwise inexplicable rise of the view—which seems illiterate to those of us

[55] A plum example is *Simpson* v *Attorney-General* [1994] 3 NZLR 667 where, had it been classified as an action in tort, an action for redress against a public authority under the New Zealand Bill of Rights Act 1990 would have failed owing to crown immunity under the Crown Proceedings Act 1950.

trained in the law of other common law jurisdictions—that the law of torts is somehow reimaginable as 'the law of accidents'.

You will notice that I have just opened up some space for Goldberg and Zipursky to resist my charge of equivocation about the law. 'True,' they might say, 'reparative damages are the only remedy available as of right in the common law of torts. We never meant to deny it. But it does not follow that this is a defining feature of the law of torts. Some legal implications of making something a tort, as you say, are not defining features of the law of torts.' This is a possible line of response. I have tried, however, to pre-empt it in this paper by suggesting that if we do not include the right to reparative damages as one of its defining features, the law of torts is insufficiently differentiated from some nearby branches of law, notably but not only the law of equitable wrongs. Goldberg and Zipursky may reply that this is a question-begging enterprise. It is an open question how much differentiation one needs, or at least how much differentiation one should expect to achieve before concluding that the rest is an accident of history. I agree. In a sense, indeed, everything we are discussing is an accident of history. The law could have developed in other ways and we could have ended up with differently differentiated areas of law. There need never have been a law of torts; it is an accident of history that there is, and that there is a law of contract, of trusts, of unjust enrichment, etc. All I would add is that the law of torts, for all its happenstance, has not simply bequeathed a more or less miscellaneous list of torts. It has also bequeathed a more or less miscellaneous list of features in virtue of which, according to the law, these qualify as torts, a list which I have tried to summarize as (a) to (f). Why add 'accident of history' to the list? The list itself is the accident of history.

This brings us to a second reason, related to the first, for stopping to identify the defining features of tort law. As areas of law take shape, they also take root. Each develops its own way of differentiating itself and its own related way of accounting for itself, a rationale, or more often a set of connected but partly competing rationales, for its own existence. There are then, as it were, local narratives available to the courts in justifying particular features of the law in that area, as well as in justifying changes to those features of the law. Sometimes these changes include changes to the very criteria by which the relevant area of the law is identified, and thus differentiated from other nearby areas. There is no timelessness and no inevitability to these differentiations. But that is not to say that they can be casually dispensed with. You may think that if some rational resources are good for the law's development, then more rational resources must be better, so that breaking down the boundaries between areas of law can only increase the richness of the available narratives, and hence make for law that is increasingly responsive to reality, or decreasingly cut off from it. Not so. Narrative coherence is not scalable.[56] Growing indifferent to the established legal differences between torts and equitable wrongs, or becoming rationalistically fixated with harmonizing contract with tort, is apt to create an incomprehensible *brouhaha*: not a more unified narrative, not a bigger choice of narratives, but no intelligible narrative at all. And with no narrative, no future for development of the law by legal argumentation.

This is not a manifesto for keeping the law as it is. The law of torts is the common law's main offering for dealing with quite a wide range of social problems and personal conflicts. We may reasonably wonder whether it is (still) up to the task of dealing with them, or whether it needs to be reformed or replaced. Before we can work out whether it is up to the task, however, we need to know what exactly it is. This brings us to a third reason for caring about the defining features of tort law. How can there be tort law reform if we have lost sight of what tort law is? If politicians and pundits think it is 'the law of accidents' won't they just run amuck with their so-called reform proposals, aiming at the wrong targets, firing in crazy directions, and doing more collateral damage to the law in the process than will ever be compensated by any improvements that they may secure? Yes, they will, and they do. Many well-meaning people proposing improvements to the law of torts fall at the very first hurdle of not having much idea what the law of torts is, maybe thinking of it as another name for 'compensation culture' or 'ambulance-chasing lawyers' or 'class-action racketeering'. I do not suggest for one moment that Goldberg and Zipursky's conceptual work, let alone my own, will help to

[56] For useful reflections, see Barbara Levenbook, 'The Role of Coherence in Legal Reasoning', *Law and Philosophy* 3 (1984), 355.

solve this problem. Possibly the people who harbour such wild misconceptions are not much interested in being put right, or do not have the time or inclination or patience to read the scholarly literature, or even to have it explained to them. But scholarly writing about the law does not have to justify itself by showing its actual influence on anybody. It has to justify itself by showing that its influence would be good if, by chance, it had any. Subject to the narrow criticisms I have made in this paper, Goldberg and Zipursky's joint work on tort law amply meets this condition.

2

WHAT IS TORT LAW FOR? THE PLACE OF CORRECTIVE JUSTICE

1. The ends of tort law

What is tort law for? This may strike some as a leading question. It may seem to predispose us towards what Ernest Weinrib calls a 'functionalist' answer: an answer that makes tort law the servant of some 'external end', such as the minimization of suffering, the compensation of injuries, or the prevention of accidents. According to functionalists, says Weinrib,

> the justificatory worth of the [law's] goals is independent of and external to the law that they justify. To continue with the tort example, deterring accidents and compensating accident victims are socially desirable quite apart from tort law.... If tort law forwards them, so much the better. The goals, however, are independently justifiable and do not derive their validity from tort law.[1]

Isn't it possible, as Weinrib replies to the functionalists, that tort law is 'its own end'? To put it less cryptically, isn't it possible that tort law has some ends that are internal to it in the sense that tort law helps to constitute them, and not merely to serve them? Yes, it is possible. But the question 'what is tort law for?' does not suggest otherwise. It is not a functionalist question in Weinrib's sense. True, it is a teleological question. It assumes that tort law is the kind of thing that has ends. But it does not assume that these ends are exclusively or mainly 'external'. At any rate, I ask the question without building in that assumption. For above all I want to assess the anti-functionalist answer to it that Weinrib himself endorses. What tort law is for, according to Weinrib, is to do justice between the parties to a tort case. More specifically, it is to do *corrective* justice between the parties to a tort case. Corrective justice is a special kind of justice that, according to Weinrib, the

[1] Ernest Weinrib, *The Idea of Private Law* (Cambridge, Mass 1995), 4.

Torts and Other Wrongs. John Gardner, Oxford University Press (2019). © John Gardner
DOI: 10.1093/oso/9780198852940.003.0002

law of torts helps to constitute, and not merely to serve. To that extent, tort law exists for its own special end.

The question 'what is tort law for?' may also seem to harbour an elementary ambiguity. In Jules Coleman's words:

> There is an important and familiar distinction between theoretical explanations and theoretical justifications. While both can illuminate or deepen our understanding, explanations do so by telling us what the nature of a thing is, or by telling us why things are as they are; by contrast, justifications seek to defend or legitimate certain kinds of things—for example, actions, rules, courses of conduct, practices, institutions, and the like.[2]

In asking what tort law is for, is one asking for an explanation or a justification? The choice, it seems to me, is a false one. True, not all explanations are justifications. But all justifications are explanations. To justify something is to explain it rationally. It is to set out some or all of the reasons why it is as it is.[3] Anyone who tries to explain anything in terms of reasons for it cannot but be concerned with the justification of that thing. Coleman himself, like Weinrib, seeks to explain tort law in terms of corrective justice. Since 'corrective justice' designates a kind of reason—or more precisely, a kind of norm, norms being givers of reasons—this is an unavoidably justificatory enterprise.

Both Coleman and Weinrib shy away from presenting their enterprises as justificatory. Weinrib claims that tort law itself is a justificatory enterprise, but he equivocates about whether he,

[2] Jules Coleman, *The Practice of Principle* (Oxford 2001), 3.

[3] See my 'Justifications and Reasons' in Gardner, *Offences and Defences* (Oxford 2007). Strictly speaking, justification is but one type of rational explanation. The other type is excuse. Rational explanation is in turn but one type of teleological explanation. Non-rational but teleological explanations include the explanation of plant behaviour as phototropic. Plants are goal-oriented creatures with no rationality, and hence the goals of which are not open to rational scrutiny. Teleological explanations are in turn a sub-class of causal explanations, using 'causal' in its broad Aristotelian sense. Often, however, 'causal' is used in a narrow sense to refer only to those broadly causal explanations that are non-teleological. Causal explanations in this narrow sense do not cite a goal to be achieved in the future but an explanatory factor in the past. Many errors in many fields of inquiry come of (a) recasting rational explanations as causal in the narrow sense or (b) treating 'functional' explanation as a *tertium quid* between rational explanation and causal explanation in the narrow sense, when there is no such *tertium quid*.

in invoking corrective justice, is in turn attempting to justify the justificatory enterprise of tort law.[4] Coleman is more forthright. He denies that his enterprise of explaining tort law in terms of corrective justice is a justificatory one.[5] Why? Because he wants to emphasize that he is remaining aloof from two important questions. First, he is remaining aloof from the question of whether any norms of corrective justice are sound norms. Secondly, he is remaining aloof from the question of whether those norms of corrective justice that are sound, if any, have enough force to support the retention of tort law in the face of well-known objections to it (e.g. its hugely expensive litigation industry, its consequent encouragement of disproportionately risk-averse behaviour, its corollary stimulation of ambulance-chasing, claim-harvesting, and other miserable types of money-grubbing behaviour, its tendency to instill in each of us a sense that someone, meaning someone else, must always be to blame, and its perverse incentivization—to be discussed in section 3 below—of justice-evading behaviour).

Coleman is certainly entitled to remain aloof from these questions. But he should not conclude that his enterprise is non-justificatory. To see why, consider his own remarks about economists of law who try to remain aloof from similar questions about the force of economic reasons:

> [W]e could wonder why we should be concerned about which liability rules are [economically] efficient. There must be a policy reason behind interests; and as long as there is, the question of the normative roots of efficiency will still be with us. Still, there is a difference between saying: If you want to promote utility or wealth then these are the rules you should adopt; and saying: Because these rules would promote utility or wealth . . . we should adopt them.[6]

There is clearly a difference between these two statements. But equally clearly it is not the difference between a non-justificatory statement and a justificatory one. Both are statements about what should be done and why, and hence both are justificatory. They

[4] See John Gardner, 'The Purity and Priority of Private Law', *University of Toronto Law Journal* 46 (1996), 459 at 464.

[5] Coleman, *The Practice of Principle*, above note 2, 5–6.

[6] Jules Coleman, 'Efficiency, Utility, and Wealth Maximisation' in Coleman, *Markets, Morals and the Law* (Cambridge 1988), 95 at 359n64.

differ only in that the first is noncommittal, whereas the second is committal. A committal justificatory statement or inquiry is a statement or inquiry about what is justified. A noncommittal justificatory statement or inquiry is a statement or inquiry about what would be justified if certain conditions were to hold, leaving open the question of whether they do indeed hold. Coleman's inquiry fits the latter specification. He is asking whether, *if* the relevant norms of corrective justice were sound, and *if* all else were equal, tort law would be justified.[7] His answer is yes. To my way of thinking, this makes 'corrective justice' Coleman's provisional answer to the question 'what is tort law for?', understood as a justificatory question. I say 'provisional' because of course he still has the option of concluding that the relevant norms of corrective justice are unsound, or that, although sound, they lack sufficient force to repel some or all of the plethora of competing considerations that militate against the retention of some or even all of the law of torts.

Coleman argues, indeed, that corrective justice can supply a *complete* answer to the question 'what is tort law for?' He argues that 'the theory' (viz. corrective justice) provides 'a complete account of what it purports to explain' (viz. the law of torts).[8] Here he does not mean to retreat from his noncommittal justificatory stance. He only means to fortify his noncommittal justificatory claim. He means: If the relevant norms of corrective justice were sound, and if all else were equal, then norms of corrective justice would be *all that one needs* to justify the main (he calls them 'structural') features of the law of torts.

Here too Coleman and Weinrib converge. As Weinrib puts the point, 'the analysis of tort law in terms of possible aims such as compensation or deterrence is incompatible with the understanding of tort law as the operation of corrective justice'.[9] At first sight this claim seems unrelated to Coleman's. It suggests that, in justifying tort law, no extra considerations *can* be conjoined with norms of corrective justice, not that no extra considerations *need* be conjoined with norms of corrective justice. But it turns out that Weinrib regards the latter claim as inseparable from the

[7] *The Practice of Principle*, above note 2, 5.
[8] Ibid, 34.
[9] *The Idea of Private Law*, above note 1, 212.

former. Both are aspects of what Weinrib calls the 'autonomy' of private law as a way of doing justice.[10] So Weinrib's claim is stronger than Coleman's, but it still commits Weinrib, with Coleman, to the completeness of 'corrective justice' as an answer to the question of what tort law is for.

This emphasis on completeness strikes me as peculiar. It seems to me that the first task of both authors, even by their own lights, is to establish the necessity rather than the sufficiency of invoking corrective justice in explaining what tort law is for. Can one explain what tort law is for *without* invoking corrective justice? After all, the main challenges that both authors are trying to fend off are from functionalists,[11] including many in the 'law and economics' tradition, who claim that they can provide complete rational explanations (committal or noncommittal justifications) of tort law from which norms of corrective justice have been excised, usually by reducing them to considerations of other, more purely functionalist, types. One does nothing to refute such claims by showing that one can equally provide complete rational explanations (committal or noncommittal justifications) of tort law from which all considerations *except* considerations of corrective justice have been excised. What would refute the functionalist claim, however, is a demonstration that any complete explanation of tort law—whatever other considerations it may invoke—cannot but invoke considerations of corrective justice. Considerations of corrective justice cannot be reduced out. They are necessary even if not sufficient.

In what follows I will build on the work of Coleman and Weinrib to explore, and ultimately to affirm, this latter view.

2. Corrective justice as a form of justice

Norms of justice are moral norms of a distinctive type. They are norms for tackling *allocative* moral questions, questions about who is to get how much of what. Some people think of all moral questions, or at least all moral questions relevant to politics and law, as

[10] Ibid, ch 8 (and *passim*).

[11] Coleman too dubs them 'functionalists', meaning roughly the same by that as Weinrib does: *The Practice of Principle*, above note 2, 13ff.

allocative. But that is a mistake. As a rule, allocative questions are forced upon us only when people make competing claims to assignable goods. Many morally significant goods, including many relevant to politics and law, are either not competed for or not assignable. They include goods such as living in a peaceful world and not being tortured. If one of us lives in a peaceful world then we all do, so this good is not assignable. And in principle there is an unlimited amount of non-torture to go round, so there need be no competition for it. Of course it does not follow that there are no questions of justice that bear on the resort to torture or on the quest for a peaceful world. The point is only that many moral questions about the resort to torture and the quest for a peaceful world are not questions of justice. If, for example, we say of someone who was tortured by the secret police that her treatment was unjust, she might well say, if her moral sensitivity has been left intact, that this misses the point and marginalizes her grievance. She is not complaining that she was the wrong person to be picked out for torture, that she was a victim of some kind of misallocation by the secret police, that she of all people should not have been tortured. She is complaining that torture should not have been used at all, against anyone. Her complaint is one of barbarity, never mind any incidental injustices involved in it.

H L A Hart made much of this point in his famous treatment of the justification of punishment.[12] He argued that the question of how to distribute punishments should be regarded as a question of justice. But not so the question of whether to have a practice of punishing in the first place, he thought, for that is not an allocative question. Or is it? Arguably punishment is a special case. Arguably punishing, unlike torturing, is an essentially allocative action, such that one cannot separate the question of whether to indulge in it at all from the question of how to distribute it. Punishment, unlike torture, is by its nature exacted *for* something (viz. for some wrong or supposed wrong). So anyone who begins their evening out by saying 'let's punish some people tonight' is making no sense until we get an answer to the question 'Punish them for what? What are they supposed to have

[12] See his 'Prolegomenon to the Principles of Punishment' in H L A Hart, *Punishment and Responsibility* (Oxford 1968).

done?' This question is already an allocative question, a question that calls for some rational linking of punishments to the people who will receive them. So arguably, *pace* Hart, one cannot raise any allocation-independent questions about the justification of punishment. Arguably all norms regulating punishment are norms of justice, even though there is no competition for punishment.[13] That, at any rate, is one major objection to Hart's thesis. Convincing or not, it shows that the justification of punishment is a problematic choice for illustrating the distinction between norms of justice and other moral norms. On the other hand, Hart is clearly right to think that there is such a distinction, and right in the way he draws it: norms of justice, he rightly sees, are norms for tackling allocative moral questions. 'They are concerned,' in Hart's own formulation, 'with the adjustment of claims between a multiplicity of persons.'[14]

Hart's treatment is also problematic in another way. The particular norm of justice that Hart regards as the only sound one for allocating punishment does not strictly speaking allocate punishment at all. A norm of justice is one that mentions a *ground* for allocating whatever it is that it allocates. A ground for allocating is a condition of allocation that is also a reason for that allocation. That I am a wrongdoer, most people think, is not just a condition but a reason for punishing me. I should be punished only if *and because* I am a wrongdoer. So there is a sound norm of justice, most people think, according to which wrongdoing grounds punishment (subject to competing considerations, such as excuses). Hart dissents. He accepts that I should be punished only if I am a wrongdoer but he denies that I should be punished *because* I am a wrongdoer. My being a wrongdoer is no reason to punish me. Rather, my not being a wrongdoer is a reason *not* to punish me (as well as a sufficient condition of my non-punishment). Therefore justice, according to Hart, only gives a ground for non-punishment. It gives no ground for punishment.

[13] This is the thesis that Anthony Quinton was groping towards in 'On Punishment', *Analysis* 14 (1954), 512. I am grateful to Les Green for helping me to see how my earlier (more unreservedly Humean) understanding of the domain of justice was too narrow in this respect. Green discusses the issue in his so-far unpublished paper 'The Germ of Justice'.

[14] 'Prolegomenon to the Principles of Punishment', above note 12, 21.

To put the point more formally, there is for Hart no sound norm of justice according to which wrongdoing grounds punishment (even allowing for competing considerations). This idea is well captured by saying that Hart is no retributivist: he endorses no norm of retributive justice, but only a norm of distributive justice that incidentally regulates the allocation of punishment. The norm regulates the allocation of punishment incidentally to regulating the allocation of non-punishment. The idea is not well captured by saying that Hart endorses a 'negative' norm of retributive justice. A norm of retributive justice, if that expression means anything, is a norm according to which (subject to competing considerations) wrongdoing grounds punishment. And Hart endorses no such norm.[15]

Norms of justice, to put the lesson concisely and more generally, answer questions about who is to get how much[16] of what *and why* (i.e. on what grounds). As we have just discovered, norms fitting this description can be divided into various types. Aristotle famously taught us to distinguish, at the top level of the classification, between norms of distributive justice and norms of corrective justice.[17] One may well doubt Aristotle's suggestion that every norm of justice is either a norm of distributive justice or a norm of corrective justice. In the light of what we just learned about punishment, shouldn't we treat norms of retributive justice as *sui generis*, and not a mere sub-class of norms of distributive justice?[18] Besides, don't norms of procedural justice (e.g. *audi alterem*

[15] For elaboration of these points see my critical introduction to the second edition of Hart's *Punishment and Responsibility* (Oxford 2008), xxiv–vi.

[16] Where the possible answers include 'all of it' and 'none of it'. I spell this out to avoid a misunderstanding that arose in conversation with Ben Zipursky. Ben thought that, if Jones is convicted and punished for Smith's crime, this is not, on my account, an injustice. Why? Because there is no question of how much punishment Jones, as opposed to Smith, should get. But I say there is such a question. There must be such a question because there is an answer: Jones should get none of it whereas Smith should get all of it. Jones' punishment, in other words, was misallocated to Smith.

[17] EN 1130^{b}30ff.

[18] This is Rawls' point in *A Theory of Justice* (Cambridge, Mass 1971), 314–15. Some, taking the point for granted, try to preserve the Aristotelian dichotomy by assimilating retributive justice to corrective justice instead. See e.g. J P Day, 'Retributive Punishment', *Mind* 87 (1978), 498.

partem, nemo in sua causa iudex) constitute a distinct type, neither distributive not corrective?[19]

Arguably so. Be that as it may, however, norms of distributive justice and norms of corrective justice stand to each other in an interesting and important contrast, which Aristotle expressed in vivid mathematical terms. Norms of distributive justice are to be understood on the 'geometric' model of division. There are several potential holders of certain goods or ills and the question is how to divide the goods or ills up among them.[20] Norms of corrective justice, on the other hand, are to be understood on the 'arithmetic' model of addition and subtraction. Only two potential holders are in play at a time. One of them has gained certain goods or ills from, or lost certain goods or ills to, the other. The question is whether and how the transaction is to be reversed, undone, counteracted. Should we add what has been subtracted, subtract what has been added, or leave things as they are?[21] Of course the result of the addition or subtraction could always still be represented as a division of the spoils: gains are divided 100:0 against the person who gained by the transaction, say, or losses are divided 60:40 in favour of the person who lost by it (imagine that she was contributorily negligent or failed to mitigate her loss). But this representation of the result as a division fails to bring out that the result depended on a special kind of norm designed to tackle a special kind of allocative question.[22] Something has already shifted between the two parties. The question of corrective justice is not the question of whether and to what extent and in what form and on what ground it should now be allocated among them *full stop*, but the question of whether and to what extent and in what form and on what ground it should now be allocated *back* from one party to the other, reversing a transaction that took

[19] I replied with a qualified 'yes' in my 'The Virtue of Justice and the Character of Law', *Current Legal Problems* 53 (2000), 1.

[20] EN 1131^{b}12–15. [21] EN 1132^{a}1–6.

[22] Cf. Wojciech Sadurski, 'Social Justice and Legal Justice', *Law and Philosophy* 3 (1984), 329. Sadurski argues (at 334ff) that corrective justice collapses into distributive justice. His argument proceeds mainly by reading 'distributive' broadly to mean 'allocative', and hence to include all of justice. (He also errs by stretching corrective justice in the characteristic Thomist way so that it becomes unrecognizable as corrective: see note 28 below.)

place between them. A norm of corrective justice is a norm that regulates (by giving a ground for) the reversal of at least some transactions.

Misinterpretations of this contrast abound. Perhaps the most common misinterpretation is the one which portrays norms of corrective justice as somehow more *personal* than norms of distributive justice. For some this means (a): conformity with norms of corrective justice is a matter of agent-relative concern (I am rationally concerned only with the extent of my own conformity); whereas conformity with norms of distributive justice is a matter of agent-neutral concern (we are each rationally concerned with the extent of everyone's conformity).[23] For others it means (b): a norm of corrective justice only regulates the actions of the person from whom the transfer back is to be made, so only that person can conform or fail to conform with such a norm; whereas a norm of distributive justice regulates the actions of others apart from the person from whom the transfer is to be made (the state, for example, might conform or fail to conform to such a norm by transferring something from me to you).[24] Propositions (a) and (b) had better not be true if 'doing corrective justice' is to be a possible answer to the question 'what is tort law for?' Only if my conformity with a norm of corrective justice can be of concern to people other than me, contrary to (a), can it be of concern to the law. And only if someone other than me can conform or fail to conform with a norm of corrective justice in my case, contrary to (b), can the law be bound by a norm of corrective justice to take something from me and transfer it back to you without my co-operation (e.g. by ordering the attachment of my earnings or bank accounts, or the seizure of my car or house).

We can rescue the law's role in doing corrective justice through these latter enforcement devices if we weaken proposition (b) so that it turns into proposition (c): a norm of corrective justice only

[23] Stephen Perry, 'The Mixed Conception of Corrective Justice', *Harvard Journal of Law and Public Policy* 15 (1992), 917 at 919–20.

[24] Jules Coleman, *Risks and Wrongs* (Cambridge 1992), 310–11 and 318. Departing from the usage of most moral philosophers, Coleman labels this the agent-relative/agent-neutral distinction, inviting confusion between (b) and (a).

regulates the actions of the person from whom the transfer back is to be made *or another person acting on behalf of that person*. And (c) strikes me as true. To explain how corrective justice can be done as between two parties without the co-operation of the party from whom the transfer back is to be made we need to explain the possibility of vicarious agency: how there can be an agent who acts on my behalf, such that on occasions I can be regarded as having conformed to norms of corrective justice even though it was someone else that did the allocating back for me. Explaining this possibility is a tricky task which I will not be undertaking here.[25] My interest here is different. Does proposition (c) mark a difference between corrective justice and distributive justice? I know of no reason to think that it does. Proposition (c) is also true, *mutatis mutandis*, of norms of distributive justice. When the law secures redistribution of wealth or income through taxation, it does so on behalf of those from whom it levies the taxes. It acts as their vicarious agent in securing their conformity—more precisely, in securing that they will count as having conformed—to those norms of distributive justice that apply to them anyway.[26] So norms of distributive justice are neither less nor more personal than norms of corrective justice. Both types of norms call for conformity by the person from whom the allocation is to be made, or by someone else acting on that person's behalf. And conformity with both types of norms, we should add, is a matter of agent-neutral concern: be it corrective or be it distributive, an injustice perpetrated by anyone is in principle everyone's business, and anyone at all has reason to help in securing its avoidance (whether by the agent himself or by another person acting on his

[25] It is best pursued by thinking first about the role of liability insurance in private law. How can my duties of corrective justice be performed on my behalf by my insurer? Armed with an answer to the question we can begin to see how my duties of corrective justice could also, in default of performance by me or my insurer, be performed on my behalf by my bank or my employer or a bailiff, etc., acting with the law's authorization. I have had an initial stab at thinking about what it means to act on behalf of someone in my 'Some Types of Law' in Douglas Edlin (ed), *Common Law Theory* (Cambridge 2007).

[26] The most sustained defence of this view is by G A Cohen. For a good start, see his 'If You're an Egalitarian, How Come You're So Rich?', *Journal of Ethics* 4 (2000), 1, especially the critique of Dworkin at 17–19.

behalf). Seen in this light, norms of corrective justice are no more personal than norms of distributive justice.

A second and perhaps more pernicious misinterpretation of the contrast between corrective and distributive justice would have it that norms of corrective justice are sensitive to the past (they set 'backward-looking' grounds of allocation) whereas norms of distributive justice look to the future (they set 'forward-looking' grounds of allocation). The mistake here was decisively exposed by Robert Nozick. Nozick established that, on its most familiar interpretation, the everyday norm 'finders keepers' is a norm of distributive justice, not a norm of corrective justice.[27] True, it is a norm for dividing up goods along what Nozick called 'historical' as opposed to 'end-result' lines. It effects a division that is sensitive to the past, viz. to the fact that different people found different goods. But still the norm answers the geometric question of whether and why things should be allocated among people *full stop*, not the arithmetic question of whether and why things should be allocated *back* from one person to another. Couldn't we, under some imaginable circumstances, turn 'finders keepers' into a norm of corrective justice? Couldn't we imagine a world in which, so far as competed-for and assignable goods are concerned, there are no *res nullius* and no *res derelictae*? Everything is already someone's. Every act of finding is therefore an act of taking from another. Under these conditions wouldn't 'finders keepers' become a (negative) norm of corrective justice with the following content: 'when things are taken from someone else by finding, the transaction between them stands and is not to be reversed'? No it wouldn't. The proposed norm still wouldn't mention any ground for allocating anything back. It would merely deny that a taking is such a ground. Anyone who asserted 'finders keepers' under these conditions would not be asserting the existence of a 'negative' norm of corrective justice, any more than Hart is asserting the existence of a 'negative' norm of retributive justice. There is no such thing. Such a person would merely be denying that there is any corrective justice to be done in the case.

Nozick's observations are also of great value in exposing a third misinterpretation of the contrast between distributive and

[27] Robert Nozick, *Anarchy, State, and Utopia* (New York 1974), 153–5.

corrective justice. Since norms of corrective justice regulate bipartite allocations—allocations back from just one party to just one other party at a time—one may easily slip into thinking that all norms that regulate bipartite allocations are norms of corrective justice. Weinrib goes down this road, and he has the Thomistic reconstruction of Aristotle for company.[28] Once again, however, Nozick has exposed the error decisively. As well as 'finders keepers', his norm of justice applicable to *res nullius* and *res derelictae*, Nozick offers a further norm of justice applicable to things that have already been found. Roughly, the norm is 'surrenderers losers'. A second way for things to be justly allocated, he says, is for them to be voluntarily sold or gifted by those who justly acquired them (whether under 'finders keepers' or under 'surrenderers losers' itself). All of this, Nozick rightly points out, belongs to the theory of distributive justice. It is all about allocation *tout court*. 'Surrenders losers' never gives us a ground for allocating anything back. On the contrary: inasmuch as it regulates allocations back, it only ever gives us a ground for *not* allocating back. And there is, as we just saw, no such thing as a negative norm of corrective justice. In his world, as Nozick points out, the norms of distributive justice 'finders keepers' and 'surrenderers losers' only need to be supplemented by a norm of corrective justice when someone takes what I originally found *without* my having surrendered it. Now the question is: am I morally entitled to have it back? Nozick's own answer was famously 'yes'. If I found something that was nobody's, and then someone else took it from me by finding it again, without my having surrendered it, I am entitled to have it back on the ground that it was taken from me.[29] 'Finders keepers' and 'surrenders losers' were Nozick's main norms of distributive justice; 'takers returners' was his main norm of corrective justice. Yet both 'surrenders losers' and 'takers returners' regulate only bipartite allocations. This is enough to show that what distinguishes a norm of corrective justice is not the mere fact that it regulates bipartite allocations. An

[28] *The Idea of Private Law*, above note 9, e.g. at 64–5. See similarly John Finnis, 'Thomistic Reconstruction of Corrective Justice as "Commutative Justice"' in his *Natural Law and Natural Rights* (Oxford 1980).

[29] *Anarchy, State, and Utopia*, above note 27, 230–1.

interesting implication is that tort law could have the sole end of doing justice between the parties to a tort case without being restricted to doing *corrective* justice between the parties. Justice between the parties might also include an element of (local) distributive justice. This cannot be ruled out by the essentially bipartite character of the case. If it is to be ruled out, it must be ruled out on some other basis.[30]

Nozick's important insights about the difference between norms of corrective justice and norms of distributive justice have been widely ignored. Probably this is because most people doubt whether his favoured norms of justice are sound, or even close to sound. They suspect, in my view rightly, that a 'finders keepers'/'surrenders losers'/'takers returners' world is a world rife with heinous injustices. But this suspicion is irrelevant to the lessons we just learned. It is one question whether a certain norm of justice is a norm of corrective justice or a norm of distributive justice. It is a completely separate question whether it is a *sound* norm of justice, such that by relying on it and conforming to it we would, all else being equal, be acting justly. The difference between norms of distributive justice and norms of corrective justice lies in the fact that they regulate different subject matters. Norms of distributive justice regulate the allocation of goods among people together with the grounds of such allocations ('division'). Norms of corrective justice regulate the allocation of goods back from one person to another together with the grounds of such allocations back ('addition and subtraction'). But no norm is made sound or unsound simply by virtue of what it regulates. To be a sound norm it also has to do a *good job* of regulating whatever it regulates. There needs to be an adequate case for regulating that subject matter by that norm.

You may be tempted to say in response that norms of justice are sound by definition. But that is a subtle distortion of the truth. It is true that whatever is just is to that extent and in that respect analytically worth pursuing. It is admittedly contradictory to say: That solution is just but it has nothing going for it, morally

[30] I will be discussing whether this should be ruled out in chapter 3.

speaking.[31] But this is because a solution is just if and only if it is in conformity with a sound norm of justice. If it is in conformity with a norm of justice, but the norm is unsound (like 'finders keepers'), then it is not a just solution. So norms of justice are not analytically sound. 'Sound norm of justice' is no tautology; 'unsound norm of justice' is no oxymoron.

This brings us to our first doubt about 'corrective justice' as an answer to the question 'what is tort law for?' Possibly, to provide an adequate account of what tort law is for, one needs to invoke a norm of corrective justice. But that can only be the first step. The next step has to be to show what the norm of corrective justice that one invoked has going for it. One should not imagine that this task is restricted to showing what this norm has going for it as compared with other norms of corrective justice. One also needs to be aware that possibly no norms of corrective justice are sound. Perhaps the only sound norms of justice are norms of distributive justice. Perhaps the just person is one who approaches every allocative problem as if no transactions have ever taken place and hence everything is still available for first allocation. This is more radical than the familiar proposal (yielding a perennial sophomoric objection to tort law) that it cannot be correctively just to give back to the original holder what the original holder did not justly hold before the transaction that is being reversed. That proposal invokes no norm of corrective justice, for it does not give any ground for allocating anything back. It merely sets a necessary condition for any norm of corrective justice to meet before it can be sound, and hence a sufficient condition for such a norm to be unsound. The more radical suggestion before us now is that every single norm of corrective justice is unsound, never mind what extra conditions it meets. Everything that is up for allocation—including the losses that are at stake in a tort case—should be regarded as *res nullius* or *res derelictae*, and should be allocated as if for the first time. True, this would be a surprising conclusion, but still one needs to show what exactly would be wrong with it. So one cannot satisfy oneself with answering the question 'what is tort law for?' simply by citing a norm of corrective justice. One has to

[31] Cf. Matthew Kramer, 'Justice as Constancy', *Law and Philosophy* 16 (1997), 561 who denies (e.g. at 569) that unjust acts are analytically objectionable.

go on to the next step of explaining what this norm of corrective justice itself is for, what the norm has going for it, what makes it sound. And 'corrective justice' clearly cannot be the answer to this further question. Why not? Because 'corrective justice' still just names a type of norm distinguished by the subject matter that it regulates. We have still not been told what case there is for having or conforming to any such norm, what makes any norm of corrective justice sound.

So far, this is just another way of saying that 'corrective justice' is a studiously noncommittal answer to the question 'what is tort law for?' It leaves open whether the law of torts is worth retaining, and merely tells us that *if* the law of torts is worth retaining, that is at least partly because it lives up to some norm of corrective justice that is worth living up to. But possibly our doubt about 'corrective justice' as an answer to the question 'what is tort law for?' can be deepened. On closer inspection, it may seem that the answer 'corrective justice' can't even take us the first step in understanding what tort law is for. Once we see that norms of corrective justice are differentiated from other norms only by what they regulate, we see that some legal norms are themselves norms of corrective justice. The norm of tort law according to which (legally recognized) wrongdoers are required to pay reparative damages in respect of those (legally recognized) losses that they wrongfully occasion,[32] on the ground that they wrongfully occasioned those losses, is one such. It is a norm by which some people are to get back at least some of what they lost from the person at whose hands they lost it. As Coleman himself says: 'These features of tort law are plain to anyone without the benefit of theory.'[33] So when people ask 'what is tort law for?', they are already asking, by necessary implication, what the legal norm of corrective justice itself is for. That norm is part of the law, 'plain to anyone'. Corrective justice, in other words, is part of the thing that needs

[32] I say 'occasion' rather than 'cause' to accommodate the huge late-twentieth century extension of personal (as opposed to vicarious) tort liability that was heralded by *Dorset Yacht Co.* v *Home Office* [1970] AC 1004. I tend to think this was a wrong turning in the law—that *Dorset Yacht* should have been treated as a vicarious liability case—but the argument is irrelevant here.

[33] *The Practice of Principle*, above note 2, 21.

to be rationally explained, part of the *explanandum*. So how can Coleman, or anyone else, think that it is (even the beginning of) the rational explanation?

The most powerful version of this critique is owed to Richard Posner.[34] A 'corrective justice' account of tort law cannot conceivably be a rival, Posner argues, to an economic analysis of tort law. To cite corrective justice is merely to remind us of one thing that has to be justified when we justify tort law. It does nothing to actually justify it. An economic analysis, by contrast, makes some effort to justify this feature of tort law. It has a go at showing what tort law's norm of corrective justice might have going for it. As Posner puts the point:

> Economic analysis supplies a reason why the duty to rectify wrongs, and the corollary principle of distributive neutrality in rectification, is (depending on the cost of rectification) a part of the concept of justice. Corrective justice is an instrument for maximizing wealth, and in the normative economic theory of the state—or at least in that version of the theory that I espouse—wealth maximization is the ultimate objective of the just state.[35]

So the problem with 'corrective justice', for Posner, is not that it supplies only the beginning of an answer to the question 'what is tort law for?' The problem is that it is merely a restatement of the question, because tort law is (on any sensible view, including the economic view) partly constituted by the legal norm of corrective justice that awards reparative damages against tortfeasors in the wake of their torts. The real question, with which economic analysts grapple heroically, but their 'corrective justice' opponents seem curiously reluctant even to mention, is: What is tort law's norm of corrective justice for? What does it have going for it? The answer espoused by Posner himself may be asinine, the typical answer of one who knows the price of everything and the value of nothing. But at least it is an answer. Whereas 'corrective justice', as it stands, is no answer at all.

[34] Richard Posner, 'The Concept of Corrective Justice in Recent Theories of Tort Law', *Journal of Legal Studies* 10 (1981), 187.

[35] Ibid, 206.

3. Corrective justice as an instrument of corrective justice

Posner's critique goes too far. It is true that tort law already includes a norm of corrective justice, the norm according to which (legally recognized) wrongdoers are required to pay reparative damages in respect of those (legally recognized) losses that they wrongfully occasion, on the ground that they wrongfully occasioned them. But a possible view is that, in accounting for this legal norm of corrective justice, one must rely on a further norm of corrective justice the force of which is not merely legal, i.e. a *moral* norm of corrective justice. One must rely, perhaps, on a counterpart moral norm whereby wrongdoers are morally required to pay reparative damages in respect of those losses that they wrongfully occasion. Such a moral norm is what many writers seem to have in mind when they offer 'corrective justice' as an answer to the question 'what is tort law for?' Of course in giving this answer these writers haven't yet got very far. As I just made clear, they still have to explain what their moral norm of corrective justice, in turn, is for—what it has going for it. But nor are they simply standing still, as Posner's critique suggests. They have made a preliminary move. They have mentioned something other than the *explanandum*. The *explanandum* is a legal norm of corrective justice; the proposed rational explanation begins, although it obviously can't end, with a counterpart moral norm of corrective justice.

How exactly could these two norms of corrective justice be related, such that the moral one needs to be relied upon in explaining the legal one? Weinrib and Coleman both argue that it must be understood as a constitutive relationship. The legal norm of corrective justice serves its moral counterpart by giving shape to it, by determining at least some of its applications. Weinrib's version of this thesis is more ambitious than Coleman's. Weinrib thinks that the counterpart moral norm of corrective justice is owed entirely to the law. Morality would not contain a norm of reparation for wrongfully occasioned losses at all were there no law giving shape to it. '[W]here practical reason formulates ethical duties,' says Weinrib, 'juridical ones have already taken hold.'[36] Coleman's claim is more modest. Morality would have a norm of reparation for wrongfully occasioned losses only in a relatively indeterminate form were it not for tort law's constitutive intervention. Social practices like tort law, for Coleman, 'turn abstract ideals into regulative principles; they turn virtue to duty'.[37] There is a significant disagreement here. The disagreement is small, however, when compared with what is agreed. Weinrib and Coleman agree that, in explaining what tort law is for, one must resist the instrumental overtone of the question, much trumpeted by legal economists. In its tackling of allocative moral questions, one must think of tort law as performing a constitutive as opposed to an instrumental role. Tort law's way of contributing to a sound moral solution to such questions is by being a component part of the solution, not by helping to make the attainment of the solution more probable or more 'efficient'. This is the core of their broader objection to 'functionalism', their resistance to thinking of tort law as the servant, whether instrumentally or otherwise, of any end that can be specified independently of tort law's contribution to it.[38]

Here begins a second doubt about 'corrective justice' as an answer to the question 'what is tort law for?' Suppose we grant Weinrib and Coleman their point that, thanks to the corrective justice norm of tort law, people often have moral obligations of reparation different from (because more determinate than) those that they would have without tort law's intervention. Let's allow, in other words, that tort law often helps to constitute the correctively just solution. What doesn't follow is that tort law's norm of corrective justice should not be evaluated as an instrument. On the contrary, to fulfill its morally constitutive role, tort law's norm of corrective justice *must* be evaluated as an instrument. It must be evaluated as an instrument of improved conformity with the very moral norm that it helps to constitute. To see why,

[36] *The Idea of Private Law*, above note 1, 110.

[37] *The Practice of Principle*, above note 2, 54.

[38] Tort law could be an expression of some attitude or ideology, which would give it an external end that it serves non-instrumentally. See Gardner, 'The Purity and Priority of Private Law', above note 4, 459–60.

think about some other laws that are supposed to lend more determinacy to counterpart moral norms.

Quite apart from the law, for example, one has a moral obligation not to drive one's car dangerously. The law attempts to make this obligation more determinate by, for example, setting up traffic lights, road markings, and speed limits. If the law does this with sound judgment, the proper application of the relevant moral norm is changed in the process. A manoeuvre that would not count as dangerous driving apart from the legal force of the lane markings at the mouth of the Lincoln Tunnel may well count as dangerous driving—and hence a breach of the moral norm forbidding dangerous driving—once the lane markings are in place. But this holds only if the law proceeds with sound judgment. It holds only if relying on the lane markings assists those who rely on them to avoid violating the original moral norm. If the mouth of the Lincoln Tunnel has profoundly confusing lane markings, reliance on which only serves to make road accidents more likely, failing to observe the lane markings is not a legally constituted way of driving dangerously. It is not immoral under the 'dangerous driving' heading. That is because, if the lane markings are profoundly confusing, driving according to the lane markings does not and would not help to reduce the incidence of dangerous driving.

The lesson of the case is simple. A legal norm cannot play its partly constitutive role in relation to a moral norm unless it also has some instrumental role to play in relation to the same moral norm, unless conformity with the legal norm would help to secure conformity with the moral norm of which the legal norm is supposed to be partly constitutive. This formulation deliberately leaves open the question of how much help the law has to give before it can be morally constitutive. Does it need to be helpful only in this case, or in all possible cases, or in most actual cases, etc.? And when it is helpful, does it need to be helpful on balance—more of a help than a hindrance—or will helpfulness in some small respect, readily outweighed, suffice? And help relative to what baseline? Does it need to be an instrument of better action than there would be in a world without any law, or only a better action than there would be in a world without this particular law? If without this particular law, then with what law instead, if any? These questions (and others like them) are important in fine-tuning the thesis that the law's morally constitutive role depends on its morally instrumental role. But all these questions presuppose that the thesis is true, that when people's doing what they are legally bound to do would not help people to do what they are morally bound to do, the law by which they are legally bound does not help to determine—and hence to constitute—what they are morally bound to do.

The case of the confusing lane markings at the mouth of the Lincoln Tunnel is a case of a directly self-defeating legal norm. The law fails as an instrument of its own moral purpose even though (and perhaps even because) people conform to it. In other cases, legal norms are indirectly self-defeating.[39] The law would be a successful instrument of its own moral purpose if only it were conformed to; but it fails as an instrument of its own moral purpose because it sets up perverse incentives that tend to encourage people to violate it. Many critics think that criminal laws prohibiting drug dealing tend to exhibit this failing. The illegality of drug dealing forces it underground where excesses cannot be checked and potential profit is very high. The net result, some claim, is more drug dealing and morally worse drug dealing than would go on if such activities were decriminalized. In such a case, unlike the case of the road markings, it is possible that the law does have a constitutive effect on the moral norm that it seeks to serve. Possibly some acts that would not be morally wrong but for such a law are made morally wrong by it. But it still does not follow that the legal norm escapes further instrumental scrutiny. It is not enough to say, in defence of the law, that drug dealing is morally wrong and that is what the law (with its morally constitutive extra determinacy) prohibits. The question must also be asked whether the law that prohibits drug dealing actually helps to reduce the incidence of drug dealing. If not, it is a failure in its own terms. Never mind that it would be a morally impeccable law if only people would comply with it. It is an indirectly self-defeating law because it encourages people not to comply with it. It retards rather than advances the cause of conformity with the

[39] On the two types of self-defeatingness, see Derek Parfit, *Reasons and Persons* (Oxford 1984), chs 1–4.

very moral norms that it helps to constitute. All else being equal (i.e. in the absence of any other good consequences) it should be removed from the statute book.

No legal norm is exempt from this kind of instrumental scrutiny. Tort law's norm of corrective justice must be subjected to it too. We need to ask: Does this norm advance the cause of conformity with the moral norm of corrective justice that, according to Weinrib and Coleman, it helps to constitute? If not then one cannot make a good case for the legal norm by relying on the moral norm. Giving the answer 'corrective justice' to the question 'what is tort law for?' therefore does not exempt one from showing that the law is instrumentally sound. Nor, therefore, does it exempt one from answering the empirical questions associated with its instrumental justification. Is it the case that the more one legally requires of people that they pay reparative damages for their wrongs, the more they do so? Or is there a point at which the law becomes self-defeating, a point at which diminishing returns turn into negative returns? And if the law is self-defeating, is this because, even when people do what the law requires in the name of corrective justice, less corrective justice is done; or is it because the law is encouraging its own violation, with the consequence that less corrective justice is done? Is the law, in other words, directly or indirectly self-defeating? Notice that these are not just any old empirical questions about the law's instrumentality. We are bracketing out other consequences that tort law's norm of corrective justice may have apart from its consequences for conformity with the moral norm of corrective justice that it is supposed to help to constitute. We are querying its efficiency only relative to that moral norm. But still we are querying its efficiency. There is no possible way of looking at tort law that escapes the question of its efficiency. It follows that 'corrective justice' as an answer to the question 'what is tort law for?' cannot be, as Weinrib and Coleman like to think, an answer that *rivals* 'efficiency'. The answer 'corrective justice' tells us, rather, what it is that the law of torts is supposed to be efficient *at*. It is supposed to be efficient at securing that people conform to a certain (partly legally constituted) moral norm of corrective justice. If it is not efficient at this job then, from the point of view of corrective justice itself, the law of torts should be abolished forthwith.

4. Prevention before correction?

Tort law's norm of corrective justice and its counterpart moral norm both regulate the reversal of wrongful transactions on the ground of their wrongfulness. The transaction was wrongful and that is why, in tort law, it calls for correction. The same is true in the law relating to breach of contract: a breach of contract is a wrong and that is why, according to contract law, correction is in order. This is a feature shared by many but not all norms of corrective justice. Sometimes, as in the law of unjust enrichment, a transaction need not be wrongful in order to call for correction. In such cases the only relevant wrong is that of failing to correct the transaction, or perhaps (differently) that of transacting without correcting.[40] In the law of unjust enrichment there need be no prior wrong that explains why the correction is called for. Nevertheless correction is called for and the norm that regulates the correction is a norm of corrective justice.[41]

This distinction between corrective justice in tort law and corrective justice in the law of unjust enrichment already hints at another worry about 'corrective justice' as an answer to the question 'what is tort law for?' In tort law, unlike the law of unjust enrichment, there are prior wrongs that call for correction. Surely tort law has some institutional responsibility in relation to these prior wrongs other than that of helping to correct them? As well as helping to secure that people conform to a certain (legally recognized and partly legally constituted) moral norm of corrective justice, isn't there a necessary role for tort law in securing that people don't commit certain (legally recognized and partly legally constituted) wrongs in the first place, so that there is less for tort law to correct? Wouldn't it be better, even from the perspective

[40] Bob Goodin mistakenly assimilates the law of torts to this model when he writes that, in tort law, 'compensation serves to right *what would otherwise count as* wrongful injuries'. Robert E Goodin, 'Theories of Compensation', *Oxford Journal of Legal Studies* 9 (1989), 56 (emphasis added).

[41] Coleman denies this, dividing the 'restitutionary justice' of unjust enrichment from the truly corrective justice of tort law: *Risks and Wrongs*, above note 24, 371. Weinrib, by contrast, joins me in regarding both tort law and the law of unjust enrichment as sites for the doing of corrective justice: *The Idea of Private Law*, above note 1, 140–1.

of tort law itself, if there were *less* correcting to do thanks to the fact that fewer legally recognized wrongs, fewer torts, had been committed? So wouldn't we more naturally think of 'corrective justice' as only a secondary *raison d'être* of tort law, and only a secondary answer to the question of what tort law is for, a 'secondary provision[] for a breakdown in case the primary intended peremptory reasons are not accepted as such'?[42] Tort law, you might think, is first and foremost there to assist in the constitution of various moral norms bearing on how we should transact with each other, and in helping to see to it that we do indeed transact with each other in conformity with these moral norms. Only where that fails, you might think, does tort law need to fall back on its norm of corrective justice as a way of shifting the losses associated with the wrongful transaction back where they came from. The need to resort to a norm of corrective justice, in short, represents a partial failure for tort law, even in its own terms.

Weinrib tries to anticipate and avoid this line of criticism by suggesting that the prior wrongs—the torts themselves—are also violations of norms of corrective justice. In his words, 'corrective justice serves a normative function: a transaction is required, on pain of rectification, to conform to its contours.'[43] In tort law, in other words, corrective justice is only ever called upon to rectify a prior corrective injustice. But this is a non-starter. Most torts are not injustices at all, let alone corrective injustices. They are violations of norms of honesty, considerateness, trustworthiness, loyalty, humanity, and so on.[44] True, one could commit a tort of conversion that consists in a wrongful failure to return an object not wrongfully acquired. In this case the tort which tort law corrects is indeed a prior corrective injustice, a wrongful failure, under the law of unjust enrichment, to return goods that had not

[42] The words are H L A Hart's, from 'Commands and Authoritative Legal Reasons' in his *Essays on Bentham* (Oxford 1982), 254.

[43] *The Idea of Private Law*, above note 9, 76. Again Coleman contents himself with a more modest proposal, viz. that corrective justice 'imposes constraints on what [the torts themselves] can be': *The Practice of Principle*, above note 2, 34. Coleman's proposal is sound but does not help to answer the objection currently under consideration.

[44] For searching discussion, see Hanoch Sheinman, 'The First Virtue of the Law Courts and the First Virtue of the Law', *Legal Theory* 13 (2007), 101.

been wrongfully acquired. But it is hard to see how a tort of nuisance, defamation, inducing breach of contract, or trespass to land could ever be a corrective injustice. The only corrective injustice, where these torts are concerned, comes later when one fails to pay the reparative damages for their commission.

But isn't Weinrib here overlooking a much more obvious answer to the criticism that corrective justice is at best a second best to the prevention of the torts themselves? The law of torts clearly does seek to reduce the commission of torts. And it clearly does so, above all, by using its norm of corrective justice. By use of this norm it transfers some losses associated with the commission of torts onto those who committed them, thereby at least partly restoring those who suffered those losses to the position they would have been in had the tort not been committed. As well as correcting torts that have already been committed, this practice is apt systematically to deter the commission of torts that have not yet been committed. Even a casual observer cannot but see the dramatic effects of this strategy in controlling the behaviour of potential tortfeasors today. Many public bodies and corporations have become almost pathologically fixated with not committing torts, mainly because of the potential legal consequences of doing so, including but not limited to potentially vast liabilities to pay reparative damages to those whom they wrong. There is of course empirical research to be done on how well-targeted this deterrence is. Experience suggests that tort law deters many acts that are not tortious as well as many that are (the so-called 'chilling effect').[45] But this does not detract from the plausibility of the hypothesis that tort law's norm of corrective justice does a great deal to deter the commission of torts. This is what gives economic analysts of law the confidence that, even without empirical research, they can explain tort law's norm of corrective justice without invoking any counterpart moral norm of corrective justice. On their view tort law's norm of corrective justice

[45] The 'chilling effect' is most often mentioned in connection with the inhibition of free speech, e.g. by the tort of libel. But the problem is a broader one that afflicts law in general, and tort law in particular. For analysis, see Frederick Schauer, 'Fear, Risk and the First Amendment: Unraveling the "Chilling Effect"', *Boston University Law Review* 58 (1978), 685.

is mainly a deterrent device directed at potential tortfeasors. Its success in securing that actual tortfeasors bear the losses they have already wrongfully occasioned—its corrective success—is important mainly as a means of securing that, in future, fewer torts are committed, with the result that there will be fewer occasions, in future, for actual tortfeasors to bear the losses they wrongfully occasioned. The point of the legal norm of corrective justice is, in short, to have less need for the legal norm of corrective justice.

Now we can see that Weinrib wasn't overlooking this much more obvious answer so much as trying to preempt it. For it leads straight back to Posner's harsh criticism of 'corrective justice' as an answer to the question 'what is tort law for?' It purports to explain tort law's norm of corrective justice without mentioning any further norm of corrective justice that tort law's norm of corrective justice might exist to serve. So it leaves 'corrective justice' to play a role in tort law only as part of the *explanandum*, not as part of the explanation.

As I said before, this attack goes too far. Without a doubt the role of tort law's norm of corrective justice in deterring future torts is a morally important role. It is part of the point of tort law's indigenous norm of corrective justice. So it is part of what tort law is for. If Coleman and Weinrib deny this they are plainly mistaken. But if Coleman and Weinrib merely claim—as I suggested they should claim—that this deterrence story cannot be the *whole* story of what tort law is for, then they are spot on. The moral norm of corrective justice cannot so easily be sidelined. Why? Coleman and Weinrib are looking in the right direction when they stress the morally constitutive role of law. When legal norms regulate some activity, and conforming to the legal norms would help one to conform to the moral norms that regulate that activity, then the legal norms *necessarily* provide extra content to the moral norms. Well-judged and well-observed road markings cannot but change what counts as dangerous driving, and hence what is prohibited by the moral norm prohibiting dangerous driving. Such constitution and reconstitution of counterpart moral norms is an unavoidable by-product of sound law-making. It follows that the law of torts cannot include a sound norm of corrective justice without there also being a moral norm of corrective justice that the legal norm of corrective justice helps to constitute. And once there is such a moral norm of corrective justice, the law of torts cannot be justified without pointing to the role that the law of torts plays in securing conformity with that very same moral norm. So the question of how the legal norm is justified inevitably leads to the question of how the moral norm is justified. If one cannot justify the moral norm whereby wrongdoers pay reparation for their wrongs, one also cannot justify its legal counterpart. So the task remains of explaining what this moral norm of corrective justice is for, such that there is a moral case for the law to serve it.

You may object that there is no question of how a moral norm is to be justified. It is part of the nature of a moral norm that, if it exists, it is a sound norm. This is one important way in which moral norms differ from legal ones. Unjustified legal norms are still legal norms; they still bind in the eyes of the law. Unjustified moral norms, by contrast, are no more than putative moral norms, supposed moral norms, would-be moral norms. They do not bind anyone morally. They are not moral norms but only what people mistakenly take to be moral norms. So if we have already concluded that the moral norm whereby wrongdoers must pay reparation for their wrongs exists, we must have concluded that it is a sound norm. I reply: That much is true. But on closer inspection we have not yet established that the moral norm whereby wrongdoers must pay reparation for their wrongs exists. We have only established that, *if* there is such a moral norm, and *if* the law of torts is not directly self-defeating in the contribution it makes to conformity with that moral norm, *then* the law of torts helps to constitute (determine the application of) that moral norm, and *thus* the moral norm must be invoked (and its soundness relied upon) in defending the law of torts. We still need to decide whether the moral norm is sound in order to decide whether it exists. For as the imaginary objector rightly points out, there is no such thing as an unsound moral norm. Unless it is sound it is only a supposed moral norm and it is incapable of lending moral justification to anything.

So what—we finally get to ask—makes this moral norm of corrective justice a sound one? Couldn't it be that the prevention of wrongs (or a similar 'external' goal) comes back in here as the main case for having the *moral* norm of corrective justice? I have explored this proposal and its limitations in detail elsewhere.[46] In the end it is unsatisfying. It works only when several artificial assumptions are made. The most important is the assumption that the moral norm of corrective justice is also a *social* norm, i.e. a norm that is widely used. It must be widely used before people in general can be deterred from wrongdoing by the prospect of its use. This has a curious implication. It has the implication that, all else being equal, the less people use the norm in question, the less case there is for them to use it. Collectively, we can release ourselves from the norm by ignoring it. It may be said that this implication is inconsistent with the very idea of a moral norm. Isn't it built into the idea of a moral norm that it binds us irrespective of whether anyone's behaviour conforms to it, irrespective of whether anyone uses it, indeed irrespective of whether anyone is even aware of its existence?[47] Certainly this can be an overtone of the word 'moral' in some contexts. In this sense moral norms are to be contrasted with 'mere' social norms, understood as norms that bind us only inasmuch as they are in social use. But we need not insist on this stark contrast here. All we need insist upon here are two more modest proposals: (1) that at least some moral norms are binding irrespective of the extent to which they are in social use; and (2) that a satisfying defence of the moral norm whereby wrongdoers owe reparation for their wrongs will be a defence that puts it in this class of use-independent moral norms. It is proposal (2) that makes the wrong-prevention defence of the moral norm so unsatisfying.

Unsatisfying perhaps. But what more satisfying alternative is on the table? Remember that the question at this stage has become: What could any norm of corrective justice, even a moral one, possibly be for? What could possibly be its *telos*, its rationale, an intelligible case for its existence? 'The prevention of the very wrongs that the norm would have us correct' may be a terrible answer, but it is at least an answer. Whereas 'corrective justice', as

[46] See chapter 4.

[47] This is the special feature of morality, or at any rate of the morality of justice, championed by G A Cohen in his *Rescuing Justice and Equality* (Cambridge, Mass 2008), part II.

I have shown, is at this point in the investigation no answer at all. It is true but explanatorily vacuous to say that the *telos* of a moral norm of corrective justice is corrective justice. It can only mean something like: Every sound norm of corrective justice is such that, by conforming to it, we make our actions in one respect, namely in a corrective respect, just. We still need to know what could possibly make such a norm sound.

5. The continuity of the corrective

The 'prevention' rationale for norms of corrective justice is unsatisfying. Yet our exploration of it—especially of the idea that doing corrective justice in the wake of a tort is at best a second best to the prevention of the tort itself—also points us in a new and more promising direction. It draws our attention back to the tort itself, the wrong that calls for correction. Up to now we may have been tempted to think of norms of corrective justice as calling for a rationale that is specific to norms of corrective justice. In looking for this special 'corrective justice' rationale, it may seem, we need—we can—no longer be much interested in the norm that was violated in committing the original wrong. *Pace* Weinrib, it was not typically a norm of justice at all, never mind a norm of corrective justice. Of course, we cannot but be interested in it in one respect. The obligation of reparation is grounded in (comes into existence on condition of and by reason of) this other norm's violation. That is our corrective justice interest in it. Yet as we gain that interest in it, we lose interest in it in another way. We lose interest in it for its own normative content and force. It is no use to us now as a source of guidance about what to do. The clock cannot literally be turned back so that violation is replaced by conformity. It is too late now for conformity. So isn't it also too late to worry—to worry rationally—about what the original norm required us to do?

Not necessarily. Consider this example devised by Neil MacCormick.[48] I promise to take my children to the beach today,

[48] Neil MacCormick, 'The Obligation of Reparation' in his *Legal Right and Social Democracy* (Oxford 1982), 212. MacCormick is unfortunately distracted by special features of the example—particularly that the breaking of the promise was justified—and is drawn to conclusions somewhat at odds with mine.

but an emergency intervenes and I renege on the deal. Let's say I was amply justified in doing so. One of my students, let's say, was in some kind of serious and urgent trouble from which only I could extricate him, and only by devoting most of the day to it. In spite of this ample justification for letting the children down today I am now bound, without having to make a further promise, to take them to the beach at the next suitable opportunity (if there is one). Suppose a suitable opportunity is tomorrow. Am I bound to take them to the beach tomorrow for reasons that are entirely different from the reasons that I had to take them to the beach today? Surely not. Why me? Why the children? Why the beach? Why tomorrow? Clearly there is some sense in which my broken promise continues to exert a hold over me after I break it, a sense in which it continues to shape what I am bound to do. Of course, it is too late for me to keep my promise perfectly. I promised to take the children to the beach today and today is gone. But is it also too late for some kind of *im*perfect performance? I can't make it today, but I can still take them to the beach some time, and if it can't be today, well tomorrow is close, and the closer to perfect performance of my promise, you might think, the better. There is an element of continuity here, something that carries through from my original obligation into my obligation now. Was the former discharged (i.e. put to an end) by its breach? Perhaps not entirely. It seems to leave some traces of itself, some echo, behind for later.

By contrasting perfect and imperfect performances, I have already raised one candidate explanation. Perhaps the later obligation is the very same obligation as the earlier one, an obligation remaining in place after violation, awaiting whatever residual performance is still feasible? Perhaps, in other words, there is one norm (the norm created by the promise to the children), with which there can be partial as well as complete conformity? This alluring idea quickly runs into grave problems of its own. It is not for nothing that contract and tort lawyers often speak of the obligation of reparation as a 'secondary obligation' which arises out of breach of a 'primary obligation' (meaning a breach of contract or tort).[49] This way of talking and thinking reflects the fact

[49] e.g. *Photo Production Ltd* v *Securicor Transport Ltd* [1980] AC 827 per Lord Diplock at 850. On a more sceptical note, at least in respect of torts, Peter Birks,

that obligations (and more generally norms) are individuated according to the action that they make obligatory (or, in the case of other norms, empower or permit).[50] Where a new action becomes obligatory only if and because another obligatory action was not taken, then what we have necessarily qualifies as a new obligation, viz. a new one that is grounded in breach of the old one. So when there is talk—as there sometimes is in contract law—of 'partial' or 'substantial' performance—this cannot be interpreted to mean that particular obligations in a contract have been imperfectly performed. It must be interpreted to mean, rather, that some of the obligations in a contract were performed, and others were not performed, with the implication that *the contract as a whole*—understood as a set of obligations—was imperfectly performed.[51]

And yet there can clearly be graver and less grave breaches of the same contractual term, more and less egregious commissions of the same tort, and generally more and less significant breaches of one and the same obligation. How are we to make sense of these ideas, if they can't be explained in terms of partial performance? One may be tempted to think that the crucial distinction here is between legal and moral assessment: that legally there is either a violation or not, whereas morally it may be appraised as more or less significant. But this is not the distinction we need here. Our remarks about the individuation of obligations apply equally in the bare moral case of the children and their abandoned trip to

'Definition and Division: A Meditation on *Institutes 3.13*' in Birks (ed), *The Classification of Obligations* (Oxford 1997).

[50] This should not be read as a denial of the existence of so-called 'imperfect obligations', here meaning those which leave the obligation-holder with discretion as to the mode of performance. These too are individuated according to the action that they make obligatory. I have an obligation to meet the children out of school. Shall I go by bus or by bicycle? Either way it is the action of meeting the children out of school that is obligatory. The example helps us to see that all obligations are (more or less) imperfect in the relevant sense. I have an obligation to lock the door at 7pm precisely. Shall I do it with my left hand or my right hand? Quickly or slowly? While humming *La Marseillaise* or not? For a fuller argument, see George Rainbolt, 'Perfect and Imperfect Obligations', *Philosophical Studies* 98 (2000), 233.

[51] So substantial performance is only possible, in the common law of contract, when a contract is 'severable': *Hoenig* v *Isaacs* [1952] 2 All ER 176.

the beach. Here too, without a legal issue in sight, the obligation to go to the beach on the next suitable occasion is a different obligation, because it calls for a different action, from the original obligation to go to the beach today. The performance of the second obligation is not part-performance of the first. And yet the violation of the first obligation is to some extent mitigated—rendered less morally troubling—by the performance of the second. How?

The answer is that while an obligation is either performed or not performed, those reasons in favour of the action that contribute to its obligatoriness can each be conformed to more or less perfectly. This proposition leads us, eventually, to an understanding of what corrective justice is for. But before we get to that point, the proposition needs some unpacking.

An obligation is not a reason, but the fact that one has an obligation is a reason—a reason of special force[52]—for doing whatever one has an obligation to do. However, it is not only a reason for doing that very thing. Reasons are individuated differently from obligations.[53] Every reason for action is potentially a reason for multiple actions. This is true even of the fact that one has an obligation, understood as a reason for action. Suppose that I have an obligation to pay for my bus journey before I make it. I perform this obligation if and only if I pay for my bus journey before I make it. And the fact that I have this obligation is a reason to do exactly that. A reason, as I said, of special force. Yet the fact that I have this obligation is also a reason for me to do various other things short of performing it, assuming that I intend to take the bus. It is a reason to keep some loose change in my pocket, to hunt in my pocket for my loose change when I get to the bus stop, to state my destination clearly to the driver or else to tender what

[52] I endorse Joseph Raz's view according to which the fact that one has an obligation to ϕ is a protected reason to ϕ, meaning a reason to ϕ that is also a reason not to act for at least some reasons not to ϕ. Joseph Raz, 'Promises and Obligations' in P M S Hacker and J Raz (eds), *Law, Morality, and Society* (Oxford 1977). (The fact that I have an obligation to ϕ is also a categorical reason to ϕ but that feature affects its scope, not its force.)

[53] One important formalization of the difference—he presents it as a difference between reasons and requirements—is that of John Broome in 'Normative Requirements' *Ratio*, 12 (1999), 398. Unfortunately his formalization leads him to the conclusion that being required does not entail having a reason.

I already know to be the correct fare, and so forth. None of these is itself an obligatory action. Yet the fact that I have an obligation to pay in advance for my bus journey is a reason for each of these actions. The reason—the fact that I have the obligation—counts in favour of these further actions because these further actions contribute instrumentally to my performing the obligation (by, for example, enabling, facilitating, or encouraging me to do it). Other actions, we may note, contribute constitutively rather than instrumentally to my doing so. For example, I contribute constitutively to performing my obligation if, lacking the money to pay my fare upfront, I don't take the bus at all. Likewise if, having paid too little, I get off at the earlier stop to which the fare I have paid would take me, and walk the rest. Again neither of these actions is itself obligatory (imagine that there are other possibilities, such as borrowing the excess fare from another passenger before continuing)[54] and yet the fact that I have the obligation remains a reason to do these things because they contribute to my performing it.

But what if, perhaps owing to a confusion between myself and the driver, I do end up making a journey beyond the one I paid for at the start? My original obligation is, we should now be able to agree, discharged (put to an end) by its breach. *Ex hypothesi* it was an obligation to pay upfront and now it is too late for me to pay upfront. Consequently, the fact of my having the obligation has also lost its ability to serve as a reason for my doing, or anyone's doing, any of the things that remain available to be done.[55] Not only is it too late for me to perform my obligation; it is also too late, by necessary implication, for any of my actions,

[54] I include this caveat because (I tend to think) it is derivatively obligatory to do whatever is both necessary and sufficient to do whatever one already has an obligation to do. To rule out an obligation derived in this way, I am ruling the sufficient acts in the example to be unnecessary. For the problem, if not the solution, see A J Kenny, 'Practical Inference', *Analysis* 26 (1966), 65.

[55] I should perhaps say 'an operative reason for action' because it may still serve in the minor or auxiliary premises of a practical syllogism. It may also, of course, serve as a presupposition of another operative reason for action. For example, that I breached an obligation (an operative reason for action after my breach) presupposes that I had an obligation. In such a case I might report just part of the now-operative reason by saying 'But I had an obligation!'.

or indeed anyone else's actions, to contribute instrumentally or constitutively to my performing my obligation. And yet, all else being equal, I clearly still have an obligation to pay, which is now an obligation to pay in arrears rather than to pay in advance for the journey. Why? The new obligation exists because, quite apart from the now non-conformable reason that was the fact of my having an obligation to pay upfront, there are further reasons *why* I had an obligation to pay upfront that are not necessarily non-conformable. I still conform, at least in part, to at least some of these further reasons if I pay in arrears. One such reason, let's suppose, is that my having (in common with all other bus passengers) this obligation to pay upfront helps to see to it that the bus company gets paid for the services it provides, and hence is enabled or encouraged to provide them. I can still help to advance this aim—and hence at least partly conform to this reason—if I pay for the journey later, either by presenting the extra money to the driver at the end of my journey, or by sending it to the bus company once I get home. Naturally, other reasons may countervail. (Such a lot of paperwork for such a tiny sum! I will only get the driver into trouble!) The reason to pay up only counts for as much as it counts for. My point is that, still being available for conformity, it counts for something.

Similarly, the avoidance of my children's disappointment may figure in the rationale of an obligation that I owe them. If I breach the obligation, let us suppose, I will not be able to avoid their disappointment altogether. But I can still do something to curtail their disappointment. My reason not to have disappointed them full stop is also a reason to minimize their disappointment if I cannot but disappoint them. Reasons, unlike obligations, allow for imperfect conformity. Since we can't go to the beach today, how about tomorrow? Or the next sunny day? Or, if there's no sunny day soon, how about the ice rink instead?

To generalize: Once the time for performance of a primary obligation is past, so that it can no longer be performed, one can often nevertheless still contribute to satisfaction of some or all of the reasons that added up to make the action obligatory. Those reasons, not having been satisfied by performance of the primary obligation, are still with us awaiting satisfaction and since they cannot now be satisfied by performance of that obligation, they call for satisfaction in some other way. They call for next-best satisfaction, the closest to full satisfaction that is still available. We need to know the rationale of the obligation, of course, so that we can work out what counts as next best. But once we have it we also have the rationale, all else being equal, for a secondary obligation, which is an obligation to do the next-best thing. If all else is equal, the reasons that were capable of justifying a primary obligation are also capable of justifying a secondary one. I will call this the 'obligation-in, obligation-out' principle. And the explanation for it that I have just sketched out I will call the 'continuity thesis'.[56] It is the thesis that the secondary obligation is a rational echo of the primary obligation, for it exists to serve, so far as may still be done, the reasons for the primary obligation that was not performed when its performance was due.

How does the continuity thesis help us to solve the problem of reparation for wrongs? How does it help to make a case for moral norms of corrective justice? Like this. The normal reason why one has an obligation to pay for the losses that one wrongfully occasioned (i.e. that one occasioned in breach of obligation) is that this constitutes the best still-available conformity with, or satisfaction of, the reasons why one had that obligation. Or to put it more tersely, the reasons why one must pay for the losses that one occasions are the very same reasons why one must not occasion those losses in the first place, when it is true that one must not occasion them. One's reparative act is in at least partial conformity with the original reasons, and if one was bound to conform to the original reason then *ceteris paribus* one is now bound, in turn, to engage in the reparative act. Obligation in, obligation out. For this purpose it matters not whether the obligation in, the primary obligation, is an obligation of corrective justice, or indeed an obligation of justice at all. The fact that one is in some measure making up for one's failure to perform it,

[56] My earlier interpretation of the continuity thesis, in previous drafts of this paper and elsewhere, was much improved by reading Joseph Raz, 'Personal Practical Conflicts' in Peter Baumann and Monika Betzler (eds), *Practical Conflicts: New Philosophical Essays* (Cambridge 2004), 172 at 189–93, and also by reading unpublished work by Matthew Henken.

namely by redressing the losses that one occasioned, is enough to make the obligation out, the secondary obligation, an obligation of corrective justice.

We can see here the beginnings of an explanation for the distinction, mentioned earlier, between the two classes of cases in which correction may be called for. Some transactions need not be wrongful in order to call for correction. They are wrongful only if they go uncorrected. The ones we have been focusing on, however, call for correction because they are wrongful. In the former class of cases, the corrected transaction leaves too few reasons unsatisfied, or leaves them too insignificantly unsatisfied, to make the transaction wrongful. By correcting, one mitigates what would otherwise be a wrong to the point at which it is no longer a wrong, no longer a breach of obligation. One has an obligation to correct precisely because *otherwise*—in the absence of correction—one commits a wrong. In the cases we have been focusing on, however, which are characteristic of the law of torts and the law of breach of contract, such preemptive correction is ruled out. The reasons not to do whatever one did, the thing that now calls for correction, suffice to make that action wrongful even if it is corrected. That is because all possible means of correction, even if conscientiously and promptly implemented, still leave too great a rational remainder behind, too much in the way of unsatisfied or imperfectly satisfied reasons, for the wrongdoing to have been averted by the act of correction alone. In such cases, even if the best corrective justice is done—even if we have truly second-best rational conformity—there remains enough rational nonconformity to make it obligatory not to have done what one did in the first place, and hence to make it wrongful to have done it. And once we have got this much of a remainder, we mustn't forget to bootstrap in the extra reason for action that consists in the very fact that it was obligatory not to have done what one did, a reason that (as we saw) eludes any kind of even partially-conforming action once the obligation has been breached, and hence increases still further the gap between what one should have done and what one can now do by way of correction. What grounds the obligation to correct is now clearly a wrong. One has an obligation to correct on condition of and by reason of one's breach of another obligation.

Inevitably, when we fall back to the next-best way of satisfying reasons that apply to us we leave behind some remainder, however slight, of unsatisfied reason.[57] That is true in both classes of cases that I just mentioned. What becomes of the remainder? When the same question came up in passing near the start of this section, I said that a reason belonging to the remainder has 'lost its ability to serve as a reason for my doing, or anyone's doing, any of the things that remain available to be done'. I carefully did not say that it lost its ability to serve as a reason for action. The reason remains a reason to perform actions that, if only they were still open to me, would contribute to my conformity with the reason. It is merely that there are now no such actions open to me; any further conformity to the reason is blocked. The reason for action then makes its force felt as a reason for regret and (depending on the details of the case) for various other emotions that respond to those shortfalls in rational conformity that are already *fait accompli*, meaning that no further corrective actions will mitigate, let alone extinguish, them.[58]

This claim runs up against a common view that assimilates the rationality of emotions to practical rationality.[59] It says that once a reason is remaindered, in the sense just explained, it cannot be a

[57] In other words, breach-plus-correction cannot be the rational equivalent of performance. Here we bid farewell to the 'efficient breach' fallacy made popular by O W Holmes in *The Common Law* (Boston 1881), 300–1. Yet we also cast doubt on anti-Holmesian attempts, e.g. in *Ruxley Electronics and Construction Ltd* v *Forsyth* [1996] AC 344, to fill the gap between breach-plus-correction and performance with an extra measure of damages to reflect the so-called 'performance interest'. The gap cannot be filled.

[58] I am not suggesting, of course, that there are no practical consequences of having such emotions. There can be reasons to express such emotions to others, e.g. by confessing or apologizing. Such expression should not be mistaken for further correction according to the continuity thesis. (See further Raz, 'Personal Practical Conflicts', above note 56, 189–90.) The case for expressing an emotion depends on whether one has that emotion to express, or at least a case to feign it. Not so the case for correction under the continuity thesis. Some quasi-reparative acts (e.g. sending flowers) are best understood as ways of apologizing, and hence depend for their success on the having or feigning of a suitable emotion. There is little use in the law's getting involved here as it cannot do the having or feigning on the wrongdoer's behalf.

[59] I have criticized this view at length in my 'The Logic of Excuses and the Rationality of Emotions', *Journal of Value Inquiry* 43 (2009), 315.

reason for regret or other emotions. One needs a further reason to dwell on the past, a reason that does not, so to speak, simply come down to one from the past but is a new reason now. Anything else is unproductive, and hence irrational.

The blanket association of rationality with productivity is a corruption. To show that regret, guilt, and remorse are rational one need not show that there are further reasons now why one should dwell upon the reasons that one did not conform to. That one did not do (even if one could not have done) as the reasons would have had one do means that they are still there, still exerting their pull, and still sufficient, all else being equal, to make one's regret, guilt, or remorse rational. Naturally one may raise new rational objections to the regret, guilt, or remorse. One may object, for instance, that always dwelling on the past is painful, energy-sapping, annoying to others, a waste of valuable time, etc. It is certainly true that everything in one's life is subject to a rolling programme of re-assessment in terms of the ever-changing landscape of reasons, and these often include reasons to move on from the past. All that I am adding is that, through all of this, the original reasons that were not satisfied when they could have been satisfied are still there. There was something one had reason to do, it is now too late, and the reason to do it is now, without further ado, a reason to regret—in some cases to feel guilty or remorseful—that one did not do it.[60]

Perhaps the relative contemporary neglect of the continuity thesis as an explanation of our obligations of corrective justice owes something to the exaggerated association of rationality with productivity. Of course, this association is most closely associated with economists, and more broadly with the utilitarian tradition in moral philosophy out of which the distinct discipline of economics grew. But its appeal may well be broader.[61] It may afflict even some anti-utilitarians, *malgré lui*. Having doubted the rationality of unproductive regret, practically-minded people

[60] A view of the significance of rational remainders similar to mine, and to which I owe a great deal, is that of Bernard Williams. See, e.g., his 'Politics and Moral Character' in Williams, *Moral Luck* (Cambridge 1981).

[61] For a defence free of utilitarian trappings, see Rudiger Bittner, 'Is It Reasonable to Regret Things One Did?', *Journal of Philosophy* 89 (1992), 262.

(and who is more practically-minded than a lawyer?) may tar reparation, as represented by the continuity thesis, with the same brush. Here as with one's emotions, they may say, one needs a further reason to dwell on the past, a reason that does not come down to one from the past but is a new reason starting from now. It is a reason borne of the violation, and hence specific to the post-violation world. This line of thought compounds the economistic mistake of associating rationality exclusively with productivity by failing to notice productivity when it is looking one straight in the eye. The post-violation world, according to the continuity thesis, is defective in respect of someone's conformity with reasons and in this respect it cries out for improvement. It cries out for whatever conformity with the same reasons can now, belatedly, be mustered. What one produces thereby is a greater measure of reason-conformity. What could be more productive, more practically rational? So why would one insist, as a condition of rationality, on some *further* productivity in continuing to have and to use the reason when it is still possible to be productive relative to it, in the sense of part-conforming to it? Why would one need, as it were, an *independent* case for doing corrective justice? The case for doing corrective justice according to the continuity thesis is not, after all, the same as the case for regret, remorse, and guilt. It is in a way the opposite case. These emotions are rendered rational, all else being equal, by the impossibility of making things better, by the impossibility of restoring what was lost by what one did. Corrective justice, by contrast, is rendered rational, all else being equal, by the residual possibility of doing so, i.e. by the residual possibility of restoring things, at least in some measure, to where they would have been had one not occasioned their loss.

6. Continuity in tort law: doubts and responses

The normal reason to pay for the losses that one wrongfully occasioned, according to the continuity thesis, is that this constitutes the best still-available measure of conformity with the reasons that one did not conform to in committing the wrong. Can this thesis help us to understand what tort law is for? Certainly it can.

Let me mention, and attempt to allay, a few possible doubts about the thesis's suitability for this task.

First doubt. My only examples of the continuity thesis at work, in section 5, were examples of failures to perform promissory, or at any rate voluntarily-incurred, obligations. I promised to take my children to the beach, but didn't. I was contractually bound to pay my fare upfront on the bus, but didn't. Isn't this emphasis on voluntary obligations telling? The continuity thesis seems to hold in these cases, you may say, only because we naturally interpret the promise or contractual term to include a fallback provision.[62] We interpret the promise to take the children to the beach today as a promise to take them today or, failing that, as soon as practicable. We interpret the contractual term requiring payment of the fare upfront as requiring payment upfront or, failing that, as soon as practicable. That mode of interpretation could possibly help to explain some reparative obligations in the law of contract. But how could we extend it to the law of torts?

First response. True, we naturally interpret a promise or contract as including fallback provisions. But why? The answer is: because it naturally does include such provisions. When we have a primary obligation to ϕ at *t1*, but do not ϕ at *t1*, we acquire, all else being equal, a secondary obligation to come as close as we now can to ϕing at *t1*, where closeness is determined by the reasons for the original obligation. This may involve nearly ϕing at *t2*, or precisely ϕing at *t3*, or (eventually) doing something at *t27* that has something in common with ϕing. Because different acts at different times may have different things in common with ϕing, all of which are rationally salient, there may sometimes be doubts about which of several rival fallback performances we are to opt for. That being so there may sometimes, in the context of a promise or contract, be a need for those involved to settle for one of the rival fallbacks by making a fresh promise or contract about where to go from here. Sometimes, alternatively, one may look for additional information about the original promise or contract to help one identify what would be the best fallback. If, for example, an agreement was made

[62] See Barbara Herman, 'Obligation and Performance' in her *The Practice of Moral Judgment* (Cambridge, Mass 1993).

with a specified purpose, the specification of the purpose helps one to select from among various rival fallbacks: all else being equal, the next-best way of honouring the contract would be the one that was next-best at serving the purpose. Here we are interpreting the agreement.

But it is not thanks to the interpretation of the agreement that we are bound to do the next-best thing. Rather, it is because we are anyway bound to do the next-best thing, according to the continuity thesis, that we need to interpret the agreement to find out what that next-best thing is. We have the obligation anyway: we have it without needing an agreement to have it (which does not mean that we cannot agree to something different). In tort law we may face similar difficulties in deciding which measure of conformity is the best that remains possible. There, unlike the law of contract, we do not have original agreements to interpret. The norm that we violated was not owed to an agreement. So instead we try to interpret the law of torts itself, or the relevant part of it, hoping to find some clue as to why the tortious behaviour was tortious, from which we can draw conclusions about what would count as an appropriate remedy. The asymmetries between tort and contract here are irrelevant to our present inquiry. It is the symmetry that is relevant. In both settings there can be a need for interpretation because we need to work out how best to correct the wrong, for which purpose we need a rational explanation of its wrongfulness. The continuity thesis holds symmetrically in the two contexts.

Second doubt. The examples of voluntary obligations held another clear advantage in illustrating the force of the continuity thesis. They were examples of *positive* obligations, obligations to confer benefits (taking children to the beach, paying a bus fare). So it is not hard to see how, upon their violation, there could arise positive obligations to take next-best steps. But the obligations that tort law places upon us are largely negative: obligations not to enter another's land without permission, obligations not to injure another by failing to take reasonable care for her safety, and so on. No conferral of benefits is called for. So how come, upon violation, the norms of tort law require the conferral of a benefit, namely the payment of reparative damages? How can a negative obligation mutate into a positive one like this?

Second response. The distinction between negative and positive obligations is relatively superficial. Take the obligation (breach of which constitutes the tort of negligence at common law) not to injure another by failing to take reasonable care not to injure her. One way to fulfill this obligation is to not injure anybody. But if we do injure somebody, what would count as a next-best course of action? It is too late not to injure. It is also too late to injure less. Is there something else to do? At this point, we need to know more about the rationale for the norm. We need to know why we have the original obligation. Suppose that our injuring people is regulated by the law, in part, because injuries, or what the law classifies as injuries, reduce people's quality of life. Then (all else being equal) the less the reduction in quality of life that an injurer leaves behind, the closer she comes to doing what her obligation existed to have her do. By way of reparation she should pay such things as medical bills (to expedite return of quality of life) and loss of earnings (to limit further consequential slippage in quality of life). Such reparative payment is not the same as not injuring, or injuring less, but in one salient respect—according to one possible reason for the norm against injuring—it might well be the next best thing. Of course there may be other reasons for not injuring apart from this one (e.g. the avoidance of suffering) and they may point towards a different remedial action (e.g. payment for distracting entertainments). Then we are back at the issues discussed in the first response above. Be that as it may, the fact that an obligation is negative does not mean that the reasons for it are incapable of being reasons (and hence as yielding an obligation) to take positive steps as second best when the original obligation is breached.

Third doubt. But can there really be norms such that whether we conform to them or fail to conform to them depends on whether someone is injured (killed, deprived, etc.) as a result of what we do? And even if there can be, are the primary obligations of tort law like this? If not, how can the payment of money damages to cover losses ever, let alone normally, count as a way of correcting the breach of a primary obligation in tort? How do the damages relate to the wrong if the wrong is not partly constituted by the resulting losses that the damages are supposed to repair?[63]

[63] This challenge can also be addressed to Weinrib, who distinguishes the plaintiff's 'factual loss' from his or her 'normative loss': *The Idea of Private Law*,

Third response. There are wrongs that are partly constituted by resulting losses, and some torts are wrongs of this type.[64] The tort of negligence is an example. One does not commit the tort of negligence if one merely fails to take reasonable care not to injure someone; one must actually injure someone *by* failing to take reasonable care not to injure that someone. The resulting losses are a constituent of the tort itself; the norm regulates one's bringing them about. But it is true that many torts (trespass, libel, conspiracy, misfeasance in public office) are not constituted by their resulting losses. All the losses associated with them are *consequential* losses. And even result-constituted torts like negligence can carry additional consequential losses, some of which may be recoverable in the law of torts.

The reallocation of such consequential losses from the defendant to the plaintiff is explained by much the same considerations that were set out in the second response above. What counts as fallback conformity with a norm after its violation is not dictated directly by the constituents of the norm. It depends on the reasons why the norm has those constituents, which often include instrumental reasons. Consequential losses are recoverable in tort because and to the extent that the avoidance of such consequential losses is among the reasons for the tort's being the tort that it is, with the constituents that it has. This explains why different types of consequential losses are recoverable in respect of different torts (e.g. pure economic losses are not recoverable in a suit for negligence, but they are recoverable in a suit for inducing breach of contract). Some torts are torts in order to protect against some types of consequences, and others to protect against other types.[65]

above note 1, 115ff. The response that follows seems, however, to be unavailable to Weinrib (he seems to deny the factual loss both a constitutive and a justificatory role in relation to the normative loss). I am not clear what his alternative response to the challenge is.

[64] See chapter 5 below; also John Gardner, 'The Wrongdoing that Gets Results', *Philosophical Perspectives* 18 (2004), 53.

[65] Where the common law tort of breach of statutory duty is concerned, the consequences to be protected against are determined, not by the purpose of the tort's existence, but by the purpose of the particular statutory duty, a.k.a. the 'mischief of the statute': *Gorris* v *Scott* [1874] 9 LR (Exch) 125.

Fourth doubt. In MacCormick's example of the broken promise to go to the beach, the breach was said to be justified. And yet the continuity thesis apparently still applied. In the example of the underpaid bus fare, it was not made clear whether the underpayment was justified or not. Possibly it was only excused; possibly not even that. So justification seems to be irrelevant to the application of the continuity thesis: fallback conformity to the violated norm is called for irrespective of *why* the violated norm was violated. Surely, however, justification is not irrelevant to the law of torts? Surely damages are only due in tort law (or at any rate would only be due in a morally sound tort law) for actions that are wrong in the sense of unjustified? Perhaps one can go further. Perhaps they are only due in tort law (or would only be due in a morally sound tort law) for actions that are wrong in the sense of unjustified *and* unexcused (i.e. faultless wrongs). But be that as it may: justification, at any rate, surely can't be thought irrelevant to tort liability?

Fourth response. That a norm-violation was justified is indeed irrelevant to the application of the continuity thesis, and at the deepest level it is equally irrelevant to the law of torts. Torts are wrongs—breaches of obligation—and one owes damages for their commission even if one's wrong was justified, never mind excused. True, there are some torts, such as the tort of negligence, that are not committed if one acted with certain justifications. That one acted with reasonable (i.e. justified)[66] care means that one did not commit this tort. These are special cases. At first sight they are paradoxical, in a way that was famously pointed out by W D Ross.[67] If one did no wrong, Ross pointed out, one has nothing to justify and nothing to excuse. It follows that the question of whether one did wrong must be answered without reference to one's fault, i.e. without yet raising questions of justification and excuse. Ross was onto something here, but he overlooked various logical possibilities. Why could there not be a wrong that one commits by committing, without justification, some other, lesser, wrong? And why could there not be a wrong that one commits

[66] I argued for this equation in my 'The Mysterious Case of the Reasonable Person', now chapter 8 of this book.

[67] W D Ross, *The Right and the Good* (Oxford 1930), 45.

by acting, without justification, in a way that does not conform to some other (non-obligatory) reason? The second possibility here requires us to abandon Ross's premiss that wrongs are the only things that call for justification. But we should indeed reject this premiss. It is too strong. Both the mooted possibilities are indeed possible. And some torts—such as the tort of negligence—must be interpreted as realizations of one or other of them. One commits these complex torts by failing to conform to a norm that regulates unjustified nonconformity with some other norms or some other reasons, not themselves norm-given, that are recognized by law.

This line of thought gives justification an occasional and derivative role in the law of torts. In general one owes reparative damages for torts as wrongs, never mind whether they are justified.[68] In some complex cases, however, one's action is a tortious wrong only if it is unjustified. One often encounters confusion on this score owing to the fact that we use the word 'wrong' sometimes to mean unjustified. 'I acted wrongly' usually means 'I did an unjustified thing'. But 'I committed a wrong' or 'I acted wrongfully' usually means 'I breached an obligation'. On these interpretations it is possible to commit a wrong or to act wrongfully without acting wrongly, and to act wrongly without committing a wrong or acting wrongfully. Tort law is concerned with the wrongs one committed, one's wrongful actions. It is only sometimes and derivatively concerned with whether one acted wrongly (because some wrongs are committed only by acting wrongly). The continuity thesis likewise. It is concerned with the continuing pull of reasons to be satisfied, even when their prior nonsatisfaction or undersatisfaction was amply justified. Indeed, as MacCormick points out, one way in which one can justify committing the particular wrong one committed, in a situation of conflicting obligations, is by pointing to the fact that the wrong one committed

[68] This is the lesson of *Vincent* v *Lake Erie Transportation Co.* 109 Minn. 456, 124 N.W. 221 (1910), interpreted as a trespass case, which in my view is what it is. There are those who interpret it as an unjust enrichment case in order to resist its lesson. For a good catalogue of possible interpretations (siding, ultimately, with the same one as me) see Arthur Ripstein, 'Tort Law in a Liberal State', *Journal of Tort Law* 1 (2007), issue 2, article 3, downloadable at http://www.bepress.com/jtl/vol1/iss2/art3.

was the easier of the two to repair by later conformity with its rationale. The kids can wait a day or two to go to the beach. The beach will still be there. The student in trouble cannot, *ex hypothesi*, wait a day to be rescued.[69] One wrongs the children, but one is justified in doing so thanks to the relative reparability of that wrong. This justification for wronging the children does not affect, but on the contrary presupposes, the application of the continuity thesis.

Fifth doubt. If the continuity thesis applies to tort law, why doesn't tort law sometimes require next-best conformity other than by way of payment of money damages? Why is this kind of payment regarded by law as the only possible fallback?

Fifth response. This is partly because of the feature discussed in the second response above. The obligations imposed by the law of torts are mainly negative obligations. Once there is injury there cannot possibly be no injury. Once there is failure of care there cannot possibly be no failure of care. Positive obligations are in this respect somewhat different. Where there has been no delivery, there can still be a (belated) delivery. Where there has been no start to the building works there can still be a (belated) start to the building works. This can sometimes allow courts to be more creative in the remedies they give for breach of contract, at any rate where time was not of the essence. Even in such cases, however, the courts may be reluctant to give remedies other than money awards. The reasons are those that the courts themselves give. It is normally easier to supervise performance of an obligation to pay money than it is to supervise the performance of other kinds of remedial obligation. It is also normally easier to bypass an uncooperative defendant where money payments are concerned, for example, by garnishment of earnings or bank accounts. It is also less oppressive to make money awards in cases in which parties who have already fallen out would now be required to collaborate in completing other remedial obligations. Such considerations play a major role in determining how somewhat indeterminate moral obligations, such as moral obligations of corrective justice, should be made more determinate in the law. There is nothing about obligations of corrective justice, or any other obligations,

[69] MacCormick, 'The Obligation of Reparation', above note 48, 213.

that prevents them from being rendered more determinate by the law in a way that is sensitive to the various costs and benefits of different ways of doing so. Here the economists clearly have a niche.

Sixth doubt. There has been no mention anywhere of the rights of the person wronged. Surely it is of the essence of the law of torts that it protects the plaintiff's rights by conferring on him further (remedial) rights against the defendant? And surely, as Weinrib says, 'corrective justice singles out a particular plaintiff and a particular defendant and makes the duties of one correlative to the rights of the other'?[70] This being so, how is it possible to explain what tort law is for in terms of corrective justice without once mentioning anyone's rights?

Sixth response. True, I did not mention rights but their role is explained by what I said. In section 4 I said, for example, that 'the reasons why one must pay for the losses that one occasions are the very same reasons why one must not occasion those losses in the first place'. In the context of the law of torts the primary obligation of the tortfeasor, the one that she violates when she commits the tort, is always justified by the interest of the person wronged (together with such other considerations as support the protection of that interest by the imposition of that obligation).[71] It follows that the primary obligation of the tortfeasor, the one that she violates by her tort, is always a rights-based obligation. This explains why, when that right is violated, the person wronged also has, in the law of torts, a right to reparative damages. If the primary obligation is rights-based then so is the secondary obligation, for both—by the continuity thesis—must share the same rationale. Recall the obligation-in, obligation-out principle? By the same logic we could now add the 'right-in, right-out' principle: whoever has a primary right (e.g. a right not to be libeled) also gets a secondary right (a right to reparative damages in a libel suit) upon violation of that primary right.

You may think that this is enough to show that the primary obligation in the law of torts must be an obligation of justice after

[70] Weinrib, *The Idea of Private Law*, above note 1, 76.

[71] On the significance of the parenthetical words, see Joseph Raz, 'Rights and Individual Well-being' in his *Ethics in the Public Domain* (Oxford 1994).

all. Isn't a question of rights always a question of justice? So it is often thought.[72] But the thought is mistaken. The obligation not to torture has, as part of its rationale, the interests of the person who is not to be tortured. Indeed the interests of the person who is not to be tortured suffice to justify the obligation not to torture. We each have, in short, a right not to be tortured. Yet the obligation not to torture that is based on this right is not an obligation of justice. It is an obligation of humanity. Not every right we have is an allocative right, i.e. a right of justice.[73] Nor is the whole of justice taken up with rights. On the other hand, my right to reparation for a violation of my rights is a right of justice. It requires a reallocation of losses as between me and my torturer. Even though it is not an injustice that my torturer does to me when he violates my right not to be tortured, there is a corrective injustice that he does to me if he violates my right to have him make good my consequent losses, if any, afterwards.

Seventh doubt. Surely the proposed explanation is too narrow to explain the whole of the law of reparative damages? Maybe it explains what are known as special damages (damages for loss of earnings, for medical bills, for repairs to houses, etc.) but how does it apply to so-called 'general damages' (damages for pain and suffering, for bereavement, for loss of amenity, etc.)?[74]

Seventh response. For the most part, the continuity thesis does not explain general damages. By and large they are not reparative in the strictest sense. They are paid in respect of certain irreparable results or consequences of a tort or breach of contract. As such, they cannot be explained directly by the continuity thesis. They require a different rationale. In my view they exist mainly to assuage frustration, resentment, and other kinds of ill-feeling that afflict plaintiffs. Thereby, often enough, they serve as a way to take the heat out of plaintiff-defendant conflicts. How do they

[72] See e.g. Finnis, *Natural Law and Natural Rights*, above note 28, 232; Nicholas Wollerstorff, *Justice: Rights and Wrongs* (Princeton 2008), 10.

[73] For a defence of this view, see my 'The Virtue of Charity and its Foils' in Charles Mitchell and Sue Moody (eds), *Foundations of Charity* (Oxford 2000). Compare Finnis, *Natural Law and Natural Rights*, above note 28, 163–4, discussing the torture example and placing it under the 'justice' heading.

[74] For full articulation of this doubt, see John Goldberg, 'Two Conceptions of Tort Damages: Fair v Full Compensation', *DePaul Law Review* 55 (2006), 435.

do this? Is it just that a cash windfall, which might equally be a lottery win or a tax refund, takes one's mind off one's pain or distracts one from hating one's injurer? No. It matters that the payment of general damages takes a quasi-reparative form, being paid by or on behalf of the tortfeasor, being pegged to results or consequences of the tort, being quantified (notionally) according to the severity of the result or consequence in question, and so on. It matters, in other words, that some of the implications of the continuity thesis are preserved in the norms regulating general damages even though the continuity thesis does not strictly apply. Thereby some of the placatory social meaning of effecting reparation according to the continuity thesis spills over; general damages bask in the reflected glory of special damages. It is no accident that special damages have this glory. It comes of the fact that correcting a wrong, in accordance with the continuity thesis, is also a way of mitigating a wrong. This gives reparative damages a distinct placatory potential. It is not hard to exploit and extend this potential by creating neighbouring categories of quasi-reparative damages (officially classified as 'reparative') that can be awarded for irreparable losses.

One may accept this line of thought while at the same time being sceptical about at least some of the extension. One may regret that people have come to expect, and are often granted, various kinds of awards that go beyond the strictly reparative. My own sense is that this has got out of hand in the jurisdictions with which I am familiar. In the United States tort law is clearly a major direct contributor to the excess, with the unprincipled use of so-called 'punitive damages' by juries turning the law of torts into a ridiculous combination of lottery and pillory. But even in England, where both juries and punitive damages in tort cases are thankfully rare, the ideology of 'compensation'—shorn of any strictly reparative objectives—has had an unhappy effect on public culture. This is only partly a direct consequence of tort law's own native doctrines. It is also partly the result of an intellectually immature body of public law, partly the result of a receding welfare state, and partly the result of aspects of civil procedure (notably the English rules as to costs) which aggravate the chilling effect of tort law itself, and lead to all sorts of spurious payouts to bribe potential plaintiffs out of pursuing speculative litigation. Is this a price we must pay for improved access to justice? Perhaps. Or perhaps we are forgetting that the pursuit of justice can be self-defeating: that attempting to do justice or have justice done can increase the incidence of injustice (even if nobody is mistaken about what would count as a relevant justice or injustice). Corrective justice too can be counterproductively pursued, and increasing access to it, at least beyond a certain point, might add to the counterproductivity. In which case what we are giving is access to injustice.

7. Putting corrective justice in its place

In the following tantalizing passage, which seems to sit rather awkwardly with the rest of his argument, Weinrib comes close to embracing the continuity thesis as an explanation of what corrective justice is for, and therefore (because he thinks this is the same thing) an explanation what tort law is for:

> When the defendant … breaches a duty correlative to the plaintiff's right, the plaintiff is entitled to reparation. The remedy reflects the fact that even after the commission of the tort the defendant remains subject to the duty with respect to the plaintiff's right. The defendant's breach of the duty not to interfere with the embodiment of the plaintiff's right does not, of course, bring the duty to an end, for if it did, the duty would—absurdly—be discharged by its breach. With the materialization of wrongful injury, the only way the defendant can discharge his or her obligation respecting the plaintiff's right is to undo the effects of the breach of duty. Just as the plaintiff's right constitutes the subject matter of the defendant's duty, so the wrongful interference with the right entails the duty to repair. Thus tort law places the defendant under the obligation to restore the plaintiff, so far as possible, to the position the plaintiff would have been in had the wrong not been committed.[75]

In the bulk of this passage, the obligation of reparation is presented as the same obligation as the original obligation, breach of which constituted the tort. It merely now falls, *tant pis*, to be discharged in a second-best way, by payment of reparation. But

[75] *The Idea of Private Law*, above note 1, 135. Similarly, Arthur Ripstein, 'As If It Had Never Happened', *William and Mary Law Review* 48 (2007), 1957 at 1979: '[t]he normative situation is unchanged' by the wrong.

in the last sentence, the proposal changes. Payment of reparation is now due because the law of torts imposes a new obligation—an obligation of corrective justice. This *volte face* is hard to make sense of. In particular, the 'thus' at the start of the final sentence seems perverse. If the obligation already exists (by entailment, no less) how can it also be imposed by tort law?

One reason why the passage seems to sit awkwardly with the rest of Weinrib's argument is that, if it were true that the so-called secondary obligation is always the same obligation as the primary one, then there would be no norms of corrective justice. We would have no need of them. The norm creating the primary obligation would be the only moral norm we would need; the rest of the work would be done by logic (entailment). Perhaps this threat of corrective justice's imminent redundancy explains Weinrib's otherwise undermotivated thesis that the primary obligation is itself an obligation of corrective justice. For with this thesis in place, the claim that the primary and secondary obligations are one and the same does not have the unfortunate side-effect of making norms of corrective justice redundant. At any rate, their redundancy is postponed. Or perhaps—a rival possibility—what Weinrib is saying in the passage just quoted is this. Perhaps he is saying that the only norms of corrective justice that exist are those that the law creates to give additional determinacy to what would otherwise be the indeterminate remedial entailments of the primary norm. This would help to explain another Weinribian thesis that otherwise seems undermotivated, namely his thesis that moral norms of corrective justice are owed entirely to the law. His point, we may now think, is not that there are no reparative obligations in morality apart from the law. There are, but they are obligations already entailed by the primary moral norm that is breached. Only when the law intervenes to sharpen them up do they become reparative norms in their own right, and hence corrective justice begins to occupy its own normative space.

If these manoeuvres seem forced, we are now in a better position to understand why. In this passage Weinrib reaches out for, but does not quite grasp, the continuity thesis. He imagines a continuity in the obligation itself. The primary obligation and the secondary one are one and the same. In fact, as we saw, the continuity is only in the reasons why the two obligations exist.

Their common rationale is what links them. Uncovering this is in one way good news for Weinrib. It rescues the morality of corrective justice from the oblivion or near-oblivion that his own distorted version of the continuity thesis would inflict upon it. On the other hand, it also deprives Weinrib of his doctrine of the autonomy of corrective justice. It shows that we need reasons from beyond the morality of corrective justice to explain the morality of corrective justice. We need to know the reasons why certain obligations, not being obligations of corrective justice, exist. For these are none other than the primary obligations of tort law, the rationale of which is also, in each case, the rationale for the secondary obligations of tort law to which breach of the primary obligations gives rise. These secondary obligations are, and cannot but be, obligations of corrective justice. So there is no tort law without corrective justice. On the other hand there has to be more to tort law than corrective justice. And there is also corrective justice beyond tort law, and indeed beyond law. It exists in raw morality too, in the raw morality of trips to the beach, students in trouble, and disappointed children. Private law can (and may be needed to) make such obligations more determinate than they would be in their raw moral form, but it is not needed to bring them into existence in the first place.

3

WHAT IS TORT LAW FOR? THE PLACE OF DISTRIBUTIVE JUSTICE

1. Distributive justice in a corrective context

[P]rinciples of distributive justice designed to cover the distribution of the benefits and burdens of economic activity among individuals in a society ... have been the dominant source of Anglo-American debate about distributive justice over the last four decades.[1]

So they have. It is hardly surprising, then, that when we think about distributive justice and the law of torts, the issues that first spring to mind concern tort law's impact on, and sensitivity to, the distribution of resources (or wherewithal) across the wider population. Should tort damages be calculated on the basis of the plaintiff's lost earnings even where those earnings were obscenely high or obscenely low? Shouldn't there be a ceiling and a floor? Even with a ceiling and a floor, doesn't tort law create incentives to divert risks onto the disadvantaged, thereby compounding their disadvantage? Moving our attention from disparities among plaintiffs to disparities among defendants, shouldn't the precautions against accidents expected of the well-heeled be greater than those expected of humbler folk? At any rate, shouldn't the relative burden of meeting the costs of safety, in the defendant's particular circumstances, be relevant to the stringency of the defendant's tort-law duties? In general, shouldn't the choices of those with more limited options be treated differently by the law of torts, and by the law generally, from the choices of those better furnished with alternatives?

Putting such questions of (what we might call) 'socio-economic justice' centre stage, notes Tsachi Keren-Paz, are at least 'two streams of scholarship' about the law of torts:

[1] Julian Lamont and Christi Favor, 'Distributive Justice' in Edward N Zalta (ed), *The Stanford Encyclopedia of Philosophy* (Stanford 2008, fall edition) <http://plato.stanford.edu/archives/fall2008/entries/justice-distributive/>.

Torts and Other Wrongs. John Gardner, Oxford University Press (2019). © John Gardner
DOI: 10.1093/oso/9780198852940.003.0003

The first stream attempts to defend the relevance and legitimacy of using private law for (limited) redistributive purposes. The other ... is the one trying to employ tort law progressively, with an ambition to be sensitive to ... the interests of disadvantaged groups in society.[2]

In his excellent book on distributive justice in tort law, Keren-Paz assesses and augments both streams of scholarship. In this essay, by contrast, I will not assess or augment either of them. That is not because I disagree with them. On the contrary: I believe that the questions listed in the previous paragraph are pressing. If it turns out to be true that the law of torts has what Keren-Paz calls a 'regressive bias',[3] i.e. that it has worse impacts on the less well-off, we ought to be striving to put that right, subject to the obvious imperative to make sure that we don't end up doing more harm than good in the attempt.

I mention this imperative, even though it is obvious, because it is easily forgotten by those with a zeal for reform. Eliminating one set of regressive allocations does not always help the cause of securing progressive allocations across the board. The temptation to phase out regressive non-means-tested distributions of public money, such as universal childcare benefits, higher education and transport subsidies, and blanket legal aid for criminal defendants, has already done great harm to the political sustainability of the (generally progressive) welfare state in Europe. Denying the middle classes a direct return on the welfare benefit system weakens the broad consensus in its favour and hence opens the way to dismantling it, as today's right-wing politicians have gleefully come to realize. That is one reason why they like to brand non-means-tested benefits and subsidies as 'regressive': so that they can dupe unsuspecting progressive voters, and even progressive politicians, into an unholy alliance that will not have progressive consequences in the longer run. Before we support overhauling or abolishing a regressive law of torts, we had better be sure that we are not likewise playing into the hands of those who would like to see less protection for the vulnerable.

[2] Tsachi Keren-Paz, *Torts, Egalitarianism and Distributive Justice* (Aldershot 2007), 2.

[3] Ibid, 67.

But that, to repeat, will not be my topic here. I will not be concerned with the desirability of changing the law of torts to cure or alleviate, or otherwise to respond to, distributive injustices that could equally exist quite apart from the law of torts, such as those that concern Keren-Paz. I will be concerned, rather, with problems of distributive justice that come into being only because the law of torts exists. And I will be less interested in working out how these problems should be solved than in establishing *that they are there*: that tort law creates, and cannot avoid dealing with, distributive problems of its own.

This may have incidental implications for Keren-Paz's project. One of the possible ways in which we may do more harm than good in reforming tort law, if I am right, is in rushing to mitigate tort law's 'regressive bias' without regard to the more specialized distributive tasks that are thrown up by tort law itself. Again, I leave it to others to assess how much importance to attach to these more specialized distributive tasks. My role will be limited to sketching out what they (or some of them) are.

In carving out this role for myself I am reacting mainly to those, led by Ernest Weinrib, who regard all considerations of distributive justice as 'extrinsic' or 'alien' to the law of torts. 'Corrective justice is the form of the private law relationship,'[4] claims Weinrib, and there can be no 'combining [of] distributive and corrective considerations within a single relationship'.[5]

In the previous chapter, I offered some support to the first of these two claims. I argued that 'any complete explanation of tort law—whatever other considerations it may invoke—cannot but invoke considerations of corrective justice'.[6] The reason I gave was this. Some legal norms central to the law of torts are themselves norms of corrective justice, and it follows, I argued, that they can be assessed only in the light of their contribution to the doing of corrective justice. This was, briefly encapsulated, my argument:

> [T]he law of torts cannot include a sound norm of corrective justice without there also being a moral norm of corrective justice that the legal norm of corrective justice helps to constitute. And once there is such a moral norm of corrective justice, the law of torts cannot be justified

[4] Ernest Weinrib, *The Idea of Private Law* (Cambridge, Mass 1995), 75.

[5] Ibid, 163. [6] See chapter 2 above.

without pointing to the role that the law of torts plays in securing conformity with that very same moral norm.[7]

'Cannot be fully justified without' does not, however, entail 'can be fully justified by'. So there is nothing here to lend credence to Weinrib's second claim, the claim that the 'immanence of corrective justice in tort law'[8] tells against 'the introduction of distributive considerations' into tort-law thinking.[9]

In what follows I will resist this second claim. Indeed I will defend an almost diametrically opposed claim: that certain questions of distributive justice are central to the law of torts, and cannot but be faced by those who administer and develop it, *precisely because* the law of torts is a site of corrective justice.

Those with pigeonholing instincts may be tempted to label this a 'mixed' or 'pluralistic' explanation of tort law. Since I think that every pro and every con of every action or practice counts in its assessment, and that no amount of theorizing can properly eradicate the ultimate diversity of pros and cons, I am hardly in a position to object to these as designations of my wider outlook on life.[10] At the same time, the interplay of corrective and distributive concerns that I will be investigating here is not well described as a mere mixture, or a mere plurality. I endorse (and regard what follows as helping to develop and finesse) Peter Cane's thesis that 'corrective justice provides the structure of tort law within which distributive justice operates'.[11] In my version of this thesis,[12] as we will see, the place of corrective justice in tort law enjoys some kind of explanatory priority. So this chapter will presuppose

[7] Ibid, 52–3. [8] Weinrib, *The Idea of Private Law*, above note 4, 171.

[9] Ibid, 74.

[10] Even for Gardner, '[p]resumably, coherence would count towards soundness,' hopes Weinrib in the conclusion of his *Corrective Justice* (Oxford 2012), 336. Not so. Any justification has to be coherent in the thin sense of intelligible. But Weinribian unity (or Dworkinian integrity) is not, in my eyes, any kind of plus. Reality, including moral reality, is fragmentary.

[11] Peter Cane, 'Distributive Justice in Tort Law', *New Zealand Law Review* [2001], 401 at 413.

[12] Which may well differ from Cane's. For him 'corrective justice is a "formal" principle whereas distributive justice is a "material" principle' (ibid, 416). I have argued that there are no formal principles of justice: John Gardner, *Law as a Leap of Faith* (Oxford 2012), ch 10.

and rely on the main findings of chapter 2. Yet the implication is not that the pursuit of distributive justice is the pursuit of a goal extrinsic to tort law in the sense given to that expression by Weinrib. The specialized distributive goals for tort law that we will be studying here are not goals 'independent of ... the law that they [help to] justify'.[13] Nor are they goals the achievement of which is 'socially desirable quite apart from tort law'.[14] They are distributive goals that the specifically corrective context of tort law brings into being, and the pursuit of which apart from that context (or something very like it) would be unimaginable, perhaps even unintelligible.

2. The distribution of correction

As I emphasized at the end of chapter 2, there are rights to and duties of corrective justice that exist independently of the law, and independently of any other kind of use, observance, recognition, or adoption by anyone. They exist (as I put it) 'in the raw morality of trips to the beach, students in trouble, and disappointed children'.[15] In the situations I had in mind, a moral duty owed to another person, a rightholder, goes unperformed. Even though the time for performing the duty is past, the reasons why that ('primary') duty to the rightholder existed (as well as the reason constituted by the fact that it was a duty) still exert their force as reasons for some fallback action, which is the subject of a new ('secondary') duty to the same rightholder. By performing the secondary duty—say, providing a new treat in substitution for a missed outing—one reduces the deficit in one's reason-conformity that was left by one's nonperformance. I called this thesis, the thesis that the secondary duty exists for the reasons that were left unsatisfied by the nonperformance of the primary duty, the 'continuity thesis'.

By their nature, raw moral rights and duties are not allocated by anybody. They exist, as I said, irrespective of their use, observance, recognition, or adoption. There is therefore no question of anyone's having such rights and duties either justly or unjustly.

13 Weinrib, *The Idea of Private Law*, above note 4, 4.

14 Ibid.

15 See chapter 2 above at 78.

Even when they are raw duties of justice it is neither just nor unjust that they are the duties of justice one happens to have. So there is in the context of morality in the raw nothing analogous to the problem that, in the context of legal decision-making, Guido Calabresi and Douglas Melamed call 'the problem of entitlement', the problem of how rights and duties are to be distributed as between 'two or more people, or two or more groups of people' with 'conflicting interests'.[16] It makes no sense to ask what distribution of raw moral rights and duties would be just, even when the interests that they serve conflict, because raw moral rights and duties are incapable of being distributed. They come and go with the reasons for and against their existence, and irrespective (to repeat one more time) of their use, observance, recognition, or adoption. In this context, and to this extent, Weinrib is quite right to say that 'corrective justice operates on entitlements without addressing the justice of the underlying distribution'.[17] With morality in the raw, there is no such thing as the justice of the underlying distribution, because nothing relevant has been distributed.[18]

Things are, however, very different with the law. Legal rights and legal duties, as Calabresi and Melamed rightly assume, are respectively *conferred* and *imposed* by someone. Calabresi and Melamed focus on 'decisions' to confer and impose them. This is too narrow. There are also many accidental conferrals and impositions of legal rights and duties, notably by custom *in foro* and in the tacit premises of judicial argument.[19] Nevertheless, Calabresi and Melamed are right to think that conferral and imposition (whether intentional or accidental) is how legal rights and duties respectively come into existence. Rights and duties must be

[16] Guido Calabresi and Douglas Melamed, 'Property Rules, Liability Rules, and Inalienability: One View of the Cathedral', *Harvard Law Review* 85 (1972), 1089 at 1090.

[17] *The Idea of Private Law*, above note 4, 80.

[18] Which should not be mistaken for the proposition that there are no raw moral rights and duties of distributive justice. There most certainly are. They bear on the distribution of things other than raw moral rights and duties. For a compelling defence of their existence against 'constructivist' doubters, see G A Cohen, *Rescuing Justice and Equality* (Cambridge, Mass 2008).

[19] See my *Law as a Leap of Faith*, above note 12, especially ch 3.

used, observed, recognized, or adopted by someone in order to be part of the law. I will call the process of making them part of the law, intentionally or accidentally, their 'institutionalization'. In chapter 2 I concentrated on the role that institutionalization can play, when it is done well, in augmenting and refining the raw morality of corrective justice, in particular by 'determining at least some of its applications'.[20] (The implication being: the raw moral position is no longer the whole moral position.) Here I want to focus, instead, on one sub-question that arises when we ask whether the institutionalization of corrective justice has been 'done well', namely whether it has been done *justly*. Unlike some people I know,[21] I don't think this is the only sub-question that arises. The institutionalization of corrective justice also needs to be done prudently, sensitively, humanely, efficiently, honestly, and so forth, sometimes at the expense of its justice. For present purposes, however, it is the question of justice that interests us. And this question of justice, it seems to me, is not a question of corrective justice. The relevant question of corrective justice has *ex hypothesi* already been answered. There is a moral duty of corrective justice in the neighbourhood, and it is now a candidate for institutionalization. The relevant question of justice now is: How do we allocate the institutionalization? How do we distribute, across the vast range of candidate wrongdoers and candidate persons wronged, the numerous possible sets of legal arrangements to support the doing of corrective justice as between them?

Here is how the question arises, more specifically, in the law of torts. It is part of the nature of a tort that designating some wrong as a tort—classifying it as a legal wrong under the 'tort' heading—entails creating a legal right to corrective justice in favour of those who are wronged.[22] This legal right is a complex one. Its incidents include not only the wrongdoer's legal duty to repair, but also a largely undirected[23] legal power for the person wronged to determine whether that legal duty is concretized

[20] See chapter 2 above at 44.

[21] eg John Finnis, in *Natural Law and Natural Rights* (Oxford 1980), ch 7.

[22] This is a point of law. I defended it as a valid one in chapter 1.

[23] An undirected legal power is a legal power that is not coupled with legal duties regulating its exercise. See Joseph Raz, 'The Inner Logic of the Law' in his *Ethics in the Public Domain* (pbk ed, Oxford 1994), 238 at 241ff.

and enforced through the courts, with a consequent duty on the courts to assist, when that power is validly exercised by the issue of proceedings.[24] When this right is conferred, public authority (the authority of the court) is put at the disposal of the wronged person. When the rule of law prevails, moreover, the authority is laid on partly at public expense (in that the court does not recoup its full running costs from its users, and may also arrange for other user costs to be subsidized). The wronged person, in short, is given a right not only against the wrongdoer but also against the court, a right to conscript the court (and its officers) in his or her quest for corrective justice against the wrongdoer.

In deciding whether something should be a tort, then, it is never enough to conclude that it is a wrong calling for repair. It is not even enough to conclude that it should be *recognized by the law* as a wrong calling for repair. The question that must be confronted, in addition, is whether the law should give it *this kind of recognition*—the tort-law kind of recognition—complete with its generous terms for power-sharing and cost-sharing as between the aggrieved party and the legal system. That question is a question of distributive justice. The law is selecting some people for a measure of official support in their personal affairs that most other clients of the welfare state can only dream of. Even among those who have been wronged, not all can possibly enjoy this level of support in putting things right, and the question is always live of who should be the privileged ones who qualify for it. That mirrors the question we ask when we ask who should get the latest cancer drugs, or who should get sent on the most effective offender-rehabilitation courses. Even for those who say that 'user pays' is the best (most just) solution, there is no doubt that such problems of how to allocate scarce medical and social services fall under the heading of distributive justice.[25] Why

[24] This complex legal power is rightly emphasized (although sometimes wrongly overemphasized) by John Goldberg and Ben Zipursky in their joint and solo writings on tort law, a mature conspectus of which is their 'Torts as Wrongs', *Texas Law Review* 88 (2010), 917.

[25] Occasionally talk of 'distributive justice' is taken to conceal a leaning towards *re*distribution. But it is better to follow Nozick in treating redistributive and non-redistributive norms as competing within the space of distributive justice: Robert Nozick, *Anarchy, State, and Utopia* (New York 1974), 153ff. See my discussion in chapter 2 above at 38–40.

doubt that the same is true regarding the allocation of scarce judicial services? The difference lies not in the character of the allocation. The difference lies in what is being allocated. What is being allocated, when we allocate rights to issue proceedings in torts, is access to a special apparatus for the doing of justice in another form, viz. corrective justice. It is one question whether corrective justice is being dispensed in the courts. It is a further question whether the system justly distributes access to the corrective justice it dispenses.

My locating the courts among the diverse public services of the welfare state may be taken to suggest that I have come back round, in spite of myself, to focusing on the overall 'distribution of the benefits and burdens of economic activity among individuals in a society'.[26] You may think, in particular, that I am assuming a scarcity of publicly provided legal services that arises only from the cost of supplying them in competition with other calls on public funds. But that is a simplification. The potential economic strain of funding the courts and access to them clearly cannot be ignored. But even if money were no object, we should still be sparing in handing out legal rights because of the cultural costs of excessive juridification, i.e. of turning too much of our lives over to the law.[27] The rule of law favours access to justice, but it also favours the existence of non-juridified space in which people can readily steer clear of the law.[28] So even if there were plentiful funding, we would still be forced by the rule of law to confront the question of how to distribute legal rights and duties as between many potential plaintiffs and defendants, respect for whose moral rights and duties could potentially be well-served by their institutionalization, and the institutionalization of which would not be ruled out on other grounds,[29] but not all of whose

[26] Lamont and Favor, 'Distributive Justice', above note 1.

[27] For valuable critical reflections on juridification, see the essays in Gunther Teubner (ed), *Juridification of Social Spheres* (Berlin 1987).

[28] I discuss other implications for the law of torts of this desideratum of the rule of law in chapter 6 of this volume. In chapter 10, meanwhile, I discuss various additional factors that turn the doing of justice into a scarce resource.

[29] I am thinking of the harm principle (a norm of toleration, not of justice) and similar moral norms that place independent restrictions on the use of law as an instrument for improving moral conformity. See Joseph Raz, 'Autonomy,

moral rights and duties it would be advisable, even if it were humanly possible, to institutionalize simultaneously.

It might be thought that such a distributive question can properly be live for legislators, but not for judges. Judges in tort cases should only do 'justice between the parties'. But where the rule of law prevails, doing justice between the parties, in the relevant sense, cannot but entail consideration of whether the plaintiff belongs to a class of people who should enjoy a right to proceed in tort against the defendant. Under the rule of law judges must decide cases according to law, which means (minimally) that they must not separate the rule from the ruling, either by declaring what the rule is or will henceforth be while declining to apply it to the case in hand, or by denying that there is a rule.[30] It follows that no judge may rule in favour of any plaintiff except by locating the plaintiff within a class of imaginable plaintiffs who would, according to the judge, be entitled to the same ruling. To determine which class this is, it is not enough for judges to settle whether the plaintiff has been wronged by the defendant and whether corrective justice could now be done. They must also confront the question of whether corrective justice should be done with the aid of tort law, which is only one possible mechanism among many (indeed, among many found in the law). And that cannot but be confronted as a distributive question: How do we dole out the right to proceed in tort among various candidate classes? Do we ask which class deserves the right most, which has most to gain from it, which is least likely to abuse the right, which is best-placed to make use of it for the public good, which needs it most, which can have it at least cost to the upholding of legal certainty, or what?

In England, to be sure, it took primary legislation to confer adequate tort-law rights on trespassers injured by the negligence of the occupiers of land.[31] But there would have been nothing improper or even unusual about such rights having been developed

Toleration, and the Harm Principle' in Ruth Gavison (ed), *Issues in Contemporary Legal Philosophy* (Oxford 1987).

30 I discuss this requirement further in Gardner, *Law as a Leap of Faith*, above note 12, ch 8.

31 Occupiers' Liability Act 1984.

at common law by the following line of thought: the fact that trespassers are themselves tortfeasors has been disproportionately visited upon them by too often denying them causes of action in tort for wrongs committed against them by occupiers; so some of the cases denying them such causes of action should be overruled or distinguished, reining in an over-harsh version of the *ex turpi causa non oritur actio* defence. Notice that it was a closely analogous line of thought by which the modern law of negligence came of age in *Donoghue* v *Stevenson*:[32] the fact that retail consumers are not in privity of contract with manufacturers and wholesalers (argued the majority in the House of Lords) has been disproportionately visited upon them by too often denying them causes of action in tort for wrongs committed against them by manufacturers and wholesalers; some of the cases denying them such causes of action should thus be overruled or distinguished, reining in an over-harsh version of the doctrine of privity of contract. The 'disproportion' in both examples is clearly a distributive one. It means something like 'comparatively undeserved'. Plaintiffs of a certain class (trespassers and strangers to contracts) have been given undeservedly little in the distribution of causes of action in tort as compared with plaintiffs of other classes (lawful visitors and parties to contracts respectively). This shows how, in attempting corrective justice between the parties in a tort case, judges may also (often inexplicitly) be attempting distributive justice between classes of parties in the allocation of access to tort law's apparatus for doing corrective justice. It shows, indeed, that whenever there is a question before them of which acts ought to be classed as torts, judges cannot avoid attempting such distributive justice.

This reveals that the scarcity of law as a public resource is not the only reason, and may not even be the most important reason, why attempts at distributive justice are inevitable in the law of torts. Attempts at distributive justice are also inevitable because the law of torts is part of the common law, and in the common law the standard way for judges to develop the law is by making comparisons between different classes of plaintiffs, and between different classes of defendants. 'People of class P have an established cause of action against people of class D,' argues a plaintiff.

[32] [1932] AC 562.

'Is the difference between people of class P and people like me, call us class P′, really so great that we should have no cause of action against people of class D at all?' Or: 'People like me, in class P, have an established cause of action against people of class D. Is the difference between people of class D and people of class D′ really so great that we should have no cause of action against people of class D′ at all?' It may have been the pervasiveness of this kind of argument in the common law that led H L A Hart to the famous but mistaken thesis that 'we have, in the bare notion of applying a general rule of law, the germ at least of justice'.[33] In the cases I am thinking of, the judges are certainly generalizing, but they are not merely applying a rule. They are forging a new rule by generalizing from an existing one, and doing so on the ground that, in their view, it would be unjust for one class of persons to enjoy recourse to tort law (recourse taken to be justified) that is denied to a neighbouring class. Legislatures, unlike judges, are not constrained to work in this way. They may create new causes of action without building on existing ones. But that does not show that they are not attempting a just distribution of tort law rights and duties. It only shows that not all distributors proceed by comparing what they are asked to bestow with what has already been bestowed.

When courts or legislatures recognize new causes of action in tort, or extend existing causes of action, they are distributing legal rights and duties to new classes of potential plaintiffs and potential defendants. In the first place they are distributing new primary legal duties, breaches of which will count not just as legally recognized wrongs but more specifically as *torts*, violating not just any legal rights but legal rights *in the law of torts*. In placing these legal rights in the law of torts—in making the breaches of primary duty tortious—courts and legislatures also unavoidably distribute associated secondary duties. These are legal duties of corrective justice—to be more exact, duties of repair—that arise from breach of the primary legal duties and are owed to the same rightholder. As already noted, these duties are bundled with

[33] H L A Hart, *The Concept of Law* (Oxford 1961), 202. For a thorough critique of this remark, see David Lyons, 'On Formal Justice', *Cornell Law Review* (1972), 58 (1973), 833. See also my *Law as a Leap of Faith*, above note 12, ch 10.

generous powers on the part of the rightholder to concretize and enforce them through the courts. Nevertheless, what is distributed remains something irreducibly corrective. And that lends a certain explanatory priority to corrective over distributive justice in what Weinrib might call the 'immanent rationality' of tort law.[34] We need to grasp the essentially corrective ingredient in tort law in order to grasp the whole package deal, the structured normative arrangement, that tort law is in the distinctive business of distributing—a deal, indeed, that would not even be up for distribution without tort law.

Calabresi and Melamed are sometimes remembered as having denied this. They are remembered as having assigned to the law the task of distributing only 'the set of initial entitlements',[35] understood (in the context and idiom of tort law) as the set of primary duties, breach of which constitutes a tort. The secondary (corrective) duties of tort law are sometimes imagined to have been, for Calabresi and Melamed, automatic implications of the initial entitlements. In other words, Calabresi and Melamed are often associated with something like my 'continuity thesis'. Doing corrective justice is responding belatedly to the reasons that one should have responded to in the first place, in not committing the tort. In combination with the Calabresi and Melamed view that these first-place reasons are reasons for the allocation of 'initial entitlements', this lures one into what might be called the 'deflationary view' of corrective justice. Corrective justice is revealed not to be a distinct form of justice, but merely distributive justice redone following a disruptive intervention (that was not itself licensed by distributive justice). And from here it is a short step to what, in chapter 2, I called 'a perennial student objection to tort law',[36] namely that it cannot be just to restore a distribution that was not itself just.

We should not be so quick to sign up to this perennial student objection to tort law, for the deflationary view of corrective

[34] *The Idea of Private Law*, above note 4, e.g. 206.

[35] 'Property Rules, Liability Rules, and Inalienability', above note 16, 1097.

[36] See p 41 above. For a properly worked-out version of the objection, see James Nickel, 'Justice in Compensation', *William and Mary Law Review* 18 (1976), 379 at 381ff.

justice is false. It is false in raw morality, as we already saw, because in raw morality there is no question of distributing initial entitlements and so no question of restoring their initial distribution. And it is also false, we can now add, in the law. In the law, quite apart from the question of which primary duties (=which 'initial entitlements') to recognize, there is the further question of how to deal with the breach of those legally recognized primary duties, and in particular whether to institutionalize a secondary duty of corrective justice. If one locates the primary duties in the law of torts, as we saw, one inevitably includes a secondary duty of corrective justice as a part of the 'tort law' package. But one need not use the law of torts, and more generally one need not grant a secondary duty of corrective justice. One may choose a different (non-corrective) legal response to some legal wrongs, or indeed no legal response at all. So there are always two questions for the court or legislature: which 'initial entitlements' to include in the law, and how to respond—correctively or otherwise—to their violation.

It follows that the corrective duties are not mere automatic implications of the initial entitlements, whether by the logic of the continuity thesis or otherwise. They are distinct entitlements that also need to be distributed by the law. And this, indeed, is what Calabresi and Melamed say. They emphasize 'the [twin] problems of selecting the initial entitlements *and the modes of protecting these entitlements*'.[37] Indeed one way to read their famous article is as a critique of the view that corrective remedies are automatically in order, i.e. that they just follow without further ado from the disruption of initial entitlements. There is always the further question, when initial entitlements are disrupted, of whether and how the law should respond to the disruption. As Calabresi and Melamed express the question:

> Why ... cannot society limit itself to the property rule? To do this it would need only to protect and enforce the initial entitlements from all attacks, perhaps through criminal sanctions, and to enforce voluntary contracts for their transfer. Why do we need liability rules at all?[38]

[37] 'Property Rules, Liability Rules, and Inalienability', above note 16, 1089, emphasis added.

[38] Ibid, 1106.

Calabresi and Melamed have their own answer. They see many advantages in choosing the tort-law route for protecting property rights. It follows that they reject the idea that there are no other routes. In protecting property rights by law, they notice, having a tort of trespass is but one option among many. Indeed, even when it comes to recognizing duties of non-trespass in the law, having a tort of trespass is but one option among many. The tort lawyer's slogan '*ubi ius, ibi remedium*' may serve well as a recommendation but it bespeaks no rational inevitability.[39]

Does all this cast doubt on the relevance to the law of torts of the continuity thesis, which does bespeak a kind of rational inevitability? Are we quietly backing away from the conclusions of chapter 2? Not at all. It is one question why, as rational beings, we would want to do corrective justice, and want to see corrective justice done, and the doing of it supported. The continuity thesis helps us to see why. But it is another question when and how, if at all, we should actually support the doing of corrective justice. Here we may have cause to reflect on the desirability of using the law (or other similar institutional systems) as a method of support. And as I have explained, we cannot but encounter that question of desirability as, at least partly, a question of distributive justice. Legal support for the doing of corrective justice is a scarce good. What Rawls calls 'the circumstances of justice' obtain in respect of it.[40] Moreover the courts constantly face the question, in common law systems, of why one class of plaintiffs should have a cause of action while another nearby class does not, or why one class of defendants should be suable while another nearby class is not. Which plaintiff-classes should be supported as against which defendant-classes? Which corrective justice is to be chosen for legal recognition? That is clearly a distributive problem.

[39] On the interpretation of the slogan, see Ted Sampsell-Jones, 'The Myth of *Ashby* v *White*', *University of St Thomas Law Journal* 8 (2010), 40.

[40] John Rawls, *A Theory of Justice* (Cambridge, Mass 1971), 110ff. The circumstances in question are 'moderate scarcity' and 'conflict of interests'. I should stress that I do not follow Rawls in thinking, if this is what he thinks, that questions of distributive justice are never forced on us outside these circumstances. I agree, however, that they are always forced on us in these circumstances. See my *Law as a Leap of Faith*, above note 12, 264–7.

3. Distributive justice between the parties

Not all questions of justice arising in tort cases are questions of justice between the parties to those cases. As we have seen, there is also the ever-present question of how to distribute, among imaginable classes of potential parties, tort law's special apparatus for doing or helping to do justice between them. That, I have claimed, is a question of distributive justice. This claim still leaves open, however, the possibility that justice between the parties, the justice that tort law's special apparatus is there to facilitate, is always and only corrective. Weinrib argues that it is. As promised in chapter 2,[41] I will argue the opposite. Corrective justice is always justice between the parties, but justice between the parties is not always corrective. Some of it is distributive. And such 'localized' distributive justice (as it is known[42]) has a key role to play, I will argue, in the doing of justice between the parties in tort law.

Problems of localized distributive justice arise in raw morality as readily as they do in the law. Here is an example that could be considered under either heading. Having lured Prey to a remote abandoned factory, Hunter engineers a situation such that Prey must blind Hunter if she is to avoid being blinded by Hunter. As Hunter planned, the two of them are now suspended above a tank filled with an eyesight-destroying chemical. The only way Prey has to stop Hunter pushing Prey into the tank is for Prey to push Hunter into the tank instead. Indeed, Hunter's plunge will lift Prey clear, and *vice versa*. Thanks to Hunter, there is now a scarcity of future eyesight as between the two of them. They are competing, winner takes all, for the future capacity to see. Who gets to blind whom and thereby keep her own sight?

The problem has many aspects and morality gives us more than one way to think about it. But one way that morality gives us to think about it is as a problem of justice. Albeit in respect of a single interaction, Hunter has contrived the circumstances of justice as between herself and Prey. There is no escaping the need for allocation as between the two of them. So what *form* of justice

[41] See p 40 above.

[42] Following Stephen Perry, 'The Moral Foundations of Tort Law', *Iowa Law Review* 77 (1991), 449 at 461.

is called for? To borrow Weinrib's own criteria of classification, it is clearly not yet a problem about 'what the doer of harm owes to the sufferer of harm'.[43] Nobody has yet been harmed. The problem does not yet have 'the shape of corrective justice'.[44] Rather, it is a problem having 'the shape of distributive justice', a problem about how to 'divid[e] a benefit or burden among a group'.[45] It matters not that the only possible division of the relevant burden (loss of sight) as between Prey and Hunter is an all-or-nothing division (because the burden cannot be shared). Nor does it matter that Prey and Hunter together constitute a group with only two members. Clearly, neither the size of the group nor the shareability of the burden makes a difference to the form of justice that falls to be done.

According to a popular view, justice forbids Hunter from blinding Prey but it does not forbid Prey from blinding Hunter, and that is because it was Hunter who made it the case, by her wrongdoing, that one of them has to be blinded. Here, tweaked to eliminate some distracting specificity, is Jeff McMahan's nice formulation of the relevant distributive norm:

> [I]n cases in which a person's [wrongful] action … has made it inevitable that someone must suffer harm, it is normally permissible, as a matter of justice, to ensure that it is the [wrongdoer] who is harmed rather than allowing the costs of his wrongful action to be imposed on the [other(s) on whom they might instead have fallen].[46]

Let's call this the 'responsibility' norm of distributive justice, meaning thereby to emphasize the fact that the norm makes a distribution of costs turn on their causal attribution. The causal element of the responsibility norm, like many other elements of it, calls for further elaboration, which I will not offer here. I will also play down some doubts I have about the responsibility norm's soundness, at least as a raw moral norm. All I will do here is treat the norm as sound for the purpose of argument.

The main case for doing so is that, even in its indeterminacy, one can readily see the potential application of the responsibility

[43] *The Idea of Private Law*, above note 4, 73. [44] Ibid. [45] Ibid.

[46] Jeff McMahan, 'Self-Defense and the Problem of the Innocent Attacker', *Ethics* 104 (1994) 252 at 259.

norm to tort litigation.[47] Like Hunter and Prey, Plaintiff and Defendant are caught up in a zero-sum situation, in which each wins if and only if the other loses. If Plaintiff is in the right, it was Defendant who, by his wrongdoing, put them in that zero-sum situation. By committing the tort, Defendant 'made it inevitable' that one of them must come out of the conflict a loser. So one might well think: that is why it is permissible for Plaintiff to insist on damages, and why the court is required, if Plaintiff insists, to award them. Tort litigation, one might think, is an occasion for doing localized distributive justice, and the responsibility norm regulates it, and (if sound) justifies its characteristic features.

The objection to this view is well-known. Tort litigation is not conducted in an abandoned factory. When Hunter confronts Prey, the two of them are cut off from civilization. There are only two candidates for blinding. But back in ordinary life, there are many other potential loss-bearers around apart from Plaintiff and Defendant. By handing the problem over to litigation, we have taken a preemptive step to localize, as opposed to socializing, the problem. We are turning what might have been a zero-sum interaction among many (played out, say, through general taxation and social insurance) into a zero-sum interaction between just two litigants. Why? There is nothing in the relevant distributive norm to explain it. As Stephen Perry says,

> the localized nature of the distributive scheme is arbitrary and unjustified; there is no basis for limiting the group of potential loss-bearers to the injurer and the victim alone.[48]

I hasten to add that Perry does not mean that there is no basis for the localization *full stop*. He only means that there is no basis, in whatever norm we use to do localized distributive justice, to explain why it is only localized distributive justice that we are doing. Perhaps the responsibility norm, applied across the wider population, would still end up casting Defendant as the loser and Plaintiff as the winner. The question is only why we are not applying it across the wider population, but instead applying it as

[47] As McMahan also notes: ibid, 279. See also Perry, 'The Moral Foundations of Tort Law', above note 42, 499.

[48] 'The Moral Foundations of Tort Law', above note 42, 471.

between Plaintiff and Defendant alone. The answer, as Perry notes, can only be for some 'extraneous reasons',[49] i.e. reasons not provided by the responsibility norm itself.

When we hear talk of 'extraneous reasons', our Weinribian alarm-bells may ring. We may imagine economists queueing up to show that localizing a conflict, even with generous social support through the judicial system, is cheaper than socializing it through the taxation and welfare benefit systems.[50] And maybe it is, and surely that would be relevant to our thinking about institutional arrangements for responding to the conflict. But it is premature to be thinking like that. We are leaping over the most obvious 'extraneous reasons' that would support the localizing of the problem of distributive justice before us, namely: reasons to do (and to support the doing of) corrective justice. These reasons are extraneous, not of course relative to the law of torts, but relative to the responsibility norm, which is a norm of distributive justice. They are the same reasons why Defendant should not have done what he did to Plaintiff, reasons why his doing it counted as a wrong against Plaintiff. Since the wrong has been done, at least some of these reasons have been left unsatisfied. They now exert their force as reasons for Defendant to do right by Plaintiff in some fallback way, as well as can now be achieved. They are reasons for corrective justice to be done, reasons *inter alia* to pay reparative damages, and they explain (together with some institutional facts) why Plaintiff and Defendant are caught up in the zero-sum conflict that is tort litigation. So they also explain why we might be confronted with questions of distributive justice that are already pre-localized, that already assume the context of a bilateral zero-sum conflict. To quote Cane again, 'corrective justice provides the structure of tort law within which distributive justice operates'.[51] Once again, it is corrective justice that has the explanatory priority.

The responsibility of wrongdoers is surely already central to corrective justice. So one might wonder why, once we are

[49] Ibid, 468.

[50] See e.g. Richard Posner, 'A Theory of Negligence Law', *Journal of Legal Studies* 1 (1972), 29 at 48–9.

[51] 'Distributive Justice in Tort Law', above note 11.

admittedly doing corrective justice between the parties, we should be drawn into applying the responsibility norm of distributive justice between the parties as well, albeit only as a subsidiary concern. Isn't that just duplicative? Far from it. One important reason why not is that, unlike the zero-sum conflict over the distribution of future eyesight between Hunter and Prey, the zero-sum conflict over the distribution of losses between Plaintiff and Defendant is not necessarily a winner-takes-all conflict. Once we are proposing to deal with the losses by an award of money damages—and we always are in the law of torts—the losses can be shared between Defendant and Plaintiff. Determining how to effect such sharing in particular cases, it seems to me, is the main function of several doctrines of the law of torts, notably those of mitigation and remoteness of damage, and the modernized law of contributory negligence. Interpreted as devices to effect loss-sharing, these doctrines lack a corrective-justice rationale. Corrective justice, as Aristotle explains, knows only addition and subtraction. It has no room for division, which is the business of distributive justice.[52] True, our responsibility norm, formulated by McMahan with all-or-nothing conflicts in mind, does not yet attend to cases of shareable loss. Tweaking it to do so would, however, make it even more conspicuously a norm of distributive justice, a norm for 'dividing a benefit or burden among a group'.[53] And it would therefore reveal even more clearly the distinct role that considerations of localized distributive justice have to play in tort adjudication.

You may say that I have not shown that these considerations should be playing any role in tort adjudication. You may say: if mitigation and remoteness of damage and contributory negligence are doctrines that exist to do distributive justice between the parties, so much the worse for them. They are alien doctrines that do not belong in tort law. But it seems to me, on the

[52] EN 1131^{b}12–15, 1132^{a}1–6. For discussion see chapter 2, at 35.

[53] What needs to be added, most conspicuously, is some kind of proportionality condition. As stated by McMahan the norm would allow us to dump everything on the wrongdoer, e.g. to ruin him in order to avoid each of us paying a penny. For discussion see McMahan, 'Self-Defense and the Problem of the Innocent Attacker', above note 46, 261–4.

contrary, that tort law cannot properly abdicate responsibility for tackling the local conflicts that are turned into zero-sum, and hence distributive, conflicts by tort law itself. Tort law offers an apparatus for the doing of corrective justice—litigation—that creates the circumstances of localized distributive justice. The courts may as a consequence be faced with collisions, perhaps endemic collisions, between sound corrective norms and sound distributive norms. Different legal systems, and different judges and courts of the same legal system, may reasonably deal with the collisions in different ways. But all must grapple with the fact that the collisions are theirs to deal with, built into the fabric of the law of torts, not imposed upon it from without, and with no other place to go. That is because, as John Finnis explains:

> [W]hether the subject-matter of [an] act of adjudication be a problem of distributive or [corrective] justice, the act of adjudication itself is always a matter for distributive justice. For the submission of an issue to the judge itself creates a kind of *common* subject-matter, the *lis inter partes*, which must be allocated between parties, the gain of one party being the loss of the other.[54]

4. On 'risk-distributive' justice

My 'continuity thesis' has been taken to task for a certain quietism in respect of distribution.[55] Nick McBride cannot conceive of a morality that would require me to pay millions of pounds to a shabby looking elderly man who I carelessly run down, because the man turns out to be Mick Jagger and I ran him down just before he was about to embark on a worldwide Rolling Stones reunion tour.[56]

To say this is, in a way, just to say that one cannot conceive of a morality of duty. When I owe you (or Jagger) a duty there are

[54] *Natural Law and Natural Rights*, above note 21, 179. Finnis says 'commutative' where I have inserted 'corrective'. See also my *Law as a Leap of Faith*, above note 12, ch 10.

[55] Note that this section was rewritten in 2019.

[56] Nick McBride, 'Not a Principle of Justice?' in Sarah Green and Alan Bogg (eds), *Illegality after Patel v Mirza* (Oxford 2018), 85 at 89.

always from the outset some costs that are mine to bear: inconvenience, say, or stress or insecurity or expense. That is in the nature of a duty: the duty-bearer does not get to rely upon all of the reasons that point in favour of nonperformance; some are excluded from her consideration. When she does not perform her duty, and the question arises of what would be her fallback duty, the duty-bearer still does not get to rely on those excluded reasons. Doing her duty was expensive before, but it is more expensive now. Yet duty calls, never mind the expense.

And yet the Jagger example also shows how quickly things can get out of hand with this idea. It is one question what duties I might have towards Jagger. It is another question what help others, including the law, should give me in upholding those duties. The second (distributive) question immediately raises problems of proportionality. 'Full' recovery of losses, as John Goldberg puts it, may sometimes exceed 'fair' recovery.[57] The law already acknowledges this fact in remoteness of damage, mitigation, and contributory negligence cases. It would take only modest changes in the law's remoteness-of-damage doctrine to acknowledge the same fact in the Jagger case. The doctrine at the moment assigns the risk of an unforeseeably high-value accident *victim* to the defendant. By contrast, it assigns to the plaintiff the risk of an unforeseeably high-value accident *type*.[58] These are ordinary choices of local legal policy. They clearly could have been otherwise, and are otherwise in some legal systems.

What does it mean to say, in these situations, that the law 'assigns the risk'? Thinking of the problems that I traversed in section 3 above, Tony Honoré writes:

> [T]he person who, in a situation of uncertainty, has a degree of control over how it will turn out, and who stands to gain if it goes in his favour, must bear the risk that it will turn out to harm another.[59]

[57] John Goldberg, 'Two Conceptions of Tort Damages: Fair v Full Compensation' *DePaul Law Review* 55 (2006), 435.

[58] *Hughes* v *Lord Advocate* [1963] AC 837.

[59] Tony Honoré, 'The Morality of Tort Law: Questions and Answers' in his *Responsibility and Fault* (Oxford 1999), 67 at 81.

And thinking of my section 2 topic he says, influentially:[60]

> To justify [the social or legal upholding of] corrective justice involves appealing at a certain stage to the just *distribution of risk* in a society. Corrective justice is a genuine form of justice only [when and] because the just distribution of risks requires people of full capacity to bear the risk of being held responsible for harming others by their conduct. [61]

Broadly, I share these views. In the originally published version of this chapter I resisted Honoré's conceptualization of them as matters of risk-distribution. I now think that my criticisms were petty. It is indeed useful to think of the law as distributing (legal) risks, and useful to think of private law as distributing risks of legal liability. Are those risks always risks of liability to be required to do corrective justice? No. As the second quoted remark from Honoré makes clear, outcome-responsibility is ultimately just one possible basis of risk-distribution, one with a special hold over the private-law imagination. Yet even in private law other bases are sometimes admitted. For example, there is a rather elastic principle of 'assumption of risk', which renders certain defendants non-contractual insurers against certain losses irrespective of any causal contribution they may have made to those losses. Some people think that modern strict liability torts, or some of them, are best understood on this model.[62] There may still be said by the law to be wrongfully occasioned losses but that is now mainly a way of paying lip-service to the idea that we are still inside the law of torts.[63] If this basis of risk-distribution were more openly

[60] Among those conspicuously influenced by Honoré on this point are Arthur Ripstein, 'Private Law and Private Narratives' in Peter Cane and John Gardner (eds), *Relating to Responsibility* (Oxford 2001) and Jenny Steele, *Risks and Legal Theory* (Oxford 2004), 87ff.

[61] 'The Morality of Tort Law: Questions and Answers', above note 59, 80. I add the words in the first set of square brackets because Honoré makes clear that he is not thinking of the raw morality of corrective justice so much as its social and legal implementations. I add the words in the second set of square brackets to reduce the length of the quotation, which in the original goes on to endorse a concrete 'when' proposal that need not detain us here.

[62] See e.g. Joseph Raz, 'Responsibility and the Negligence Standard', *Oxford Journal of Legal Studies* 30 (2010), 1 at 8–9.

[63] In chapter 5 below I stand up for a more classical analysis of strict liability torts.

acknowledged to be a rival to the causal basis, we might perhaps find it more natural to think of private law as a system for doing distributive justice, in which distribution of risks to those who occasion losses is merely the dominant, not the only, basis of distribution. Then we could still say, with Cane, that 'corrective justice provides the structure of tort law within which distributive justice operates'. Yet now we could surely also find some truth in the converse proposition: distributive justice provides the structure of tort law within which corrective justice operates.

4

BACKWARDS AND FORWARDS WITH TORT LAW

1. Torts as wrongs

Here is a lawyer's view of the law of torts. We might call it the 'textbook' view. A tort, on this view, is a kind of legal wrong, a breach of a legal obligation on the part of the tortfeasor. This ('primary') legal obligation, unlike a contractual obligation, is not created by the exercise of the tortfeasor's own legal power to bind herself. Rather it is imposed directly by the law. But, like a contractual obligation, it is owed to somebody in particular, some rightholder whose rights are violated by the commission of the wrong. This right-violation has legal consequences for both the tortfeasor and the rightholder. It places the tortfeasor under a new ('secondary') legal obligation towards the rightholder, namely an obligation of reparation. It also confers on the rightholder a legal power to enforce this new obligation against the tortfeasor by applying to the court for an award of damages against the tortfeasor. Such an award crystallizes the tortfeasor's secondary legal obligation of reparation (by putting a money figure on it) and thereby activates further powers of enforcement (those available for liquidated debts). In principle the rightholder could also have enforced the original primary obligation against the tortfeasor by applying to the court for an injunction before the tort was committed. An injunction would have crystallized the primary legal obligation (by specifying more exactly which action would count as a violation of it), and would also have activated further powers of enforcement (penalties for contempt of court). But whereas a court retains discretion to deny the rightholder an injunction to crystallize and enforce the primary obligation, the court has no discretion to deny her an award of damages to crystallize and enforce the secondary obligation. If she makes out her case in tort, the court has a legal obligation to make her an award of damages,

Torts and Other Wrongs. John Gardner, Oxford University Press (2019). © John Gardner
DOI: 10.1093/oso/9780198852940.003.0004

even if only a nominal one.[1] Thanks to her original (primary) legal right having been violated by the tortfeasor, to put it another way, the rightholder not only gains a new (secondary) legal right against the tortfeasor but also gains—for the first time—a legal right to be assisted by the court in the enforcement of her legal rights against the tortfeasor.

In sketching this view I have not separated the essential from the inessential nor the central from the peripheral. If the aim were to distinguish the law of torts from other parts of the law, what I have just said would be incomplete in some respects and too elaborate in others. But one feature that I picked out is clearly pivotal. Everything else turns on it. A tort, according to the textbook view, is a kind of legal wrong. It is the breach of a primary legal obligation by the tortfeasor. That somebody's (performed or anticipated) action qualifies as the breach of one of tort law's primary obligations is what lends legal consequences to that action so far as tort law is concerned. Both the rightholder and the court accordingly need to rely upon the legally wrongful character of the tortfeasor's (performed or anticipated) action in making the legal case for the award of damages or the issue of an injunction. They must identify it as the breach of a primary legal obligation. If they do not then they have not made out a case in the law of torts. For they have not identified a tort.

Some theorists are suspicious about the textbook view of the law of torts precisely because it makes this feature pivotal. They doubt whether there really are primary legal obligations in tort law. They say that in spite of appearances torts are not really wrongs at all. Here I will not go through all the colourful and clever but uniformly fallacious arguments that have been given for favouring this revisionist conclusion. But let me mention one particularly influential and particularly confused line of thought. It begins from the observation that many potential tortfeasors—perhaps more than ever before in this age of the

[1] Hence the practice of giving contemptuous damages—a farthing, say—to those making out unmeritorious but legally successful claims in tort. It is true of all rights (moral as well as legal) that relying on them can be unjustifiable or even inexcusable. Nevertheless they are rights and those against whom they are held remain bound by them. Cf. Aristotle *NE* 1137^{b}35 commenting on those who are 'sticklers for their rights in a bad way'.

ruthless multinational corporation—do not think of their so-called 'primary legal obligations' as obligatory and do not rely on them as obligations when they think about what to do. In fact they don't engage with the law of torts in terms of obligations at all, whether primary or secondary. If they give the law of torts any credence, what many potential tortfeasors worry about, and rely upon in thinking about what to do, are their potential legal *liabilities*—in other words, the legal powers that others may exercise against them. So why hold out for the view that potential tortfeasors *have* obligations in the law of torts? Why not regard all the law's talk of obligations as verbiage, and switch over to thinking of the law of torts as a system of legal liabilities, unencumbered by obligations? It is no answer to say that the liabilities that potential tortfeasors worry about are none other than liabilities to have their obligations crystallized and enforced, so that there must be obligations in the law of torts. This doesn't get us where we need to be. It leaves open that there are no obligations in the law of torts until they are crystallized by a court. In which case a tort—not yet injuncted—is not yet a breach of any obligation, and the textbook view still fails.

This challenge to the textbook view misses something really obvious, or at any rate really obvious to lawyers. Even if few (or for that matter no) potential tortfeasors rely on the fact that they have obligations in the law of torts, plenty of other people *do* rely on that fact. In particular, those who have the associated legal powers of crystallization and enforcement—rightholders bringing cases in tort and courts hearing cases in tort—rely extensively and systematically on the existence of the tortfeasor's primary legal obligation. For unless they identify someone's (performed or anticipated) action as the breach of such an obligation there is no case in tort for rightholders to bring or for courts to hear. A primary obligation and an action constituting its breach have to be identified to get the legal arguments started. That is the very point that is pivotal to the textbook view. So the revisionists face the following counter-challenge on behalf of the textbook view: How come what figures in the reasoning of potential tortfeasors should admittedly be regarded as pivotal to the law of torts, whereas what figures in the reasoning of the courts and those who argue cases before the courts should not be?

It is tolerably clear what the revisionists are thinking here. They are thinking of legal systems as systems of incentives, and legal obligations, in particular, as incentives to those who are bound by them. If those who are supposedly bound do not attend to their supposed obligations in their practical reasoning, the revisionist thinks, then there are no such obligations for there are none of the definitive effects of such obligations. By failing to incentivize, the law fails to obligate. But this conclusion is wide of the mark. Although legal obligations often do come bundled with incentives for their performance, legal obligations are not incentives and are not validated as obligations by their incentive effects. They are validated as obligations by their *normative* effects (including their effectiveness in furnishing legal arguments for the creation by law of incentives for conformity with them).[2] It is no skin off the law's nose, in general, if those who have legal obligations never attend to those obligations in their reasoning. They may even be anarchists for all the law cares. So long as people do whatever they have a legal obligation to do—so long as in their actions they conform to the legal norm—it is all the same to the law whether they do so for legal reasons, for moral reasons, for prudential reasons, or indeed for no reason at all.

Normally, in short, we have no legal obligation, nor even a legal reason, to attend to legal obligations, or any other legal reasons, in our reasoning. But there are exceptions. The main exceptions are those that apply to officials of the legal system (including acting officials such as plaintiffs in civil suits). Some officials have a legal obligation to reason legally. Some have legal powers that are validly exercised only if exercised for legal reasons. Some are legally empowered to acquire further legal powers or rights only if they establish or at least assert legal reasons why they should acquire them. So if we want to know whether a certain legal obligation exists, there is normally no reason to be especially interested in the reasoning of those (non-officials) who are said to be bound by it. But there is often a reason to be interested in the reasoning of legal officials who rely on the existence of that legal obligation in

[2] On the justificatory relationship between obligations and incentives, see P M S Hacker, 'Sanction Theories of Duty' in A W B Simpson (ed), *Oxford Essays in Jurisprudence: Second Series* (Oxford 1973)

fulfilling their own legal obligations or exercising their own legal powers or making a legal case for the extension of their own legal powers or rights.

The central role of official law-users in determining the incidence of legal obligations and powers was emphasized by H L A Hart. Hart is most commonly remembered for the application of this point to the law of the constitution, where (he argued) all legal systems need official law-users (law-applying officials) to settle the incidence of ultimate legal obligations and powers.[3] But Hart's main insight applies no less to the law of torts. If we want confirmation of the existence of primary legal obligations in the law of torts, we should be focusing not on the reasoning of potential tortfeasors but on the reasoning of the courts and the rightholders who appear before them. And in this reasoning we cannot deny the pivotal role of the tort itself. Some (performed or anticipated) action on the part of an alleged tortfeasor has to be identified as a breach of one of tort law's primary legal obligations or else a tort case never gets off the ground. The alleged tortfeasor has no case to answer.

2. Law and economics

Possibly some members of the so-called 'law and economics' movement think of legal systems as systems of incentives. If they do, then the difference between them and most other legal theorists is not that the economists are assessing the law against their own specialized economic benchmarks. The difference between them and most other legal theorists, rather, is that they are not assessing the law at all. The law has dropped out of their world. All they can see are certain accessories of the law, namely the incentives that are sometimes but not always attached to legal obligations and liabilities. Talk of legal obligations and liabilities is therefore of no interest to them except as a euphemistic (perhaps efficiently euphemistic, but still euphemistic) way of talking about threats, predictions, expectations, and deprivations.

[3] H L A Hart, *The Concept of Law* (2nd ed, Oxford 1994), 98–9

But I doubt whether many legal economists consistently lose sight of the law in this way. More often, in the law and economics literature, the law is taken and assessed at face value. It is held to be made up of the very obligations and liabilities that legal officials rely upon in their legal reasoning and that make their way, accordingly, into the legal textbooks. The mainstream legal economists' question is whether people's having these legal obligations and liabilities—understood not as incentives but as normative positions—is economically defensible.[4] Of course, the economic defence of a norm, like other purely instrumental defences of it, must be sensitive to the extent of conformity with it by those to whom it applies, and securing such conformity may sometimes require the addition of incentives. But this is where economists of law tend to wear their lawyers' hats for a moment. They often make the simplifying assumption, for the sake of conducting their economic assessments, that what the law says goes. The economic defensibility of a legal norm is then its economic defensibility assuming perfect, or at least very extensive, implementation. So, for example, the primary and secondary obligations of potential tortfeasors are apt to be treated as economically defensible if and only if conformity with them by all and only those who are bound by them would be economically defensible. And the enforcement powers of rightholders and courts in respect of breaches of those obligations are apt to be treated as economically defensible if and only if the valid exercise of those powers on every available occasion by all and only those who have them would be economically defensible. And so forth. If it turned out that in fact the legal norm in question were widely disregarded, its economic merits and demerits would call for radical reassessment.[5]

[4] Consider the titles alone of the following articles, picked at random from a much longer list: George L Priest, 'The Common Law Process and the Selection of Efficient Legal Rules', *Journal of Legal Studies* 6 (1977), 65; Ian Ayres and Robert Gertner, 'Strategic Contractual Inefficiency and the Optimal Choice of Legal Rules', *Yale Law Journal* 101 (1992), 729; Louis Kaplow and Steven Shavell, 'Property Rules versus Liability Rules: an Economic Analysis', *Harvard Law Review* 109 (1996), 713.

[5] On the effects of varying the conformity assumptions in economic analysis of law, see Lewis Kornhuaser, 'The Economic Analysis of Law' in Edward N Zalta (ed), *The Stanford Encyclopaedia of Philosophy* (winter 2001 edition), http://plato.stanford.edu/archives/win2001/entries/legal-econanalysis/.

With or without these simplifying assumptions in place, the question of whether the law is economically defensible could of course be asked with more or less dispositive ambitions. Some who ask it may suppose that the only considerations relevant to assessing the law are economic considerations, so that all and only those legal obligations and liabilities that are economically defensible are defensible *tout court*.[6] Others may think, less embarrassingly, that discovering whether the law is economically defensible is part but only part of the job of discovering whether the law is defensible *tout court*. Some non-economic strengths in the law, on this view, might make up for its economic deficiencies.[7] Still other economists of law, out of abundant caution, may wish to keep their distance from both of these views by saying that they are invoking economic considerations entirely noncommittally. For all they know, economic considerations will turn out to be irrelevant to the defence of the law, but still it is interesting to see to what extent—if they were relevant—such considerations *could* be used to defend the law. To what extent does the law say what economic thinking would have it say? Tackling this question may help to expose the blind-spots as well as the insights of economic thinking about law, and so may be interesting even to those who are sceptical about the ultimate importance of economic considerations. The question may also be interesting to those who want to investigate what considerations (for better or worse) influence law-makers, such as judges and legislators. That the law says what economic thinking would have it say does not of course show that any law-maker is thinking economically. Nor, for that matter, *vice versa*. It may all be a coincidence. But it may be a legitimate working hypothesis that how law-makers think will show up, albeit approximately, in the laws they make.

[6] Richard Posner, 'Utilitarianism, Economics, and Legal Theory', *Journal of Legal Studies* 8 (1979), 103; Bruce Johnsen, 'Wealth *is* Value', *Journal of Legal Studies* 15 (1986), 263; Louis Kaplow and Steven Shavell, 'Fairness versus Welfare', *Harvard Law Review* 114 (2001), 961. Kaplow and Shavell have a slightly more sophisticated idea of what counts as an economic consideration.

[7] Guido Calabresi, *The Costs of Accidents* (New Haven 1970), e.g. 291–2. This also seems to have become Posner's view by the time of, e.g., 'Wealth Maximisation and Tort Law: a Philosophical Inquiry' in D Owen (ed), *Philosophical Foundations of Tort Law* (Oxford 1995).

Coupled with other plausible hypotheses about the institutional influence of prevailing social ideologies, this may give some scholars a reason to investigate the extent to which legal norms are amenable to an economic justification, without themselves advancing or endorsing that justification.

Legal economists in this noncommittal vein sometimes like to present themselves as engaged in a radically different enterprise from their more committal peers. Their work, they may say, is 'explanation' or 'analysis', not 'justification' or 'defence'. It belongs to 'positive' rather than 'normative' economics.[8] But these are notorious false contrasts. Anyone who explains or analyses legal norms in terms of 'considerations' (also known as reasons) cannot but be concerned with the justifiability or defensibility of those norms. In that sense, their project cannot be other than normative. The only caveat is that a concern with justifiability can in principle be a detached concern. Possibly some people working in the law-and-economics tradition want to know whether certain laws are economically justifiable in the same detached way that I (an atheist who sees nothing wrong with sex outside marriage and who objects to both corporal and capital punishment) might want to know whether stoning adulteresses to death really is justifiable according to Islamic teachings.[9] If it turns out that such an abhorrent action is justifiable according to Islamic teachings, then (I would say) so much the worse for Islamic teachings. It does not follow that my interest in those teachings was not an interest in their justificatory force. On the contrary: I judge them to be deficient teachings precisely because of what is justifiable according to them.

To put it another way, the issue of whether the law of torts is economically defensible has to be kept distinct from the question

[8] For invocations of this contrast aimed at insulating the 'positive' enterprise, see Richard Posner, *Economic Analysis of Law* (2nd ed., Boston 1977), 17–19; Jules Coleman, 'Efficiency, Utility, and Wealth Maximisation' *Hofstra Law Review* 8 (1980), 509 at 547; David Friedman, 'A Positive Account of Property Rights', *Social Philosophy and Policy* 11 (1994), 1 at 15; Mark Geistfeld, 'Economics, Moral Philosophy and the Positive Analysis of Tort Law' in G Postema (ed), *Philosophy and the Law of Torts* (Cambridge 2001), 250 at 252.

[9] This example was brought to mind by the case of Amina Lawal: 'Woman faces death by stoning "after weaning"', *The Guardian*, 20 August 2002.

of whether an economic defence of the law of torts is a defence worth wanting. Corresponding to these two distinct questions, there are two types of objections to the so-called 'economic analysis of tort law'. On the one hand (a) there are objections to the dispiriting economic theory of value that the economic analysis implicates. Are economic considerations really the only ones, or even the main ones, that matter? Isn't there a lot more to life than can be represented by anyone's 'utility function', or measured, even approximately, by their ability-and-willingness to pay? On the other hand (b) there are objections that concede for the sake of argument that economic considerations are indeed the only ones that matter, and then proceed to argue that the obligations and liabilities of tort law are not defensible in terms of such considerations, or in terms of such considerations alone, so that an economic analysis of tort law fails. Naturally a type (b) objection leaves a major hostage to fortune. Those who offer an economic analysis of tort law may reply that, since their analysis fails to show the law of torts in a defensible light, the law of torts is indefensible as it stands and calls for reform or abolition. At that point critics of the economic analysis are forced back to a type (a) objection. But at least they are forced back in a way that prevents supporters of the economic analysis from denying that they really are committed to the dispiriting theory of value that their analysis implicates. They can no longer parade the justificatory detachment of the 'mere' social scientist who does not personally endorse the values that he or she invokes. So in this way we can smoke out the disingenuous minority of legal economists who do personally advocate the dispiriting economic theory of value even as they insist—with a hurt look on their faces—that all they are doing is 'positive' economics.

A great deal of philosophical energy and ingenuity has been invested in building type (b) objections to the economic analysis of tort law, objections that attempt to show the inadequacy of economic considerations to explain the main features of the law of torts. Some writers have strange ideas about what counts as a 'main feature' for this purpose. Many arguments rage, for example, about the adequacy of an economic analysis of the law's negligence standard, even though negligence is but one constituent among many of some but not all torts. Other arguments rage about the adequacy of an economic analysis of the legal idea of proximate causation, even though proximate causation is again just one constituent among many of some but not all torts. I will leave these distracting local difficulties on one side. They do not belong to the general part of the law of torts. They bear on what list of primary obligations would feature in the law of torts, were it economically defended. My interest here will be in a prior question: Can an economic analyst explain the pivotal role of primary obligations in the law of torts *at all*, never mind which primary obligations end up on the list?

3. Coleman's twin objections

In *The Practice of Principle* Jules Coleman sketches two important and closely related type (b) objections to the economic analysis of tort law. Both challenge the ability of the economic analyst to accord primary obligations—never mind which particular primary obligations—their proper place relative to secondary obligations in the argumentative logic of tort law. Here are Coleman's most trenchant renditions of the two objections:

[*First objection:*] These [economic] accounts do not use efficiency to discover an independent class of duties that are analytically prior to our liability practices. In the standard economic analysis, there is no boundary, as it were, between what the duties are and what the liability practices should be. What counts as a 'duty' or a 'wrong' in a standard economic account depends on an assessment of what the consequences are of imposing liability in a given case. Duty and wrong, as independent categories, are doing no work in the story. So while in principle we could have an efficiency theory of duties, what economists offer is not an efficiency theory of duties at all, but an efficiency theory of liability or cost allocation.[10]

[*Second objection:*] How then does the economist account for the fact that in the typical tort suit the victim sues the injurer and not the alleged cheapest cost avoider? How does one square the forward-looking goal of tort law (on the economic model) with the backward-looking structure of tort law? The economist cannot appeal to the obvious answer that the victim believes the injurer harmed him wrongfully and in doing

[10] Jules Coleman, *The Practice of Principle* (Oxford 2001), 35.

so incurred a duty to make good the victim's losses. In the economist's account, the victim sues the injurer because the cost of searching for those in the best position to reduce the costs of future accidents is too high.[11]

These two objections might easily be collapsed. But the first is more radical than the second, and Coleman is right to set it apart. The second objection only doubts the ability of legal economists to justify tort law's secondary obligations. As pure instrumentalists about norms, legal economists insist that a secondary obligation can only be justified by the good consequences of its being incurred. According to Coleman, this means that legal economists cannot explain the law's justification of a secondary obligation, which points not to the good consequences of its being incurred ('forward-looking'), but to the fact that a primary obligation was already violated ('backward-looking'). Coleman's first objection, however, goes further and doubts whether legal economists can properly account for the primary obligation itself. A purely instrumental justification of the primary obligation as a way of bringing optimal secondary obligations into existence cannot, claims Coleman, account for the primary obligation *as* a primary obligation. If this is true then the difficulty that economic analysts have in explaining the legal justification of a secondary obligation by reference to the breach of a primary obligation is the least of their problems. They cannot even explain why, in tort law, the primary obligation is there to breach.

You may wonder whether the first objection's greater radicalism isn't promptly surrendered in Coleman's concession that economic analysts could 'in principle' offer an economic defence of at least some primary obligations suitable for use in the law of torts ('an efficiency theory of duties'). Doesn't this concession instantly take all the sting out of his first objection, understood as a type (b) objection to the economic analysis of tort law? The problem, it seems, is not that economic analysis lacks the resources adequately to account for tort law's primary obligations. The problem is merely that legal economists 'standard[ly]' fail to use these resources, and so drop the primary obligations out of their

[11] Ibid, 18. This encapsulates an objection originally advanced by Coleman in 'The Economic Structure of Tort Law' *Yale Law Journal* 97 (1988), 1233.

picture of tort law. In the process they inflict unnecessary damage on their own positions. But I don't think that Coleman means to concede this much. I suspect he only means to make a more limited concession that I also made in the previous section. An economic study of the law of torts, as I mentioned, could readily tackle the following question about the tortfeasor's primary obligations: Are the tortfeasor's primary obligations economically defensible assuming perfect or at least very widespread conformity, i.e. on the footing that they are rarely if ever breached? The problem is that nobody would regard an affirmative answer to this question, without more, as an adequate economic defence of the law of torts. In addition we would need to know the answer to this follow-up question: Are tort law's *secondary* obligations (assuming perfect or at least widespread conformity with these) economically defensible as legal consequences of the breach of tort law's primary obligations (now necessarily assuming significant nonconformity with these)? The charge against the economic analysts, as framed in Coleman's first objection, is that they cannot but let the follow-up question swallow the original question, and in the process destroy any prospect of an adequate economic defence of tort law's primary obligations. At any rate, this is the intended force that I will ascribe to the first objection in the discussion that follows. And it is with the first objection that we will begin.

4. Forwards from the primary obligation

(i) Policy and legitimacy. The impact of Coleman's first objection, if sound, goes beyond the destabilization of the economic analysis of tort law. It also has implications for the workaday tort lawyer's reliance on 'policy arguments' in debates about where the primary obligations of tort law should begin and end. In this context 'policy argument' is a technical lawyers' expression. It refers to an argument for or against recognizing certain acts as falling under certain legal norms (e.g. as meeting the legal test for causation) on the strength of the legal consequences of such recognition (e.g. a wider or narrower net of tort liabilities), and the extra-legal consequences, in turn, of those legal consequences (e.g. the possible

bankrupting of local authorities or insurance companies, or the possible absence of recourse for victims of large-scale pharmaceutical accidents involving multiple manufacturers). Not all instrumental arguments about what should qualify as a primary obligation in tort law are policy arguments. Even for economists, the classification of a given action as legal obligatory may have good and bad consequences quite apart from the good and bad extra-legal consequences of the legal consequences of its classification. Nevertheless, it is hard to deny that the most important extra-legal consequences of classifying a given action as legally obligatory are those that are consequences of the legal liability that attaches to a failure to perform the obligation. So if they can't put policy arguments in the driving seat, legal economists and others seeking a purely instrumental defence of the law of torts have little to say for themselves. This is the unhappy state of speechlessness that Coleman's first objection seeks to reduce them to.

Coleman is not the only theorist of tort law to challenge the ability of policy arguments to establish the content of tort law's primary obligations. Most familiar objections, however, are objections to the *legitimacy* of *judicial resort* to policy arguments.[12] When judges are attaching legal consequences to people's actions, the story goes, their job is to ensure that justice is done between the parties. The further non-legal consequences of their doing so (the consequent availability and cost of insurance, the consequent increases in public expenditure, the consequent shift in negotiating power between consumers and producers, etc.) are problems for other institutions, such as legislators, to worry about. Such separation-of-powers objections are open to a range of relatively straightforward replies on behalf of those who advance policy arguments. The most important is the reply made famous by John Rawls and extensively exhibited in the work of modern game theorists.[13] Justification is rarely transparent. That a certain judicial

[12] For different versions, see Ronald Dworkin, 'Principle, Policy, Procedure' in his *A Matter of Principle* (Cambridge, Mass 1984), 72 at 73–4, and Ernest Weinrib, *The Idea of Private Law* (Cambridge, Mass 1995), 210–14.

[13] John Rawls, 'Two Concepts of Rules', *Philosophical Review* 64 (1955), 3.

decision is ultimately justified by policy arguments in its favour does not entail that the judge should be aware of those policy arguments, still less rely on them. It suffices that the judge relies on legal or moral norms, reliance upon which is in turn justified by policy arguments. There is no reason to imagine that such norms will disclose the policy arguments that justify reliance upon them, let alone instruct or authorize judges to *use* those policy arguments. So the claim that it is illegitimate for judges to resort to policy arguments need not detract from the importance of such arguments in determining what judges are to do. In other words, the contrast between policy arguments and arguments of justice is a false one: those who see to it that justice is done between the parties may well in the process be doing the very thing that, unbeknown to them, the assembled policy arguments would have them do.

We will be coming back to this line of thought when we turn to Coleman's second objection. For present purposes, however, we can make do with a simpler reply to those who offer separation-of-powers objections to the use of policy arguments in determining the content of tort law's primary obligations. The simpler reply is that there is no reason to assume that the content of tort law's primary obligations is wholly or even mainly the business of judges. True, some torts are torts at common law, which have been shaped by successive judicial decisions. But many are statutory torts, or common law torts modified by statute. Indeed one of the common law's most enduringly important torts—breach of statutory duty—is explicitly organized around the idea that the content of the relevant primary obligation should be determined, in large measure, by legislation. So if the problem with policy arguments were only a problem with the legitimacy of judicial resort to such arguments, the obvious answer would be this: Nothing about the law of torts requires that the question of what actions are to count as tortious be left wholly or mainly to judges. Indeed who should decide what actions are to count as tortious is itself a matter amenable to policy argument, turning on a determination of who is best placed to give effect to the policy arguments for and against counting certain actions as tortious (whether by relying on those policy arguments or otherwise).

(ii) A problem of circularity? Coleman knows all this. His first objection, accordingly, is not an objection to the legitimacy of judicial resort to policy arguments (or to the legitimacy of anything, for that matter). Coleman objects, rather, to something in the *logic* of policy arguments. On the simplest interpretation of what he is saying, his charge is one of vicious circularity. In the law of torts, as I mentioned earlier, the primary obligation has justificatory priority. Its existence and breach have to be relied upon in arguing that a secondary obligation has been incurred, and hence in making a case that the rightholder is entitled to the crystallizing and enforcing assistance of the court. But when policy arguments are being employed, the secondary obligation, with its attendant liabilities, seems instead to assume justificatory priority over the primary. One needs to furnish arguments for the incurring of a secondary obligation, with its attendant liabilities, in order to establish that what the defendant did should indeed be counted as a breach of a primary obligation. Can the latter order of argumentation be squared with the former? For Coleman, simply interpreted, the answer is no. There is a vicious circle in treating primary obligations as justified by the very thing that primary obligations also serve to justify.

There is something immediately paradoxical about this 'circularity' challenge. Another way to express the idea that primary obligations have justificatory priority in the law of torts is to say that, in the law of torts, the incurring of a secondary obligation, with its attendant liabilities, is a *legal consequence* of the breach of a primary obligation. When legislatures or courts create new primary obligations in the law of torts (i.e. when they hold additional actions to be tortious) they also create, by operation of law, new secondary legal obligations that arise in the event of the primary obligation's breach, and new rights for rightholders in search of judicial assistance with the crystallization and enforcement of those secondary obligations. Legislatures and courts cannot avoid creating these legal consequences except by not creating any new primary legal obligations in the law of torts. How can it possibly be viciously circular to regard these legal consequences as relevant to the question of whether to create new primary legal obligations? And if they are relevant to *whether*, then surely also to *which*? Surely the case for or against creating a certain primary obligation cannot *but* be affected by the legal consequences of doing so? Far from casting doubt on the logical acceptability of policy arguments, then, the justificatory priority of primary legal obligations seems to be the very thing that makes policy arguments so central to any credible debate about which primary legal obligations we should have: new primary obligations justify new secondary obligations, so the various arguments for and against having such new secondary obligations must surely be relevant to the arguments for and against having the new primary obligations.

We can make the flavour of paradox here more intense if we apply Coleman's first objection in another (non-institutional) context. Consider, for example, the morality of promising. One may well suppose that the existence of a moral power to incur moral obligations by promising is justified, at least in part, by the case for people's incurring those moral obligations by promising. How else would one go about defending the power to promise if one did not rest one's case on the defensibility of promising's having the moral consequences that promising has, viz. the incurring of new moral obligations? At the same time, the very fact that the incurring of a new moral obligation is a moral consequence of the exercise of the power means that one necessarily relies on the exercise of the power in defending the incurring of the obligation. Is this viciously circular? Coleman's first objection seems to suggest that it is. So long as one grants that the incurring of the obligation is the moral consequence of the exercise of the power, applying Coleman's first objection, the existence of the power cannot be defended in turn by pointing to the value of its giving rise to that same obligation. For in that defence one puts the obligation before the power in one's order of argumentation, but at the same time one puts the power before the obligation. They cannot both come before each other in the order of argumentation. So we are left—it seems—with a bit of a justificatory vacuum in the morality of promising. How on earth are we now going to set about justifying the existence of the moral power to promise?

Something has gone wrong here, and it does not take long to work out what it is. The existence of the power to promise is one thing, and its exercise is quite another. There is no vicious circle—no circle at all—in holding that the *existence* of the power to promise is justifiable only because the obligations incurred by promising are justifiable obligations, while also holding that each such obligation is justifiable, in return, only thanks to the *exercise* of the same (justifiable) power. So there is no logical obstacle to defending the existence of the power to promise by arguing that the moral consequences of the exercise of that power would be defensible consequences. And exactly the same point can be made regarding the primary and secondary obligations of tort law. The existence of the primary obligations is one thing, and their breach is another. There is nothing circular in holding that the *existence* of the primary obligation not to defame or cause a nuisance is justifiable only because the secondary obligations of reparation that would arise from the legal recognition of these acts as tortious would be justifiable, while also holding that tort law's secondary obligations of reparation are justifiable, in return, only thanks to the *breach* of the same (*ex hypothesi* justifiable) primary obligations. So there is no logical obstacle to defending the primary obligations of tort law by arguing that the legal consequences of the breach of such obligations—the secondary obligations and attendant liabilities—would be (independently) defensible. One may properly begin by defending the secondary obligations and attendant liabilities, and then proceed to defend the primary obligations by showing them to be the very primary obligations, breach of which would happily have, among its legal consequences, the same secondary obligations and attendant liabilities that one just defended. That the legal justification for the secondary obligation then looks backwards to the breach of the primary obligation, while the policy justification for the secondary obligation looks forwards to its consequences is a separate problem, not a problem of circularity but a problem of incongruity. It is the problem raised in Coleman's second objection, to which we will be turning shortly.

(iii) Moral unintelligibility. The knock-down character of this refutation leads to the suspicion that Coleman's first objection has been uncharitably interpreted. I can think of just one alternative interpretation. It is hinted at in Coleman's addition of scare-quotes around the words 'duty' and 'wrong' as, in his view, these words are used by many legal economists. On this interpretation,

Coleman's first objection is not that policy arguments are circular and hence can justify *nothing* in the space of primary obligations. Rather it is that policy arguments are uncontainable and can justify *just about anything* in the space of primary obligations. In particular they can justify 'obligations' that are not obligations, hence 'wrongs' that are not wrongs, hence a law of 'torts' that is not a law of torts.[14]

How so? As ordinary non-doctrinaire observers of legal argument we naturally imagine policy arguments being used to adjudicate small-scale disagreements of the kind that tort lawyers constantly have about what action should count as a tort. (What should be the standard of care in the tort of negligence? Should the unreasonable creation of a personal risk of death be a tort even where the risk does not materialize? Should there ever be strict tort liability?) Many economic analysts of law indulge in this kind of micro-adjudication, taking the rest of the existing law of torts for granted in the background.[15] But suppose one takes *nothing* in the existing law of torts for granted. Instead one looks in an uncontained way for the liability norms that would have the best consequences and works back to decide what is to count as a tort. It may turn out, for all one can tell at the outset, that one or other of the following liability norms—among infinitely many alternatives—will turn out to have the best consequences: the injured rightholder's family must have reparative damages awarded against them; the person who will least miss the money must have reparative damages awarded against her; the person of whom we can make the most spectacular example must

[14] This interpretation would bring Coleman's thinking in one respect closer to Weinrib's. Weinrib also claims that those who resort to policy arguments do not respect the very idea of a tort: *The Idea of Private Law*, above note 12, at 218–22. However Weinrib invokes a highly idealized notion of a tort, laced with common law romanticism, to get this claim off the ground. Coleman does not need and does not use any such idealizing measures.

[15] For example, Posner's famous economic defence of the law governing the tort of negligence ('A Theory of Negligence', *Journal of Legal Studies* 1 (1972), 29) proceeds as follows. Legal norm A is defended economically while norms B, C and D are held constant. Then norm B is defended economically while norms A, C and D are held constant. And so on. In a neat illustration of the fallacy of composition, these several defences of A, B, C, and D are then paraded as adding up to a defence of the system of norms A+B+C+D.

have reparative damages awarded against him. So far as policy arguments are concerned, then, we should be considering all of the following as possible torts: being a member of an injured rightholder's family, being the person who will least miss the money, being the person of whom the most spectacular example can be made. But none of these is a possible tort, because none of them is a possible breach of an obligation. And that in turn is because none of the following is a possible obligation: not being a member of an injured rightholder's family; not being the person who will least miss the money; not being the person of whom the most spectacular example can be made. What this shows is that, by pursuing policy arguments at large, we may end up not with a law of torts in which primary obligations are breached, but rather with a law of 'torts' in which 'primary obligations' are 'breached'. This is because it is a matter of indifference, so far as policy arguments are concerned, whether there are *really* any primary obligations to be breached. All that matters from the point of view of policy arguments is that there be consequentially optimal liability norms such that liabilities to pay reparative damages are always conditional upon whatever they should be conditional upon in order to ensure that they are consequentially optimal, be that the breach of a primary obligation or something else altogether.

The general strategy of this objection is sound. Not just any old thing can be a legal obligation. There are limits to the law's ability, in the fashion of Humpty Dumpty, to make things legally obligatory simply by designating them as legally obligatory. Legal obligations must also satisfy what I like to call the 'moral intelligibility' condition. They must be such that, if only the law were justified, they would be moral obligations. Or to put the same point another way, it must make sense for those who regard the law as having a claim on their allegiance to regard their legal obligations as being among their moral obligations. Many theorists rely on this 'moral intelligibility' condition to attack various aspects of the law of torts as it exists today: its resort to strict liability, for instance, or its use of impersonal standards of care. There can be—it is said—no such thing as a moral obligation to avoid injuring people irrespective of how much care one takes (as in strict liability), or a moral obligation to take more care than one is personally able to take (as with impersonal standards of care). So there can be no such thing as a legal obligation to do these things either. There can only be a legal 'obligation'.[16] For myself, I do not believe that strict liability or impersonal standards of care fall foul of the moral intelligibility condition.[17] But I certainly agree that some things fall foul of it. In particular, the law cannot make something obligatory if that something is not among the conceivable actions of any rational agent. And the following are not among the conceivable actions of any rational agent, because they are not *actions* at all: not being a member of an injured rightholder's family; not being the person who will least miss the money; not being the person of whom the most spectacular example can be made. So any argument by which such things are advocated or even countenanced as primary obligations of the law of torts does indeed violate the moral intelligibility condition. Such an argument yields 'obligations' that are not obligations, 'wrongs' that are not wrongs, and hence 'torts' that are not torts.

So far so good for Coleman's first objection, as reinterpreted. Yet the soundness of the general strategy still leaves us asking whether it counts as a success when directed against the economist's inevitable emphasis on policy arguments as the way to justify tort law's primary obligations. Is it true that policy arguments are doomed to be indifferent as between a liability norm which makes liability to have reparative damages awarded against one a legal consequence of the prior breach of a primary obligation, and one that does not? It seems to me that the answer must depend on a study of *particular* policy arguments. If there are any policy arguments in favour of having liabilities that are legal consequences of breached primary obligations, then obviously these policy arguments are not indifferent as between a liability norm which makes liability to have reparative damages awarded against one a legal consequence of the prior breach of a

[16] See e.g. Stephen Perry, 'Libertarianism, Entitlement, and Responsibility', *Philosophy and Public Affairs* 26 (1997), 351 at 352 ('There can be no *ex ante* duty, except in the most formal sense, not to cause harm to others.'); Arthur Ripstein, 'Justice and Responsibility', *Canadian Journal of Law and Jurisprudence*, 17 (2004) 361, 374 ('One cannot be responsible for an unforeseeable injury because one person cannot owe another a duty to avoid them.').

[17] See chapter 5 below.

primary obligation, and one that does not. We are simply looking for good non-legal (e.g. economic) consequences of making liability a legal consequence of some legal wrong done in the past. How can the existence of such good consequences be ruled out *a priori*, without even asking what they are supposed to be? How can we be sure, without detailed interrogation of the merits that are claimed for it, that there are no forward-looking merits in a legal norm that sets a backward-looking condition of liability?

Here our attempt to make good Coleman's first objection returns us once again to his second objection. Legal justification for the secondary obligation (with its attendant liabilities) looks backwards to the breach of the primary obligation. But any economic justification of the secondary obligation (with its attendant liabilities) necessarily looks forwards to the good economic consequences of its being incurred. How can a backward-looking legal justification be squared with a forward-looking economic justification? That is the question posed in Coleman's second objection. But it is also the question on which the success of Coleman's first objection turns, no matter how we interpret it. So Coleman's first objection stands or falls with his second. Although more radical, the first objection is not autonomous: the first cannot succeed if the second fails. With that in mind, I turn now to the second objection.

4. Backwards from the secondary obligation

(i) The supposed inconstancy of the instrumentalist. In pitting the economist's 'forward-looking' preoccupations against the law's 'backward-looking' features, Coleman's second objection echoes a stock criticism of instrumental defences of tort law. But he takes pains to distance himself from the vulgar version of this criticism, which he rightly regards as confused. It is often claimed that pure instrumentalists about practical reasoning, including but not restricted to legal economists, are incapable of explaining why the incurring of a secondary obligation should be conditional (whether necessarily or sufficiently) on a primary obligation already having been committed at an earlier time. For a pure instrumentalist, an act is made wrong by its costs, meaning its actual or

expected bad consequences. If these costs have not yet been incurred then the wrong has not yet been committed. The corollary is that once the wrong has been committed these costs are sunk. Nothing anyone can do will save them. But there are other costs that might still be saved, including the costs of future wrongs that might still be prevented. Instrumental rationality would have one orientate what one does entirely towards the saving of these unsunk costs. How can this instrumental orientation towards the saving of unsunk costs be squared with making what is to be done conditional on sunk costs, as tort law does? Sometimes, to be sure, getting someone to pay reparative damages in the wake of their own wrongdoing, or maybe (vicariously) in the wake of someone else's wrongdoing, might be the least costly way of deterring or otherwise preventing future wrongs, and thereby saving further costs. But this makes the past commission of a wrong only *inconstantly* relevant to instrumental thinking. Its relevance varies from case to case. On other occasions the best way to minimize further costs may be to get someone to bear the sunk costs irrespective of whether they, or indeed anyone else, committed a wrong. So there is nothing here that could justify the kind of stance that the law of torts takes, in which the relationship between one's breach of a primary obligation and one's incurring of a secondary obligation is constant, the former being a standing condition (necessary and defeasibly sufficient) of the latter.

The confusion in this line of thought is evident. From the bold charge that pure instrumentalists cannot justify attaching legal consequences to wrongs already committed, the argument quickly retreats to the more modest allegation that they cannot do so with the law's measure of constancy, i.e. in every case to which the legal norm under discussion applies. And that more modest allegation itself turns out, on closer inspection, to be just another rehearsal of the view that pure instrumentalists about practical reasoning can't stand up for *any* constancy in norms, but must always license departure from any norm as soon as it requires or permits actions that would not be instrumentally defensible were it not for the norm's existence. I already mentioned John Rawls' famous demolition of this view.[18] I will not flog a dead horse by

[18] Rawls, 'Two Concepts of Rules', above note 13.

demolishing it again here. Suffice it to say that if it were sound it would rule out the economic analysis of *any* law, not only those with a backward-looking aspect, since every law, being a norm capable of application to more than one case, sometimes requires or permits actions that would not be economically optimal were it not for that law's existence.[19]

Coleman rightly has no truck with such overkill.[20] He sees that economists and other believers in the pure instrumentality of norms can readily account for normative constancy, including the constancy of the legal norm (which I will call the 'linking norm') whereby my breach of a primary obligation is a standing condition of my incurring a secondary obligation. They can do this by pointing to the various extra economies that come of using this norm instead of engaging in unconstrained economic (or more broadly instrumental) reasoning. In particular, as Coleman notes, they can reduce the high cost of 'searching for those in the best position to reduce the costs of future accidents' by narrowing their search, and looking only among wrongdoers. In looking only among wrongdoers they can also, as Coleman might usefully have added, enlist aggrieved rightholders as temporary enforcement officials at reduced cost as compared with disinterested regulators.[21] Either of these considerations, or *a fortiori* both together, could in principle yield a sound economic case for the linking norm to be part of the law. Naturally, economists of law still have to do the work to show that the cost-savings involved are sufficient to justify the law's use of that norm in the face of its undoubted costs (notably the costs involved in litigation). But this is beside the point. Once we start basing our type (b) objections to the economic analysis of tort law on the accuracy of the costings used by its exponents, we have effectively conceded defeat. We are reduced to fighting economic arguments with economic arguments.

[19] With the obvious exception of a law prohibiting whatever action would not be economically optimal were it not for that law's existence.

[20] Contrast the interpretation of Coleman's position in Christopher Kutz, 'Pragmatism Regained', *Michigan Law Review* 100 (2002), 2001 at 2008–9.

[21] Cf. Posner, 'A Theory of Negligence', above note 15, 48.

(ii) From condition to reason. Once Coleman concedes that economists of law can defend the linking norm, what is left of his second objection? Here is one tempting answer: It is not enough for legal economists to defend the linking norm. In the law of torts, the breach of a primary obligation is not only a standing condition of the incurring of the secondary obligation, but also a *reason why* the secondary obligation is incurred. And this, one might think, is a tougher nut for economists of law to crack. So far as economic thinking is concerned, reasons all lie in the future, in the consequences of what one does (including the consequences of having a norm that regulates one's doing it). But in tort law, one reason for my incurring a secondary obligation—my past breach of a primary obligation—always lies in the past at the time when the secondary obligation is incurred.

It is true that my past breach of the primary obligation is regarded by the law as a reason for, and not only a standing legal condition of, my incurring a secondary obligation. The breach is needed to make the *case* in law. But this fact alone is still not enough to put legal economists on the back foot. For the linking norm itself—now seen to be economically defensible—automatically turns the breach of the primary obligation into a reason for the incurring of the secondary obligation. If a wrongdoer says: 'Give me one good reason why I should be the one to incur a secondary obligation in the law of torts,' the economist may reply: 'Because you breached a primary obligation and an economically defensible legal norm picks those who breach primary obligations as the right people to incur secondary obligations.' Here the wrongdoer's breach of a primary obligation, his wrongdoing, is given as a reason for his incurring a secondary obligation. And the linking norm is what makes it a reason. Even though its costs are sunk, a wrong already committed is turned, by its mention in an economically defensible norm, into an economically intelligible reason for the subsequent payability of damages. So there is no incongruity to be found here between the backward-looking legal reasons and the forward-looking economic reasons.

(iii) From reason to ground. Coleman is unsatisfied, and it seems to me rightly unsatisfied, with this way of forging a rational relationship between my breach of the primary obligation and my

incurring of the secondary obligation. In the foregoing story, the breach of a primary obligation becomes a legal reason for the incurring of a secondary obligation because it is a standing legal condition of the incurring of the secondary obligation. But in the law of torts, notices Coleman, the relationship goes the other way. The breach of a primary obligation is a standing legal condition of the incurring of a secondary obligation because it is a legal reason for the incurring of the secondary. This is what is sometimes conveyed by saying that the breach of primary obligation 'grounds' the secondary obligation and its associated liabilities. The breach of primary obligation is what gets the case for the secondary obligation up and running. In the law's eyes the breach of a primary obligation is the only possible reason for a secondary obligation to be incurred, and a defeasibly sufficient reason at that. This is reflected in—as opposed to being a reflection of—the linking norm that makes the breach of a primary obligation into a standing condition (necessary and defeasibly sufficient) for the incurring of the secondary.

This, if I understand it right, is what really lies at the heart of Coleman's second objection to the economic analysis of tort law. Although it echoes the stock criticism, it avoids the traps into which vulgar versions of that criticism fall. Unfortunately, it falls into other traps of its own making. To see how, consider what Coleman offers by way of alternative to an economic analysis of tort law, namely 'the sort of explanation offered by the principle of corrective justice'.[22] The main feature such an explanation is supposed to have going for it, as against an economic analysis, is its invulnerability to Coleman's second objection. Thanks to this invulnerability, claims Coleman, corrective justice 'can provide an account of what tort law is, in a way that economic analysis fails to do'.[23] But can it really?

What Coleman calls 'the principle of corrective justice' is the principle that 'individuals who are responsible for the wrongful losses of others have a duty to repair the losses'.[24] We could likewise designate as 'a norm of corrective justice' any norm under which

[22] *The Practice of Principle*, above note 10, 15.

[23] Ibid.

[24] Ibid.

those who are responsible for the wrongful losses of others have a duty to repair those losses. Applying these criteria, the linking norm is already, without further ado, a norm of corrective justice. It attaches secondary legal obligations (=duties to repair losses) to those who breach primary legal obligations, or who are vicariously liable in law for the breaching of primary legal obligations by others (=those who are responsible for wrongful losses). Now, as we saw and as Coleman concedes, economic analysts *do* have the resources to mount an adequate defence of the linking norm. It follows that at least one norm of corrective justice, namely tort law's own norm of corrective justice, is economically defensible. So in what sense is a corrective justice account, in Coleman's view, a *rival* to an economic one? Why isn't a good economic analysis of tort law *also* a corrective justice account of tort law?[25]

Coleman must mean something like this. He must mean that there is a further norm of corrective justice at work in the law of torts, quite apart from the law's own norm. This we could call the 'moral' norm of corrective justice. The law relies upon this moral norm, which it regards as a norm not of its own making, in defending its own norm of corrective justice. The moral norm, we may glean from Coleman's formulations, picks out wrongdoing as a necessary and defeasibly sufficient condition for amends to be owed. So thanks to this moral norm the fact that a wrong has been committed becomes a moral reason for amends to be owed. The law in turn cites this moral reason as the reason why, by the law's own norm of corrective justice, (legally recognized) wrongdoing is a necessary and defeasibly sufficient condition for the owing of (legally specified) amends. In this 'corrective justice' story, the wrong having been committed becomes the ground of the ensuing reparative obligations in the law of torts. The wrongdoing is a moral reason for the making of amends which becomes a legal condition of the making of amends only by virtue of the law's recognition of it as a moral reason. So it is a condition because it is a reason. It is not a reason only because it is a condition. And here we have the respect in which the 'corrective justice' story rivals the economic one. The economic story cannot find a

[25] For more on this theme see Richard Posner 'The Concept of Corrective Justice in Recent Theories of Tort Law', *Journal of Legal Studies* 10 (1981), 187.

rational significance for the wrong's commission apart from that conferred by the law's own norm, whereas the 'corrective justice' story can: the wrongdoing is given rational significance by a moral norm recognized by law, invoked in the legal justification of the legal norm.

But here we come to the crunch for Coleman's first objection. Since the thoughtful economic analyst can admittedly defend the legal norm of corrective justice, why can't she equally defend its moral counterpart in much the same way? I can't think of any obstacle in principle to her doing so. Arguably the existence of such a moral norm, if it were widely conformed to, would help to reduce the duration and intensity of economically wasteful disputes. Arguably the moral norm's existence, if it were widely conformed to, would also give people greater confidence about investing in economically productive activity.[26] One can quibble about the details here, as before, but these sample economic considerations are already enough to show that at the very least a moral norm of corrective justice is open in principle to economic defence. That being so, economic analysts of tort law plainly do have the argumentative wherewithal, *pace* Coleman, to provide a corrective justice defence of tort law's own norm of corrective justice. They can go on to defend the legal norm by relying on the (*ex hypothesi* economically defensible) moral norm and in the process provide an economic defence of the legal position whereby

[26] Recently the Swiss conglomerate Nestlé argued that (with or without the imprimatur of the law) the government of Ethiopia had a moral obligation to pay the company reparative damages for the nonconsensual and uncompensated (and hence according to Nestlé wrongful) expropriation of one of its Ethiopian subsidiaries in an earlier nationalization programme: 'Nestlé claims £3.7m from famine-hit Ethiopia', *The Guardian*, 19 December 2002. The Nestlé argument for the existence of this moral obligation was a purely economic one: that any government that denied the existence of such an obligation (or failed to perform it having granted its existence) would be undermining the confidence of prospective investors and hence failing to maximize economic value. I shared with many the view that Nestlé's demand for damages was base. But this was not because the economic considerations the company mentioned were incapable of justifying the moral norm of corrective justice that it identified, nor because the norm did not apply. It was simply because there were conflicting moral norms (of mercy and humanity) which were more important in the circumstances. Nestlé was therefore being a mean-spirited stickler for its rights (see note 1 above).

the commission of the wrong is a ground of, and not merely a condition of or a reason for, the payability of reparative damages. This move completely disarms Coleman's second objection. In the process his parasitic first objection is also neutralized.

5. Doing without law and economics

In an effort to re-arm Coleman's second objection you may say that the two sample economic defences of the moral norm of corrective justice that I just suggested suffer from a common weakness, namely that they are admittedly capable of defending that norm economically only 'if it were widely conformed to'. This proviso should not surprise us. I already mentioned that economic defences of legal norms tend to be conducted against the background of strong assumptions about conformity: typically, it is assumed for the sake of argument that what the law says goes. Much the same goes for economic defences of moral norms: typically, the economic defence of a moral norm is conducted on the footing that it is successfully implemented—if not completely then at least widely—as a social norm.[27]

In the case of legal norms, such an assumption turns out to be relatively innocent. One need not be a pure instrumentalist about the justification of norms to believe that the justification of a legal norm is subject to at least one instrumental condition. The condition is that the existence of the legal norm must serve to improve people's actions enough to warrant all the trouble and intrusion of regulating the matter by law. In the case of a legal norm that attempts to implement a moral norm—in the way that Coleman envisages the legal norm of corrective justice implementing the moral norm of corrective justice—the normal way to show that the moral norm meets this condition is to show that conformity to the moral norm is sufficiently improved by the existence of

[27] See e.g. Richard Posner and Eric Rasmusen, 'Creating and Enforcing Norms, with Special Reference to Sanctions', *International Review of Law and Economics* 19 (1999), 369; Saul Levmore 'Norms as Supplements', *Virginia Law Review* 86 (2000), 1989. The assumption of successful implementation is not gratuitous. When moral norms are not social norms Rawls' argument in 'Two Concepts of Rules', above note 13, does not apply. See the first few footnotes of John Rawls, 'Justice as Fairness', *Philosophical Review* 67 (1958), 164.

the legal norm. The improvement may either be direct (enough people successfully use the legal norm to help them conform to the corresponding moral norm) or indirect (the legal norm is relied upon in making a case for the application of other legal norms, such as liability norms, that in turn help to secure that enough people conform to the moral norm). All of this should be common ground to defenders of legal norms, be they pure instrumentalists or otherwise. Normally, when anyone tries to defend a legal norm they are taking its successful implementation for granted, and they are entitled to assume that others are doing the same.

But the same does not go for moral norms. Moral norms are not all of them social norms and many are valid irrespective of the extent to which they are implemented. I tend to think that this is true of the moral norm whereby those who commit wrongs should make amends to those whom they wrong. It applies even where nobody conforms to it, where nobody relies on it in argument, even where it has been long forgotten. So I tend to think that the economic defence of this moral norm is a fifth wheel: it defends a moral norm that remains valid quite irrespective of its economic defence. That should not surprise us. As rational agents, people (considered *en masse*) tend to want what they anyway have reason to want, although not necessarily in proportion to their reason to want it. They have reason to want reparation from wrongdoers for wrongs that were committed against them, that reason being the independently valid moral norm whereby wrongdoers should pay them such reparation. So not surprisingly people often do want reparation. And not surprisingly this shows up in the economic assessment of the very moral norm that gives people reason to want it. The moral norm has epiphenomenal economic appeal: it has appeal as a reflection of what people want, but what mainly explains their wanting it is the moral norm according to which they should anyway want it, whatever its economic appeal.

This is not the place to explain where this moral norm gets its force. That is for another day. Suffice it to say, here, that the explanation could not possibly provide any comfort for Coleman. Why not? First, because Coleman himself joins the legal economists in holding that the moral norm of corrective justice is valid only where it is, in large measure, successfully implemented.

'Social practices,' he says, 'turn abstract ideals into regulative principles; they turn virtue to duty.'[28] But secondly, and more importantly, because my objection to the economic analysis of law is not a type (b) objection, which is what Coleman is looking for. Coleman wants to show that an economic defence of the law of torts cannot but be inadequate to the task. The legal economist lacks the resources to account for what is going on in tort law. My own view, by contrast, is that the legal economist has all the resources she needs to account for what is going on it tort law. The real question, however, is why the law of torts needs the legal economist, except at the margins to defend it against specifically economic objections. For the law of torts has ample moral support already, assuming only that it meets the instrumental condition I mentioned, i.e. that its norms do indeed improve people's actions enough to warrant all the trouble and intrusion of regulating the matter by law.

I hope I have made it tolerably clear that, in my view, there can be no successful type (b) objection to the economic analysis of tort law. Coleman's attempts to make good such objections are the best we have, but still, as we have seen, they fail. That is because legal economists can in principle account for any norm that can be accounted for. To show that their explanation fails one is always reduced in the end to arguing that they got their costings wrong, and once the argument gets to that point the war is over. If one wants to defeat the economic analysis of tort law in a less pyrrhic way, one has no alternative but to mount a type (a) objection. One must establish that the economic analysis rests on a bad theory of value. This one does by exploring what really matters in life, for what really matters in life is also, by and large, what really matters in law. In the process of exploring this one will discover that whatever success the economic analysis of law enjoys in explaining the norms of the law of torts is mainly as follower, not as leader: what really matters is mainly tracked, not constituted, by whatever economic goods tort law may yield (and even that, I hasten to add, only very incompletely).

[28] *The Practice of Principle*, above note 10, 54.

5

OBLIGATIONS AND OUTCOMES IN THE LAW OF TORTS

I

'Under strict liability,' according to Alan Brudner,

> one has no right to act in ways that happen to injure another. Since, however, all action carries the risk of such injury, strict liability means that I have a right that you be governed in all your actions by concern for my welfare, and you have the same right over me. No doubt there is a mutuality of care here; but it is the mutual care of extreme altruists who, because they claim no worth as independent selves, can neither give nor receive effective confirmation of worth and hence can require no valid right to care. By contrast a fault [i.e. negligence] requirement establishes a reciprocity of care between selves.[1]

Brudner casts his argument in terms of the potential plaintiff's rights, but (to avoid some distractions further down the line) I am going to reframe it in terms of the potential defendant's obligations (also known as her duties). True enough, P's rights against D are not the same thing as D's obligations towards P. A right is not an obligation; rather, it is the ground of (one or more) obligations.[2] All the same, there is nothing that counts as the *violation* of a right other than a failure to perform (one or more of) the obligations that it grounds. Thus the conditions under which D violates P's rights—the conditions under which D *wrongs* P—are identical to the conditions under which D fails to perform (one or more of) his obligations towards P. It follows that, if our interest is in what it takes for D to wrong P, and in the liability to which such wrongs may give rise in law, the important differences between rights-talk and obligations-talk can largely be put on one side.

[1] Alan Brudner, *The Unity of the Common Law* (Berkeley 1995), 190. For a similar line of thought, see Ernest Weinrib, *The Idea of Private Law* (Cambridge, Mass 1995), 182–3.

[2] Joseph Raz, *The Morality of Freedom* (Oxford 1986), ch 7.

Torts and Other Wrongs. John Gardner, Oxford University Press (2019). © John Gardner
DOI: 10.1093/oso/9780198852940.003.0005

It seems to me, accordingly, that we can faithfully recast Brudner's argument in the following terms. When the law imposes strict liability on D for actions of D's that injured P, says Brudner, it asserts that D had (and failed to perform) an obligation to take extreme care not to injure P—such extreme care not to injure P, indeed, that D would have effaced himself entirely in performing the obligation. In demanding that D have acted so entirely self-effacingly for the sake of P, the law undermines its own position that P in turn owes the same obligation to take extreme care not to injure D. How could the existence of this reciprocal obligation be defended when, by the law's own reckoning, D clearly counts for so little?

This argument against the legal imposition of strict liability fails. I do not mean that it fails in its striking moral claims inspired by Kant and Hegel. Maybe Brudner is right that there comes a point at which one person takes such extreme care not to injure another that in the process she effaces herself entirely. Maybe Brudner is also right that there is something obnoxious about effacing oneself entirely in this way, or at least about being under an obligation to do it, or at the very least about being authoritatively held to be under an obligation to do it. And maybe that obnoxiousness comes, as Brudner suggests, of the fact that the self-effacing action is performed for reasons that cannot consistently be universalized to include the scenario in which D's and P's positions are reversed. Maybe Brudner is also right that, for this reason if no other, the law should not hold anyone to be under an obligation to take self-effacingly extreme care not to injure another. Let all of this be true. The problem remains that it still does not add up to an argument against the legal imposition of strict liability unless it is also true, as Brudner asserts right at the start of the argument, that in imposing strict liability on D for actions of D's that injured P, the law holds D to have been under (and to have failed to perform) an obligation to take extreme care not injure P. And sadly this doctrinal premiss (as I will call it) is not true. In fact, it is an inversion of the truth.

The truth is that when the law imposes strict liability on D for actions of D's that injured P, it asserts that D had (and failed to perform) a straightforward obligation *not to injure P*. D would have performed this obligation not to injure P—and hence would have avoided the strictest of strict liabilities—if and only if she had not injured P. Now, not injuring P, and therein performing her obligation, is something that D might have done entirely fortuitously, without taking the slightest care, let alone extreme care, not to injure P. (Perhaps P just happens not to step off the pavement as D careers drunkenly and obliviously past in her car.) Conversely, injuring P, and therein failing to perform her obligation, is something that D might have done in spite of having taken the most extreme conceivable care not to do so, even to the point of total self-effacement that so worries Brudner. (Perhaps P has an unprecedented allergic reaction to all the cotton wool D spent the whole day laboriously wrapping him up in.) Under a regime of strict liability for D's injuring P there could be no liability in the first case where no care at all is taken, whereas there could be liability in the second where every conceivable care is taken. When strict liability is at stake, in other words, the law does not give two hoots *either way* about the care that D took. The most inhuman lack of care does not count against her but by the same token the most superhuman investment of care does not count in her favour. It is this double-edged obliviousness to D's precautions that lawyers have in mind when they call liability by the evocative name 'strict'. So strict liability is not, as Brudner suggests, a variant of negligence-based liability in which the standard of obligatory care has been cranked up to an awesome level. It is a quite unrelated mode of liability in which the law does not care about care-taking, and therefore does not treat the bestowing of care—*any care at all*—as having been obligatory. Correspondingly, no measure of self-effacement at all is called for in performing the obligation.

You may object that in these remarks I am interpreting Brudner's doctrinal premiss uncharitably by interpreting it *too* doctrinally. I am attributing to him the clearly mistaken view that D's legal obligation, nonperformance of which gives rise to D's strict liability, is an obligation to take extreme, self-effacing care not to injure P. But what Brudner is actually suggesting (you may say in his defence) is that D's declared legal obligation—admittedly a straightforward obligation not to injure P, for the performance of which taking care is admittedly neither necessary nor sufficient—effectively puts D under another (legally undisclosed) obligation as well, namely a morally obnoxious obligation to take extreme care not to injure P. To be exact, isn't Brudner's real point that taking the most extreme conceivable care, to the point of total self-effacement, is the only way that D has to perform his straightforward legal obligation not to injure P? And that being so, doesn't the very logic of practical rationality dictate that D also has a second, derivative obligation to take that most extreme conceivable care? To will the end, surely, is to will the means; and to will that the end (D's not injuring P) be obligatory is surely, by the same token, to will the derivative obligatoriness of the only way (D's taking ever-such-extreme care not to injure P). It is the obnoxiousness of this latter derivative obligation that, on this more charitable reading of Brudner, casts shame on the former (parent) obligation, and hence casts shame on the strict liability that is based on the former obligation's nonperformance.

I doubt whether this is really a more charitable reading. The proposed argument is open to challenge at virtually every step. Consider, for a start, the step ascribed to the very logic of practical rationality. Should we agree that an action γ is derivatively obligatory for a given agent D whenever another action ϕ is obligatory for D and γing constitutes D's only way of ϕing? On some interpretation of the proposal we clearly should. But which interpretation? We need to know what 'D's only way' means. Minimally, it sets a sufficiency condition:

(*s*) D's γing would contribute to D's ϕing.

Clearly it also sets a necessity condition:

(*n*) no action but D's γing would contribute to D's ϕing.

But should we also read in an availability condition, such as:

(*a*) D has the capacity and opportunity to γ?

And how about an intentionality condition, such as:

(*i*) γing would count as a way for D to avoid ϕing by trying to avoid ϕing?

It is tempting, but mistaken, to incorporate conditions (*a*) and (*i*). To do so is prematurely to build specialized moral ideals—we might call them 'legality ideals', or 'rule of law ideals'—into the very logic of practical rationality. The effect of doing so in the present context is to grant premature credence to the idea that taking extreme, self-effacing care not to injure P is the only way for D to avoid injuring P. If we could free ourselves from the constraints of (*a*) and (*i*), however, there turn out to be plenty of other ways. That D will not encounter P at all as he weaves his drunken way home in the car is surely a perfectly realistic prospect. So why isn't this realistic prospect billed, in the proposed 'charitable' reconstruction of Brudner's argument, as an alternative available means of D's not injuring P, with the result that D's taking ever-such-great care not to injure P is not left as his only way of not injuring P? By knocking out some of the competition in advance—namely all ways of *un*intentionally ϕing—the reading in of condition (*i*) makes it systematically easier for γing to be declared D's only way of ϕing. The condition therefore makes it easier than it would otherwise be to generate a derivative obligation to γ (e.g. to take care not to injure) out of an existing obligation to ϕ (e.g. not to injure).

Probably it will be later in this paper, if ever, before I am able to persuade the reader that (*a*) and (*i*) do not belong to the very logic of practical rationality. So let's turn our attention instead to the further interpretation of (*s*). To understand (*s*), we clearly have to unpack the relevant idea of a 'contribution' to D's ϕing. The basic idea we are looking for here is that of *making it more likely* that D ϕs. After all, for Brudner's purpose—the purpose of evaluating rival legal standards or rules—it is not enough to derive, as an object of evaluation, a one-off obligation on D to take ever-such-extreme care not to injure P as a means of not injuring P. What is needed is a *standard* or *rule* according to which D is to take ever-such-extreme care not to injure P as a means of not injuring P. So our interest is not in D's possible one-off failures and successes in not injuring P by taking ever-such-extreme care not to. Our interest is in his *prospect* of failure and success, his *tendency* to succeed when he conforms to the advertised standard or rule, the *probability* of his not injuring P in the process. Thus the acid question facing Brudner's rearguard defenders is: Is it really the case that D always continues to improve the probability of his not injuring P, the more care he takes not to injure P? Is D's taking ever-such-extreme care not to injure P in *that* sense making a contribution to his not injuring P?

To that question the answer is a resounding no. In principle there always comes a point at which D's taking further care not to injure P does nothing to improve the probability of his not injuring P. Indeed, in principle there always comes a (further) point at which D's taking further care not to injure P is positively counterproductive. The further care D takes not to injure P, beyond this point, actually makes it more, not less, likely that D will injure P. Like other moral virtues, to put the point in familiar Aristotelian terms, the virtue of caution lies in a mean between deficiency and excess. Excessive caution, or at any rate one kind of excessive caution,[3] is the caution that fails in its own terms, the caution that tends to precipitate the very eventualities that the excessively cautious person was taking such pains to avoid. In this vein, we are all familiar with the self-defeating menaces that are the overcautious driver, the overprotective parent, and the oversolicitous lover. Set alongside their all-too-careless counterparts these characters are of course genuinely admirable.[4] But our admiration for them is tinged with pity and frustration. That is because (discounting the secondary success, the bittersweet moral victory, that lies in the mere fact of their being admirable) these too-careful characters are alas no more *successful* at what they do than their all-too-careless counterparts—and that is in spite of, nay *because* of, all the care they take to do it. Their taking such care, put simply, is not a means to their actually doing what they are taking such care to do. On the contrary it is a means to their doing the opposite. So if they have a straightforward obligation not to hurt some other person (say), that obligation yields—on any credible view of the logic of practical rationality—no derivative obligation on them to take the extreme care that they irrationally imagine they should take. Why, it does not even yield a derivative *reason* to take such extreme care. What it yields, on

[3] Perhaps there are other kinds. Couldn't one be overcautious either in being self-defeatingly cautious or in being, as Brudner emphasizes, self-*effacingly* cautious? I wonder whether the latter fault is strictly speaking an instance of overcaution, as opposed to an instance of cravenness or slavishness (that being the virtue of humility taken to a self-defeating point).

[4] I do not mean that they are admirable in spite of their fault. I mean that their fault is an admirable one. It does not follow that it is any the less a fault or that the conduct exhibiting it is any the less wrong or blameworthy. On the logic of admirable yet blameworthy wrongdoing, see Michael Stocker, *Plural and Conflicting Values* (Oxford 1990), ch 2.

the contrary, is a reason, and perhaps sometimes even an obligation, *not* to take such extreme care. It is a salutary reminder of the extent of reason's cunning that a straightforward obligation not to injure P, far from yielding an obligation to take ever-so-much care not to injure P, could in principle yield a derivative obligation to do exactly the opposite, i.e. to proceed without taking very much care, or in extreme cases maybe even any care at all, not to injure P.[5]

II

I mention such dramatic and hard-to-envisage cases mainly to bring home this message. The highest level of productive care (as we might call that point beyond which taking further care makes one no more likely to do what one is taking care to do) is not a constant. It varies from activity to activity. If one must walk across a bed of hot coals it is probably best, as a rule, to be entirely careless where one places one's feet, since any care one takes (e.g. to avoid sharp coals) will, as a rule, just slow one's progress and intensify one's pain. Here the highest level of productive care is on the low side. On the other hand, if one is walking a tightrope very great care in placing one's feet is as a rule exactly what is called for, so I am told, and the highest level of productive care is very high. Thus the overcautious types we mentioned might be, in that respect, good tightrope-walkers but bad hot-coals-walkers. There are in other words very dramatic variations in where the mean of caution lies, as we shift from activity to activity. In principle, however, a highest level of productive care always lurks somewhere. Even in tightrope-walking there comes a point at which one's ever more elaborate precautions against falling (lessons in concentration, extra checks on the rope, intensive practice sessions all afternoon, etc.) tend to stop helping one walk the rope, and soon enough (thanks to the extra stress and tiredness they bring on, etc.) they become the very things that precipitate one's fall. So a straightforward obligation on D not to fall from his tightrope could not—*pace* Brudner's would-be

[5] The most important modern study of this phenomenon of self-defeating endeavour is Derek Parfit's *Reasons and Persons* (Oxford 1984), part 1.

charitable interpreters—yield a derivative obligation on D to take ever-such-extreme care not to fall from his tightrope. What it might yield is a derivative obligation on A to take all *reasonable* (i.e. productive) care not to fall from the tightrope, where this is contrasted with the *unreasonable* (i.e. excessive) care not to fall from the tightrope that would actually hasten A's falling.

When I say 'reasonable care' here, do I mean reasonable care as this is understood by lawyers—namely the care that all and only the negligent fail to take? Something close. What I have been calling the highest level of productive care is indeed one of the central determinants of what counts, in law, as the negligent pursuit of this or that activity. To be sure, it is not the only determinant. Even an extra measure of productive care is not regarded as an extra measure of reasonable care, and so is not required to avoid negligence-based liability, if it is too difficult or costly for D to lay on. But Brudner's argument plays up the difficulties and costs to D of laying on additional measures of care, without noticing that there is always, at the highest level of productive care, an independent cap on the rationality (and hence the derivative obligatoriness) of D's incurring those difficulties and costs. Because of this cap, there is no possibility of a straightforward standardized legal obligation on D not to injure P yielding a derivative standardized obligation on D to take ever-such-extreme measures of care not to injure P. If the obligation not to injure P yields any derivative obligation to take care at all, it is at most an obligation to take all *productive* measures of care—all care that contributes by making it more likely that one will avoid what one cares to avoid—and that often means, *pace* Brudner, only very modest measures of care. In principle, as I said, it might sometimes mean no measures of care at all.

These remarks were supposed to help bring out the rational relationship between negligence-based (or fault) liability on the one hand and strict liability on the other. Essentially, the obligation that one is held to have under a regime of fault liability is an obligation *to take productive care to do* that which, under a regime of strict liability, one would merely have a straightforward unadorned obligation *to do*. As well as bringing out the connection between the two modes of liability, however, this last formulation also helps to bring out the simple ineliminable qualitative contrast between them. The contrast is but one instance of a larger contrast that turns out to be at stake in many of the deepest puzzles of moral and political philosophy. Elsewhere,[6] I have coined some terminology to mark the larger contrast. I have called it the contrast between obligations to *try* and obligations to *succeed*. An obligation to succeed is a straightforward obligation to ϕ, for the performance of which only one's actually ϕing matters, never mind what steps one takes (if any) with a view to ϕing. An obligation to try is the converse case: only the steps one takes with a view to ϕing are relevant to whether one performs the obligation, never mind whether one actually ϕs thereby. On this account, a straightforward obligation not to injure P—the obligation that D is held to have been under (and to have failed to perform) when she is held strictly liable for injuring P—is a straightforward example of an obligation to succeed. By contrast what the law calls D's 'duty of care' to P—the obligation to take care not to injure P, nonperformance of which puts D at fault and grounds D's fault liability—is a straightforward example of an obligation to try.

Or maybe not so straightforward? Some lawyers, in my experience, are resistant to the suggestion that an obligation to take care is an obligation to try. On the one hand, it is said, no amount of trying is logically *sufficient* to perform one's obligation to take care in law, for the legal standard of negligence is an impersonal (or 'objective') standard and this means that, for at least some people, try as they might they will not perform their legal obligation. On the other hand, it is said, no amount of trying is logically *necessary* to perform one's obligation to take care in law. One takes reasonable care not to injure in the relevant sense just as long as one acts in ways that actually reduce the risk of injury one poses to an acceptable level, even if one was not at all concerned, or motivated, to reduce the risk. These objections combine to portray the legal obligation to take care as just another obligation to succeed—to be exact, an obligation to succeed in not behaving too riskily, never mind what one was trying to do—and hence they purport to eliminate the 'ineliminable qualitative contrast' that I drew

[6] In John Gardner, 'The Purity and Priority of Private Law', *University of Toronto Law Journal* 46 (1996), 459 at 486.

between strict liability and fault liability. Both of the objections misfire, however, and my contrast stands uneliminated.

Regarding the first objection: If some people do not perform their obligation to take care however hard they try, this does not go to show that it is not an obligation to try. It only goes to show that it is an obligation to try harder (more assiduously) than they are capable of trying. True, an obligation to try harder than one is capable of trying is a problematic obligation. In particular, it runs up against what I set out as condition (*a*) above, namely the 'availability' condition for deriving one obligation from another. But recall that I am urging caution about condition (*a*). More generally I urge caution about the assumption that 'ought' implies 'can'.[7] But even if there is reason to make this assumption regarding obligations more broadly, there is no reason to think that the assumption applies any the less to obligations to succeed than it does to obligations to try. The point is that the distinction between obligations that one has only on condition that one has the capacity to perform them and obligations (if there be any) that are not subject to this condition is a distinction that *cuts across* the distinction between obligations to try and obligations to succeed.[8] That one lacks the capacity to perform one's obligation does not entail that one has an obligation to succeed rather than an obligation to try. Rather, it remains an obligation to try if the explanation of why one lacks the capacity to perform it is that one lacks assiduousness, i.e. the capacity to try hard enough.

As for the second objection: According to this objection, negligence is a matter of the injurious tendency of one's action, and in assessing that injurious tendency intended effects (those one was trying to achieve) are regarded, through the lens of the law's negligence test, as being completely on a par with side-effects. All are relevant according only to their foreseeability, not according to whether or not the agent literally 'cared' (here meaning 'tried')

[7] The assumption is often ascribed to Kant but much of Kant's work was devoted to refuting it in the sense in which it is usually ascribed to him and widely but mistakenly assumed to be true. Cf. note 41 below.

[8] Those who think that 'obligations to succeed that I have the capacity to perform' is inevitably an empty set are confusing the capacity to perform with the capacity to guarantee performance. Cf. Michael Moore, 'Authority, Law, and Razian Reasons', *Southern California Law Review* 62 (1989), 827 at 875.

to bring them about or avoid them. Trying assiduously enough to avoid injuring is admittedly *one* way to avoid being negligent; but one can also avoid being negligent by (fortuitously) posing only acceptable risks of injury by one's conduct. So we are often told by, for example, those who have an economistic interpretation of the law. But is this the real legal position? I think not. Let's concede—although the matter is more complicated than it looks—that the law doesn't locate D's negligence in the fact that he tried to do what he tried to do.[9] But it nevertheless clearly does locate D's negligence in what he meanwhile *didn't* try to do. The whole point is that D didn't *take sufficient care to avert* (limit, reduce, control) the injurious side-effects of his endeavours. The words 'to avert' here mean 'in order to avert', 'with a view to averting', or (in other words) 'intending to avert'. What else could be meant by them? Taking care is an essentially intentional action. One cannot take care not to ϕ without trying not to ϕ. That is also the law's position. Negligence in law is a failure to try assiduously enough to avert (limit, reduce, control) the unwelcome side-effects of one's (otherwise valuable) endeavours. It follows that the obligation that one fails to perform when one acts negligently is indeed an obligation to try. The nonperformance of an obligation to try is what gives rise to fault liability in law, just as the nonperformance of an obligation to succeed is what gives rise to strict liability. The contrast between the two is as basic as they come.

And yet, doubts persist. In spite of its name, it may be objected, the law's 'duty of care' does not require of D that she literally takes any care at all. It only asks of D that she take whatever 'precautions' someone who was taking enough care would take. That someone is the law's famous 'reasonable person'. The reasonable person takes the right amount of care and all that is required of D, to avoid liability for negligence, is that she emulate the resulting actions. So, for example, the reasonable person drives within the lane markings on the road. She is paying attention. Is D paying attention? One analysis has it that the law does not care whether D pays attention as long as she too is driving within the lane

[9] The complications are brilliantly exposed in John Finnis's 'Allocating Risks and Suffering: Some Hidden Traps', *Cleveland State Law Review* 38 (1990), 193.

markings on the road, i.e. so long as she does what the reasonable person would have done.

Is this really the law? In the law of negligence, as opposed to a strict liability context, is something as minimal as 'driving within the lane markings on the road' really all that the law requires of D? Once we have observed the lane movements of D's car, does it really make no difference to D's position in the law of negligence whether, for example, D is sending a text message on his mobile phone at the time? Or reading the billboards? Or showing off to his girlfriend who is sitting in the passenger seat? If any of these things makes a difference then the law's expression 'taking precautions' needs to be given an intentionalistic reading no less than 'taking care'. It is all about what steps D was taking (or failing to take) *in order to* avert, or *with a view to* averting, an accident. Negligence in law remains a failure to try assiduously enough to avert (limit, reduce, control) the unwelcome side-effects of one's (otherwise valuable) endeavours. The obligation that one fails to perform when one acts negligently remains an obligation to try. What we are witnessing with the introduction of the 'reasonable person' standard is mainly the law's helping itself to an additional measure of elasticity, or indeterminacy, in the exact shape of the duty of care. D is still judged by the care that he himself takes.

III

Brudner's failed objection to the legal imposition of strict liability was notable for having virtually turned on its head the most common objection to strict liability in the law. Brudner's objection proceeded from the thought that to avoid incurring strict liability, one needs to exercise the most extreme conceivable care. By contrast, the common objection focuses on the fact that, when strict liability is at issue, the law does not give two hoots how much care one takes. This common objection in turn comes in two variants. I will call them the *moral intelligibility* variant and the *institutional fairness* variant. According to the institutional fairness variant, it is unfair (or contrary to the rule of law, or something along those lines) to ground legal liability in nonperformance of an obligation to succeed, since this makes it impossible even in principle for people to plan their lives according to whether their actions will or will not attract legal liability. For they cannot possibly know this until they know how their actions turn out—as successes or failures—by which time it is too late to reconsider whether to perform them. Unfair? You may think so. But if you sign up to the other variant of the objection—the moral intelligibility variant—you do not even get as far as asking whether the legal enforcement of obligations to succeed is unfair. For what you deny, in a sense, is the very possibility of there being obligations to succeed, be they enforced or not. Of course, this is not to deny that the law *asserts* the existence of unperformed obligations to succeed whenever it imposes strict liability. That cannot be denied. Nor is it denied that the law may have its reasons for imposing the liability and hence for asserting the existence of the underlying obligations. Naturally it may. What is denied is that the law's assertion of the existence of the obligations can be made morally intelligible. For morally speaking—i.e. apart from the law—there is and can be no such thing as an obligation to succeed. Or so the objection goes. Strict liability, as Thomas Nagel famously put it, 'may have its legal uses but seems irrational as a moral position'.[10]

At first sight this second variant of the common objection seems to miss the target completely. If the assertion of an obligation to succeed 'has its legal uses', why is it an objection to those legal uses that obligations to succeed could not possibly exist *apart* from the law? Why should the law care whether its assertions are morally intelligible so long as they are legally useful? The answer, of course, is that the law by its very nature claims to bind people morally; it purports to tell them what they *really* ought to do, not merely what they ought to do according to law.[11] Legal obligations, in short, are would-be moral obligations. What this means is that, if they are to be defended as legal obligations, they have

[10] Thomas Nagel, 'Moral Luck', *Proceedings of the Aristotelian Society Supplementary Volume* 50 (1976), 137; reprinted in his collection *Mortal Questions* (Cambridge 1979), 24 at 31 (to which page references below refer).

[11] For two largely complementary defences of the thesis that such claims form part of the very nature of law, see Joseph Raz, *The Authority of Law* (Oxford 1979), chs 1 and 2, and John Finnis, *Natural Law and Natural Rights* (Oxford 1980), chs 1 and 11.

to be defended as would-be moral obligations, i.e. inspected in a moral light. It does not follow, of course, that defensible legal obligations all need to be institutionalizations of moral obligations that already exist apart from the law (the nonperformance of which would be *malum in se*). Defensible legal obligations are often new moral obligations created by law (the nonperformance of which is *malum prohibitum*), and in principle the creation of these new moral obligations can be defended perfectly adequately by relying on the usefulness (the consequential advantages) of the liability regime thereby brought into being.[12] But the creation of such legal obligations always remains subject to the following constraint: On pain of indefensibility as legal obligations, they must be obligations that could conceivably have existed apart from the law. On pain of indefensibility, it must always *make sense* to say of any legal obligation 'this is your moral obligation'. Otherwise it is impossible to judge legal obligations as would-be moral obligations. So if, as many are wont to argue, it never makes sense to say of an obligation to succeed 'this is your moral obligation', then the assertion of obligations to succeed in law is always indefensible, whatever their 'legal uses'. Although rarely spelt out, this is the moral intelligibility variant of the common objection to the legal imposition of strict liability.

These lines of argument are invoked to discredit strict liability. But as I expressed them it seems that they also bite, in the process, against some other kinds of legal liability. Take, for example, liability for the tort of negligence at common law. In spite of its name, the tort of negligence is not the simple tort of acting negligently towards P. It is the more complex tort of injuring P *by* acting negligently towards P. To put it another way, although one has a legal obligation to take reasonable care not to injure P (the 'duty of care'), breach of this straightforward obligation to try is not a tort. It is not a legally actionable breach of obligation. What is legally actionable, and is a tort, is the breach of a more complex

[12] Thus when I say 'moral' here I do not mean 'moral' in the narrow technical sense often favoured in recent tort theory, which is by way of contrast with 'economic' or 'policy-oriented'. Contrast, e.g., Ernest Weinrib's anti-*mala-prohibita* invocation of 'moral' in 'Towards a Moral Theory of Negligence Law', *Law and Philosophy* 2 (1983), 37.

obligation, namely the obligation *not to injure P by* not taking reasonable care not to injure P. This is not, as you can see by the italicized words, a straightforward obligation to try. Rather it is a kind of hybrid trying-succeeding obligation. More than one kind of hybrid trying-succeeding obligation is, of course, logically possible. One kind of hybrid would be an obligation to *succeed-by-trying*—an obligation, for instance, to take reasonable care not to injure P and (thereby) to avoid injuring P. This is obviously a tall order. One would fail to perform this hybrid obligation if *either* one did not take the correct measure of care not to injure P *or* one did in fact injure P. But the hybrid obligation, nonperformance of which constitutes the tort of negligence, is not a hybrid of this 'tall-order' kind. It is the converse case. One commits the tort of negligence only if one *both* failed to take the correct measure of care not to injure P *and* one did in fact injure P. The obligation at stake is not an obligation to succeed by trying but an obligation *not to fail for want of trying*. We might call this a 'short-order' as opposed to a 'tall-order' hybrid. It is more readily performed than either a straightforward obligation to try or a straightforward obligation to succeed, all else being equal, since there are always two alternative ways of performing it: either by trying to the requisite extent (whether successfully or not) or else by succeeding (whether or not by trying).

The fact that it is more readily performed than either a straightforward obligation to try or a straightforward obligation to succeed does not entail, however, that the presence of such a hybrid obligation in the law is also easier to defend. True, one can quickly nuance the institutional fairness argument so that it cuts against the legal enforcement of straightforward obligations to succeed (i.e. strict liability) but not against the legal enforcement of short-order hybrids (as in the action for negligence at common law). The institutional fairness argument is indeed most often ventured asymmetrically, with the focus on helping those who want to be sure in advance that they will *not* incur any liability, rather than on helping the perhaps more eccentric types who want to be sure in advance that they will incur it. Since taking the legally specified measure of care is logically *sufficient* to extinguish liability for the tort of negligence, one can plan to steer clear of that liability just as readily as one could plan to steer clear of liability for nonperformance of a simple obligation to take the specified measure of care (i.e. a straightforward obligation to try). True, taking a legally specified measure of care is not logically *necessary* to extinguish liability for the tort of negligence, since that liability could also be extinguished by the happy fortuity that one injured nobody by one's carelessness. But naturally this possibility is no skin off the nose of people who merely want to plan safely to avoid the liability, for they only need to know what investment of care would be sufficient to do so. If these people are the only ones that the institutional fairness argument seeks to protect, then that argument cuts against strict liability (the legal enforcement of straightforward obligations to succeed) but not against liability for the tort of negligence (the legal enforcement of short-order hybrid obligations not to fail for want of trying).

Matters are not so clear-cut, however, when we come to the moral intelligibility objection. If straightforward obligations to succeed (and hence strict liability torts) turn out to be morally unintelligible, could obligations not to fail for want of trying (and hence the tort of negligence at common law) nevertheless turn out to be morally intelligible?[13] The final answer to this question depends, of course, on what exactly it is that is said to *make* obligations to succeed morally unintelligible. For the time being, however, our interest is not in the answer. Our interest is in the question itself. As followers of modern policy debates about the law of torts, especially those that rage in the North American law schools, we are all accustomed to think of the history of modern tort policy as a struggle for supremacy between the reigning tort of negligence on the one hand, and, on the other hand, the upstart strict liability torts (on the *Rylands* v *Fletcher*[14] model) that occasionally surface, or are promoted, as pretenders to its throne (nowadays, for example, in the field of products liability). In the mentality of modern tort law and tort theory, to defend the one is implicitly to attack the other. But our question puts a completely different complexion on the relationship between them. It shows that in another dimension the tort of negligence may on the contrary have its moral fate *bound up* with that of its strict

[13] See Nagel, 'Moral Luck', above note 10, 28–9.

[14] (1866) LR 1 Ex 265; [1868] LR 3 HL 330.

liability rivals. For the tort of negligence and its strict liability rivals on the *Rylands* v *Fletcher* model stand together in opposition to another little-noticed but increasingly powerful pretender, a model of tort liability in the incurring of which it matters not one jot whether D actually injured P, but *only* how much care D took that P not be injured. The really stark contrast is, of course, the contrast between this kind of 'bare negligence' tort (which consists in nonperformance of a straightforward obligation to try, never mind one's success) and a strict liability tort (which consists in nonperformance of a straightforward obligation to succeed, never mind whether or to what extent one tried). In this contrast, the tort of negligence at common law is logically non-aligned. It consists in the nonperformance of a hybrid trying-succeeding obligation (to be exact, an obligation not to fail for want of trying), and hence shares as much and as little of its logical structure with strict liability torts as it does with bare negligence torts.

But is it also *morally* non-aligned? There are two dramatically contrasting ways of thinking about the moral intelligibility, and hence the defensibility, of the tort of negligence at common law. It is possible to take compromise positions intermediate between them but they represent the two magnetic poles of the debate, the first of which has lately proved more magnetic than the second. The first interpretation—the one which has come into the ascendant in the late-twentieth-century literature—would have it that the tort of negligence is essentially a variation on the theme of a bare negligence tort. The essence of D's wrong, morally speaking, lies in his failure to take adequate care not to injure P. The extra condition that P have actually been injured by D's failure to take care is regarded, correspondingly, as morally secondary. Its defence is accordingly apt to be a parasitic defence, i.e. one that presupposes that the real moral wrong has already been done to P. Thus the extra condition is collaterally defended as, for example, a *locus standi* condition calculated to optimize the incidence of litigation in respect of the wrong,[15] or as a way of ensuring that compensation for the wrong will in principle be quantifiable without resort to excessive speculation about

[15] See, most obviously, Richard Posner's influential 'A Theory of Negligence' *Journal of Legal Studies* 1 (1972) 29 at 46–52.

probabilities. But by the same token the door is left open to allowing the extra condition that P be injured by D to be eliminated or watered down while leaving the central moral theme of the tort in place. On this interpretation, one can imagine modifying the tort such that in some cases (e.g. mass injuries arising from multi-manufacturer pharmaceuticals or industry-wide environmental hazards) it is no longer a condition of D's liability for the tort of negligence that D actually injured P, but only (say) that P was injured and D was one of a finite group of careless operators who may well have injured her, or even (say) that P was not injured at all but only left insufficiently protected against injury by D and his fellow operators. These are regarded, on the first of the two contrasting interpretations that I have in mind, as relatively marginal adjustments to a tort, the moral essence of which lies in nonperformance of a straightforward obligation to try, viz. the common law's famous duty of care.

But on the other interpretation that I have in mind these adjustments are far from marginal. They represent the most dramatic possible abrogation of the moral foundation of the tort of negligence. For in spite of the tort's misleading name, the moral essence of D's tort in a negligence case is really just that he injured P. In other words, the tort of negligence at common law is morally speaking a variation on the strict liability model of a tort, in which what is of the essence is what one actually does (injures P), never mind what one merely tries to do (one's not taking adequate care not to injure P). The extra condition that D not have taken adequate care not to injure P is regarded, correspondingly, as morally secondary. Its defence is accordingly apt to be a parasitic defence, i.e. one that presupposes that the real moral wrong has already been done to P. The negligence condition is defended, for example, as one that is needed merely to meet the institutional fairness objection. The moral wrong one does is essentially just to injure P, but it is unfair to hold D liable for that wrong without providing a way in which D could have taken steps to guard himself against incurring the liability. Thus the extra condition of fault is grafted on to the tort for institutional reasons. Or some such parasitic, morally secondary reasons. Correspondingly the negligence condition could in principle be removed in appropriate cases without eating away at the moral foundations of the tort. Where someone embarks on ultra-hazardous activities, for example, they may be regarded as having been put on fair warning of their liability for the injuries they do merely by the fact that their activities were ultra-hazardous. They could plan not to incur the liability simply enough, by giving up the blasting or the chemical processing that is creating the hazard. So under some conditions—for example, those prevailing in *Rylands* v *Fletcher*—the extra negligence condition may defensibly be dropped, and then we are left with the moral essence of the tort, which emerges as the simple unadorned wrong of *D injuring P*.[16] Or so goes the rival—and nowadays markedly contrarian—interpretation of the tort of negligence.

IV

We owe to Tony Honoré the most important modern attempt to rehabilitate this contrarian interpretation of the tort of negligence at common law.[17] When we put the tort of negligence

[16] We can see here one reason why Brudner may have thought that strict tort liability demands of D that he be entirely self-effacing. It is not because tort liability is strict but because in modern legal systems it is typically strict *and conditional*, i.e. it is a strict liability that arises only when one is engaged in certain pursuits, such as blasting and manufacturing consumer products. These extra conditions are needed to meet the problem of institutional fairness. To guarantee avoiding the strict liability, it is logically sufficient (but notice: not necessary) that one give up the pursuit in question. Now surely *that* would be a huge (self-effacing) burden for one to bear? True, but one cannot plead this as an objection to the liability's being strict. Suppose, in response, the law called one's bluff. Suppose it removed the condition and left one with an unconditional strict liability instead, applicable as much to car-driving and hairdressing as to blasting and consumer manufacturing. Then the law would have met one's objection head on by removing one's reason to give up the blasting in favour of, say, hairdressing. Yet rather than eliminating strict liability the law's reaction would have expanded it to take in hairdressing as well. The point I am making is that if strict liability in modern tort law seems to require that one efface oneself by taking extreme measures to avoid liability, that is usually because there is not enough of it around to make the self-effacement utterly fruitless.

[17] Largely in the papers collected in his *Responsibility and Fault* (Oxford 1999), although anticipated in the preface to the second edition of H L A Hart and Tony Honoré, *Causation in the Law* (Oxford 1985). In the following footnotes, all references to papers reprinted in *Responsibility and Fault* use the pagination of the reprint.

side by side with modern strict liability torts, argues Honoré, the first feature that calls for our defensive or critical attention is not the much-discussed feature that divides the two ('fault' v 'no-fault'), but the less-widely-remarked-upon feature that they both have in common, namely what Honoré calls their shared element of *outcome responsibility*. Depending as it does on the moral defensibility of outcome responsibility, the tort of negligence is in the same boat, morally speaking, as a strict liability tort. The tort of negligence is essentially a variation on the theme of a strict liability tort, in which the basic wrong lies in D's actually injuring P. Accordingly, those who want to defend the tort of negligence at common law had better begin by defending, not attacking, the morality of strict liability. There is plenty of time to part company with enthusiasts for strict liability later, when one comes to the question of what *further* conditions must be met before legal liability is justified. In answer to that question, enthusiasts for strict liability may say 'anything but a fault condition' while enthusiasts for the tort of negligence may say 'a fault condition'. That polarization is for later. Before that, according to Honoré, comes the morally more basic problem of understanding the common ground that unites the two competing sets of enthusiasts against everyone else, namely the moral significance that they agree in attaching to *D's actually injuring P*—the element of outcome responsibility.

It should be said that Honoré's first articulation of this contrarian line of thought suffered from an equivocation. At first he made the wrong connection between strict liability and liability for the tort of negligence. He said that it was the *objective standard of care* in the tort of negligence which gave that tort an affinity with strict liability torts. 'For the objective standard of competence,' he wrote in his first major venture into the subject, 'imposes a form of strict liability on that minority of shortcomers who cannot achieve it.'[18] We have already seen that this is a mistake. To defend strict liability is to defend, minimally, the moral intelligibility of straightforward obligations to succeed. An obligation to

[18] Tony Honoré, 'Responsibility and Luck', *Law Quarterly Review* 104 (1988), 530, reprinted in his *Responsibility and Fault*, above note 17, 14 at 22.

try harder than one is capable of trying, of the kind that is created when 'shortcomers' encounter the objective standard of care, is not an obligation to succeed. It remains an obligation to try. As we saw already, the distinction between obligations to try and obligations to succeed *cuts across* the distinction between obligations that one has only to the extent that one has the capacity to perform them and obligations (if there be any) that are not subject to this condition. The problem of strict liability correspondingly cuts across, rather than tracking, the problem of the objective standard of care in the tort of negligence. By lumping the two together Honoré equivocated about which of the two problems he was really trying to tackle.

Honoré was led astray here by his instinct to interpret the common objection to strict liability as an objection to the intelligibility (or, on its other variant, the fairness) of the law's exposing people to 'moral luck', i.e. luck in whether they come up to scratch in what they do and hence in what judgments they are properly open to. Surely, he reasoned, not only strict liability but also the objective standard of negligence can be objected to on this ground? True enough—if the objection makes sense. But, as Nagel established, it does not. There can be no such thing as a coherent general objection to our being exposed to moral luck. Attempts to explicate such an objection are an object lesson in the hazards of argumentative overkill. For what counts as luck is always, Nagel shows, luck *only relative to some baseline or other*. Whenever something is held to be luck, there is necessarily something else that is held *not* to be luck, and it is only relative to this second thing that the first counts as lucky or unlucky. The problem with a general objection to our exposure to moral luck is that *everything* we do is entirely a matter of luck relative to *some* baseline or other. Even when I maliciously attempt to do away with my professional rival—on any credible view an action that is open to some moral judgment—my doing so is luck relative to some baselines (e.g. the baseline of my genetic make-up, which pre-programmed no such behaviour and was compatible with my leading a life without any such attempt). It follows that to object to moral luck *tout court* is to object to morality *tout court*. Indeed it is to object to judging people's actions by any standards at all. As Nagel himself puts it: 'The area of genuine agency, and therefore of legitimate moral judgment, seems to shrink under this scrutiny to an extensionless point.'[19]

Misreading Nagel's tone here, some took it that they were supposed to endorse the conclusion of this sentence, and to regard morality itself as having been discredited by Nagel's demonstration that there is no place for morality to hide from luck. But in fact Nagel's argument is a classic *reductio*. The conclusion is absurd—agency *does* have some reach and moral judgment *does* have some area of application—so something must have gone wrong in the premisses.[20] What went wrong, Nagel showed, was the instinct to formulate as a general objection to the intelligibility (or fairness) of exposing people to 'moral luck' what were really different people's quite different and unrelated objections to the use of different baselines as the baselines for our moral judgments. Some people think that the question of whether we come up to scratch in what we do should be relativized (baselined) to our own personal capacities, and in the light of that view they rebel at objective standards of care as used in the law. Some think—an overlapping constituency, I suspect—that the question of whether we come up to scratch in what we do should be relativized (baselined) to the possible limits of trying, and in the light of that view they rebel at strict liability. Each of these suggested baselines needs to be defended, and for that matter objected to, on its own merits. Maybe refusing to acknowledge one or other or both of these baselines as fixing the proper boundaries of moral judgment is morally unintelligible or institutionally unfair. But the observation that in refusing to acknowledge them we expose people to 'moral luck' does absolutely nothing to tell us *what it is* that would make such reliance either unintelligible or unfair. For (as Nagel shows) we are automatically exposed to moral luck, against some baseline, just in virtue of the fact that our actions are held up to judgment at all. The so-called 'problem of moral luck' (like the so-called 'problem of free will' with which it is supposedly connected) is therefore a pseudo-problem.[21] It represents the bundling

[19] 'Moral Luck', above note 10, 35.

[20] Even if you don't accept the assertions, Nagel and Honoré do. So maybe I should say that the argument is a classic *reductio* for their purposes.

[21] An irony: Bernard Williams and Tom Nagel conjured up 'the problem of moral luck' as a topic for their joint Aristotelian Society seminar in 1976. Both of

together of various different problems about the grounds of moral judgment that have nothing at all in common save that they are all problems about the grounds of moral judgment. Two of these problems—and they are as distinct from each other as it is possible for two problems to be—are the problem of the objective standard of care (can there be moral obligations to do more than one is capable of doing—whether in the way of succeeding or trying—and if so should they be legally enforced?) and the problem of strict liability (can there be straightforward moral obligations to succeed—whether within or beyond the limits of one's capacities—and if so should they be legally enforced?)

Fortunately it did not take Honoré long to recover from the effects of this distracting conflation. A few pages later he puts it behind him and trenchantly captures the real respect in which the tort of negligence is morally aligned with strict liability torts of the *Rylands* v *Fletcher* variety, and to that extent stands or falls with them. It turns out to have nothing to do with the objective standard of care. Rather, explains Honoré,

> [s]trict liability is one species of enhanced responsibility for outcomes. This does not entail that whenever a harmful outcome is properly allocated to someone, this justifies imposing on him a strict liability to compensate for that outcome.... [R]esponsibility for a harmful outcome should not automatically involve a legal duty to compensate. An extra element is needed to ground the legal sanction. Sometimes [as in the tort of negligence at common law] the extra element is fault.... For strict liability [as under *Rylands* v *Fletcher*] the extra element is usually that the conduct of the harm doer carries a special risk of harm of the sort that has in fact come about.[22]

There admittedly comes a point at which one needs to decide what further conditions, if any, one will insist upon for legal liability: maybe (objective) fault, as in the tort of negligence, maybe not, as under *Rylands* v *Fletcher*. But that little internecine squabble is for later. First, in the order of moral argument, comes

them showed, in their different ways, that there is no such problem. Yet strangely the problem took off while its agreed dissolution was forgotten. Williams' eponymous paper appears before Nagel's in the original periodical printing (above note 10), and is reprinted in Bernard Williams, *Moral Luck* (Cambridge 1981).

[22] 'Responsibility and Luck', above note 18, 27.

the question of what kind of standard these further conditions of liability are supposed to be grafted onto, and why. In the tort of negligence and *Rylands* v *Fletcher* torts alike, argues Honoré, the underlying standard is a standard of outcome responsibility, a standard which attaches a person (D) to the way his actions actually turn out (say, with P's being injured).

I think Honoré chooses the label 'outcome responsibility' to designate the issue that he is interested in here because the label's intriguing ambiguities correspond to some intriguing ambiguities in the issue itself, and these Honoré understandably wants to keep alive for investigation. For a start, talk of an action's 'outcome' equivocates nicely between a reference to an action's *consequences* and a reference to (what some philosophers call) its *results*.[23] The consequences of an action are what they sound like: they are eventualities that follow an action and that are also causally connected to it. Results are different. They are the causal *constituents* of actions, i.e. they do not follow the action but form part of it.[24] P's death, for example, is a consequence of D's trying to kill P. On the other hand P's death is a result of D's actually killing P, because the action of killing P (unlike the action of trying to kill P) is partly constituted by P's dying. Until P is dead, D hasn't killed him but has only tried to. Death is a consequence of the one action and a result of the other, but it is perfectly natural to say, in the intentionally ambiguous terminology chosen by Honoré, that it is the 'outcome' of them both.

As for 'responsibility', this is a notoriously multivocal term.[25] For Honoré's purpose, the interesting ambiguity that it harbours is this one. In some contexts 'my responsibility' means something very close to 'my liability'. Being responsible in this sense means facing the adverse normative consequences of having failed to

[23] This useful terminology is G H von Wright's, from his *Norm and Action* (London 1963), 39ff. The distinction is interestingly nuanced in Anthony Kenny, *Will, Freedom and Power* (Oxford 1975), 54ff.

[24] I call a result a 'causal' constituent because the action of which it forms part is an action of causing that result (or occasioning it, or provoking it, or inducing it, or standing in some other causal relationship to it).

[25] The best study of the various concepts of responsibility and the relationships among them remains H L A Hart, 'Varieties of Responsibility', *Law Quarterly Review* 83 (1967), 346.

perform one's obligations (such as being subject to a power of punishment or being subject to a new obligation to pay compensation or apologise). But on other occasions 'my responsibility' refers to something else: it refers to the obligations themselves rather than to the normative consequences of their nonperformance. Thus failing in one's legal responsibility (=obligation) may have, as one of its legal consequences, legal responsibility (=liability). Actually, to be strict, a responsibility in the 'obligation' sense is not exactly the same as an obligation, so the '=' in the first set of parentheses here is slightly misleading. Rather, a responsibility in this sense, like a right, is the *ground* of (one or more) obligations.[26] Often, indeed, D's obligations to P are grounded in the combination of P's rights and D's responsibilities. But just as we did with rights, we may put this subtlety on one side for present purposes. That is because just as there is nothing that counts as D violating P's rights other than D failing to perform her obligations to P, so there is nothing that counts as D failing to fulfil her responsibilities to P other than D failing to perform the associated obligations. Thus if we are interested in the ingredients of D's *wrongs*—for instance, her torts or breaches of contract—the difference between an obligation and the responsibility that grounds it need not concern us. Nor, for that matter, need we concern ourselves with the similarly tangential conceptual wedge that can be driven between liability and responsibility-in-the-liability-sense. We have grasped the pertinent aspects of the two concepts of responsibility that bear on Honoré's discussion if we think of them as responsibility (≈liability) and responsibility (≈obligation).

These twin ambiguities—outcome (=consequence? =result?) and responsibility (≈liability? ≈obligation?)—combine nicely to provide Honoré with the ambiguity in the expression 'outcome responsibility' that he wants to preserve for the purposes of his discussion. One of the issues that he is interested in under this heading is the issue of whether it is *fair* to hold people responsible (≈liable), whether in law or in other social settings (e.g. games, professional codes of practice, traditional codes of honour, etc.),

[26] This explains why, as Hart notices but does not satisfactorily explain (ibid, 347), some obligations are not associated with any responsibilities, while others are associated with more than one. The same goes for rights.

for the actual (as opposed to intended or projected) outcomes (=consequences *or* results) of their actions. The other issue he is interested in under the 'outcome responsibility' heading is the issue of whether we can really *have* responsibilities (≈obligations) to perform actions defined in terms of their outcomes (=results). It does not take long to see that these two issues correspond to the two variants I mentioned of the common objection to strict liability. The first corresponds to the institutional fairness variant, which was an objection to (legal or other) liability based on nonperformance of obligations to succeed. Honoré notices that if the institutional fairness variant of the objection is successful, it bites not only against forms of liability that depend on what one did-including-results (i.e. one's success) but likewise against forms of liability that depend on what happened when one did it (the actual consequences of one's actions). Thus he rightly reads the institutional fairness objection as an objection to outcome (=results *or* consequences) responsibility (≈liability). The other issue he is interested in is, however, the deeper one of the two. It is the issue of whether it can ever be one's responsibility (≈obligation) to perform actions that have a certain outcome (=result). Only if it can be do we ever get to the further question of the fairness of making us legally (or otherwise) liable when we fail to perform such obligations. This deeper issue is the very same one that is raised by those who deny the moral intelligibility of obligations to succeed. To deny the moral intelligibility of obligations to succeed is to deny the very possibility of outcome responsibility in Honoré's second sense, never mind its fairness. It is to deny that our responsibilities (≈obligations) really do extend beyond our merely trying to do things so as to include our actually succeeding in doing them (i.e. acting with specified results). Hence it is to deny that we can make morally intelligible a law that asserts that our responsibilities do so extend.

Corresponding to these two different explanations of what outcome responsibility is,[27] Honoré offers two quite different defences of it. One, designed to meet the institutional fairness

[27] Stephen Perry calls them respectively the 'social' and the 'personhood' senses of outcome responsibility: 'Honoré on Responsibility for Outcomes' in Peter Cane and John Gardner (eds), *Relating to Responsibility* (Oxford 2001).

objection, is his well-known and carefully crafted 'betting' argument. Action is by its nature a gamble, he says: some you win, some you lose. Facing liability when you lose is only half of the story of outcome responsibility; the other half includes all the *positive* normative consequences (admittedly mostly laid on extra-legally) that flow from doing what you do successfully. So long as the mechanism really does cut both ways in social life taken as a whole, one has no complaint of unfairness merely because the law concentrates on the down side.[28] Although I agree that this argument is sufficient to its task, I also tend to think that it is unnecessary. In my view, one can overcome the institutional fairness objection to (at any rate some pockets of) strict liability in the law with far less elaborate manoeuvres that leave fewer hostages to fortune.[29] But I am not going to pursue this matter in what

[28] 'Responsibility and Luck', above note 18, 24–9. Let me mention just one point about the 'betting' argument in passing, because it supplements some remarks I have already made about the structure of Honoré's enterprise. In pursuing the 'betting' argument, it seems to me, Honoré gradually slips back into his initial mistake of confusing objections to strict liability with objections to the objective standard of care. As the 'betting' argument proceeds he starts to engage with an imaginary objector who says: some lose more than they win and some win more than they lose. How is that fair? Honoré responds with an (implausibly) optimistic view of ordinary people's failure rates that is supposed to marginalize the problem of net losers (at 28). He should have responded much more robustly by saying that the new imaginary objector was changing the subject and alleging a totally different unfairness. The new imaginary objector was objecting to the unfairness of the law's failure to relativize legal liability to people's varying capacities. Honoré's 'betting' argument was not, however, a defence of the law's failure to relativize to capacities. It was a defence of the law's refusal to ignore the importance of success as well as the importance of trying. All that one can ask of the betting argument is that it eliminate the unfairness that it was devised to eliminate, viz. the unfairness of outcome responsibility. That it leaves another supposed unfairness untouched is not, so to speak, its problem. I say 'supposed' unfairness because I believe that, barring special cases, there is nothing unfair about people being held up to standards that personally they are unable to meet. The robust (and correct) answer to this complaint of unfairness is that, barring special cases (e.g. young infants and the seriously mentally ill), people *should* be able to meet the standards in question and have no complaint if they are judged by them when they cannot.

[29] In my view one overcomes the objections simply by putting potential Ds on fair warning that they are embarking on an activity (e.g. blasting) in respect of which strict liability applies to them. Cf. note 16 above on the 'ultra-hazardous activities' condition as a fair warning condition.

remains of this paper. Instead I am going to focus my attention on Honoré's second argument.

This second argument is offered not as a rebuttal of the institutional fairness objection but rather as a response to the moral intelligibility objection. Can one even make sense of the idea that people have obligations to succeed? Can one make sense of the idea, in other words, that they are outcome-responsible in the second of Honoré's two senses? Not only can one make sense of this idea, answers Honoré. More to the point, *one cannot manage without it*. It is not the presence of outcome responsibility that makes no sense, but rather its absence:

> [O]utcome allocation can be defended on grounds deeper than the overall balance of benefit over burden; and so, in its wake, can strict liability. For outcome allocation is crucial to our identity as persons; and unless we were persons who possessed an identity, the question of whether it was fair to subject us to responsibility could not arise. If actions and outcomes were not ascribed to us on the basis of our bodily movements and their mental accompaniments, we could have no continuing history or character. There would indeed be bodies, and associated with them minds. Each would possess a certain continuity. They could be labelled A, B, C. But having decided nothing and done nothing these entities would hardly be people.[30]

This approach to the problem is exciting and unusual. The approach is to fight fire with fire. If the absence of outcome responsibility really makes no sense then its presence can't *but* make sense, and those who think it unintelligible must therefore be thinking fallaciously. Honoré's remarks therefore hold out the tantalizing promise of a philosophical role reversal, with 'moral intelligibility' objectors to the legal enforcement of obligations to succeed finding themselves, for once, in the defensive position, with their own challenge thrown back at their feet. Nor is the challenger content with rescuing obligations to succeed from oblivion; he also aims to elevate them, in the process, to a kind of moral priority. Remember Brudner's view that a regime of strict liability takes us to the point of total self-effacement, to the point at which, as agents, we are obliterated from the world? On

[30] 'Responsibility and Luck', above note 18, 29.

the contrary, according to Honoré. A regime of strict liability represents the starkest possible *reaffirmation* of our agency and its importance in the world, because the simple idea at the heart of strict liability—the idea of outcome responsibility—is the idea that we leave traces of ourselves forever imprinted on history, in the form of the countless welcome and unwelcome events that were (as Honoré puts it elsewhere) 'unequivocally our doing'.[31] In what we merely try to do this imprint is lacking, and the power of our agency is therefore but meanly represented. In that sense, trying to ϕ is secondary. Success—actually ϕing—is primary. 'It is only this primary outcome responsibility,' observes Honoré, 'that can explain why we (rightly) judge murder more severely than attempted murder, and causing death by dangerous driving more severely than dangerous driving.'[32] And it is only this primary outcome responsibility—he could have added—that puts the requisite moral distance between someone who merely fails to take an adequate measure of care not to injure P, but fortunately leaves P uninjured, and someone who fails to take that same adequate measure of care, by the same margin, *and actually injures P in the process*. For first and foremost, the deeper argument goes, we are what we do—complete with results.

V

This deeper argument of Honoré's is never developed to the same level of specificity as his 'betting' argument. In subsequent writings, indeed, Honoré has preserved the speculative and exploratory tone of the words just quoted.[33] It is the tone of a philosophical promissory note. For this reason the force of Honoré's remarks—the decisive argument that they tantalizingly promise—has never been fully brought home to those who doubt the moral possibility, let alone the moral priority, of straightforward obligations to succeed. Yet Honoré's remarks do alert us to the basic steps of

[31] *Causation in the Law*, above note 17, lxxxi.

[32] 'Responsibility and Luck', above note 18, 31.

[33] For instance, in Tony Honoré, 'The Morality of Tort Law: Questions and Answers' in D G Owen (ed), *Philosophical Foundations of Tort Law* (Oxford 1995), also reprinted as ch 4 of Honoré, *Responsibility and Fault*, above note 17, 76–7.

just such a decisive argument. True, the argument does not quite establish the moral intelligibility of straightforward obligations to succeed, let alone their moral priority over obligations to try. What it does establish, when fully spelt out, is the moral intelligibility of *reasons* to succeed, and one important sense in which those reasons have moral priority over mere *reasons* to try. With this much established, the most important source of doubt about the possibility of straightforward obligations to succeed—namely scepticism about the independent rational salience of success—is roundly dispatched. Of course, at this point the question may still in principle be raised of whether these reasons to succeed with their special moral priority can ever be *categorical mandatory* reasons to succeed—that is to say, obligations.[34] But once we see that there are indeed moral reasons to succeed and that they are in one way more basic than moral reasons to try, the available arguments for doubting that they can be categorical and/or mandatory reasons are few and unconvincing. Maybe more convincing ones could be found. But the challenge to find more convincing ones is at any rate decisively thrown at the feet of the doubters, as Honoré promised us that it would be.

To see the real strength of Honoré's argument, one needs to focus on nothing so much as its apparent weakness. 'Having decided nothing and done nothing,' concludes Honoré briskly, 'these entities would hardly be people.' Surely this conclusion goes much too far, much too fast? In the first place, for the purpose of telling the story of our lives we can surely insist on the significance of the events out in the world that were 'our doing', without allowing that this significance was necessarily a moral significance? Can't things be part of the story of what we did, in an autobiographically pertinent sense, without being part of the story of our *right*doing and our *wrong*doing? Couldn't what we do *full stop* include our successes (and failures) and yet what we do *wrong* or what we do *qua moral agents* only extend as far as our attempts (and neglects)?[35] But even if we postpone this first

[34] On obligations as categorical mandatory reasons, see John Gardner and Timothy Macklem, 'Reasons' in Jules Coleman and Scott Shapiro (eds), *The Oxford Handbook of Jurisprudence and the Philosophy of Law* (Oxford 2002).

[35] This is the gist of the response to Honoré proposed by Arthur Ripstein in his contribution to Peter Cane and John Gardner (eds), *Relating to Responsibility*

worry for a moment—which is exactly what I propose to do—there is a second, and possibly more alarming, one. Honoré seems to be claiming that if one excises results from the story of our rightdoing and wrongdoing, it is not only the case that there was nothing we did (in the sense of nothing out in the world that was our doing) but also nothing we *decided*. Surely, on the contrary, what we *decided* is among the things that are left over when we excise from the scope of our moral agency those events in the world that were our doing in Honoré's sense? Deciding, to put it another way, belongs to the 'trying' side of the trying/succeeding divide. That reminds us that there is after all a story left over when results are excised from the story of our moral agency. It is the story of our trying, a story of our endeavour rather than our achievement. And our deciding belongs to that very story. So how can it be said, as Honoré says, that in the absence of outcome responsibility we would have *decided* nothing as well as done nothing, so that there would be *no* story left of us as human agents, as opposed to a *different* one?

Let me explain how exactly it can be said. Deciding, and for that matter trying, are actions of a logically parasitic type. One does not merely decide full stop or try full stop. Necessarily, one decides to ϕ or tries to ϕ, where ϕing is another action. So necessarily there exists, whenever one tries or decides, some further action ϕ such that one decides or tries, as the case may be, to perform it. What is more, the kind of parasitism involved here is a distinctively *rational* kind of parasitism. The 'to' in the expressions 'trying to' and 'deciding to' (like that in 'taking care to') is the familiar intention-implicating 'to' that we also find in the expressions 'with a view to', 'in order to', and 'intending to'. To be exact, trying to ϕ is acting with a view to ϕing, while deciding to ϕ is (one way of) preparing oneself, with a view to ϕing, to act with a view to ϕing (roughly, it is trying to make it the case that one will try to ϕ). In these characterizations, acting 'with a view to ϕing' means, in turn, acting for the reason (*inter alia*) that one's action will (supposedly) contribute to one's ϕing.

(Oxford 2001). Ripstein distinguishes the undoubted 'first-person' importance of outcomes (results, successes, achievements) from their possible 'third person' (or moral) irrelevance.

That one's action will contribute to one's ϕing is a reason for that action, however, only if one also has a reason to ϕ. Thus to act for the reason that one's action will (supposedly) contribute to one's ϕing is possible only if one is prepared to regard or treat oneself, at least for present purposes, as having a reason to ϕ. This is not an optional extra. Someone who really thinks that they have no possible reason not to injure P—i.e. no possible reason to *succeed* in not injuring P—cannot conceivably try not to injure P or decide not to injure P, for they cannot conceivably act or prepare to act for the reason that what they do will not injure P. Accordingly, if it is impossible to make sense of the idea of a reason to ϕ—where ϕ signifies the successful action which one is trying or deciding to perform—it is also impossible to make sense of the idea of a reason to try to ϕ or to decide to ϕ. Honoré is right, then, to think that if our success turns out to be rationally insignificant across the board, then our trying and deciding (etc.) cannot but be rationally insignificant too. Assuming, then, that his conclusion is about rational significance—about what belongs to the story of our lives *as rational agents*—he is spot on. To deny that success can have independent rational significance is to leave us without *any* story of our lives as practical reasoners. It is not merely to leave us with a story of our lives as practical reasoners that omits our successes and failures but includes our attempts, decisions, precautions, neglects, etc. For the latter story depends for its intelligibility on our granting the intelligibility of a more complete—or dare I say morally richer?—story in which our successes and failures are registered as rationally significant too.

An unargued assumption of many moral philosophers as well as almost all economists and decision theorists—and I suspect also of most lawyers—is that a reason to ϕ is the very same thing as a reason to try to ϕ. Indeed the statement 'D has a reason to ϕ' is often promptly interpreted, without explanation, as 'D has a reason to try to ϕ'. But the above remarks already show that this is a serious mistake. A reason to try to ϕ is not a reason to ϕ but a reason to act for the reason (*inter alia*) that one's so acting will (supposedly) contribute to one's ϕing. This difference makes possible a variety of important asymmetries between one's reasons to ϕ and one's reasons to try to ϕ. I will mention three.

(i) Where acting with a view to ϕing would not contribute to one's ϕing, one has reasons to ϕ (i.e. reasons to succeed) without corresponding reasons to try. I am on a clifftop miles from anywhere looking down helplessly on a man drowning in the stormy sea below.[36] Because no amount of trying would bring me closer to success, my reasons to save the man do not yield any reasons to try to save him. Yet I still have the same reasons to save him that I would have if doing so were perfectly straightforward. That is why the situation is so horrifying. If my reasons to save him were eliminated by the impossibility of my doing so then my not saving him would be nothing to me; it would leave no trace on my life as an agent; I could walk away without compunction. As it is I am merely blocked from doing as these reasons would have me do because there is no contributory action—including trying to save—that I have any (derivative) reasons to perform. The situation is an unusually stark variant of a common one in which one has more reason to succeed than one has (derivative) reason to try, thanks to the fact that one's prospects of succeeding by trying are limited.[37]

(ii) I add 'derivative' in parentheses here because I do not mean to deny that one may have *additional* reasons to try that do not correspond to reasons to succeed. This is an asymmetry in the opposite direction. Just as one may have less reason to try than to succeed, so one may have more reason to try than to succeed. The extra reasons to try in such a case are non-derivative reasons to try: they are reasons to try quite apart from the contribution that trying makes to success. Suppose that it is my daughter or my brother drowning in the sea below. Then I have additional reasons to try to save her or him, since such an attempt may be an expression of love even if doomed (or perhaps: even more of an expression of love *because* it is doomed). Naturally it is possible to act for these additional reasons, and possibly, in some cases, one does not express what those reasons would have one express

[36] For more on this case see my 'Justifications and Reasons' in A T H Smith and A P Simester (eds), *Harm and Culpability* (Oxford 1996).

[37] I mean one's prospects of succeeding by any amount of trying. The problem under scrutiny here is different from the problem of self-defeating endeavour encountered earlier, in which the problem was that of how *much* one tried, granting that one had every reason to try.

by one's doomed attempt unless one actually acts for them. But it is not possible to act for these additional reasons *alone*, because unless one *also* aimed at success (i.e. also acted for the derivative reason that one's trying would supposedly contribute to one's succeeding) one just wouldn't be trying—and so, obviously, one wouldn't be doing what one's non-derivative expressive reasons to try would have one do. This was why I included the parenthetical '*inter alia*' in my characterization of reasons to try: A reason to try to ϕ is not a reason to ϕ but a reason to act for the reason (*inter alia*) that one's so acting will (supposedly) contribute to one's ϕing. There are other reasons to try apart from those based on the contribution that trying makes to succeeding, and perhaps some of these other reasons to try are obligations. One can try *for* these additional reasons. But the (supposed) contribution that one's trying makes to succeeding must be among one's reasons for trying *or else one just isn't trying*.

(iii) Does it follow that there are no possible reasons to try unless it is the case that there is at least one reason to succeed, and that trying would contribute to one's success? You may think that this follows, but it doesn't quite. What follows from the foregoing is that, to have any reason to try, the agent must *believe* or *accept* that she has a reason to succeed and must *believe* or *accept* that trying would contribute to succeeding. That was why I included the parenthetical 'supposedly' in my characterization of reasons to try. I could try to save the drowning man if I mistakenly thought that I could just possibly save him and that I had a reason to do so. In this case, I could have reasons to try to save him. Of course I don't have the particular reason that I take myself to have, viz. the derivative reason. About that I am mistaken. But I might still have the non-derivative reasons, for example, that of expressing my love for him, and I can do as these reasons would have me do by acting for what I mistakenly take to be the derivative reason.

These are just a few of the many complexities that figure in the relationship between reasons to try and reasons to succeed. I mention them, in admittedly brief outline, to bring out the sense in which reasons to succeed are 'primary' (to use Honoré's word) as well as the sense in which they are not. Reasons to succeed are primary in the sense that the *intelligibility* of reasons to try depends on the *independent intelligibility* of reasons to succeed.

If there can be no such thing as a straightforward non-derivative reason to succeed then there can be no such thing as a derivative reason to try. From this it follows that there can be no such thing as trying (or deciding, intending, aiming, etc.), and thus there can be no such thing as a non-derivative reason to try either. But once we have the possibility of derivative reasons to try on the table (by admitting that there are reasons to succeed from which those reasons derive), non-derivative reasons to try also become intelligible. Thus the case for trying is not by any means exhausted—it is not necessarily even dominated—by the case for succeeding. In that sense the story of my life as a rational agent, told as a story of endeavour, is not merely a pale shadow of the story of my life, told in terms of achievement. Both aspects have some independent significance and the full story of my life as a rational agent is the story that has room for both: it is the story of my trying (or neglecting) and my succeeding (or failing), including sometimes (double triumph) my succeeding-by-trying and sometimes (double trouble) my failing for want of trying. The last notably discouraging case is the one that the tort of negligence latches onto: the case of someone who fails for want of trying, whose action is doubly deficient in its conformity with reasons, for not only did she not succeed; judged by the applicable measure of assiduousness, she didn't even try.

This line of argument almost fulfils Honoré's promise, I believe, and does so (I hope) in the spirit in which the promise was originally intended. What Honoré was promising was an argument according to which, first, our *not* having straightforward obligations to succeed would be unintelligible (so that our having them couldn't possibly be unintelligible) and according to which, secondly, our obligations to succeed would have some kind of argumentative primacy over other obligations, such as obligations to take care. The argument just ventured meets these conditions readily, save only that it softens 'obligations' to 'reasons'. So can the argument be replicated, *mutatis mutandis*, with 'reasons' hardened back up to 'obligations'? Not quite. That is because the substitution of 'obligations' makes for additional asymmetries on top of those I labelled (i), (ii), and (iii). It is perfectly possible that obligations to try might derive from non-obligatory reasons to succeed, or that non-obligatory reasons to try might derive from obligations to succeed. Thus there being obligations to try without obligations to succeed is not made unintelligible by the same knock-down manoeuvres as made it unintelligible that there are reasons to try but no reasons to succeed. Obligations to try to ϕ could, after all, be obligations to act for the (itself non-obligatory) reason (*inter alia*) that one's so acting will (supposedly) contribute to one's ϕing. Still, after the foregoing considerations the ball is now firmly in the court of those who deny that we can be subject to obligations to succeed. If there are indeed reasons to succeed—and there are—is there any possible reason to doubt that they could be obligations to succeed, such that failing to do as they would have one do would be *wrong* and hence could properly be made *tortious* in law?

An obligation is no more and no less than a categorical mandatory reason. It is categorical in the sense that it applies to people independently of their prevailing personal goals. It is mandatory in the sense that it is a reason that operates, on at least some occasions, to the partial or total exclusion of at least some countervailing reasons. Why would anybody think that these particular properties—being categorical and being mandatory—could not be possessed by reasons to succeed, now that the possibility of reasons to succeed has been established? Commonly, in my view, the following mistake tends to steer lawyers' thoughts in that direction. They think that a reason to do something counts as *mandatory* if and only if we would be justified in attaching adverse normative consequences (legally or otherwise) to its nonperformance. Since attaching adverse normative consequences to nonperformance would be unfair in the case of a straightforward obligation to succeed (the thinking goes), it follows that there can be no such obligation. The problem with this line of thinking is that it wheels out the problem of unfairness much too early. Once we have established that an action is obligatory, it remains to be discussed whether the obligation should be enforced, or more generally whether people should have to bear any adverse normative consequences of its nonperformance. Possibly, as Honoré points out, further conditions have to be met before such measures would be justified, including measures to overcome the institutional fairness objection. We always admitted that there would be further internecine squabbles to come on this subject: what some would regard as sufficient to overcome the institutional fairness objection (e.g. the *Rylands* v *Fletcher* condition of an ultra-hazardous activity) others would regard as insufficient to meet that objection. But it is jumping the gun to use the institutional fairness objection as an objection to the very possibility of the obligation, when it is not yet a foregone conclusion that those who fail to perform it will be subject to any adverse normative consequences at all. To put it simply, the institutional fairness objection is one objection, and the moral intelligibility objection is another. One cannot have two bites at the institutional fairness objection by saying that obligations to succeed are morally unintelligible because if only they existed they would have unfair normative consequences. The proper response to this alleged unfairness is to detach the normative consequences, not to deny the intelligibility of the obligation. Those who say that they cannot detach the normative consequences because they are built into the very idea of mandatoriness have simply misunderstood the idea of mandatoriness.[38] The mandatoriness of a reason lies in the fact that it operates to the exclusion of at least some countervailing reasons. Whether one is subject to adverse normative consequences in the event that one does not do as the reason would have one do is a separate—detachable—matter.

VI

To the best of my knowledge, only one serious (philosophically credible) objection has ever been raised to the proposal that reasons to succeed can be obligatory reasons. It is Kant's famous objection. According to Kant:

> A good will is not good because of what it effects or accomplishes—because of its fitness for attaining some proposed end: it is good through its willing alone—that is good in itself. . . . Even if, by some special disfavour of destiny or by the niggardly endowment of stepmotherly nature, this will is entirely lacking in power to carry out its intentions; if

[38] To be exact they are still in the thrall of the crudest 'sanction theories' of obligation that were decisively discredited by Peter Hacker in his famous 'Sanction Theories of Duty' in A W B Simpson (ed), *Oxford Essays in Jurisprudence: Second Series* (Oxford 1973).

by its utmost effort it still accomplishes nothing, and only good will is left (not admittedly as a mere wish but by the straining of every means so far as they are in our control); even then it would still shine like a jewel for its own sake as something which has full value in itself. Usefulness or fruitlessness can neither add to, nor subtract from, this value.[39]

These remarks furnish the first and second premisses of Kant's curious argument against the moral intelligibility of obligations to succeed. It is an argument that dwells on the fact that obligations are *categorical* reasons (not conditional on the agent's prevailing personal goals) rather than the fact that they are mandatory reasons; thus it leaves fully open the possibility of mandatory non-categorical reasons to succeed. The argument, which is completed by Kant with the addition of a third premiss several pages later,[40] goes something like this:

(1) the only source of unconditional (a.k.a. moral) value in our actions is the good will;

(2) the good will infects not the whole of what we do but only that part of it that consists in our trying to do good;

(3) performing one's obligations is of unconditional (a.k.a. moral) value;

thus

(4) there can be no obligations to succeed but only obligations to try.

This objection is sometimes confused with what I earlier dismissed as the pseudo-objection to 'moral luck'. But in fact Kant's argument is much more carefully targeted and hence withstands much more critical attention. Unlike the 'moral luck' pseudo-objection, for instance, Kant's objection has no quarrel with the objective standards of trying that are at work in the legal criterion of negligence. Indeed in premiss (1) such an objective standard is explicitly set up, namely the standard of the good will, the standard of perfect moral virtue. Not everyone, Kant agrees, is capable of meeting this standard. Some people, indeed, are moral degenerates who would not recognize a moral consideration if it slapped

[39] Kant, *Groundwork of the Metaphysic of Morals* (trans. Paton New York 1964), 62.

[40] Ibid, 68.

them in the face.[41] Relative to the baseline of their attenuated moral capacities it is a stroke of bad luck that they have the moral obligations that they have, and which they are doomed by their own degeneracy to violate. So Kant's is not a version of the 'moral luck' pseudo-objection. Rather it is an objection carefully targeted against obligations to succeed. And even regarding obligations to succeed its impact turns out to be highly selective. On closer inspection Kant's third premiss calls for a modification even by the lights of his own views. In the end he only stands by the more limited claim that it must be *possible* for performing one's obligation to be an act of unconditional value. Thus possession of a good will must be sufficient, even if not always necessary, for performance of one's duties.[42] This rules out straightforward obligations to succeed, and what I called 'tall-order' hybrid obligations (obligations to succeed by trying), but it does not rule out the short-order hybrid obligation (the obligation not to fail for want of trying), nonperformance of which constitutes the tort of negligence at common law. For as we saw trying (to the legally specified degree) is sufficient, but not necessary, to perform that obligation. Thus, thanks to an important Kantian concession on the third premiss, the tort of negligence is morally intelligible to Kant. On the other hand, a strict liability tort of the *Rylands* v *Fletcher* type still is not.

I do not propose to tackle Kant's argument here. Showing that it collapses—which it does, spectacularly—is a task for another paper. Here I merely leave the argument on the file, for it seems to me that by developing Honoré's sketchy thoughts, we have now done the most important work of turning the moral intelligibility objection to strict liability back against its supporters. To

[41] Thus it is an error to associate Kant with the thesis that 'ought' implies 'can' in the way in which this thesis is normally read. In the sense in which it is normally read it is taken to mean that those who lack certain moral capacities lack the corresponding obligations. Kant believed that the doctrine worked in the opposite way. He believed that since (necessarily) everyone has the obligations it follows that fundamentally they have the moral capacities as well. *Qua* human they have it in them to be less incapable than they are. As Kant spells it out: 'Ethical duties must not be determined in accordance with the capacity to fulfil the law that is ascribed to human beings; on the contrary their moral capacity must be estimated by the the [moral] law, which commands categorically.' (Kant, *The Metaphysic of Morals* (trans Gregor, Cambridge 1996), 164.)

[42] See *Groundwork of the Metaphysic of Morals*, above note 39, 65–6.

achieve this, what we needed to do was to bear out Honoré's claim that a story of our lives as rational agents that refuses to admit the rational salience of our successes (and failures) as well as our tryings (and neglects) is an unintelligible story. It cannot even accommodate the rational salience of our tryings (and neglects) and so, in the end, comes down to no story at all. You may say, reprising an earlier worry that we postponed, that it is one thing to establish the *rational* salience of success and another to establish its *moral* salience. Maybe there are reasons to succeed but surely they need not be *moral* reasons? Possibly in some senses of the often-unhelpful word 'moral' this is true. For example, in Kant's rather technical sense, only non-derivative reasons to try could possibly be moral reasons, whereas derivative reasons to try and the reasons to succeed from which they are derived would instead be set aside as 'prudential' reasons. Such matters of classification need not detain us here. For the notion of the morally intelligible that was implicated in the moral intelligibility objection was not, you will recall, a narrow one in which moral considerations could be contrasted with prudential ones or aesthetic ones or economic ones, etc. The notion of the morally intelligible that we had in mind was merely the notion of what is intelligible apart from the law (or similar institutional arrangements) so that the law could intelligibly claim to be binding people from something other than a narrowly legal point of view. Our argument showed that reasons to succeed are indeed intelligible apart from the law—i.e. morally intelligible in the relevant sense—and that reasons to try are not morally intelligible, in the relevant sense, without them. From here it is, in my view, but a relatively short step to the conclusion that at least the first half of this conjunction still holds true when the reasons in question are obligatory. There is no special problem, in my view, with mandatory categorical reasons to succeed. But instead of making that short step here let me just leave it in the hands of others, including those who remain attached to Kant's curious argument, to try and block it. That, I think, is the way best to honour the spirit of Honoré's ground-breaking contrarian contribution to the philosophical study of the law of torts, and indeed the philosophical study of the human condition.

6

SOME RULE-OF-LAW ANXIETIES ABOUT STRICT LIABILITY IN PRIVATE LAW

1. Strict liability: why worry?

In legal parlance, strict liability is liability regardless of fault. 'Fault' here has a technical lawyers' meaning. Unpacking that meaning: strict liability is liability that attaches to someone (call her D) for something she did (call it φing), irrespective of any steps that she took in order not to φ and irrespective of whether she knew or had reason to know that she was φing.[1] Never mind that D did all that it was reasonable for her to do to avoid φing, all that she was personally capable of doing, even all that it was humanly possible to do. Never mind that she could not reasonably, possibly, imaginably have known that she was φing. She is still stuck with her strict liability for having φed. 'Liability' here, in turn, bears its lawyers' meaning. To say that D is liable is to say that another has a normative power to burden her, for example by imposing extra duties on her or taking away some of her rights. She is liable *for* φing if her having φed grounds her liability, that is, if her having φed is (a) a complete (but not necessarily conclusive) reason[2] for her to be liable, and (b) a necessary condition of her being liable. And, to repeat, her liability for φing is *strict* if and only if her having φed grounds the liability irrespective of what she could have known or done about her φing and thereby incurring the liability.

Strict liability plays a significant role in many legal systems, in both criminal law and private law. Its occasional use attracts a weary toleration from legal thinkers, but few stand up for it with enthusiasm, and few argue for its extension. Common anxieties

[1] Including any steps she took to find out whether she was about to φ.

[2] On complete reasons, see Joseph Raz, *Practical Reason and Norms* (London 1975), 22–5. On conclusive reasons, see ibid, 25–8.

Torts and Other Wrongs. John Gardner, Oxford University Press (2019). © John Gardner
DOI: 10.1093/oso/9780198852940.003.0006

about strict liability fall under two main headings. Some writers worry most about the suboptimal incentives or spurs to action that, in their view, a strict liability rule creates for those who might, or think they might, fall foul of it in the future. Others worry more about how the rule treats the particular person who has already fallen foul of it, the D who has φed. To express the difference in a familiar, if not entirely happy, terminology: some people fret mainly about the supposed *inefficiency* of strict liability, while others fret mainly about the supposed *injustice*. One reason why the terminology is not entirely happy is that it is possible for a rule to be inefficient *at* doing justice.[3] Another reason is that we might object to the way the rule treats D not because it is unjust but because it is (say) cruel or petty. Still, the terminology is revealing enough that we can live with it for now. We will return to inefficiency below. But let's start with injustice.

Injustice challenges to strict liability take more than one form. Here I will focus on those that see the injustice of strict liability as bound up with a failure, on the law's part, to conform to the ideal of the rule of law. These challenges can be contrasted with those that complain of the injustice of attaching liability to morally blameless actions. Although strict liability is no-fault liability in a special lawyers' sense of 'fault', it also extends in the process to many who are not at fault in the ordinary moral sense of 'fault', i.e. many whose actions are morally blameless. Some people think that, whatever consequences the law may attach to them, one's morally blameless actions cannot change one's moral situation for the worse; unwelcome moral consequences cannot descend upon one in the absence of moral culpability. Thus, writes Nagel, 'strict liability may have its legal uses but seems irrational as a moral position'.[4] This view gives rise, in turn, to a simple moral critique of the legal uses of strict liability. Such uses are unjust, some say, because they do not treat us as moral agents. Treating someone as a moral agent means holding him liable for what he does only if he is morally culpable in doing it.

[3] For further explanation see chapter 2 above.

[4] Thomas Nagel, 'Moral Luck' in his *Mortal Questions* (Cambridge 1979), 24 at 31.

In my view, this line of thought harbours an accumulation of errors. Most importantly, the view of moral agency that Nagel tempts us to endorse (in the end he does not endorse it himself[5]) is wrong. Morally blameless actions often do change their agent's moral situation for the worse. Often their agent is morally bound to repair, to mitigate, to apologize, or to explain.[6] Ironically, we think otherwise only if we are in the thrall of what H L A Hart calls 'a legalistic conception of morality'.[7] We project back onto morality our moral expectations of the law. And one moral expectation we have of the law is that it will live up to the ideal of the rule of law. It was Kant, first and foremost, who lured us into thinking that morality itself ('the moral law') somehow lives up to this ideal. Not so. We need law, and law that lives up to the ideal of the rule of law, partly in order to help us deal with the fact that morality often does not.[8] Here begins a quite separate kind of 'injustice' objection to strict liability, one that is specific to strict liability's 'legal uses'. It sees the injustice of strict liability as bound up with a failure on the law's part to conform to the ideal of the rule of law. This is the kind of complaint about strict liability on which—to repeat—I will focus here.

2. Guiding and goading

The ideal of the rule of law is the ideal according to which the law should be capable of guiding those who are subject to it. People should not be ambushed by the law; it should be possible for them reliably to anticipate the legal consequences of their actions and reliably to obtain or to avoid those consequences by following

[5] Ibid, 38.

[6] Explaining includes offering a justification or excuse. Once we recognize being morally bound to offer a justification or excuse as a possible moral consequence of acting, it becomes hard to deny that morally blameless actions are capable of having unwelcome moral consequences for their agents. This is one theme of my essay 'The Mark of Responsibility', the authoritative version of which appears in John Gardner, *Offences and Defences* (Oxford 2007).

[7] H L A Hart, 'Intention and Punishment' in his *Punishment and Responsibility* (Oxford 1968), 113 at 125.

[8] For detailed and memorable discussion, see Tony Honoré, 'The Dependence of Morality on Law', *Oxford Journal of Legal Studies* 13 (1993), 1.

the law. So understood, the ideal sets a wide range of disparate standards for all legal systems to live up to. The ones that mainly concern us here are standards for legal *norms* to live up to. Legal norms should not, according to the ideal of the rule of law, be secret, retroactive, unclear, impossible to conform to, or forever in a state of flux; and particular legal norms (rulings) should be applications of general legal norms (rules). Legal norms that do not live up to these standards, as Lon Fuller famously explained, are not truly capable of being *followed*.[9] That does not stop them from being legal norms (Fuller sometimes got this point wrong[10]), but it does make them deficient *qua* legal norms. One may try to follow them but, however hard one tries, one cannot be sure of avoiding their violation, and thereby avoiding the unwelcome legal consequences. If one conforms to them by trying to do so, then that is at least partly a stroke of luck.

Fuller himself argued that strict liability in the law is objectionable on rule-of-law grounds because it demands the impossible.[11] That was a slip on his part. Only very rarely is it impossible for people to do what it takes to avoid strict liability. If only D had bought less dynamite, which she had the option to do, there would have been no fatal blast; if only D had parked on a different street, which she could easily have done, nobody would have put up a 'no parking' sign in her absence; if only D had emptied the swimming pool for winter a week earlier, as she had seriously considered doing, there would have been no flood; if only D had let her home to a different tenant, and she had plenty of candidates to choose from, it would never have become a crack-den; if only D had sold her customers a different holiday, as she was poised to do, they would not have ended up in that flea-pit. In every case, a happy ending to D's misadventure was perfectly possible when she went into it. Her problem, from the point of view of the rule of law, was not one of impossibility but only of lack of assurance. It was always entirely possible that she would not φ but it was nevertheless, at the crucial time, impossible for her to *make sure* that she would not φ.

[9] Lon Fuller, *The Morality of Law* (rev ed, New Haven 1969), 33–8.

[10] Ibid, e.g. at 41.

[11] Ibid, 75–7.

Where the law imposes strict liability on D for φing (for blowing people up, for parking in a 'no parking' zone, for flooding a neighbour's land, for permitting one's property to be used for drug dealing, for providing a holiday different from the one contracted for) there is no step D could have taken, at the moment when she φed, to make sure that she wouldn't incur the liability, or even to be sure whether she would incur it. Recall that when the law imposes strict liability on D for φing, it doesn't care which steps D took to avoid φing or even whether there was any way for her to know that φing was what she was doing. And that, it may be thought, puts strict liability radically at odds with the ideal of the rule of law. One cannot follow a rule, in the relevant sense, if the rule provides one with no mechanism by which one can reliably avoid breaking it, or even find out if one is breaking it, when the time to conform to it arrives.

This is essentially H L A Hart's argument against the legal imposition of strict liability. He writes:

> Consider the law not as a system of stimuli but as what might be termed a choosing system, in which individuals can find out, in general terms at least, the costs they have to pay if they act in certain ways. This done, let us ask what value this system would have in social life and why we should regret its absence. I do not of course mean that it is a matter of indifference whether we obey the law or break it and pay the penalty. Punishment is different from a mere 'tax on a course of conduct'. What I do mean is that the conception of the law simply as goading individuals into desired courses of behaviour is inadequate and misleading; what a legal system that makes liability generally [non-strict, fault-based] does is to guide individual's choices as to behaviour by presenting them with reasons for exercising choice in the direction of obedience, but leaving them to choose.[12]

Hart goes on to divide into three the advantages of eschewing strict liability in favour of some kind of fault-based liability:

> First, we maximize the individual's power at any time to predict the likelihood that the sanctions of the criminal law will be applied to him. Secondly, we introduce the individual's choice as one of the operative

[12] Hart, 'Legal Responsibility and Excuses' in his *Punishment and Responsibility*, above note 7, 44.

factors determining whether or not these sanctions shall be applied to him. Thirdly, . . . we provide that, if the sanctions of the criminal law are applied, the pains of punishment will for each individual represent the price of some satisfaction obtained from breach of law.[13]

I have argued at length elsewhere that these passages should be read as (successfully) harnessing Hart's objection to strict liability to a wider defence of the ideal of the rule of law.[14] As well as militating against strict liability, the considerations Hart adduces also militate, in broadly Fullerian spirit, against a resort to retroactivity, obscurity, secrecy, impossibility, inconstancy, and so on. We could say that Hart adds 'strict liability' to Fuller's list, as a distinct affront or challenge to the rule of law. Strict liability laws, like secret or retrospective ones, do not guide us towards conformity; they cannot really be *followed*.

3. From criminal law to private law

Hart focuses his attention on strict criminal liability, or at any rate on strict liability to be punished. Can his argument equally be extended to private law, for example to the law of torts or breach of contract, where the normal mode of liability is not punitive ('pay[ing] the penalty') but rather reparative or restitutionary?

Clearly the argument applies in both contexts. But the change of context equally clearly makes a difference to how much weight we should attach to the argument in evaluating the relevant legal norms. Litigation in private law, unlike criminal prosecution, is zero-sum. In the criminal court there may of course be a victim of the crime and he may feel aggrieved if he does not 'get justice'. But contrary to the impression given by such familiar complaints, the main task of the criminal court is not corrective. It is not to give to the victim of wrongdoing something that it extracts from the wrongdoer. Burdens imposed on the wrongdoer (years spent in prison, fines levied, etc.) are not burdens that the victim would otherwise bear. Conversely, burdens *not* imposed on the wrongdoer (years not spent in prison, fines not levied, etc.)

[13] Ibid, 47.

[14] See my 'Introduction' in the second edition of Hart's *Punishment and Responsibility* (Oxford 2008), xxxxiv–xliv.

are not thereby borne by her victim instead. In the civil courts, when dealing with the aftermath of torts and breaches of contract, things are very different. The main task of the court is corrective. It is to give to the wronged plaintiff something that it extracts from the wronging defendant, reversing so far as possible the wrongful transaction that took place between them. There is normally a burdensome consequence of the wrong to be borne by either the plaintiff or the defendant and the court has to determine, *inter alia*, which of them is to bear it. If it is not allocated to the defendant (by an award of damages) then it is left with the plaintiff (who must absorb the costs of the wrong that an award of damages would otherwise have covered). This means that not only the defendant but also the plaintiff can be unjustly treated, and moreover in a similar way, by the legal rule under which the defendant's liability is determined.[15] In particular, the more extra protections against liability that we give to the defendant in the name of upholding the rule of law in her case, the more the plaintiff loses the protection that a less defendant-protective regime would allow her. What the defendant gains from there being fault liability, the plaintiff loses; what the defendant loses from there being strict liability, the plaintiff gains.[16]

Some writers think that this difference between criminal law and private law may be less substantial than it seems. Contrary to first impressions, they say, the criminal trial is indeed zero-sum. True, burdens not imposed on the wrongdoer (years not spent in prison, fines not levied, etc.) are not borne by his victim instead.

[15] I have argued elsewhere that this zero-sum feature inevitably brings distributive-justice questions to bear on the doing of corrective justice: see chapter 3 above at 96–9.

[16] It may be thought that this fact already militates in favour of fault-based liability (using the negligence standard) because such liability somehow puts the parties on an equal footing in their zero-sum conflict in a way that strict liability would not. See Ernest Weinrib, *The Idea of Private Law* (Cambridge, Mass 1995), 177–83, and Alan Brudner, *The Unity of the Common Law* (Berkeley 1995), 190. I do not agree, and this is not what I am arguing here. My argument here does not enable one to draw any positive conclusions about which standards for liability should be used where in the law. I am exclusively attending to the question of how the zero-sum feature of private law affects the relative importance of the ideal of the rule of law in evaluating private law standards of liability, whatever they may be.

They are, however, borne by various (usually indefinite) other people who will some day be the victims of crimes. By burdening today's wrongdoer less we are not doing our bit to prevent or deter these future crimes and so are burdening future victims more. Some say, indeed, that a necessary condition of just sentencing (although, most agree, not a sufficient one) is that no extra burdens should be imposed by the court on wrongdoers beyond those that future victims of crime can thereby be spared.[17] If that proposal is sound, should we not conclude that rule-of-law protections accorded to criminal defendants, like those accorded to private law defendants, necessarily come at the cost of protections that are thereby denied to others?

Maybe. But be that as it may, the criminal trial remains importantly different from its private-law counterpart. The burdens created by (as it were) criminal under-sentencing are generally diffuse. For the most part, they are spread thinly across a wider population of victims of later crimes, usually in unassignable proportions. True, loss-spreading among potential plaintiffs is also possible in private law, thanks to the availability and widespread use of insurance. But in private law, defendant-side burdens can also be spread thinly, and often are spread thinly, through liability insurance. Not so in criminal law. In criminal law, making the defendant personally bear the burdens of liability is an aim of the exercise, and liability insurance (or any contract of indemnification) is void.[18] The distinctive technique by which criminal law deters and prevents (and of course often punishes too) is that of the non-spreadable, and more generally non-transferable, burden. So the way in which criminal trials are zero-sum, if indeed they are, still leaves the criminal defendant uniquely exposed and in

[17] The latest and probably most philosophically ambitious defence of this view is in Victor Tadros, *The Ends of Harm* (Oxford 2012). However a similar view was defended less ambitiously by Hart in 'Prolegomenon to the Principles of Punishment', ch 1 of his *Punishment and Responsibility*, above note 7. Hart was in turn moderating the positions of Bentham and Beccaria, who came close to embracing 'no extra burdens' as a sufficient condition of just sentencing (although they might both have favoured a word other than 'just').

[18] *Askey* v *Golden Wine Company Limited* [1948] 2 All ER 35, 38; for nuanced discussion of the limits of this common law doctrine, see *Gray* v *Thames Trains* [2009] UKHL 33, especially in the speech of Lord Hoffmann.

need of enhanced protection against the possibility of being ambushed by the law.[19] The civil trial remains, in the relevant respect, a more symmetrical one than its criminal counterpart, and hence one in which the defendant-protective standards of the rule of law may well call for more compromise in the name of plaintiff protection.

I am not suggesting an exact symmetry here. Some talk as if, in a tort or breach of contract case, there is either defendant liability or plaintiff liability, so that the question is: liability for whom?[20] But there is no such thing as 'plaintiff liability'.[21] At the end of the trial there is either defendant liability or no liability. This makes a significant difference in many ways. In particular, the standards of the rule of law that we are focusing on here are standards for legal norms to live up to, including legal norms that impose liabilities. If there is no norm imposing liability, it cannot either meet or fail to meet the relevant rule-of-law standards. In respect of norms imposing liability, the plaintiff's rule-of-law interests are usually aligned with those of the defendant: both want legal norms that are open, clear, prospective, and otherwise tolerably free from the potential to ambush the unwitting. That is a public good from which both sides stand to benefit. So the complaint from aggrieved plaintiffs that we are imagining, when we think about the civil trial, is not strictly speaking that the defendant's rule-of-law gain is their *rule-of-law* loss. Rather it is that the defendant's rule-of-law gain is their loss *in other ways*; most obviously, it deprives them of a remedy for wrongdoing that the law would otherwise grant. And that consideration does militate in favour of less stringent adherence to rule-of-law standards in respect of private law norms than would be acceptable in respect of criminal law norms. Rigid adherence to the Hartian stance on strict liability (as to the related Fullerian stance on unclarity, inconstancy, retrospectivity,

[19] A possible *quid pro quo* is that if the law does not provide the relevant protection against ambush, then a contract of insurance covering criminal penalties should exceptionally be enforceable: *R* v *Northumbrian Water* ex parte *Newcastle and North Tyneside Health Authority* [1998] All ER (D) 733.

[20] Jules Coleman, 'The Morality of Strict Tort Liability' in his *Markets, Morals, and the Law* (Cambridge 1988), 166 at 175.

[21] I am disregarding the possibility of a counterclaim in which the plaintiff is cast as defendant. I am also ignoring any possible liability to pay legal costs.

secrecy, etc.) can make an otherwise symmetrical private law dispute unjustly asymmetrical. The standards that the ideal of the rule of law sets for legal norms to live up to therefore need to be less stringently or more flexibly applied to the norms of private law, or at any rate to those that make up the law relating to the treatment in court of torts and of breaches of contract.

This is not startling news. In the common law world we tolerate a radically indeterminate body of law governing the tort of negligence—a body of law that, were it transplanted into the criminal law, would constitute a grave departure from the most elementary requirements of the rule of law. One reason to have any law, as I mentioned in section 1, is to help us cope with the various ways in which morality can trip us up. Law cannot do this where its purported norm only says: morality applies here; just do the right thing. That is not the rule of law. That is not even a legal norm. That is a legal vacuum.[22] Many propositions of the law governing the tort of negligence come surprisingly close to such legal vacuity. They pass the buck back to ordinary moral reasoning in its rawest form. They invite us to think and act reasonably, meaning just as we should quite apart from the law.

In view of the relatively rudimentary level of attention to Fullerian rule-of-law standards in this ever more dominant part of the law of torts, it is perhaps slightly comic to be fretting, on Hartian rule-of-law grounds, about some relatively contained pockets of strict liability in the residue. Motes and beams come to mind. That is not, of course, a reason to think that strict liability in the law of torts, or anywhere else in private law, is nothing to worry about, or nothing to worry about so far as the rule of law is concerned. My point is only that, for reasons I have sketched out, we should and do expect less stringent compliance with the relevant rule-of-law standards for legal norms in private law than in criminal law. A Hartian rule-of-law critique of strict liability in private law should make much the same allowances that a Fullerian rule-of-law critique of the law of negligence, on the ground of its indeterminacy, would have to make for the more symmetrical setting of the private law trial.

[22] For what seems to me to be the decisive argument, see Joseph Raz, 'Incorporation by Law' in his *Between Authority and Interpretation* (Oxford 2009).

4. Commanding and commending

Stephen Smith offers a reorientated 'rule of law' objection to strict liability, one that is perhaps designed to have more force in private law settings than the Hartian objection.[23] He presents it as an objection under the 'clarity' heading, and to that extent remains faithful to the Fullerian account of the rule of law. The main thing that makes Smith's objection different from Hart's is that it is not (in the terms I introduced cautiously in section 1) an injustice objection. It is an inefficiency objection. It focuses on the suboptimal spurs to action that, in Smith's view, a strict liability rule creates for those who might, or think they might, fall foul of it, rather than on how the rule treats those who have already fallen foul of it. In one way this focus is not surprising. The ideal of the rule of law is primarily an ideal for legal efficiency, demanding of the law that it be good at guiding action.[24] The injustices that can come of failure to conform to the rule of law, such as those on which Hart is dwelling, are in a way derivative. They are consequential unjust impositions *ex post* upon people to whom the law did not (as it were) efficiently address itself *ex ante*. Possibly Smith thinks that some such unjust impositions flow from the inefficiencies with which he is primarily concerned; but his emphasis throughout is on the inefficiencies themselves, not on the injustices.

In keeping with this shift in emphasis from the *ex post* to the *ex ante*, Smith tells us that he is not objecting to strict liability as such. He is objecting to strict liability only when it is strict liability for the supposed breach of a 'strict duty'.[25] That is his name for a supposed duty not to φ that D may supposedly breach irrespective of any steps that she took in order not to φ and irrespective of whether she knew or had reason to know that she was

[23] Stephen Smith, 'Strict Duties and the Rule of Law' in Lisa Austin and Dennis Klimchuk (eds), *Private Law and the Rule of Law* (Oxford 2014), ch 8.

[24] Joseph Raz, 'The Rule of Law and its Virtue' in his *The Authority of Law* (Oxford 1979), 210 at 226. This sounds odd to a contemporary theorist of private law only because we have unwisely allowed economists to monopolize the language of efficiency. Conformity to the rule of law does not of course make the law economically efficient. It only makes it legally efficient.

[25] 'Strict Duties and the Rule of Law', above note 23, 189.

φing. This change of focus from the liability to the duty makes less difference than some may think. Strict liability is normally contrasted with fault-based liability, and fault-based liability, by its nature, can only be liability for one's own actions and omissions (including, of course, one's actions and omissions of contributing to the actions and omissions of another). To make the contrast with fault-based liability a contrast of like with like, strict liability too must be thought of as a species of liability for one's own actions and omissions. I defined it accordingly at the start of this essay: 'strict liability is [a type of] liability that attaches to someone (call her D) for something she did (call it φing)'. This means that an employer's vicarious liability for the tort of an employee, understood as arising irrespective of the employer's own contributions to the tort, does not qualify as strict.[26] Likewise an insurer's contractual liability to indemnify the torts of the insured, or of a third party, does not qualify as strict, for it does not depend on the insurer's having played a part in the commission of the tort. On the other hand, an insurer's legal liability for *breach* of the same insurance contract by *non-payment* of a sum validly claimed could be a strict liability. For now there is an action or omission by the insurer—not paying out on a valid claim—which serves as the ground of the liability.

Must D's φing always be a breach of duty if D is to be strictly liable, in law, on the ground of it? Clearly not. The plainest counterexample is the one that Hart foregrounds when he speaks of a 'tax on a course of conduct',[27] and that Fuller describes, in similar vein, as 'a kind of surcharge on the act'.[28] An import tax is levied on actions of importing and a sales tax on actions of selling. In each case the action is the ground of the liability to pay tax, and that liability is typically strict. Reasonable ignorance or reasonable effort may be defences to a further liability (e.g. a liability to pay administrative penalties) for non-reporting of a taxable

[26] Compare Lord Nicholls in *Majrowski* v *Guy's Hospital* [2006] UKHL 34: 'Vicarious liability is a common law principle of strict, no-fault liability.' This strikes me as a category mistake. If it were fault liability it could not possibly be vicarious. Therefore it makes no sense to classify it as 'no-fault' either.

[27] In the passage quoted at note 12 above.

[28] *The Morality of Law*, above note 9, 75.

import or sale, but the liability to pay the tax itself is typically unaffected by such considerations. As Fuller explains, it is possible to think of some strict liabilities in private law on this model. Strict tort liability for an ultra-hazardous activity such as blasting, for example, can be understood as 'impos[ing] on [the] blasting operations a kind of tax in the form of a rule that [the operator] must respond for any damage that results from these operations, whether or not they can be attributed to any negligence on his part'.[29] And when the strict liability is so understood, Fuller goes on to say, then what is required of the law under the rule of law 'is not that it cease commanding [actions that one cannot be sure of avoiding], but that it define as clearly as possible the kind of activity that carries a special surcharge of legal responsibility'.[30]

These remarks help us to see what Smith means when he claims not to be objecting to strict liability as such. He is leaving open the possibility that what we think of as strict tort liability might turn out to meet the requirements of the rule of law when understood on Fuller's tax model. His thesis is only that it does not meet the requirements of the rule of law when understood on the *tort* model, i.e. as liability for a wrong, a breach of duty.

Smith's objection to the existence of such a duty, however, is not Fuller's. It is not that a strict liability rule (understood on the tort model) commands something that it should not command, but that it commends something that it should not *commend*. Or rather, in Smith's turn of phrase, that the law, so understood, 'appears to recommend actions that it does not want to recommend'.[31] Smith has something like the following in mind: When the law of trespass is held to impose a strict duty not to enter another's land without permission, those who fear falling foul of the law may go to ridiculous lengths not to trespass, for example by never going anywhere, or by neglecting other duties in order to avoid a trespass even when the other duties are much more important. The law clearly does not seek this kind of overkill by its

[29] Ibid.

[30] Ibid. I have substituted the square-bracketed words here for Fuller's words 'the impossible' to reflect the point, in section 2 above, that Fuller confuses the impossibility of making sure that one will φ with the impossibility of φing.

[31] 'Strict Duties and the Rule of Law', above note 23, 189.

users, which is on any view totally unreasonable; yet the law does give people a reason to engage in it. A duty not to enter another's land without permission gives one a reason to destroy all one's opportunities to enter another's land without permission, in the same way that a duty to destroy a wasp's nest in the attic gives one a reason to blow up the whole house. The law is not being sufficiently clear in this case, thinks Smith, because it is 'sending mixed messages'.[32] It is giving people a reason to go to lengths to which, as the law well knows, it would be unreasonable for them to go. If the law only wanted them to go to reasonable lengths not to enter another's land without permission, that is what it would tell them to do. It would tell them to take reasonable steps not to φ, and then the duty, by definition, would no longer be a strict one.

This argument itself contains an element of overkill. All laws give one reasons to do things that it would be unreasonable for one to do. Many cowardly people hide behind the law to do totally unreasonable things. They evasively cite 'legal reasons'. They make it sound as if they have a legal duty not to allow nut-eating at school, ice-skating in the park, or advice-giving on the phone. In fact they have no such duty. They only have a duty to take reasonable steps to avoid injuries or losses of one kind or another, under the law of tortious negligence. The problem is that this also gives them a reason to take unreasonable steps, since one way to avoid failing to take reasonable steps is to take every imaginable step, including daft ones like banning everyone from the school or the park or the phone. This shows that the problem of 'mixed messages' to which Smith is addressing himself is not specific to strict legal duties. It applies to all legal duties.

So Smith still needs to show some way in which strict duties are especially or distinctively prone to induce overkill. The way he tries to show this is by showing that what appear to be strict duties to φ in the law are in fact duties to go to every possible length not to φ. They do not only give one a reason to engage in crazy overkill but positively *require* it of one. If there is a duty, then 'go to all lengths not to φ' is the content of the duty.

[32] Ibid.

I have argued elsewhere that the law is not telling anyone to 'go to all lengths not to φ' when it gives them a strict duty not to φ.[33] Far from telling them to go to all lengths not to φ, it is telling them that in the law's eyes it does not matter what lengths they go to. They can go to no lengths at all if they like, so long as they do not φ. And that is because, as I explained above, strict liability is liability that attaches to D for φing, irrespective of any steps that she takes not to φ. Smith resists this line of thought. He has some minor skirmishes with my previous writings along the way. He rejects my view, for example, that going to great lengths to do something is not always, or even reliably, the best way to do it. But his main resistance has deeper roots. For when Smith is faced with my affirmative view that the only thing a strict duty not to φ tells D to do is *not to* φ—i.e. that the law means exactly what it says—he does not regard that as even a candidate interpretation. He says that the law here 'cannot mean what it appears to mean'.[34] It can only mean that D has a duty to take *some set of steps towards* not φing. And if that is all it can mean, then in the name of the rule of law ('clarity') that is what it should say. It should not say to D: do not φ. It should say: take steps not to φ. Then we can openly discuss whether it should be saying 'all possible steps', or only 'all reasonable steps', or perhaps 'all the steps that D thinks reasonable', or whatever.

This explains why, when I first told you what a 'strict duty' is according to Smith, I told you that it is a *supposed* duty not to φ that D may *supposedly* breach irrespective of any steps that she took in order not to φ and irrespective of whether she knew or had reason to know that she was φing. All of this is only 'supposed' because, according to Smith, the duty cannot really be like this. Its content must be different from what we suppose.

Smith's refusal to even entertain my simple 'do not φ' interpretation of the duty seems to come most immediately of his unargued assumption that the meaning of a proposition of law can only be its meaning '[f]rom a rule of law perspective'.[35] In other words the content of the so-called 'strict duty' must be read

[33] In ch 5 above.

[34] 'Strict Duties and the Rule of Law', above note 23, 195.

[35] Ibid, 193.

in such a way as to satisfy Fuller's demand for followability, and hence cannot be read as a strict 'do not φ' duty. The law must be interpreted as guidance, and 'strict duties guide citizens to take more than reasonable care'.[36] For reasons that I gave in section 3, this manoeuvre jumps the gun. In private law there are plaintiff-side considerations that compete systematically with Fullerian rule-of-law standards for legal norms, and this fact should lead us to contemplate interpretations of some private law norms which leave them scoring pretty badly on the Fullerian scale.

Can we *only* interpret the law that governs the tort of negligence, for example, in such a way that it is as determinate as it would need to be to satisfy the tough standards that Fuller sets, the ones that we rightly insist upon in the criminal law? To do that we would need to dismiss almost every modern case on the tort of negligence, at least since *Donoghue* v *Stevenson*. It cannot be that in order to judge whether and to what extent a body of legal norms meets the relevant standards of the rule of law we can only ever begin by interpreting the body of norms so that it already meets them. That would mean that there is no law that fails to meet the standards of the rule of law. And this view, with which Fuller flirted and to which Dworkin later became wedded,[37] has long been exposed as incoherent. There cannot be standards for somebody or something to meet such that, by its nature, that same somebody or something always meets them. That is at odds with the very idea of a standard.[38]

Smith's resistance to the simple 'do not φ' interpretation of strict duties, then, rests partly on a Dworkinian mistake. Yet there seems to lurk in Smith's paper a second, deeper, cause of resistance to the simple 'do not φ' interpretation. Smith shares my view that legal duties must be morally intelligible, meaning presentable and imaginable as moral duties. 'When we try to explain legal duties,' he writes, 'our explanation should show how they could plausibly be presented as reflecting moral duties.'[39]

[36] Ibid, 194.

[37] For a notable statement, see Ronald Dworkin, 'Hart's Postscript and the Character of Political Philosophy', *Oxford Journal of Legal Studies* 24 (2004), 1 at 25.

[38] See further Timothy Macklem and John Gardner, 'Provocation and Pluralism' in Gardner, *Offences and Defences*, above note 6.

[39] 'Strict Duties and the Rule of Law', above note 23, 195.

Apparently, however, Smith does not think that moral duties can be strict duties of the 'do not φ' kind. At any rate, that seems to be the implication of the following passage:

> [T]he rule of law objection [to strict duties is] that strict duties are not what they appear to be: that is to say, they are not actually duties. Both in law and morality to say that you have a duty to do X means that you ought to plan your actions so that you do X.[40]

I think that this is false of both legal and moral duties. Smith explains why he thinks it is true of legal duties: for him they must, as we saw, be interpreted as already rule-of-law compliant. But he says nothing to explain why he thinks it is true of moral duties. The only hint he gives is in the very words just quoted. He says that his 'rule of law objection' is an objection to taking literally a supposed moral injunction ('strictly') not to do X. This suggests to me that Smith thinks that morality conforms to the requirements of the rule of law. I have already explained why I think this assumption is mistaken. The fact that moral norms are often inadequate as guides—that morality constantly ambushes us and sabotages even our well-laid plans—is one reason why we need to have law, and to live under the rule of law. Morality is rife with luck. In particular it includes many strict duties: duties not to φ, where φing is something that one cannot be sure not to do or even to know one is doing. When we φ, even totally innocently, we often owe apologies, accounts, and repairs.

The puzzle is why the same should not be true in the law. Hart gives an answer. He draws attention to one tension between strict liability and the requirements of the rule of law. Does Smith's argument draw attention to another tension between strict liability and the requirements of the rule of law? Inasmuch as Smith's answer depends on an insistence that strict duties cannot possibly be what they seem, the answer is clearly no. One cannot show a rule-of-law problem with strict duties, or with the strict liabilities that are grounded in their breach, by denying that such duties are conceptually possible. If they are conceptually impossible, the question of their desirability does not arise.

[40] Ibid, 197–8.

5. Prophylaxis and pricing

None of this goes to show that strict liability in private law is unobjectionable from the point of view of the rule of law. Smith's argument fails. But Hart's argument succeeds. It reveals genuine rule-of-law problems with strict liability, which I called assurance problems. All I added to Hart's argument was a caveat to the effect that, in the private law context, we may sometimes have to swallow our rule-of-law scruples and tolerate some assurance problems that we would not tolerate in criminal law, because in private law we have to think of extra assurance for the defendant in a zero-sum way, as extra hazard for the plaintiff.

This way of presenting what is at stake assumes that we are already at the stage where a zero-sum conflict exists, where plaintiff and defendant are locked together in the grim embrace of pending or imminent litigation. A merit of Smith's argument is that it draws our attention back to the earlier *ex ante* point at which there is still, for the potential defendant, a question of whether to risk becoming part of such a grim embrace.

Those writing about strict liability sometimes write as if the only relevant question of what to do facing the potential defendant *ex ante* is the question of whether to φ, where φing is the breach of duty that grounds the strict liability. But for the most part strict liability for φing exists, in the private law of all legal systems known to me, only where the φing takes place in the course of some specified activity or relationship—call it ψing. And in general, in such legal systems, ψing is an activity or relationship that one cannot but know one is engaged in, and moreover that one could (with enough effort) avoid getting into. So for the most part the law does provide an assurance of no liability to potential defendants at an earlier time, via a prophylactic measure, if they are willing to take the trouble to use it. Want to avoid strict liability for injuring people with your blasting operations? Fine: just don't go into the blasting business. Want to avoid strict liability for flooding your neighbour's land? Fine: just don't transport water onto your land. Want to avoid strict liability for breaches of contract? Fine: just don't enter into contracts that impose strict duties on you; undertake contractual duties only when they are of a 'best endeavours' variety. More generally, want to avoid strict liability for φing in the course of your ψing? Fine: just don't start ψing.

The law in these cases makes the strict liability a predictable cost, we might want to say, of doing certain avoidable kinds of business, or in Fullerian terms 'a kind of tax in the form of a rule that [the ψer] must respond for any damage that results from [φing in the course of ψing]'.[41] Don't want to bear the cost of φing? Fine: just stay out of the ψing business. This kind of prophylactic assurance device, in my view as in Fuller's, is capable of going a long way to meeting the assurance requirements of the rule of law, and in the process tends to mitigate, although maybe not eliminate, the Fuller-Hart rule of law anxieties we might otherwise experience about the use of strict liability in private law contexts. Moreover, the device does so without significantly shifting the risks of the regulated activities in question onto potential plaintiffs. By hypothesis, those who help themselves to the relevant prophylactic assurance devices do not embark on the regulated activities in question, and so do not impose the risks of those activities on any potential plaintiff. They might still be sued, of course—anyone at all can be sued for anything at all—and dispute might still arise in such a suit over whether their activity was, in spite of appearances, the regulated one. So the prophylactic assurance device does still create an obstacle for future plaintiffs. Nothing can save us altogether from the zero-sum quality of litigation in private law. But the addition of a prophylactic assurance device generally gives rise to less complex and speculative probative challenges than arise from the addition of a requirement to prove fault. And it also does more to guide plaintiffs into choosing different (more suitable) defendants to sue. So as a measure to bring greater rule-of-law conformity into private law without hobbling plaintiffs, the use of prophylactic assurance devices has some advantages over the use of fault standards. If fault liability in private law is nevertheless (at least sometimes) morally preferable to activity-specific strict liability, that can only be on other grounds. It is not because of the assurance demands of the rule of law.

[41] Fuller, *The Morality of Law*, above note 9, 75.

Or at least not directly. Maybe indirectly, in the following way. Where ψing is a very specialized activity, giving rise to a small pocket of strict liability in a sea of potential liabilities that are otherwise fault-based, it is relatively easy to steer clear of strict liability for ψing. There are plenty of other ways left to make a living, get around, engage in social activities, etc. As ψing gets less specific and the associated pockets of strict liability grow, the force of the argument that one could have ruled them out at an earlier stage by simply not ψing diminishes. It is one thing to say: If you want to steer clear of strict liability, don't go into the blasting business. It is quite another to say: If you want to steer clear of strict liability, don't go into business at all. It is one thing to say: If you want to steer clear of strict liability, don't say anything about other people in the newspapers. It is quite another to say: If you want to steer clear of strict liability, don't say anything about other people. Activity-specific strict liability helps to satisfy the rule-of-law demand for assurance because and to the extent that it is genuinely specific. A regime of otherwise fault-based liabilities in private law is presupposed.

Since activity-specific strict liability, when it satisfies these conditions, makes certain liabilities in private law a predictable cost of doing certain kinds of business, it is tempting to read it as not regulating the action of φing at all (the killing by blasting, the flooding by importing water onto your land, the failure to deliver on the contractually specified date, etc.). It is tempting to read it as only regulating, on the one hand, the wider activity of ψing (blasting, importing water onto your land, contracting) and, on the other hand, the legal liabilities that ensue when someone suffers harm or loss by one's ψing. On this view, when one is strictly liable in law, it is not really for one's wrongdoing. There is not really a tort or a breach of contract; those are just the lawyer's perhaps outmoded or fantastical *façons de parler*. There is no prior duty, breach of which grounds the liability. Nobody is suggesting, obviously, that one has a duty not to ψ, a duty that one breached by ψing. Rather, there is a freestanding liability that belongs to all ψers when certain harms or losses materialize from their ψing. In some ways, then, theirs is akin to the indemnity liability of an insurer, or the vicarious liability of an employer. It is a liability attached to their activities (employing, insuring) rather than their actions. In particular, there is no suggestion that they, as employers or insurers, have themselves done anything wrong. On this view the law attaches, as Fuller puts it, 'a special [kind of] liability to *entry* upon a certain *line* of conduct'.[42]

I do not doubt—in fact I have conceded already[43]—that it is possible to interpret some tort liabilities in this way, even though in doing so one awkwardly puts paid to the idea that tort liability is liability for torts, that is, for actions that the law holds to be wrongful. The question before us, however, is not whether the interpretation is (awkwardly) possible but whether one is forced to it as soon as one thinks of strict tort liability as a cost of doing certain types of business. It seems to me that one is not.

It is often suggested that one must choose between the following two ways of looking at any given tort liability. Either one thinks of it as a liability for a wrongful action of φing (the 'old' moralistic way of thinking about tort law) or one thinks of it as a mechanism for attaching a cost to the activity of ψing (the 'new' regulatory way of thinking about tort law). But these are not rival ways of thinking about the liability. They are fully compatible. Only an economist or accountant, or someone who should be an economist or accountant, would take it for granted that the cost of doing business we are talking about, when we describe strict liability as a cost of doing business, is the economic cost, meaning the price in pounds or dollars that the strictly liable ψer ends up paying. The cost that I had in mind, by contrast, was the fact of the strict tort liability itself, i.e. the fact that φing (whatever one did to avoid it and whether one knew of it or not) will now be a wrong, and a wrong recognized by law and actionable in law, because it will have been done in the course of ψing. The cost of doing business that we should be thinking of first, when we think about tort liability in the 'new' way as a mechanism for attaching costs to ψing, is the very fact of being subject to extra tort liability in the 'old' way, i.e. being at risk of committing wrongs of φing that would not qualify as wrongs were one not engaged in ψing. Any economic costs are mere consequences of that. They come and go according to the skill of one's lawyers, the scope of one's insurance policies, and the resources and resilience those

[42] Ibid. [43] Text above at note 29.

who launch proceedings against one. The tort liability, however, remains, and the non-awkward way to interpret it is as a liability for a tort of φing-while-ψing, and to think of potential liability for committing that tort as one of the costs of ψing. This is what Fuller gestures towards when he speaks of a 'special surcharge *of legal responsibility*'[44]—pointing not to the tax on ψing alone, but also to the distinctively tort-law ground for its falling due, namely that D tortiously φed in the course of ψing.

Different elements of this tort of φing-while-ψing come into the foreground depending on one's investigative preoccupations. If one is interested in how people might plan for their future liabilities, then one naturally focuses on the ψing element. If one is interested in the ground of the liability in tort, however, one naturally focuses on the φing element—the action, not the activity. The activity, ψing, is a necessary condition of liability but not, in itself, a ground of it (because not, in itself, a complete reason for it). It is perfectly understandable that many lawyers, immersed from the first day of their professional education in the ideology of the rule of law, are tempted to shift the focus of their analysis from the *ex hypothesi* unassurable φing element (killing, flooding, failure to deliver on the specified date, etc.) to the *ex hypothesi* assurable ψing element (blasting, importing water onto land, contracting). It is also understandable that, in forging such a ψing-focused analysis, lawyers often find common cause with, or take comfort in the work of, micro-economists, who are immersed from the first day of *their* professional education in the stunted psychology of the self-interested 'rational' chooser who is out to maximize economic returns for himself. The economistic ideology agrees with the legalistic ideology in focusing attention on the ψing element as opposed to the φing element. In emphasizing the importance of the φing element, the action by D that grounds the liability, I am not suggesting that we can dispense with these specialized professional ideologies. The bewildering conditions of modern life unfortunately demand ever-greater bureaucratization, an ever-more pervasive parcelling up of rational labour into distinct professions, offices, and disciplines. The occupants of such distinct professions, offices, and disciplines

44 Fuller, *The Morality of Law*, above note 9, 75.

cannot but interpret the world so that it can be marshalled and rationalized according to the defining ideology of their role. Sometimes they are led to think and talk as if the ideals built into that ideology are the most important ideals for humanity, or society, or civilization. Sometimes they are led to think and talk, wishfully, as if the world of their work, or the world as a whole, already conforms to the ideals that they, as professionals, set for it. Most often they are led to focus professional attention on the data that do conform to those ideals, and to hold them up as some kind of vindication for their professional worldview.

This is a well-known syndrome among lawyers, who naturally enough long to convince themselves and others of the nobility of what is often a murky and desolate professional life, raking and ploughing an endless 'field of pain and death'.[45] In this exercise of esteem-building, not only is the moral ideal of the rule of law casually endowed with too much importance as compared with the rest of morality; not only is the law often paraded too uncritically as already conforming to the ideal; but also the organizing categories of the law, and the relationships among them, are distorted by the urge to foreground those that conform to the ideal, and to background those that do not.[46] In the literature of the law of torts, especially but not only among those writers who self-identify as belonging to the new world of tort law as 'regulation', this syndrome is greatly in evidence in the premature rejection, marginalization, or reconstruction of strict liability, and in particular in the refusal to acknowledge (or even entertain) the existence of the strict duties, duties not to φ, the breach of which constitutes the tort.

[45] The famous phrase is Robert Cover's, from his 'Violence and the Word', *Yale Law Journal* 95 (1986), 1601 at 1601.

[46] To see all three esteem-building engines whirring simultaneously without interruption, see Ronald Dworkin, *Law's Empire* (Cambridge Mass 1986).

7

THE NEGLIGENCE STANDARD: POLITICAL NOT METAPHYSICAL

1. Institutional actions, ordinary reasons

My title echoes that of a famous article by John Rawls.[1] But the main distinction that I will be drawing and exploring in this lecture is not the one that Rawls had in mind. Rawls sought to isolate, among all valid reasons for action, those that are suitable to guide and assess the use of governmental, or perhaps more broadly institutional, power. He aimed to identify reasons that have a proper place, as he sometimes put it, in 'public justification'. The hallmark of public justification, as Rawls saw it, is that it does not cleave to any particular 'conception of the good' or 'comprehensive doctrine'. Rather, it has ecumenical appeal across a wide range of such conceptions, namely the ones that Rawls dubbed 'reasonable'.[2] Rawls thought that this ecumenical appeal made public justification somehow less *metaphysical* than other kinds of justification. I have never been sure what he meant.[3] Maybe he was using the word 'metaphysical' in what might be called the 'Glastonbury' sense, to mean something like 'mystical'. Maybe he hoped to demystify the theory of sound governmental or institutional action by demerging or abstracting it from the theory of sound action more generally. If that was his ambition, history has not smiled upon him. There is little in contemporary philosophy that more resembles an esoteric new age teaching than

[1] John Rawls, 'Justice as Fairness: Political not Metaphysical', *Philosophy & Public Affairs* 14 (1985), 223.

[2] For a short recapitulation of these ideas, see John Rawls, 'The Idea of Public Reason Revisited', *University of Chicago Law Review* 64 (1997), 765 at 786. Here Rawls speaks of 'comprehensive doctrines' where, in 'Justice as Fairness', above note 1, he had spoken of 'conceptions of the good'.

[3] His attempt to explain appears in 'Justice as Fairness', above note 1, 238–40.

Torts and Other Wrongs. John Gardner, Oxford University Press (2019). © John Gardner
DOI: 10.1093/oso/9780198852940.003.0007

the idea of a purely 'political' theory of politics, a 'political liberalism', of the kind that Rawls bequeathed to us in his later work.[4]

As this remark already reveals, I am not among those who regard governmental agents as inhabiting a world apart from the rest of us. Governmental agents answer to all valid reasons for action, just like you and me. If some claimed reason for action could never possibly contribute to the justification of what a governmental agent does, then it is not a valid reason for action and cannot contribute to the justification of what anyone does. Political morality, to put it another way, is just ordinary morality as it bears on the circumstances in which certain agents (certain officials and institutions) find themselves. These circumstances may seem a world apart at first sight. Few of us have vast armies to command, multi-million-pound healthcare budgets to spend, or a succession of strangers parading before us who face losing their liberty or their children on our say-so. Yet still these are, in the final analysis, but large-stakes examples of the same kind of responsibilities that we all have as friends, employers, teachers, neighbours, and so on. Public or private, individual or collective, personal or institutional, in law or in love, in parliament or in the supermarket, all valid reasons for action count.

It is true that they may count, among other things, in the assignment of responsibilities. It is true that when we have responsibilities we have reasons to concentrate on some reasons for action at the expense of others in connection with our own actions. Such playing up and playing down of reasons is the normal business of all rational life, or at least all human rational life—for parents and volleyball teams as much as for police officers and constitutional courts. Only rarely should one person attempt to attend even-handedly to all the applicable reasons at once in her reasoning. Apart from anything else, doing so would often be counterproductive. Focusing one's attention on a sub-set of the applicable reasons, or even relying on some simplified proxy reasons that marshal and conceal the underlying *melée* of applicable reasons, is often a better policy, with a lower error rate. That much was pointed out by Rawls himself in earlier work.[5] He

[4] See chapter 8.

[5] John Rawls, 'Two Concepts of Rules', *Philosophical Review* 64 (1955), 3.

used it to explain the rational appeal of certain rules, including responsibility-assignment rules, that lie at the heart of certain social practices. It is, however, a long way from this early Rawlsian insight to the later Rawlsian thesis that the theory of sound government (sound judging, sound legislating, sound constitution-making, etc.) can be demerged or abstracted from the theory of sound action more generally. The earlier Rawlsian argument reveals a set of reasons that are relevant to the assignment of all responsibilities if they are relevant to the assignment of any. It has no special application to the assignment of governmental or institutional responsibilities.

2. Assignable responsibility

The idea that there might be reasons to assign different responsibilities to different agents brings me closer to the topic of my lecture. It does not bring me, just yet, to the negligence standard. But at least it brings me to the conceptual space within which reflection on the negligence standard takes place.

Some people think, as I once thought,[6] that there are two senses of 'responsibility' which are both such that responsibility can be assigned differentially to different agents. They are sometimes called, following Joel Feinberg, the 'prospective' sense and the 'retrospective' sense.[7] When we talk of assigning responsibilities (plural), we are generally thinking of things that are, at the time when the responsibility arises, yet to be done. We are asking who will be the one to do those things, or at least see to it that they are done. When we talk of assigning responsibility (singular), by contrast, we are often thinking of things that were already done, or will already have been done, by the time the responsibility arises. We are asking who will be the one to face the music or pick up the pieces when the things that were supposed already to have been done were not done.

[6] John Gardner, 'Hart and Feinberg on Responsibility' in Matthew H Kramer, Claire Grant, Ben Colburn, and Antony Hatzistavrou (eds), *The Legacy of H.L.A. Hart: Legal, Political, and Moral Philosophy* (Oxford 2008), 121 at 133.

[7] Joel Feinberg, 'Responsibility for the Future', *Philosophy Research Archives* 14 (1998), 93.

We all know that the prospective and the retrospective judgments can come apart. I may end up with retrospective responsibility for failures that fell outwith the prospective responsibilities that belonged to me at the time of the failure. Suppose that I am the successor in post of the person who had some prospective responsibility. I am the new Home Secretary or the new Data Protection Officer. My predecessor was the one who was supposed to have made sure the report was delivered on time, but it wasn't done. Now I am the one who is left to face the music and pick up the pieces. Such cases may lead one to think, as I used to think, that we are already dealing with two distinct senses of the word 'responsibility', namely a prospective sense and a retrospective sense. My predecessor was responsible in the prospective sense for the delivery of the report; yet I am responsible, in the retrospective sense, for its non-delivery.

There is another way to think about such cases, however, which I now think is preferable. To assign retro*spective* responsibility is to reassign prospective responsibility retro*active*ly. When I take over a role from some delinquent predecessor and have to face the music for what that person did in the same role, the original (prospective) responsibility has become mine by reassignment. I inherited it as part of the role. Never mind that I personally wasn't around last month to have fulfilled it, at the time when it called for fulfilment. When I say 'never mind', I mean that we shouldn't think that there is any *conceptual* obstacle to the retroactive reassignment. We shouldn't think that it is blocked by 'ought implies can' or some similar luck-proofing doctrine. Life would be so much less awkward if only it were true that, whenever I ought to have done something, I was already at the time in a position to have done it and to have known that it was mine to do. Alas, the human condition is not so obliging. Yet the word 'alas' here reveals that we should worry about the retroactive reassignment in another way. The reassignment can be awkward for the person on the receiving end of it. Sometimes it might even be unfair. When it is unfair, we need a suitably strong case for doing it. Notice that this way of thinking about what is going on already concedes my main point. Prospective responsibility is conceptually capable of being retroactively reassigned and the question in any given case is only whether there is a suitably strong case for reassigning it, even at the price of some possible unfairness to the reassignee.

My conversion to this revised way of thinking about role-transfer cases is allied to my coming to understand better the implications of a thesis that I have elsewhere labelled the 'continuity thesis'.[8] According to the continuity thesis, when I fail to do what I have a duty to do, I acquire without further ado a fallback duty to do the next best thing—a duty, so far as it can still be done, to make up for my failure. Whatever reasons I failed to conform to when I failed to do my duty still await my conformity, and they are what justify and give shape to my new duty. The expression 'next best thing' in my formulation of the continuity thesis means, therefore, the next best way of conforming to the very same reasons. Since the reasons stay the same, one may be tempted to think that the fallback duty is just the original duty in a new guise.[9] But that is not so: duties are individuated according to the actions that they are duties to perform. A duty to perform a different action is a different duty. Responsibilities, however, are individuated otherwise. Alongside rights,[10] they belong to the apparatus for explaining why I have whatever duties I have. They are individuated at the level of the *reasons for* my duties. I have a responsibility inasmuch as a certain reason or set of reasons is mine to conform to. The relevant set of reasons need not be definitely specified; it may be an indefinitely specified set such as 'any reasons that bear, when the time comes, on whether and when the lights are to be switched off'. Whether definitely or indefinitely specified, however, the same reasons are reasons for several duties if they are reasons for any. If they are reasons for an original duty (e.g. a duty to switch off the lights, or to see to it that they are switched off, when the last person leaves) then, by the continuity thesis, they are also reasons for a fallback duty (e.g. a duty to go back and switch the lights off later if the lights weren't switched off at the right time). We should think of

[8] In ch 2 above.

[9] This is the way that Ernest Weinrib presents it in *The Idea of Private Law* (Cambridge, Mass 1995), 135.

[10] See Joseph Raz, 'On the Nature of Rights', *Mind* 93 (1984), 194 esp 211–12 where the relationship between rights and responsibilities is sketched.

these two duties, it seems to me, as two pay-offs or incidents of one and the same responsibility. So when someone puts it to you that you were responsible for turning off the lights (prospective) and infers that you are responsible for the lights having been left on (retrospective) we should regard them as offering, essentially, two formulations of one and the same point. They are asserting what we might most simply call your *responsibility for the lights*. Your responsibility for the lights is essentially diachronic: if the lights still being on isn't your responsibility, their being turned off wasn't any responsibility of yours; and if the lights still being on *is* your responsibility, their being turned off must have been a responsibility of yours—even if that means that we have just retroactively made it so.[11]

Not all situations in which someone is singled out to face the music or pick up the pieces in respect of another's failures fit this pattern of retroactive re-assignment. Employers, for example, do not have any responsibility assigned to them retroactively when they have to pay for the failures of their employees. Rather they already had a second-order responsibility to see to it that their employees fulfilled their first-order responsibilities as employees. The employer's responsibility here is not the acquisition of the employee's responsibility but the continuation of the employer's own. So there is nothing retroactive going on. At least that is one possible analysis.[12] Another possible analysis is that employers are akin to insurers. Possibly employers do not have a second-order responsibility to see to it that their employees fulfil their first-order responsibilities as employees any more than my motor-insurance company has a second-order responsibility to see to it that I fulfil my first-order responsibilities as a driver. True, the

[11] I am here implicitly rejecting the distinction drawn by Andrew Khoury in his 'Synchronic and Diachronic Responsibility', *Philosophical Studies* 165 (2013), 735. Unfortunately my quarrel with Khoury cannot be developed here.

[12] The analysis is often discussed, and usually rejected as out of keeping with the law, under the heading of *culpa in eligendo/in vigilando*: negligence in the selection or supervision of the employee. See e.g. Paula Giliker, *Vicarious Liability in Tort: A Comparative Perspective* (Cambridge 2010), 231–4. In my version, however, there is no mention of any *culpa* on the employer's part. That there can be no responsibility without *culpa* is the main proposition that I attempt, in this lecture, to deny.

insurance company has to pay out when I cause damage by my bad driving. But that is not because responsibility for the avoiding-or-causing of the damage has been retroactively assigned to them. All that has been assigned to them is a fresh responsibility, to pay for the damage, that arose *de novo* when I failed in my responsibility not to cause that damage. That fresh responsibility was assigned to the insurer by the contract of insurance. While there is an assignment of responsibility here, there is nothing retroactive about it. It is not that the insurer is now held to have been responsible for avoiding the damage, *hence* responsible for having done the damage, *hence* responsible for picking up the pieces now that the damage is done. No, the insurer's responsibility arises only at the pick-up-the-pieces stage, and it is not a responsibility for the damage, exactly, but only a responsibility for *paying for* the damage (i.e. for 'the damages'). Might it not be thus with employers too?

Although the differences between these various situations are fascinating, my immediate interest is in a feature that all of them share. They all highlight that responsibility, as we have been discussing it up to now, is the kind of thing that can be assigned or, if you prefer, allocated. That much is true whether you think that we have so far been discussing two different senses in which an agent can be responsible, or only one sense. To simplify our discussion I will generally foreground judgments of responsibility of the kind that Feinberg would have called prospective. I will presuppose that the deed is yet to be done. But with or without that restriction, an agent's responsibility, as we have been discussing it up to now, is the kind of thing that can be augmented or curtailed by someone's exercising a normative power over it. Sometimes I *take* responsibility for something. Responsibility is here assigned to me by my own consent or undertaking. In other cases, I am *given* responsibility or, in a different idiom, *made* responsible. Here the responsibility is assigned to me by an exercise of another's authority.

It is important not to conclude, from the fact that responsibility is assignable, that we have none of it without an act of assignment. Many of our responsibilities are ours simply because of the value of our having them, without our having taken them on and without anyone having given them to us. Parental responsibility, for example, descends upon parents without the exercise, by themselves or by others, of any normative powers. There is normally no live question of whether I consented to be a parent, or undertook to do it, etc. Parents have parental responsibility just by virtue of being parents. The question of assignment arises only when parents begin to consider leaving the children with granny for the weekend or signing them into a play scheme for the day, or (more radically) when someone begins to think of adoption, fostering, making the children wards of court, etc. The question of assignment arises, in other words, only when we begin to think about giving parental responsibility (in whole or in part, substitutively or supplementally) to people *other than* the parents.

The parenthetical words here are important. A tempting objection to the idea that responsibility is assignable is that sometimes I have a logically irreplaceable role in the fulfilment of my own responsibilities.[13] Only I can keep the promise I made, only I can atone for my own wrongs, etc. How can these responsibilities possibly be re-assigned? Answer: these are the duties, not the responsibilities. True, these particular actions, and hence these particular duties of mine, cannot by their natures be proxied.[14] But other people can be given, or can take, supplemental responsibility in respect of my performance of them (e.g. it can be their job to encourage me or compel me to do my duty). And other people can be given, or can take, supplemental or substitutive responsibility in respect of the performance of certain fallback actions (e.g. making it their job to mop up after my failures). When I say 'can be given' or 'can take' here I mean the 'can' to be read conceptually. I leave open the desirability of such assignments, and (a different matter) the effectiveness of attempts to bring them about. It is no part of my thesis that responsibility is always effectively re-assigned when someone attempts to re-assign it, let alone that attempting to re-assign it would always, or indeed often, be a good idea. My thesis is only that responsibility, as we have been discussing it up to now, is the kind of thing, the taking

[13] I thank Arash Abizadeh for pressing me on this point. Arash also wanted me to think about inalienable duties not to murder, rape, torture, etc. My remarks in the text can also be applied, with some modifications, to these.

[14] For more on proxyability, see Sanford Kadish, 'Complicity, Cause and Blame: A Study in the Interpretation of Doctrine' *California Law Review* 73 (1985), 323.

or giving of which is an intelligible proposal and an imaginable undertaking.

The taking and giving of responsibility are both of great importance in the law, the giving more fundamentally than the taking. The law claims, by its authority, to make each of us responsible for some things and not for others.[15] We may think that these authority-claims are ill-founded, at least in some cases. The law, we may think, is wrong to the point of illegitimacy in the way in which it makes accomplices responsible for certain acts of their principals, or in the way in which it limits the responsibility of company directors for some acts of their companies, or in the way in which it allows insurance to lighten the responsibility-burden of tortfeasors. We may think, in other words, that the legal position in these or similar cases is so misguided as to cast doubt on the moral effectiveness of the law's purported exercise of authority in them. We may even be anarchists who think that *all* the law's purported exercises of authority are morally ineffective, and so should be ignored, subverted, or derided rather than adhered to. But these objections, you will notice, are only to the moral effectiveness of some or all of the law's purported assignments of responsibility. They do not deny, indeed they presuppose, that responsibility is the kind of thing that could conceivably be assigned. Assigning responsibility by authority, consent, undertaking, disclaimer, etc. may not always succeed, but it is no category mistake.

3. Basic responsibility

Except when it is. At this point we need to distinguish responsibility in the sense or senses we have just been discussing (I'll call it 'assignable responsibility') from responsibility in a very different, although closely related, sense, which I like to call 'basic responsibility'.[16] Basic responsibility is what it sounds like. It is an

[15] The broader idea that law claims authority is most often associated with Joseph Raz. A useful discussion and defence is Bas van der Vossen, 'Assessing Law's Claim to Authority', *Oxford Journal of Legal Studies* 31 (2011), 481.

[16] See John Gardner, *Offences and Defences* (Oxford 2007), ch 9. Basic responsibility as I explained it was studied further by Angela Smith in 'Responsibility as

ability. More fully, it is the ability and propensity to have and to give self-explanations in the currency of reasons. The ability and the propensity are but two sides of the same coin. As beings who are able to respond to reasons we cannot avoid being disposed to respond to them. There is nowhere to hide from them. As Jean Renoir expressed the point nicely in *La Règle du Jeu*: 'sur cette terre il y a quelque chose d'effroyable, c'est que tout le monde a ses raisons'.[17] And having one's reasons is only the start. One not only responds to reasons in what one thinks, feels, wants, and does. One also responds to them again in telling the story—to oneself or others—of what one already thought, felt, wanted, and did. In saying this I do not doubt that in self-explanation people often conjure up rationalizations, making themselves look or feel better in the telling than their original reasons would have allowed them to look or feel. Of course they do. This is but one among many tragic aspects of life as a basically responsible agent. What else would one crave, as a being with the ability and propensity to respond to reasons, than to have had better reasons than, alas, one had? This already shows that basic responsibility is by no means a kind of success with reasons. It does not entail that one is wise, sensitive, or even competent in one's grasp or use of reasons. It connotes no skill and no virtue of character.[18] We all have our reasons, to be sure, but it doesn't mean we all have good or adequate or even valid reasons. Often we don't; we take things to be reasons which in fact are not, or we give some reasons more weight than they are capable of bearing. None of that is inconsistent with our basic responsibility. The question of how well we respond to reasons arises only because, and when, we are basically responsible.

Answerability', *Inquiry* 58 (2015), 99–126. I have benefited greatly from reading Smith's work on this point and several others.

[17] *La Règle du Jeu* (Paris 1939), 20:16.

[18] There is also a virtue of character called 'responsibility'. Aristotle called it *phronesis*, often translated as 'practical wisdom'. It is a kind of master-virtue. 'It is not possible to have any moral virtue without *phronesis*, nor to have *phronesis* without any [other] moral virtue,' says Aristotle at *NE* $1144^{b}30$–34. Although the concept is closely bound up with those under discussion, for reasons of space I will not be saying any more about the virtue of responsibility here.

Basic responsibility, I suggest, cannot be assigned or allocated by anyone. There is no normative power, by the exercise of which anyone can add to or subtract from it. That is not because it is impossible for any of us not to have it. Some of us lack it altogether. Well, actually, that depends on who counts as 'us'. But assuming we mean 'human beings', we might doubt the basic responsibility of very young children, those with advanced forms of dementia or severe mental illnesses, and those in comas. Surely basic responsibility is entirely lacking in at least some such cases? Yes, and that is already a matter of regret. Human beings ought to be answerable to reasons. That is part of their human *ergon*, to use the Aristotelian term, sometimes translated as 'function' but perhaps better as 'destiny'.[19] With young children, the expectation is usually that they will sooner or later come to be answerable to reasons; with the others there may be the hope, however vain, that they might. With the rest of us, however, the conditions of basic responsibility are typically met. Typically we are responsible for our actions, and for our thoughts, feelings, and wants. Typically, but not invariably. Being basically responsible doesn't mean being basically responsible for *all* your actions, thoughts, feelings, and wants. There are exceptions. Here is one. If I have a kind of severe obsessive-compulsive disorder (OCD) that propels me to wash my hands every few minutes, that may affect my basic responsibility for washing my hands every few minutes, and perhaps for some things that I failed to do while I was washing my hands. But it doesn't affect my basic responsibility for forgetting the groceries or distracting the bus driver, when my OCD did not play any part in the story.

Now OCD can often be treated, or, failing that, managed.[20] Those who suffer from it can be restored to basic responsibility in respect of the class of actions into which their OCD once propelled them, or from which it once distracted them. So I am

[19] *NE* 1097^{b}22–1098^{a}20. I explored some implications of this idea in my *Law as a Leap of Faith* (Oxford 2012), ch 6, and others (with Timothy Macklem) in 'Human Disability', *King's Law Journal* 25 (2014), 60.

[20] Martin Antony, Christine Purdon, and Laura Summerfeldt (eds), *Psychological Treatment of Obsessive-Compulsive Disorder: Fundamentals and Beyond* (Washington DC 2007).

obviously not denying that basic responsibility can be deliberately conferred or restored, or indeed taken away, by a suitable human intervention. The point is only that an exercise of a normative power over the basic responsibility is not the relevant kind of human intervention. It is a category mistake to treat basic responsibility (unlike assignable responsibility) as the kind of thing that can be imposed by an exercise of authority purporting to impose it, or likewise by giving consent to having it or undertaking to have it, or by disclaiming it, etc. Should we advise the OCD sufferer to seek relief, not from a cognitive-behavioural therapist, but from a judge or magistrate?

That is not to deny that judges have their role to play in the investigation of basic responsibility. Like assignable responsibility, basic responsibility is of great importance in the law. Every day, in the courts as in other corners of life, people are *held* responsible, *deemed* responsible, or *treated as* responsible. They also *accept* or *claim* responsibility. Clearly these expressions are sometimes used in connection with basic responsibility, and intelligibly so. That is because it is possible to make authoritative or otherwise binding determinations of fact such that, for certain purposes, certain propositions will be treated as true even if they are false. Propositions about basic responsibility are among them. Just as a court might declare a testator to be dead or proceed on the footing that he is dead, a court might declare a defendant to be basically responsible or proceed on the footing that she is basically responsible. The defendant may also admit or assert her basic responsibility, just as she may admit or assert her dyslexia or her forgetfulness. Things may then proceed in the law, and where the law has influence, as if these declarations, admissions, etc. were true. But it does not mean that they are true. That a testator is declared dead or treated as dead doesn't make him dead; that a defendant claims to be dyslexic doesn't make her dyslexic; that someone is declared or conceded to be basically responsible doesn't make her basically responsible. A normative power was exercised, but it was not a normative power to make the defendant basically responsible. It was a normative power to permit or require the court, and others covered by the doctrine of *res judicata*, to proceed *as if she were* basically responsible even if, as all involved may know, she is nothing of the kind.

The idioms of 'holding someone responsible' and 'accepting responsibility' are in particularly widespread use, and not only in the law. The reason is not hard to see. The words are equivocal and the equivocation can be advantageous. The words can easily be heard as words of assignment, indicating that someone is being made responsible when they otherwise wouldn't be. But they can just as easily be heard as indicating a proposition that one is treating, for one or more purposes, as true.[21] Sometimes it is convenient to leave it vague which of these two things one is doing in connection with responsibility. This need not be a form of concealment. It can simply be a form of economy. When I say that I 'hold you responsible' I am often trying to convey two points at once, and I want you to hear them both. I am trying to convey (a) that I regard you as basically responsible for something and (b) that I am therefore not attempting to re-assign assignable responsibility for that thing to anyone else, nor inviting you to re-assign it to anyone else. Likewise when I say that I 'accept responsibility', I may be trying to convey two things at once. I may be trying to convey (a) that I decline to contest the truth of the proposition that I am basically responsible for something, and (b) that therefore I am not attempting to re-assign assignable responsibility for that thing to anyone else, or indeed inviting you to do so. I am not trying to pass the buck.

The word 'therefore' in these explanations testifies to some connection between my being basically responsible for something and my being assignably responsible for it. What is the connection? There are several. I will mention three, themselves closely interconnected. First, the question of my basic responsibility arises principally in connection with the question of whether I acquitted myself in respect of some assignable responsibility. There we see one reason why my assignable responsibilities are called 'responsibilities'. It is because they are the things in respect of which I am the one who owes (to somebody, or to nobody

[21] For similar points about 'taking responsibility' see David Enoch, 'Being Responsible, Taking Responsibility, and Penumbral Agency' in Ulrike Heuer and Gerald Lang (eds), *Luck, Value, and Commitment: Themes from the Ethics of Bernard Williams* (Oxford 2011), s4.

in particular[22]) a self-explanation in the currency of reasons. To this end I need the ability to have and to provide such a self-explanation, i.e. I need to be basically responsible. And that brings us to the second connection. My basic responsibility for something is normally a condition of my assignable responsibility for that same thing. The word 'normally' is there to allow for special cases in which assignable responsibility for something is assigned to someone who lacks basic responsibility for that thing. The assignee may be someone who consents or undertakes to be treated as if she had been basically responsible. The assignee may also be someone regarding whom someone else has authority to make factual determinations, and who (thanks to such a determination) is treated as if she were basically responsible. These two cases are quite different in some ways. However they both reflect, by a roundabout route, the normal dependence of assignable responsibility upon basic responsibility. In both cases the assigning of assignable responsibility to someone means treating the assignee as if she were basically responsible. She is *made* responsible in one sense and that means *holding her* responsible, even if fictitiously or erroneously, in another sense.

But why does it mean that? That brings us to the third and deepest connection. In a way basic responsibility is the whole, the totality, of which assignable responsibility is but a special part. Ultimately, all reasons are mine to contend with, to respond to, and to explain myself in terms of. As a rational being I have nowhere to hide from any of them.[23] Even if a reason is such that only some other person could satisfy it (e.g. your reason to keep a promise that you made), there is always the question of what I might have done to help. In the ultimate analysis, nothing is ever 'none of my business'. Therein lies my basic responsibility. But only rarely, to repeat what I said in my opening remarks, should

[22] For doubts about 'nobody in particular' cases, some of them directed against my views, see R A Duff, *Answering for Crime: Responsibility and Liability in the Criminal Law* (Oxford 2007), 23–30.

[23] In particular, to reprise the theme of my introductory section, public office gives one no hiding place. See my 'Criminals in Uniform' in R A Duff, Lindsay Farmer, S E Marshall, Massimo Renzo, and Victor Tadros (eds), *The Constitution of Criminal Law* (Oxford 2012).

I attempt to attend even-handedly to all reasons at once. For, as George Eliot evocatively puts it in *Middlemarch*,

> If we had a keen vision and feeling of all ordinary human life, it would be like hearing the grass grow and the squirrel's heart beat, and we should die of that roar which lies on the other side of silence.[24]

For each of us, most of the time, some reasons are to be played up and others played down. That is itself explained by reasons; it represents the only reasonable way for us to engage, as finite beings, with the madding 'roar' of reasons (which proliferate even beyond the 'ordinary' humanistic ones foregrounded by Eliot).[25] At the surface of our rationality, then, we have some things that are especially our business, and others not so much. The things that are especially our business, demarcated as clusters or ranges of reasons, are our assignable responsibilities. Unlike the non-negotiable fact of our basic responsibility—hence the inescapable hold that every reason has over us—these assignable responsibilities could in principle be augmented, curtailed, replaced, or displaced by ourselves or others.

4. Political v metaphysical

It has taken us a long time to reach the distinction between the political and the metaphysical, the one that I had in mind when I gave this lecture its title. Assignable responsibility belongs to politics in the widest sense of the word. It is possible, by the use of authority, consent, or other normative powers, to assign this responsibility and to re-assign it. Remember that by calling it assignable I am not saying that it is always assigned. The same kinds of reasons that can justify assigning assignable responsibility to someone can also justify their having assignable responsibility without anyone's having assigned it. You may have assignable responsibility for switching out the lights because I gave you that job, or just because you are the last one to leave and there was nobody to assign the job. As this example reminds us, there may

24 George Eliot, *Middlemarch* (Edinburgh 1871), bk 2 ch 20.

25 For expansion of the cryptic parenthetical remark, see Timothy Macklem and John Gardner, 'Value, Interest, and Well-Being', *Utilitas* 18 (2006), 362.

be good policies and bad policies concerning the assignment or non-assignment of assignable responsibility. Some people may end up with too much of it and others with too little; there may be unfair distributions of it and inconvenient allocations of it and so on. It may be my responsibility to switch the lights out, since I signed out the key, even though it would have been better if you had signed out the key and thereby acquired responsibility for the lights. And as this case illustrates, the conditions of assignable responsibility may vary from occasion to occasion; one may find that sometimes one acquires or loses responsibility easily, and on other occasions only with difficulty. Such differences may be explained, and indeed justified, by pointing to the advantages of assigning responsibility on certain conditions on certain occasions, but not on other occasions. The whole organization (and disorganization) of our assignable responsibilities could be cast as a matter of advantage and disadvantage. Who is best doing what and seeing to what, and hence answering for what?

At least one condition, however, is less flexible. It is the basic responsibility condition. Assignable responsibility is sometimes assigned, rightly or wrongly, to people who are not basically responsible for whatever they are being assigned assignable responsibility for. However, it is assigned to nobody without at least the fiction of their basic responsibility for whatever they are being assigned the assignable responsibility for. No *making* responsible, we might say, without *holding* responsible. And what is more the conditions of basic responsibility, unlike some other conditions of assignable responsibility, do not respond to the advantages and disadvantages of those being the conditions. The conditions of basic responsibility are what they are and people meet them, when they do, irrespective of the appeal, the attractions, the merits, the value, the fittingness, of it being the case that they meet them. That is not to say that there is no value in their meeting them. It is an aspect of our human *ergon*, as I called it, that we should meet them. If we do not meet the conditions of basic responsibility, that means something is amiss with us as human beings. No explanation of what it takes to be human can omit to give a central place to the fact that humans are supposed to answer to reasons, and that even when we don't, we still ought to. In that sense basic responsibility can be thought of as a 'metaphysical' truth. It belongs, if it belongs anywhere, to an explanation of what makes human beings fit to have assignable responsibility assigned to them. Basic responsibility belongs to the relatively fixed presuppositions, if you like, of the extremely pliable politics of assignable responsibility.

5. Basic responsibility without negligence

In general, I said, we are basically responsible for our actions. How about our negligent actions? The question has a long history among lawyers, for the negligence standard has a venerable and wide-ranging role in many legal systems. The question first arises because negligent actions are by definition unintentional actions, and so are not performed for reasons. They are performed, rather, in the course of performing other actions that are performed for reasons.[26] I intentionally drive out of the side road; I thereby unintentionally, perhaps negligently, drive into the path of your car. I intentionally undertake repairs on your gas boiler; I thereby unintentionally, perhaps negligently, leave it poorly ventilated. One may wonder: How can I answer to reasons in respect of actions that I did not perform for reasons—actions, indeed, that I did not even take myself to have reasons to perform? How do *those* tragic actions fit into Jean Renoir's characterization of the human tragedy?

Personally, I do not find that a very difficult question.[27] As basically responsible agents we answer to reasons that we overlook as well as reasons that we attend to. That basic responsibility must be symmetrical on this front is revealed even when we think about

[26] Although not always deliberately. Getting oneself stung while instinctively trying to flap a wasp away from one's face is a good example of doing something unintentional—indeed counterintentional—in the course of doing something that is intentional but not deliberate. Timothy Macklem and I protested against a too-deliberate picture of rational agency in our 'Reasons' in Jules Coleman and Scott Shapiro (eds), *The Oxford Handbook of Jurisprudence and Philosophy of Law* (Oxford 2002).

[27] Others are more troubled. Recent examples: Larry Alexander and Kimberly Ferzan, 'Against Negligence Liability' in Paul Robinson, Stephen Garvey, and Kimberly Ferzan (eds), *Criminal Law Conversations* (Oxford 2009) 273; Heidi Hurd, 'Finding No Fault with Negligence' in John Oberdiek (ed), *Philosophical Foundations of the Law of Torts* (Oxford 2014).

intentional actions. I intentionally kick my neighbour's dog. Sure, I have my reasons. The dog is always bothering me and this kick, I reckon, will teach him to keep his distance. But what about all the obvious reasons not to go about kicking dogs, still less other people's dogs? Well, I didn't give those reasons any weight, or indeed any thought. In my frustration I forgot all about them and attended to just the one reason for which I acted. Does it follow that the other reasons are not my problem, that I do not answer to them? Far from it. If I hope to escape the harshest judgments that I might face as a dog-kicker, if I hope to reduce the volume of the music that I will properly face from my neighbour, from the local paper, from the RSPCA, even from the courts, I had better be able to explain why I overlooked these reasons. I had better be able to give reasons why these reasons did not occur to me or did not weigh with me. This shows how my basic responsibility extends to overlooked reasons: by extending to my explanations, in the currency of reasons, for having overlooked them. And if my basic responsibility extends this far in the case of intentional actions like dog-kicking, then why not in respect of unintentional actions like leaving your boiler inadequately ventilated or driving into the path of your car?

This, however, makes one think about a different way in which negligence might matter to basic responsibility. Could it be that I am basically responsible for unintentional actions *only* if they are negligent? That view is sometimes advanced.[28] I want to persuade you here of its untenability. To do that I first need to tell you a little more about basic responsibility.

When we explain ourselves in the currency of reasons, we often aim thereby to justify ourselves. We hope to reveal that

[28] For example, Gideon Rosen, 'Skepticism About Moral Responsibility', *Philosophical Perspectives* 18 (2004), 295; George Sher, *Who Knew? Responsibility without Awareness* (New York 2009); Joseph Raz, 'Responsibility and the Negligence Standard', *Oxford Journal of Legal Studies* 30 (2010), 1. In listing these writings I am plagued by the thought that the responsibility that their authors had in mind is not my basic kind and not even *their* basic kind. Any debate in which responsibility-talk looms large tends to be held up for want of shared conceptual foundations. All one can do is what I have done here, namely set out one's conceptual stall and await the probable response: 'That wasn't the kind of responsibility I had in mind.'

we had sufficient reasons to do as we did, or to think as we thought, or to feel as we felt, or to want as we wanted, and that was why we did so. But sometimes, at any rate where our actions are concerned, we lower our sights. Our self-explanatory aims are no more than excusatory. We concede that we were not justified in doing as we did, but we hope to reveal that we nevertheless did as we did on the strength of justified thinking, feeling, or wanting. Our reasons for acting were insufficient, we concede, but we had sufficient reasons for taking them to be sufficient or treating them as sufficient—either for taking them to exist when they did not, or for exaggerating their importance when they did. We were misled by credible testimony, or we were consumed with grief, or we were harassed and pestered to the point of losing our cool, etc. Such excuses are our first fallback when we lack justifications.[29] I am not suggesting that basically responsible people always have *good* or *adequate* or *convincing* excuses. I am suggesting that, lacking good justifications, they are disposed to *look for* good or adequate or convincing excuses, and in the process to show that they remained reason-responsive even when, in the round, they acted contrary to reason. Renoir's aphorism conveys this nicely—'tout le monde a ses raisons'—and his film plays up the following implication in fine style. Not everyone has good, adequate, convincing, or even valid reasons for what he or she does; but everyone, every basically responsible agent, has (i) what he or she takes to be some reasons for what he or she does, and (ii) some reasons, however pathetic and unconvincing, for taking them to be reasons for doing it.

The human tragedy that Renoir has in mind is the extent to which reasons to think and feel and want can draw us, quite rationally, into rational failure at the point of action, i.e. into doing what we have no, or too little, reason to do. Or if you don't like the word 'rational', which economists have stolen from the English language to use in their own technical sense for their own nefarious ends, you can substitute the friendlier word

[29] I am here reprising points I developed at greater length in my *Offences and Defences*, above note 16, ch 6.

'reasonable', the word that Rawls chose.[30] The tragedy, to put it in these friendlier terms, is that even perfect reasonableness is not enough to protect us reliably against doing something seriously unreasonable. All of us are vulnerable to being lured by thoughts, feelings, and wants that we had ample reason to harbour into doing things that we had far too little, or even no, reason to do.

Using the language of reasonableness here may draw our thoughts back to the negligence standard. And so it should. In the law, acting negligently means acting in a way in which someone would not have acted if they had taken reasonable care.[31] In common parlance, acting negligently means something simpler. It means simply acting without taking reasonable care. The difference between the two ideas is interesting and worthy of our attention. But it is not what concerns us here. What concerns us here is the 'reasonable care' standard that is common to both the legal and the extra-legal version. Is this fundamentally a justificatory standard or an excusatory one? Part of the attraction of the negligence standard, as a device for the law, is precisely its plasticity on this front. 'Reasonable care' may be interpreted to mean 'such care as leads one to reasonable action'. That makes it a quasi-justificatory standard. Or it may be interpreted to mean 'such care as one might reasonably be minded to take', where this is consistent with doing something unreasonable, thanks to reasonable misjudgment, reasonable temptation, reasonable concern, etc. This makes the standard a quasi-excusatory standard. By and large the law gravitates towards the quasi-justificatory version, but leaves itself some latitude to make quasi-excusatory allowances for error, for example for less than perfect expertise or skill or resilience. We can all think of negligence cases in

[30] Although Rawls gave it a meaning much more idiosyncratic than I have in mind: see his 'Kantian Constructivism in Moral Theory', *Journal of Philosophy* 77 (1980), 515 at 528–30.

[31] Thus the so-called 'duty of care' in the law of torts is not exactly a duty to take reasonable care. It is a duty to do whatever a taker of reasonable care would do. Ori Herstein made this point in his 'Responsibility in Negligence: Why the Duty of Care is *Not* a Duty "to Try"', *Canadian Journal of Law and Jurisprudence* 23 (2010), 403 at 412–14, criticizing my analysis in ch 5 above. I am not entirely convinced that his criticism makes as big a difference as Herstein thought. Chapter 5 has been modified slightly to explain why.

which such allowances were made.[32] We may worry that the allowances are hard to marshal into settled rules, or at any rate that the law has failed so to organize them. For someone worried about so-called 'legal certainty' that is a problem with the negligence standard. For most of the law's purposes, however, the standard's plasticity is a distinct selling-point. The negligence standard allows for quasi-excusatory allowances to be made *ad hoc*, in response to particular concatenations of facts, without having to generalize. Indeed the central role that modern tort law has found for the negligence standard owes a lot to the space that the standard leaves for unruly responses to particular concatenations of facts, not only in the making of quasi-excusatory allowances, but in various other ways as well. The negligence standard helps to block the pesky transformation of questions of fact, including questions about what we have most reason to do or think or feel or want, into questions of law, governed by rules that treat only selected features of the case as determining the answer.[33] The quasi-excusatory cases are good examples. Why are quasi-excusatory arguments allowed to figure in some negligence cases but not in others? There is, by design, very little law on the subject.

You may wonder why I have recently started to add the prefix 'quasi' in front of the words 'justificatory' and 'excusatory'. Here is the explanation. When someone claims to have taken reasonable care, they may of course be asserting that they were justified or excused in what they did. But sometimes they are saying something a bit different. They are denying that any justification or excuse is called for. They are saying that they did nothing wrong, and so don't have anything to justify or excuse. In that case, what would otherwise count as either a justification or an excuse for wrongdoing has instead been anticipated in the very ingredients of the wrong. Although non-negligence sometimes serves as a

[32] Miscellaneous common law examples: *McHale* v *Watson* (1966) 115 CLR 199; *Mullin* v *Richards* [1998] 1 WLR 1304; *Surtees* v *Kingston upon Thames Borough Council* [1992] 2 FLR 559; *Cook* v *Cook* (1986) ALR 353; *Bolam* v *Friern Hospital Management Committee* [1957] 1 WLR 582; arguably, because very close to the borderline, *Roe* v *Minister of Health* [1954] 2 QB 66.

[33] See my lengthy discussion in Chapter 9.

distinct legal defence, justificatory or excusatory, to some legal wrong that does not have negligence as an ingredient, the negligence standard is often incorporated by the law into the ingredients of the wrong. Questions that might, outside the law, be treated as arising at the stage of justification or excuse ('Why were you on the wrong side of the road anyway?' 'Why didn't you get a second opinion like I suggested?' 'What was the big hurry?' etc.) are transferred over into the determination of whether a wrong (a tort, a breach of contract, etc.) was committed by the defendant in the first place.

The explanation for this transfer is not straightforward. I will mention some aspects of it in the final section of this lecture. The explanation does not, however, make much difference to the point that I am currently developing. Whether or not incorporated into the ingredients of the wrong, the negligence standard is a reasonableness standard. One may invoke it in the course of justifying or excusing a wrong or in the course of denying that one committed a wrong. Either way one displaces the charge of negligence by pointing to the adequacy of one's reasons and that means explaining oneself in the currency of reasons. As soon as one explains oneself in the currency of reasons, one holds oneself out as having been basically responsible. If the explanation points to reasons that one actually had, either reasons for one's action or reasons for taking oneself to have reasons for that action, one was indeed basically responsible for the action. Possibly the reasons will turn out to have been adequate to acquit one of negligence, or possibly not. That is irrelevant. One is basically responsible either way, just in virtue of the fact that one was answerable to reasons in respect of the action. One's basic responsibility is confirmed, therefore, by the mere fact that the question of one's negligence arose. It did not depend on one's actually having been negligent. To adapt a terminology often favoured by lawyers, basic responsibility is basically strict responsibility. Negligence is an added extra.

6. Assigning responsibility for negligence

From the fact that basic responsibility is basically strict responsibility it does not follow, of course, that legal liability should likewise be basically strict liability. That further claim, if sound, lies a long way down the road.[34] Its soundness depends on what the ingredients of various legal wrongs should be, and on which justifications and excuses, if any, should be available to those who commit them. Possibly (although I doubt it) those who are not at least negligent should never face legal liability, for every unintentional legal wrong should either have negligence as an ingredient or non-negligence as a defence. If that is so, the explanation has nothing to do with any limit on our basic responsibility for our actions. There is no metaphysical limit in the immediate neighbourhood. If there is a limit, it is a political one. It concerns the principles on which assignable responsibility should be assigned to us by the law.

To help with further reflection on this point, consider the following remark by Neil Levy:

> It is only reasonable to demand that someone perform an action if performing that action is something they can do rationally; that is, by means of a reasoning procedure that operates over their beliefs and desires. But what agents can do rationally in this sense is a function of their internalist reasons [i.e. reasons they are aware of, or could become aware of thanks to other reasons they are aware of].[35]

I have various quarrels with what Levy says here, and with further conclusions that he draws. But here is something that he gets exactly right. Where negligence is concerned, the principal question is about *what it is reasonable to demand*. Some demands we make of basically responsible agents are unfair or unjust demands. Others are ineffective. Yet others are a sledgehammer to crack a nut. There are many possible lines of objection to the demands we make of each other. The point is that these are all lines of objection that are addressed to *us as the demanders*. They presuppose that there is someone who is doing some demanding of the agent, such that the question of the unfairness or stupidity of doing that demanding can arise. In the relevant demands, the agent may of

[34] You will hear echoes here of Tony Honoré's famous 'Responsibility and Luck', *Law Quarterly Review* 104 (1988), 530, which has influenced me greatly on the topic of this lecture and on many other topics besides.

[35] Neil Levy, *Hard Luck: How Luck Undermines Free Will and Moral Responsibility* (Oxford 2011), 128.

course mistakenly be held to be basically responsible, or she may mistakenly concede her own basic responsibility. Such a mistake may indeed be unfair or stupid on the part of the person making it. But a person's actually *being* basically responsible for an action, say an action that they did not know they were performing, is not the kind of thing that can be unfair or stupid. Nobody assigns basic responsibility to them, so there is nobody who is being unfair or stupid, let alone unreasonable, in connection with their possession of it. Basic responsibility is simply a fact of human life, such that those who lack basic responsibility are lacking something which, as human beings, they ought to have.[36] You'll see from that formulation that I don't mean basic responsibility to be somehow a value-free fact of human life. (Are there any?) As I said before, it is valuable to be basically responsible inasmuch as being basically responsible represents the partial achievement of one's human *ergon*. The point is only that our being basically responsible is not subject to certain types of evaluations. We cannot intelligibly complain, for example, that basic responsibility is unfairly distributed, such that I keep finding myself basically responsible for actions that I did not know I was performing. Nobody distributes it and so the question of the fairness of its distribution does not arise.

When parents point out to their children that 'life isn't fair', I hope they don't mean to suggest that life is *un*fair. I hope they mean to suggest that it's a mistake—a category mistake—to hold life up to the light of fairness. People can be unfair; so can institutions; so, perhaps, can societies.[37] But people and institutions and so on can qualify as unfair, or for that matter as stupid,

[36] For some excellent unpacking of these points and their implications, on a much wider philosophical front, see Angela Smith, 'On Being Responsible and Holding Responsible', *Journal of Ethics* 11 (2007), 465.

[37] Friedrich Hayek invested much in the idea that societies are not agents, and thus cannot themselves be charged with injustice/unfairness: *Law, Legislation, and Liberty, Volume 2: The Mirage of Social Justice* (London 1976), ch 9. I tend to agree. Yet Hayek paid too little attention to the obvious next point that there can be injustice in the way in which people and institutions, who clearly are agents, respond to bad social conditions. This is what we normally mean when we speak, somewhat elliptically, of 'social injustice'. We do not need to think of society as an agent in order to do it.

intolerant, mean-spirited, etc., only inasmuch as they are agents, capable of responding wrongly to reasons. What is called for is precisely basic responsibility. Only a basically responsible agent can be unfair, stupid, intolerant, and so on. Life cannot be unfair, stupid, intolerant, etc., for life is not an agent. Thinking of life as an agent, like thinking of luck as an agent, is as instance of what Ruskin branded 'the pathetic fallacy'.[38]

Inasmuch as Levy is concerned with the role of negligence in responsibility, then, it cannot be basic responsibility that he has in mind. It must be assignable responsibility. He is arguing—now without any category mistake—that it is unreasonable to assign assignable responsibilities to people which are such that they could fail in them, or could retroactively be held to have failed in them, without any negligence on their part. As a general proposition that strikes me as far-fetched. We know, because I already pointed out, that it is sometimes true that the negligence standard is incorporated into the ingredients of the wrong, such that, if one was not negligent, one did nothing wrong and one has nothing to justify or excuse oneself for. But there are also cases, as I explained, in which one offers a justification or excuse for something one did wrong, a justification or excuse that centres on the fact that one was not negligent in doing it. For that to be possible, there must be a possibility of wrongs that do not have negligence as an ingredient. There must, to put it another way, be possible assignable responsibilities that do not pass Levy's test—responsibilities, for example, for seeing to it that the parcel will actually arrive today and did actually arrive today, never mind when one thought it would arrive and what led one to think that and how reasonable it was to think that, etc. Maybe such 'strict' responsibilities are always somewhat unfairly assigned to those who have them. But as I said before, that simply points to the need for a suitably strong case for assigning them, one that suffices to overcome the objection of unfairness.

And in fact, it is hard to see the unfairness in the assignment of strict responsibilities as such. It all depends on what one thinks the consequences are going to be of failing in them. Maybe Levy, for example, is tending to think of punishment, condemnation,

[38] Ruskin, *Modern Painters, Volume III* (New York 1863), ch 12.

resentment, and all that blaming jazz. But these blaming cases are exactly the cases in which one's justifications and excuses for failing in one's responsibilities as a responsible agent should be listened to, and in suitable instances regarded as exonerating. These cases are not the right place to begin; something has gone badly wrong with our priorities if they are where we look first when we think about responsibility.[39] We should begin with apology, reparation, and restitution, and the complex psychology of blameless but responsible agency that Bernard Williams discussed under the heading of 'agent-regret'.[40] It may sometimes be unfair for people to be forced to apologize, to have damages extracted from them, to be criticized for the paucity of their feelings, and so on. But is it also unfair or otherwise rationally questionable, do you think, for them to *volunteer* their apologies, to *insist on* paying for the damage, to *merely rue* their part in the day's events, and so forth? If that doesn't seem so unfair, could the explanation be that the problem is not, after all, with the strict responsibilities themselves, but with the clumsy way in which the normative consequences of failure in such responsibilities are managed by others? Could it be too much heavy-handedness in the way the responsibilities are identified, marked, and upheld, rather than the responsibilities themselves?

To see if you think that the problem is with the responsibilities themselves, ask yourself this. Ask yourself whether you regard it as unfair that I should be the one who owes you an explanation in the currency of reasons, that I should be the one who owes you a justification or excuse, for what I did to you. If I do sometimes owe that much to you, then my blameless acts are already capable of landing me in a tricky position. They are capable of landing me in the position in which I should justify or excuse myself to you, and hence assert my blamelessness. Is that unfair? Not, it seems to me, where the assignable responsibility was mine and I was basically responsible for failing in it. Being the one to answer for failures in your assignable responsibilities

[39] J R Lucas, 'The Ascription of Actions', available at http://users.ox.ac.uk/~jrlucas/ascript.html (accessed 20 August 2016 and held on file).

[40] Bernard Williams, 'Moral Luck', *Proceedings of the Aristotelian Society Supplementary Volume* 50 (1976), 115 at 123–7.

goes with the territory of being a rational creature. *Pace* Levy, I do not owe a justification or excuse for 'an action [only] if performing that action is something [I] can do ... by means of a reasoning procedure that operates over [my] beliefs and desires'.[41] Rather, that this action was the best I could manage given my beliefs and desires, and given what led me to have those beliefs and desires, is the very thing that I will cite *in making* my justification or excuse. My basic responsibility and my assignable responsibility for what I did are both taken for granted when my justification or excuse—say my argument that I was not negligent—is put on the table.

You may say that the conclusion here is not exactly what I promised. Fundamentally, as it turns out, the negligence standard belongs neither to the conditions of basic responsibility nor to the conditions of assignable responsibility. It belongs to the world of justification and excuse that opens up once responsibility, in both senses, is established. But I'm not sure that I promised otherwise. I think I promised to conclude that, *inasmuch as* the negligence standard belongs to the conditions of responsibility at all, it belongs to the conditions of assignable responsibility, not to the conditions of basic responsibility. And that is indeed our conclusion. When the question of negligence comes up in connection with responsibility—as opposed to in connection with justification or excuse—it comes up under the heading of assignable responsibility. It bears on whose responsibility it is to do which things, always assuming that all involved are basically responsible for their actions. Do I have the assignable responsibility in law not to drive into the path of your car? No. My responsibility, at most, is not to do so negligently. Do I have the assignable responsibility in law not to leave your gas boiler poorly ventilated after I service it? Quite possibly. The case is different from the first. It could well be a breach of statutory duty case rather than a negligence case and the responsibility assigned to me by law could well be strict. But there is no doubt that I am basically responsible for my failure either way. Negligent or not, and ultimately legally liable or not, it falls to me, the benighted gas installer, to explain myself in the currency of reasons. It is no obstacle to my being in

[41] Levy, *Hard Luck*, above note 35, 128.

this position that, thanks to some fault in the venting kit or failure in my measurement gear, I wasn't to know what I had done until it was too late to have avoided it. That *is* my explanation. I was the gas installer; it was my job; my failure is mine to account for, subject only to my possessing the basic human ability to account for it.

7. Negligence and legal policy

Why might the law sometimes assign us strict responsibilities and sometimes negligence-limited responsibilities? The explanation is political, not metaphysical. Sometimes, as in the case in which I drive out in front of your car, we are both in the same role so far as the law is concerned. We are both drivers and we have, fundamentally, the same responsibilities to each other. These include the responsibility not to cause accidents. But who caused this accident? That, alas, is not so clear. Or rather, insofar as it is clear, that is because of a rule that we inherit mainly from the law. It is a rule that the law uses to attach the (legally relevant) causation of accidents to particular drivers, and it attaches that causation according to negligence. That rule is not, of course, the only rule in play. Things are a bit more complicated. There are various rules of *res ipsa loquitur* that allow negligence to be deemed when certain other rules of the road, legal and otherwise, are violated. And there are various rules in the Road Traffic Act and the Highway Code and custom among road users on which the identification of negligence may turn. Yet the central organizing rule remains the negligence rule. It is needed because, without it, the situation of colliding drivers is very often too symmetrical to allow assignable responsibility, in respect of the avoidance of particular accidents, to be assigned. Even when all the more specific rules of the road are considered, often we do not have enough to determine who, for the purpose of liability to pay for the damage of the other, was the cause of the accident. The law's central rule, it seems to me, simply assigns the assignable responsibility, hence the role of accident-causer in law, to whichever of the two drivers was negligent, building the negligence in turn on failure to observe various other rules of the road, some legal, some not, about the significance of painted lines, signage, indicator lights, speed, road position, etc.

This is a common arrangement in the modern law of torts not only in the traffic case, but more generally. In other cases, however, the law may reflect an asymmetry of roles. Gas engineers and the householders for whom they provide boiler repairs do not need the negligence standard to differentiate them. They are already differentiated by the fact that only one of them is a gas engineer (or, in derivative cases, holds himself out as a gas engineer) and the law can make that differentiation without waiting to see how either person handles the interaction between them. It can assign a strict responsibility to the engineer for ensuring that the boiler is adequately ventilated. Should it do so? Many considerations including the extent of the hazard from poor ventilation, the difference in relative expertise between typical gas engineers and their typical customers, the existence of a licensing and certification scheme, the availability of professional indemnity insurance, the availability of carbon monoxide alarms, and so forth, bear on the choice of arrangements for assigning responsibility.[42]

It has not been my aim here to defend the use of the negligence standard in driving cases and the rival 'strict' standard in boiler repair cases. Indeed it has not been my aim here to defend the use of the negligence standard in some cases and not in other cases. My aim has been to show you what kind of considerations bear on the choice. Not only are considerations of this kind the ones that matter when assignable responsibility is assigned by the law. Considerations of this kind are also the ones which bear on who has assignable responsibility even before anybody, including the law, assigns it. Such considerations bear, in other words, on the role that the negligence standard plays in everyday life outside the law, as well as in the law.

I hope that you can now see what kind of considerations they are. They are, in the widest sense, political considerations. They

[42] For current English law on the subject, which I do not purport to be summarizing in the text, see the Gas Safety (Installation and Use) Regulations 1998 and the Enterprise and Regulatory Reform Act 2013, s69(3). Under the 2013 Act tort liability in respect of gas installation, and other health and safety matters, has substantially shifted away from the strict liability model that I sketched and towards a negligence model akin to the one prevailing on the roads. That is an object lesson in the politics of assignable responsibility: compared with strict liability, negligence liability is 'deregulation'.

relate to the desirability or appeal or merit or attractiveness of the arrangements whereby some people have responsibility for some things, and others have responsibility for others. They point to the fairness, the efficiency, or more generally the reasonableness, of responsibilities being carved up in that way, or in some other way. They do not relate to the tragedy of the human condition or the impossibility of our escape from our rational nature. They do not belong to the metaphysics of basic responsibility. They belong instead to the politics of assignable responsibility.

8

THE MYSTERIOUS CASE OF THE REASONABLE PERSON

1. Reasonableness and justification

Who is the 'reasonable person', that 'excellent but odious character'[1] who seems to inhabit every nook and cranny of the common law? Until I read Arthur Ripstein's extended treatment of the subject,[2] I thought I knew the answer. I generally understood the word 'reasonable', in legal contexts, to mean no more and no less than 'justified'. A reasonable action is a justified action, a reasonable belief is a justified belief, a reasonable fear is a justified fear, a reasonable measure of care is a justified measure of care, etc. By the same token, the common law's reasonable person (I fondly thought) is none other than a justified person, i.e. a person who is justified in all those aspects of her life that properly call for justification. She is justified in her actions, her beliefs, her fears, the measure of care she takes, and so on. Thus, to say that one's actions or beliefs or emotions or attitudes, etc. were those of the reasonable person is merely to say, in a typically roundabout lawyer's way, that one's actions or beliefs or emotions or attitudes, etc. were justified ones.

It may be thought that at least some of the law's uses of its reasonableness standard plainly defy this interpretation, so that it should not have taken a philosophical virtuoso like Ripstein to alert me to its deficiencies. What about the familiar cases, mentioned in even the most pedestrian of criminal-law textbooks, in which a defendant's living up to the law's reasonableness standard furnishes her only with a legal *excuse*, and not a legal justification, for what she does? For example, isn't the provocation defence to murder, which depends for its availability on the defendant's having reacted reasonably to the provocative behaviour, plainly

[1] A P Herbert, *Uncommon Law* (London 1935), 4.

[2] Arthur Ripstein, *Equality, Responsibility, and the Law* (Cambridge 1998).

Torts and Other Wrongs. John Gardner, Oxford University Press (2019). © John Gardner
DOI: 10.1093/oso/9780198852940.003.0008

an excusatory rather than a justificatory defence? True enough. But this does not yet go to show that 'reasonable', in the law of provocation, means anything other than 'justified'. To benefit from the provocation defence, the defendant must have 're-acted reasonably' only in the sense that he must have been justified in losing his temper to the point at which he was apt to kill. Naturally this does not entail that he was justified in killing. At best his justified loss of temper serves to excuse the killing. Like an unjustified action on the strength of a justified belief, an unjustified action on the strength of a justified emotion is sometimes excused. In the law's rendition of such margin-of-error excuses, the fact that the relevant belief or emotion has to be justified before it can excuse is expressed by saying that it has to be reasonable. So even here, in the realm of legal excuses, 'reasonable' still means no more and no less than 'justified'. This, at any rate, has always been my interpretation.

I will call this the *open* interpretation of the law's reasonableness standard. It does not associate that standard with any particular class of justificatory considerations nor any particular mode of justificatory argument. It leaves completely untouched the (so to speak) 'substantive' question of *which* considerations and arguments will do the justificatory trick in which legal contexts.[3] Ripstein's book, as I understand it, challenges this open interpretation of the law's reasonableness standard. I don't mean that Ripstein denies that the law's reasonableness standard is a standard of justification. The point, rather, is that he aims to represent it and defend it as one *particular* standard of justification. 'The idea of reasonable persons,' he writes near the start of the book, 'expresses a *distinctive conception* of normative justification.'[4] It is a conception, to be exact, that is 'specific to political morality, rather than dependent on a more comprehensive moral or metaphysical account'.[5]

Here (as elsewhere in the book) Ripstein echoes the Rawlsian claim that there exists a special 'public' standard of justification,

[3] A recently renewed defence of the open interpretation is Neil MacCormick, 'Reasonableness and Objectivity', *Notre Dame Law Review* 74 (1999), 1575.

[4] *Equality, Responsibility, and the Law*, above note 2, 8, emphasis added.

[5] Ibid, 12.

a standard to be invoked by those occupying official public roles such as that of judge or civil servant. The distinctiveness of this standard lies in the fact that it can be relied upon and defended without adjudicating the soundness or unsoundness of the various other standards of justification that different people may (as it were) 'privately' subscribe to. An action that is justified according to one person's private moral beliefs (or one person's 'conception of the good', to use the authentic Rawlsian expression) may well be unjustified according to another person's. In such cases, surely, at least one of the two is necessarily making at least some moral mistakes? Perhaps so.[6] But the Rawlsian public standard of justification declines to hold all of one's mistakes against one, even if they are mistakes that make a decisive difference to how one acts. For, as Ripstein explains,

> political morality, the morality governing the exercise of force, has its own standards of responsibility that may well be out of place in other moral contexts.... To talk about responsibility as political in this sense is an application of the familiar liberal strategy of separation. This strategy has its origins in Locke's *Letter Concerning Toleration*, which seeks to show how we can regard toleration as a special duty imposed by the office of magistrate, and so in no way incompatible with taking one's own religious views seriously.[7]

Ripstein's rendition of Locke's thesis emphasizes its continuity with the Rawlsian project. It foregrounds the distinction between those official (public) roles in which people are called upon to judge others and the non-official (private) roles in which they do the same. It associates the proper fulfilment of the former roles with a suspension of the standards of justification—even if, for the sake of argument, they are sound standards—that are incidents of the latter roles. For as an occupant of the former roles one properly invokes only a special public standard of justification that is not allied with any particular private moral beliefs (or conceptions of the good), whether they be sound or unsound. It is this special non-partisan public standard of justification, as

[6] Although I doubt it. I touch on some of the grounds for doubting it in my 'The Virtue of Charity and its Foils' which is ch 1 of Charles Mitchell and Sue Moody (eds), *Foundations of Charity* (Oxford 2000).

[7] *Equality, Responsibility, and the Law*, above note 2, 5, and 12–13.

opposed to any other, that Ripstein claims to find embodied in the common law's ubiquitous reasonable person.

So what *is* this special non-partisan public standard of justification? Ripstein gives it to us straight: 'the reasonable person in [the law's] sense is . . . the person whose actions display appropriate regard for both her interests and the interests of others'.[8] So now we know. Or do we? I must admit that when I encountered this short summary statement of Ripstein's central thesis, two thirds of the way through the book, it was a slightly disorientating moment for me. I had the feeling that, even though I had by this stage followed him on many exhilarating philosophical adventures and learnt much of lasting worth in the process, I had not come as far as I thought I had. I still had not grasped exactly *where* Ripstein parts company with the open interpretation of the law's reasonableness standard, and so *in what respect* the justificatory standard supported by his 'liberal strategy of separation' is supposed to be a 'distinctive' one. Indeed I began to wonder whether, in spite of his ingenious and sustained efforts, Ripstein ultimately fails to make progress with what I called the 'substantive' question, and hence (for all his other philosophical successes) fails to bring to fruition (what I took to be) the core project of his book. Let me explain why.

Any attempt to justify oneself, in any context, is an attempt to show that one did not defy the balance of reasons. More precisely, it is an attempt to show that the following three conditions were met: first, that there were reasons for one to do as one did (or think as one thought, feel as one felt, etc.); secondly, that these reasons stood *undefeated* by conflicting reasons; and, thirdly, that one did as one did (thought as one thought, felt as one felt, etc.) *for* one of these undefeated reasons. This much is built into the very idea of justification.[9] People who have different moral beliefs may disagree, of course, about which reasons stand undefeated in which conflicts of reasons. Occasionally they may

[8] Ibid, 192.

[9] The third condition is controversial. I have defended it against some objections in my 'Justifications and Reasons' in A T H Smith and A P Simester (eds), *Harm and Culpability* (Oxford 1996). But nothing that follows turns on this defence, since Ripstein's proposals all relate to conditions one and two.

even disagree about whether some factor counts as a reason at all, undefeated or otherwise. But people's disagreements on these substantive points matter to them only because they agree that if a certain reason existed and stood undefeated in a certain case, then in following that reason one was entirely[10] justified. So (with ϕing standing as a placeholder for acting, believing, desiring, hoping, feeling, deciding, and all other aspects of our lives that answer to reason and hence call for justification) we could further spell out the open interpretation of the law's reasonableness standard thus:

(J) One ϕs reasonably if and only if one ϕs with justification, i.e. if and only if one ϕs for an undefeated reason.

As we saw, Ripstein officially rejects this interpretation. He thinks that the reasonableness standard in law is a *particular* standard of justification, one that adds a measure of *substance* to (J). And here, apparently, is the substance that it adds:

(PJ) One ϕs reasonably if and only if one ϕs with *public* justification, i.e. if and only if one ϕs with 'appropriate regard for both [one's own] interests and the interests of others'.

But does this really add any substance? Does it focus our justificatory attention on some particular class of reasons or some particular way of counting them? Or does it still say as much and only as much as (J) does? What logical space, in other words, divides the injunction to act (etc.) only for an undefeated reason from the injunction to act (etc.) only with appropriate regard for everyone's interests? This I came to regard, towards the end of the book, as the enduring mystery of Ripstein's reasonable person. The reasonable person, we are told at the start, embodies not just a justificatory standard but a *particular* justificatory standard. But what exactly *is* particular, I came to wonder, about the justificatory standard that she embodies?

I will sketch six possible solutions to the mystery, which enjoy varying degrees of support in Ripstein's text. They are by no means mutually exclusive. But I am not clear how combining

[10] For simplicity's sake: Whenever I speak of justification in this paper I mean complete justification.

them would mitigate, as opposed to compounding, their several difficulties. And difficulties they certainly have.

2. Reasons and interests

Some may say that they cannot see any mystery at all. It is blindingly obvious how Ripstein's interpretation of the reasonableness standard in (PJ) departs from the open interpretation in (J). It is one thing to give *reasons* their due importance, some may say, but quite another thing to give *interests* their due importance. But in what respect, exactly, is this 'quite another thing'? One possibility is that there are interests that are not reasons, or the importance of which is not (only) their importance as reasons. The converse possibility is that there are reasons that are not interests, or the importance of which is not (only) their importance as interests. The first possibility is intriguing. Are there some things that are good for me and yet never open to intentional pursuit by anybody, myself included? Are there some blessings that can only be idly counted, and never, even in principle, sought? Maybe there are.[11] But the possibility is of little use to Ripstein. 'Displaying appropriate regard' for everyone's interests doesn't mean, for him, idly counting everyone's blessings. Rather, it means giving everyone's interests their due importance *in one's practical reasoning*, i.e. as reasons for one's actions, or at least as reasons for the beliefs or emotions or attitudes, etc. on the strength of which one acts. So interests are clearly relevant to public justification, as indeed to any kind of justification, only insofar as they are also reasons.

This leaves us with the converse possibility, the possibility that reasons are meant to be relevant to public justification, and hence to reasonableness, only insofar as they are also interests. Ripstein's thought may be that there are some reasons that are not reducible to anyone's interests, and that these are admittedly relevant to private justification but fall to be discounted on both sides of the justificatory equation (i.e. both as pros and as cons) for the purposes of public justification. Could this be what Ripstein has in mind

[11] Timothy Macklem and I have raised doubts about this possibility in our essay, 'Reasons' in Jules Coleman and Scott Shapiro (eds), *The Oxford Handbook of Jurisprudence* (Oxford 2002).

near the start of the book when he writes that the law's 'primary concern is not with the quality of a person's will or character, but with the external aspects of action'?[12] Are the 'external aspects of action' those aspects of action that affect people's interests, while the 'quality of [one's] character' is an independent evaluative variable?

I am not quite sure what to make of this contrast. Think again, if you will, about the margin-of-error excuses granted by the criminal law, such as provocation and duress. The gist of these excuses is that, although unjustified in what one did, one was justified in getting so enraged (in the case of provocation) or so terrified (in the case of duress) that one ended up doing it. Another way to put exactly the same point, and the way the law often prefers to put it, is in terms of the character traits one manifested. In doing as one did one was not being too hot-headed, one was not being too lily-livered, etc.[13] When the law invokes such standards of character—often billed as those of the reasonable person—it does no more and no less than invoke its own standard of justification for emotions (beliefs, attitudes, etc.). So if the legal standard of justification for emotions (beliefs, attitudes, etc.) is indeed a test of 'appropriate regard for interests', as Ripstein claims, then that is also, necessarily, the legal standard for judging the quality of our characters. Against this background, the suggestion that the quality of our characters is not what the reasonableness standard in (PJ) is 'primarily concerned with'—and that it is in this respect a more particular standard than that set by (J)—is a hard suggestion to fathom.

Maybe the real suggestion is that the reasonableness standard in (PJ) is not concerned with the *further* value of one's good character, meaning the value that being sturdy or temperate or diligent or honest, etc. brings to one's own life *quite apart from* the interests of oneself and others that it equips one to negotiate properly. Whether there is any such further value in a mastery of (other) values is a perennially troublesome question. I share with Aristotle and Kant the view that there is. But this view, whether

[12] *Equality, Responsibility, and the Law*, above note 2, 4.

[13] For further discussion, see my paper 'The Gist of Excuses' in *Buffalo Criminal Law Review* 1 (1988), 576.

in its Kantian or its Aristotelian variant, yields no plausible examples of reasons that are divorced from interests. If the further value in question is indeed brought *to one's own life* by one's own virtues of character then necessarily it is in one's interests, all else being equal, to be virtuous. These interests are among those that Rawls aptly calls our 'highest-order interests'.[14] They are part and parcel of our master-interest in being rational beings, beings equipped to cope with reasons (and hence with other interests). Indeed this further value that my virtues of character bring to my own life seems to be an example, not of something that is a reason for me but is not in my interests, but on the contrary an example of something that is in my interests but is not a reason for me. Can I exhibit any virtue of character in acting with a view to exhibiting that virtue? I am not sure that I can. Arguably this is just moral self-indulgence, not virtuous behaviour at all. My highest-order interests, in other words, seem not to count as reasons for me to serve them. That they are served by what I do is a blessing that can be counted but not sought (by me, in doing that thing). But this does nothing to drive a logical wedge between (J) and (PJ), given that (as I explained above) interests are clearly only relevant to (PJ) insofar as they are also reasons. What we are still looking for, in order to drive a logical wedge between (J) and (PJ), is an example of *a reason that is not equally an interest*, and a reason that accordingly figures in the balance of reasons mentioned in (J) but not (or not without some adjustment of weight) in the balance of interests mentioned in Ripstein's (PJ).

I do not deny that such reasons exist. Nobody, it seems to me, can have an interest in anything that is not valuable quite apart from his or her interest in it. To be exact, something is in one's interests only to the extent that (i) it is anyway valuable and (ii) one has the capacity to participate (or to come to participate) in its value. If something is not in many people's interests this could of course be a bad reflection on its value independently of their interests. But it could just as well be a bad reflection on the relevant people's capacities to participate in that value. Should we conclude that one's reasons to write great music or literature or

[14] See e.g. John Rawls, 'Kantian Constructivism in Moral Theory' in his *Collected Papers* (Cambridge, Mass 1999), 303 at 312.

philosophy are comprehensively at the mercy of other people's limitations? If one could equally devote one's life to writing exceptional works that few will ever be able to get anything out of, or else respectable but unexceptional works that will be accessible and enjoyable to millions, could one ever be justified in opting for the former course? True, there may be indirect effects to take account of. Perhaps one's work, although itself not widely appreciated, will contribute over time to improvements in people's critical capacities and hence create space for future exceptional work to be better appreciated (so that it better serves people's interests). Or perhaps writing for a small constituency of *cognoscenti* is also doing one's bit to contribute to the vibrancy and variety of public culture, something which is in the interests of all including those for whom one's own work and work like it will never be remotely accessible. This is an aspect of the *public* interest. These additional interests may indeed improve the interest-based case for pursuing the more purist path in one's creative work. But the question remains: *Need* one make a purely interest-based case for pursuing that path? Or is there also scope to plead the sheer quality of one's work, quite apart from anyone's interests that may be served by it, as part of the rational case for engaging in it? It seems to me that there is such scope. That being so, the balance of all interests affected by one's work is not the whole balance of reasons for and against engaging in it. Here a logical wedge *can* be driven between (J) and (PJ).

So far as I can see, however, Ripstein does not attempt to drive this particular logical wedge between (J) and (PJ) anywhere in *Equality, Responsibility and the Law*. It does not seem to be implicated in any of his examples. He gives us no reason to suppose that the law's reasonableness standard would, or should, block the argument from sheer quality where it applies, insisting on hearing a purely interest-based case instead. To discover whether it would, one would probably need to shift attention away from the private law and criminal law contexts that so interest Ripstein, and consider the use of the reasonableness standard in public law settings instead. If a public body is charged with dispensing funding to the arts, would it be acting 'as no reasonable public body would act', and hence be susceptible to *certiorari*, if it gave weight to the sheer quality of the artistic endeavours that it proposes to fund as well as the way in which these endeavours or the funding of them would impact on the various interests involved (including the public interest)? It is an interesting question which to the best of my knowledge has not been properly tested in the courts. But I see nothing in the existing legal authorities, nor for that matter in Ripstein's arguments, to suggest that the law's reasonableness standard need rule out in advance the public pursuit of sheer artistic quality or other similar objectives (e.g. accomplishment in sport). Such pursuit might, of course, be ruled out by the legal remit of *particular* public bodies, but that is not the same as its being ruled out by the reasonableness standard itself.[15] So far as I can see, the law's reasonableness standard would and should be perfectly open, in such a case, to the possibility of justification other than purely in terms of the interests affected by the impugned action (including the public interest). Thus, insofar as (PJ) does depart from (J) in the respect just discussed, we have no reason to think that (PJ) represents a superior interpretation of the law.

3. The element of risk

Perhaps the answer to our mystery lies in identifying a special way of counting the interests that count under (PJ)? Many passages in Ripstein's book are devoted to emphasizing and illustrating the relationship between reasonableness and *risk*. For instance, in his bravura discussion of the tort of negligence at common law, he writes:

> The reasonable person provides the standpoint from which a general distribution of risks can be applied to particular circumstances.... [I]n deciding liability, courts must decide whether a person showing appropriate regard would have taken a particular risk into account.[16]

We may be reminded here of an old debate about the role of probability in practical reasoning. 'It's going rain this evening',

[15] To put the point in terms of English administrative law, this would be an *Anisminic* (jurisdictional) challenge rather than a *Wednesbury* (reasonableness) challenge. The cases are *Anisminic* v *Foreign Compensation Commission* [1969] 2 AC 147 and *Associated Provincial Picture Houses* v *Wednesbury Corporation* [1948] 1 KB 223.

[16] *Equality, Responsibility, and the Law*, above note 2, 56.

I explain to my disappointed friends as I cancel my barbecue. Against all odds, the rain doesn't show up. My cancelling the barbecue turned out to be the depressing waste of a good party. So did I really have the reason I said I had to cancel my barbecue? People's conceptual intuitions diverge sharply on the point. Some think that, to the extent that reason and value go hand-in-hand, the reasons for doing anything correspond in force to the *actual* value of doing it, meaning the action's value as things turn out (in this case the depressing waste of a good party). Others go straight to the *probable* value, assessed at the time of acting, to divine the force of the reasons (in this case, the avoidance of what will probably be a depressingly bad party). On this second view, the force of the reason varies according to how probable it is at the time of performance that, if the action is performed, the value in question will materialize. Personally, I tend towards the first ('actualist') view. Does Ripstein, with his persistent emphasis on risk, perhaps lean towards the opposite ('probabilist') view? It is hard to be sure. Even actualists naturally find many subsidiary roles for probabilistic variables in practical reasoning. For example, relying on rules of thumb that mention probabilities may enable one to maximize one's conformity with certain reasons over time. Where that is so, the rules themselves serve as (further) reasons for acting in accordance with them.[17] That it is going to rain this evening is no reason for cancelling the barbecue this evening since actually it isn't going to rain. But that one should, as a rule, avoid taking serious risks of depressingly bad parties could be a perfectly valid reason for cancelling the barbecue under the conditions described, even for an actualist like me. So is Ripstein perhaps an actualist like me, but one who regards the law's reasonableness standard (at least as it figures in defining the tort of negligence) as the legal rendition of a certain sound probabilistic rule of thumb, or as the legal consolidation of various sound probabilistic rules of thumb, that maximize conformity over time with the (logically prior) reasons

[17] Some writers have contrasted 'mere' rules of thumb with real or proper rules, claiming that the former serve only as reasons to believe that one has reasons to act, and not—like real or proper rules—as reasons to act in their own right. Fred Schauer nicely outwits this way of understanding rules of thumb in his *Playing by the Rules* (Oxford 1991), 104–11, while leaving intact the original thought that a rule of thumb is a special type of rule.

we have not to do things that actually bring injury (misery, loss, etc.) to other people?[18]

The question need not detain us for long. Determining whether Ripstein is a probabilist or an actualist wouldn't in itself help us to see what the difference is supposed to be between (PJ) and (J). For there is no reason to think that the view he takes on how probabilities come to be relevant to the law's reasonableness standard (and hence to public justification) is different from the view he would take on how probabilities come to be relevant to practical reasoning (and hence to justification more generally). Nevertheless Ripstein's emphasis on probabilities points to another possible explanation of the contrast that he means to draw between (PJ) and (J). Whatever the correct resolution of the probabilism v actualism debate, that debate arises only in connection with consequence-based reasons, i.e. reasons for or against one's actions residing in the fact that those actions will or may have certain valuable or disvaluable consequences. When we turn to the *intrinsic* value or disvalue of one's actions, and the reasons to perform those actions that reside in that intrinsic value or disvalue, there is no question of being a probabilist or an actualist. This is particularly important in view of the fact that many reasons commonly thought to be consequence-based in the relevant sense are not. Rather they are reasons corresponding to the intrinsic value or disvalue of certain actions that are partly constituted by their *results* (e.g. promise-keeping, giving to charity, killing).[19] Such intrinsic results-based reasons, unlike their consequence-based peers, cannot vary in force according to the probability at the time of performance that if the action in question is performed its results will materialize. For if the results do not materialize, the action in question is not performed at all. The question of how probable it is that the results would materialize if the action were performed is then a silly question; the answer is always, of necessity, 100% certain.

It does not follow, of course, that there can be no intrinsic reasons, to the force of which probabilities are relevant. On the

[18] I defended the logical priority of such reasons in chapter 5.

[19] I borrow this semi-technical terminology of 'consequences' and 'results' from G H von Wright's *Norm and Action* (London 1963), 39–41.

contrary, my intrinsic (non-consequence-based) reasons to climb Etive Mor have greater force than my intrinsic reasons to climb Ben Nevis precisely thanks to the fact that the former climb is more risky, i.e. that my coming a cropper is more probable. I am a serious mountaineer and I need a challenge. The example helps to show that probability bears on intrinsic reasons in a different way from the way in which it bears on consequence-based reasons. In the case of consequence-based reasons it is at least plausible to think—as probabilists do think—that the greater the probability of a certain (dis)value in the event that I perform a certain action, the more reason I have (not) to perform that (one and the same) action, all else being equal. By contrast, intrinsic reasons to perform actions constituted by probabilities (e.g. super-risky as opposed to moderately risky climbs, safe as opposed to unsafe sex, gambles on the stock exchange as opposed to savings in a deposit account) are just reasons to perform different actions. There is no *further* probability variable that can be used to adjust the force of the intrinsic reasons to perform those actions. Without the probability element that goes to make them up they would not be *those* actions, and so would not be the actions that one has (*ex hypothesi*) intrinsic reasons to perform. So in respect of these non-consequence-based reasons there is no conceivable probabilism v actualism debate to be had. The probabilism v actualism debate, to repeat, is a debate about how we are to count an action's consequences, and only its consequences.[20]

These remarks bring us straight to the key question: By emphasizing probability in the way that he does (i.e. in the way that persistently implicates the actualism v probabilism debate) does Ripstein mean to eliminate all non-consequence-based reasons for action from the arena of public justification of those actions, while leaving open the importance of those non-consequence-based reasons to the justification of those same actions by non-public standards? In other words, are people's 'interests', in the sense in which the term figures in (PJ), all of them logically independent of the actions that advance or retard them, so that it

[20] Thus it is not surprising that, in modern times, the debate has been mainly an internecine one among utilitarians and their ilk. See e.g. David Braybrooke, 'The Choice Between Utilitarianisms', *American Philosophical Quarterly* 4 (1967), 28.

is always an open question whether, when those actions are performed, the interests in question will actually be advanced or retarded, and so that the advancement or retardation of those interests is always a consequence rather than a result of the action in question? Some of Ripstein's arguments in the 'tort law' chapters of his book—chapters two to four—led me to think so at first. Most significantly, he takes his arch-adversaries in those chapters to be some writers whom he strangely dubs 'libertarians' but whose relevantly objectionable disposition appears only to be that they favour a system of tort liability based on intrinsic wrongs that are partly constituted by results, to the exclusion of instrumental wrongs tailored to the minimization of bad consequences (as well as to the exclusion of hybrids straddling the two types of wrongs). One might think that the main problem with such people, if they really exist, is that they are fanatics.[21] In which case one might think that what they need to refute them is simply a firm reminder of the obvious fact that consequence-based reasons are also reasons, and can sometimes make a difference to the rules that one should follow, and hence to the wrongs that one commits. Instead, however, Ripstein appears sometimes to be replacing their fanaticism with his own rival fanaticism, according to which the whole terrain of tort liability is to be structured by probabilities—risks—understood in their distinctively consequentialist role (i.e. as they are debated in the actualism v probabilism debate). Wouldn't this be a rather extraordinary gambit? Since the most crazy thing about these so-called libertarians appears to be the fat wedge that they drive between (J) and their version of (PJ) (according to which no consequences count) it seems unpromising to respond by conjuring up a version of (PJ)

[21] Do they exist? Ripstein identifies only Richard Epstein by name as being a 'libertarian' in his approach to tort law. However Epstein always conceded that once one has identified an intrinsic wrong (e.g. D's hitting P) the question of justification (a.k.a. reasonableness) may remain to be considered under the heading of defences, and here the (probable) consequences of D's action *do* count (in at least some cases) insofar as they lean in his favour. That being so, the difference between Epstein and Ripstein seems to be mainly that Ripstein carries over into the definition of the wrong matters that Epstein regards as extraneous to it, but still in principle relevant to the associated liability. See Richard Epstein, 'A Theory of Strict Liability', *Journal of Legal Studies* 2 (1973), 151.

that drives an equally large wedge on the opposite side (so that nothing *but* consequences counts). A more obvious reaction, you might think, would be to stick with (J) in its raw form, driving no wedge at all, and allowing that *all* practical reasons, be they consequence-based or otherwise, are in principle relevant to the shape of tort law as a whole, and to the shape of its reasonableness standard in particular.

Just a little further reading reveals, however, that Ripstein is not the fanatic consequentialist that I have just described. He is not even close. Even in the early 'tort' chapters there are many signs that people's interests, in the (PJ) sense that we are looking for, are at least sometimes non-consequence-based reasons for action. Or at least, there are many signs that in Ripstein's view people have interests in respect of their *own* actions other than those that reside in the consequences of those actions, and these intrinsic interests in their own actions people can in principle plead by way of justification, under the reasonableness standard in (PJ), for what they do to other people. Thus:

> [F]rom the perspective of the reasonable person, injuries are differentiated in part on the basis of the burden to liberty that precautions against them pose. Each person accepts a certain level of risk in return for a measure of liberty; each accepts a restriction on liberty in return for a measure of security.[22]

We will be coming back to these particular interests in liberty and security under heading (4) below. Suffice it to say, for the moment, that an interest in being at liberty to perform a certain action is hard to reduce to an interest in that very same action's consequences, and Ripstein does not seem to mean it to be so reduced. It is not long, indeed, before Ripstein goes further still down the non-consequentialist road. When he shifts his attention to criminal law doctrine he reveals that in his view people's interests in respect even of *other people's* actions need not reside in the consequences of those actions. His excellent discussion of rape, in particular, makes clear that he includes as interests pertinent to the law's reasonableness standard at least some interests that are not logically independent of the action that retards or advances

[22] *Equality, Responsibility, and the Law*, above note 2, 51.

them. That sexual intercourse is an 'essentially consensual activity' in which we have a legally relevant interest *qua* consensual means that rape has as its *result*, not as its consequence, a setback to the victim's interest for the purpose of (PJ).[23] So in spite of his strong reaction to the so-called 'libertarians' in chapter two, Ripstein eventually joins them in recognizing the legal importance of intrinsic wrongs, including intrinsic wrongs constituted by results, even if (for some reason that I have failed to grasp) he regards such wrongs as having a more central role in the criminal law than in the law of torts. So there is no sign here of a logical gap emerging between (J) and (PJ). The latter, it seems, is not designed to be more narrowly consequentialist than the former.

4. A further element of risk

Even when he shifts his attention to the criminal law, Ripstein endeavours to maintain his claim that 'the reasonable person provides the standpoint from which a general distribution of risks can be applied to particular circumstances'. How does he do it? Consider these passages from his valuable discussion of self-defence as a justification:

> Asking whether the assailant really did pose a threat is a ... misleading line of inquiry. Suppose I come at you, firing a loaded gun. Unbeknownst to either of us, the remaining bullets in the chamber are flawed, and will not fire. Such an attack must pass any test of reasonable fear, even if chance events make it turn out that I do not pose a mortal danger to you. To put the point differently, we might say that imminent attacks do not always materialize. Rather, an attack is imminent if it is sufficiently likely to happen, even if, for reasons unknown to the parties involved, it would not actually have happened.[24]
>
> [To summarize:] the person who behaves in a way that others would reasonably take to be life-threatening is posing a threat to that person's life [in the sense that matters to the law]. As a result, defensive actions against such a person are justified.[25]

Ripstein seems to be making two proposals here. One is that, for the purposes of the law's reasonableness standard, justification is

[23] Ibid, 204–5. [24] Ibid, 193. [25] Ibid, 196.

largely probabilistic rather than actualistic, in the sense explained under heading (2) above. The reasons for and against an action, insofar as they lie in the consequences of that action, lie not in its actual consequences but in its probable consequences, with the rational importance of each probable consequence adjusted according to the probability, assessed at the time of action, that it will eventuate. But to this he now adds a second, and entirely detachable, proposal. The second proposal is that, for the purposes of the law's reasonableness standard, the probability at any given time of any consequence eventuating is a function of the then-available reasons for the agent who is being judged by that standard to *believe* that it will eventuate. For the purposes of justification according to the law's reasonableness standard, in other words, probability is to be equated with *foreseeability* to the person claiming justification. So it is not to be held against the pre-emptive self-defender in Ripstein's example (call her D) that (thanks to the already-present flaw in the remaining bullets that makes them incapable of being fired) there is, at the time when she acts, no *real* probability of her being shot. The shooting is still 'sufficiently likely to happen' in the sense that matters to Ripstein, because according to the evidence available to D at the time it still *seems* sufficiently likely to happen. The available evidence (as Ripstein goes on to formulate his test) 'would lead a reasonable person to suppose', as D does suppose, that she is very likely to be shot if she takes no pre-emptive action, and the legal justification of her self-defensive reaction is, Ripstein clearly thinks, to be assessed relative to that reasonable person's supposition.[26] So there is a type of risk that matters pervasively to the law even in cases of intrinsic wrongdoing, and it is *epistemic* risk. It is the risk of having false beliefs about the facts, including (but not restricted to) the risk of having false beliefs about risks.[27] Thus even where one's action is wrong for reasons that need have nothing to do with the risk that one poses (e.g. in cases of rape) in acting one

[26] Ibid, 196.

[27] An excellent and relevant discussion of the differences between epistemic risk and 'objective' risk (as he calls it) is Stephen Perry's in 'Risk, Harm and Responsibility' in D G Owen (ed), *Philosophical Foundations of Tort Law* (Oxford 1995), 321 at 322–9.

is still subject to the risk that unbeknown to one one's action is wrong—because one makes a mistake about the circumstances in which one acts—and this risk properly becomes the new focus of one's justificatory arguments.

The second of Ripstein's two proposals—the equating of probability with foreseeability—is foreshadowed, as one would expect, in his discussion of the law of torts.[28] But only here in the discussion of criminal law do we see its crucial importance. By this equation those who act on reasonable (justified) beliefs are deemed to have performed reasonable (justified) actions, on condition that if those beliefs had been true their actions would indeed have been reasonable (justified). To my way of thinking, this proposal rides roughshod over the fundamental distinction between a justification and an excuse, the distinction that I tried to sketch out at the start of this paper. But maybe—you will say—riding roughshod over that distinction is the whole point of Ripstein's remarks. Isn't this where Ripstein's alignment with Rawls becomes most important? In Rawls' own work, after all, the standard of reasonableness is applied primarily to people's *conceptions of the good*, i.e. to their moral beliefs.[29] So on one plausible (but controversial) reading, Rawls' own version of (PJ) goes something like this. If people's actions are performed on the strength of justified moral beliefs which, if true, would serve to justify those actions, then those same actions are *publicly* justified even if, as it happens, the beliefs are false and so (privately) the actions would only count as excused, not justified.[30] Could this test, or something like it, be the one that Ripstein too has in mind for his version of (PJ)? If so, then we have been looking at the wrong words in Ripstein's summary statement of (PJ) to see how it differs from (J). Ripstein's thought is not that by referring to 'interests' (PJ) takes in a narrower range of reasons than (J), but

[28] For example, *Equality, Responsibility, and the Law*, above note 2, 104.

[29] For more discussion of Rawls' test see Joseph Raz, 'Disagreement in Politics', *American Journal of Jurisprudence* 43 (1998), 25 at 32–7.

[30] For passages supporting this interpretation see e.g. Rawls, 'The Priority of Right and Ideas of the Good' in his *Collected Papers*, above note 14, 449 at 459–65, 'The Domain of the Political and Overlapping Consensus' in *Collected Papers*, 473 at 475–8, and 'The Idea of Public Reason Revisited' in *Collected Papers*, 573 at 593–4 and 607–8.

rather that displaying 'appropriate regard' for reasons as required by (PJ) is not the same as giving them their correct weight or force as would normally be required by (J). It is a matter of giving them the weight or force that, quite possibly mistakenly, but at least with justification, one believes them to have.

Yet there are several question marks over this explanation. To my mind it does more to deepen than it does to dispel the mystery. Let me mention a few of the new puzzles that arise if we interpret Ripstein's (PJ) along these lines.

First, those mistakes, the defensive value of which Ripstein seems prepared to upgrade from excusatory to justificatory, are only reasonable mistakes *of fact*, not reasonable *moral* mistakes, i.e. mistakes about the relative importance of the interests that are at stake, given the facts as one reasonably believes them to be. Possibly Ripstein even goes so far as to deny that mistakes of the latter type *can* be reasonable mistakes. At any rate, to give people the benefit of such mistakes, he thinks, would be to allow each of us 'unilaterally [to] set the terms of his interaction with others', a measure which is (he thinks) the very antithesis of the reasonableness standard.[31] In this verdict Ripstein sides with the common law tradition (which does not make any concessions to moral as opposed to factual mistakes under the heading of reasonableness) against Rawls (for whom the most important use of the reasonableness standard is, on the contrary, to make concessions to people's moral mistakes). This makes one wonder how exactly the latitude for justificatory error that Ripstein allows in the case of the self-defender faced with the gun is supposed to contribute to the broadly Rawlsian rendition of the 'liberal strategy of separation' that Ripstein endorses earlier in the book. It also raises the suspicion that *pace* Ripstein, the most important issue is not whether one embraces the standard of reasonableness, or how one interprets it, but *what one applies it to*. Rawls and Ripstein are, after all, poles apart on the question of exoneration through error. Although both look kindly on action from reasonable mistaken belief, by elevating it under certain conditions from excused to justified, in doing so they each have in mind a different kind of mistake. That both happen to invoke the standard

[31] *Equality, Responsibility, and the Law*, above note 2, 181.

of reasonableness only goes to show, one may be tempted to conclude, that *anyone* can invoke that standard, for as it turns out the standard is none other than the entirely ecumenical 'open' standard mentioned in (J).

Secondly, in the first passage I quoted, Ripstein only says of D that, in view of her reasonable but mistaken assessment of the risk, her *fear* was reasonable. Perhaps so. But this is not the same as saying that her self-defensive *actions* were reasonable. She may have acted unjustifiably on the strength of justified fear, in which case her actions are still at most excusable. Is the reference to 'reasonable fear' rather than 'reasonable self-defensive action' just a slip of Ripstein's pen? Or is it that he *assumes* that actions out of reasonable (and hence justified) fear are reasonable (and hence justified) actions? If the latter then he would appear to assume his own conclusion (or rather the neo-Rawlsian conclusion that we are currently ascribing to him) namely that (some) excusatory arguments fall to be upgraded to justificatory ones for the purposes of official public judgment. Once again one may be led to wonder: In his concern to lend some substance to the reasonableness standard, does Ripstein sometimes overlook how much turns on what exactly it is that falls to be judged by that standard? In that vein, I wondered whether his equation of probability with foreseeability may garner some of its plausibility, at least to a lawyer's mind, from the well-known feature of the tort of negligence that one does not commit that tort so long as one takes all reasonable precautions against all reasonably foreseeable eventualities, never mind what care one takes against those eventualities that are probable but (thanks to the paucity of available evidence) not reasonably foreseeable.[32] Ripstein seems inclined to build this complex circumscription from the law of negligence into the law's reasonableness standard more generally. But isn't it more plausible to think that it is a circumscription local to the tort of negligence and its various offshoots? Why should we grant that probability (insofar as it is relevant at all) should also be equated with foreseeability in cases in which the question is not one of reasonable care, but rather one of (say) reasonable anger or reasonable belief or reasonable reliance? If we resile from this more

[32] *Roe* v *Minister of Health* [1954] 2 QB 66.

general equation (as I think we should) then the logical space that we had just hoped to find between (J) and (PJ), namely the space between 'giving correct weight' and 'displaying appropriate regard', promptly evaporates.

Thirdly, even if we are tempted by Ripstein's view that D's actions are to be classed as reasonable (and hence justified) actions, the explanation may partly stem from reasons that are in play *other* than the one on which Ripstein focuses our attention. Arguably someone who is prepared to go around firing guns at people, faulty or otherwise, fully deserves his comeuppance when someone eventually fires back. Arguably people who show attenuated concern for others are morally estopped from complaining when attenuated concern is shown for them. And so forth. Of course the criminal law does not let our self-defender act *for* these reasons. She must act for the sake of self-defence. But it does not follow that, when she does act for the sake of self-defence, the case for her having done so is not enhanced by these other reasons which have nothing directly to do with the risk she imagined was posed to her, on the strength of which she acts. Arguably, indeed, these independent reasons are among the reasons why people are given the legal right to act in self-defence in the first place. It means that one may be inclined to regard the case sketched by Ripstein as sitting quite near to the borderline between justification and excuse quite independently of Ripstein's explanation of how it comes to be there. Ripstein presents the case as one in which a justificatory drift comes of the fact that a reasonable person would think the attack life-threatening. This is what entitles D, thinks Ripstein, to a public upgrade of her defence from excuse to justification. But the justificatory drift which makes such an upgrade tempting might equally come from quite separate undercurrents in the story, lending spurious plausibility to the thesis that, for the purposes of public justification according to (PJ), people are to be judged on the facts (including probabilities) as they reasonably believed them to be rather than on the facts *tout court*.

Finally, one may well ask: What would be the *benefit* to reasonably mistaken self-defenders like D of upgrading from excuse to justification a line of defence to a criminal charge which is (by common consent) to be allowed to them anyway? One can immediately see the possible value for Rawls of treating all reasonable conceptions of the good as if they were correct. This move grounds a constitutional doctrine of non-discrimination as between true moral beliefs and false but reasonable moral beliefs. To be exact, on the Rawlsian doctrine, public officials may not count people's reasonable moral beliefs against them (nor indeed their actions on the strength of those beliefs) merely because the beliefs in question are false ones. But what corresponding advantage does Ripstein's doctrine confer on anyone, given that an acquittal for D is admittedly going to be the result whether or not his doctrine holds? One answer might be that it matters not only *that* one is acquitted but *why* one is acquitted. True enough. An acquittal based on justification is worth more to any self-respecting human being than an acquittal based on excuse.[33] But by the same token no self-respecting human being is going to be much cheered by her excuse being *deemed* to be a justification for public purposes. Being self-respecting, she wants to be *really* justified, not to be condescended to by having the public standard of justification dropped down a notch or two so that she finds it easier to meet it. There is no self-respect in living up to a standard that was manipulated to make it easier for one to live up to it. My general impression is that these considerations of self-respect do not in any case cut much ice with Ripstein, any more than (in spite of his protestations) they cut much ice with Rawls. Both authors tend to think, as many lawyers do, that what really matters is whether one ends up incurring liability (or some other adverse normative consequence), never mind how low the law would have one stoop, morally speaking, to avoid it. In keeping with that outlook, Ripstein's only suggestion as to why it matters publicly to assimilate the case of the self-defender faced with the gun to justification rather than to excuse seems to be that this might affect the incidence of *tort* liability. 'Consent and self-defence,' Ripstein writes, 'differ from other defenses to a criminal charge in that the successful defense will also be sufficient to defend against a tort action.'[34] Maybe they do. Yet it is far from clear why, in order to hold that some pleas of *mistaken* self-defence are likewise sufficient to defend against a tort action, one must go to the length

[33] See further my discussion in 'The Gist of Excuses', above note 13.

[34] *Equality, Responsibility, and the Law*, above note 2, 190.

of making an official shift in the boundary between justification and excuse. It seems likely to me that just as some justificatory arguments do *not* avail in tort, some excusatory arguments *do* avail in tort. Whether a defensive argument avails in tort does not depend, so far as I can see, on whether it is a justificatory or an excusatory argument. It turns on other factors. To some of these factors I will be returning under heading (6) below. For present purposes the point is only that in order to give D a full defence to an action in tort, it is surely not necessary to deem her actions to have been justified according to the special public standard in (PJ), if they would not have been justified anyway according to the more ecumenical standard in (J). An excuse may already suffice.

5. Liberty and security

As we saw before, Ripstein sometimes mentions two particular interests that he regards as being implicated in the common law's reasonableness standard, namely people's interests in liberty and security. On first encounter I took these merely to be his stock examples of interests that might be at stake alongside countless others. But after they had been mentioned over and again, especially but not only in the chapters on the law of torts, I came to think that perhaps these were meant to be regarded as the *only* interests relevant to the law's reasonableness standard. So maybe this proposal takes to the heart of the intended difference between (PJ) and (J):

> The basic strategy for dividing risks [so far as the reasonableness standard in (PJ) is concerned] is to look to the interests in both liberty and security that all are presumed to share. If neither liberty nor security interests are to totally cancel the significance of the other, some balance must be struck between them.[35]

I find it hard to assess this proposal, and will comment on it only rather sketchily. That is because Ripstein never fully explains why these particular interests rather than others have been singled out for attention, and consequently never spells out how broadly or narrowly they are to be conceived. True, he tells us that the

[35] Ibid, 50.

two interests mentioned have been singled out to play something like the role that Rawls ascribes to his 'primary goods', namely to provide some kind of common currency in terms of which to compare and negotiate (what are thought to be) people's widely divergent and often incommensurable ultimate interests when those interests come into conflict.[36] That being so, Ripstein's narrowing of attention to liberty and security provokes many of the same anxieties that were already provoked by Rawls' narrowing of attention to primary goods.[37] But it also raises additional questions. Why is Ripstein's list of interests mentioned in the passage just quoted so much shorter than Rawls' list of primary goods? Why is it shorter than the list of primary goods that Ripstein himself seems to embrace when he comes to discuss *social* justice at the end of the book?[38] What has happened to what Rawls called 'perhaps the most important primary good', namely self-respect?[39] Are 'liberty' and 'security' the names of two interests or the names of two types of interests, such that we can go on to provide longer lists of interests that fall under them? It is clearly a shorter list than Rawls' list of primary goods but is it a narrower one too?

Here is the only explicit measure of clarification that I could find in *Equality, Responsibility and the Law*:

> Most liberty and security interests are utterly uncontroversial. Security from bodily injury is obviously important, as is the liberty to come and go one pleases. In order to fill out the idea of protecting people equally, though, a more detailed account is required. The amount of care that is required of a person is set in relation to specific risks. In general the fact that my injury might causes you some injury is not sufficient to require me to take care. Nor is the fact that my liberty is at stake sufficient to require you to bear risks. Instead the question is whether or not I exercise appropriate care with respect to specific risks.[40]

[36] Ibid, 273.

[37] For instance, those of Thomas Nagel in 'Rawls on Justice', *Philosophical Review* 82 (1973), 220 at 228–30, and those of Amartya Sen, 'Equality of What?' in his *Choice, Welfare and Measurement* (Oxford 1982), 353 at 364–7,

[38] Ripstein, *Equality, Responsibility, and the Law*, above note 2, 273–8.

[39] John Rawls, *A Theory of Justice* (Cambridge, Mass 1971), 386.

[40] *Equality, Responsibility, and the Law*, above note 2, 51.

We return under heading (5) below to Ripstein's 'idea of protecting people equally'. Right now our concern is only with the 'more detailed account' that Ripstein sets out to provide of the interests that he designates as liberty and security interests. The remarkable thing (I thought the weakest aspect of the book by a long way) is that having told us that this 'more detailed account' is required, he goes on provide no such account. Instead he changes the subject. He returns to talking about how our liberty and security interests are to be *counted* under (PJ), and so far as I could detect never tackles the quite distinct question of what exactly our liberty and security interests *are*. Even his claim that most examples of such interests are 'utterly uncontroversial' is unintelligible until we find out—as we never do, so far as I could see—what they are supposed to be uncontroversial examples *of*. The possibilities, at least on the security side, are endless. Talk of my security interests could refer (most narrowly) to my distinct interest in not having my existing life disrupted. But at the other extreme (most generally) it could refer to the whole range of my interests in what is done to me and what happens to me (what might be called my 'patient-interests'). Thus not only the disruption of my existing life but also my suffering disability, loneliness, pain, stress, homelessness, hunger, betrayal, deceit, rape—anything at all I can suffer—invades my security interests, whether or not it disrupts my life.[41] So we could be looking at a nitpickingly narrow category or a breathtakingly broad one—or anything in between—and which of these it is will make all the difference to how far (PJ) differs from (J). Will there be any patient-interests left out of the (PJ) calculation? If not then in

[41] The longer list of nasty things that may happen to me or be done to me cannot simply be embraced within the narrow security interest in not having my existing life disrupted. I have an interest in not suffering disability, betrayal, rape, and so on even if I am used to it or ignorant of it, so that my life goes on much as before. It is worth noticing that Ripstein classifies the interest in not being raped as a security interest in his *Equality, Responsibility, and the Law*, above note 2, 213 n70. I assume he means the interest in not being raped *per se*. That the interest in not being raped *per se* is a different interest from the interest in not having one's life disrupted *by* rape was the main thesis of a paper I co-wrote with Stephen Shute called 'The Wrongness of Rape' in Jeremy Horder (ed), *Oxford Essays in Jurisprudence—Fourth Series* (Oxford 2000). Are both security interests, in Ripstein's sense?

respect of patient-interests, (PJ) will simply reduce once again to (J). I do not want to claim that it does so reduce. I just want to claim that Ripstein tells us nothing that would allow us to decide whether it does so or not. So he tells us nothing that would enable us, in this dimension of patient-interests, to tell (PJ) apart from (J). This makes it hard to believe that we have found, in the special emphasis he places upon security interests, one of the core respects in which Ripstein means (PJ) to peel apart from the more ecumenical (J).

Things are a bit different when we come to liberty interests, because the concept of liberty is in some respects less elastic than that of security. Liberty interests are clearly interests we have as agents, rather than as patients. They are (as I put it before) intrinsic interests we have in our own actions. But equally clearly our liberty interests do not exhaust our possible agent-interests. Our liberty interests are interests in being able to do other things apart from the things we actually do. We are at liberty to the extent that there are such other things that we are able to do. Being 'able' to do other things in this context means, on some views, having the capacity and the opportunity to do those things and, on other views, merely having the opportunity to do them, with much debate consequently raging about what exactly is to be regarded as a lack of capacity rather than a lack of opportunity.[42] Whatever the outcome of such debates, our liberty interests in this sense clearly contrast with our patient-interests. But they also contrast with another set of agent-interests, namely our interests in doing the things that we actually *do*. As well as my liberty interest in being *able* to do so on occasions when I do not, I also have an intrinsic interest in actually doing things: an interests in participating in arts and sports that I am good at, in not betraying my friends, in having real sex rather than just the simulation of it, in spending a sunny afternoon on the beach, etc. I finally came to the conclusion, while reading *Equality, Responsibility and the Law* for a second time, that Ripstein really did intend such

[42] The debate over whether lack of capacity as well as lack of opportunity limits one's liberty is one of many debates rather arbitrarily collected under the umbrella of 'positive liberty v negative liberty' in Isaiah Berlin's 'Two Concepts of Liberty' in his *Four Essays on Liberty* (Oxford 1969), 118.

non-liberty agent-interests to be excluded from the range of things to which reasonable people would have regard according to (PJ). He never says anything that could be construed as making space for them on the reasonable person's horizons. What I found harder to fathom, because actually he never says anything about them *full stop*, was whether non-liberty agent-interests were excluded from the balance of interests under (PJ) because Ripstein does not think they exist—so that for him they would not count under (J) either—or whether they were excluded from (PJ) in spite of their known existence—thus marking a real asymmetry for Ripstein between (J) and (PJ).

You may say that it must be the latter, because we have already seen that Ripstein believes in at least some non-liberty agent-interests. But have we? True enough, we saw under heading (2) above that Ripstein believes in the existence of some intrinsic wrongs, such as rape. But that doesn't commit him to the view that the agents of intrinsic wrongs have an intrinsic interest in not committing them. It is perfectly compatible with the view that the only interests set back by the commission of intrinsic wrongs are the (security) interests of the victim in not being thus wronged. And true enough, we also saw, under heading (1) above, that Ripstein does draw attention to people's 'highest order' interests, as Rawls calls them, in the condition of their own characters. Since one's character is partly constituted by the action in which one exhibits it, it follows that Ripstein does mention some non-liberty agent-interests, and does so with a view to excluding them from the ambit of (PJ). But what is unclear (you will recall) is whether he recognizes these interests *as interests*. And even if he does (you will also recall) it is not clear that these interests could be relevant to (J), so it is not clear that their exclusion from the balance of interests under (PJ) could represent any kind of asymmetry between (J) and (PJ).

The absence of these non-liberty agent-interests from Ripstein's arguments creates a shadow difficulty for him in his handling of liberty interests themselves. Perhaps the most basic and enduring philosophical question about liberty interests is this: Can it be in one's liberty interests that one is able to perform actions, the actual performance of which would not be in one's non-liberty agent-interests? At many points in his argument, Ripstein ought to have encountered this question. At many points in his argument, he assumes that people have a liberty interest in being able to do some shabby things, and that in determining what it is reasonable for such people to do, their liberty interest in doing the shabby thing in question has to be reckoned in the balance of interests under (PJ) as a counterweight to other people's various interests in their not doing it. Take the 'restriction on liberty' that people are said to accept 'in return for a measure of security'.[43] What we are talking about here is one person's liberty to be utterly careless about other people's fates. Is that a liberty in which they have an interest, and the restriction of which they accordingly have reason to avoid? True, they may, on occasions, have patient-interests in the profits that will come to them if they do it, in the time that is freed up when they do it, etc. They then have reason to avoid their loss of profit or loss of time, etc. But that is not the issue. The issue is whether they have reason to regret this loss of liberty *as such*, i.e. the very fact that they no longer have the alternative of treating other people like dirt, irrespective of whether that is what they would actually have done. I tend to think—although the matter is complicated—that they do not have such an interest. But it does not matter so much whether we are sure about the answer. The important point is that we are sure about the question. The question is: Do we already need to have something like the reasonableness standard in place before we can work out which of their liberties people have an agent-interest in and which not? If we do need the reasonableness standard as part of this adjudication, then one thing is for sure. *Pace* Ripstein, people's liberty interests cannot be the main reasons weighing on their side in determining whether their actions towards others would count as reasonable, for until we know whether their actions towards others would count as reasonable, we do not know whether they have any liberty interest in performing them, and hence any liberty interest to weigh on their side in determining whether to perform them. The suggestion helps us to see one reason why (if we must think in terms of primary goods), self-respect might turn out to be 'the most important primary good'. For our liberty interests, on the proposed account, are interests only in being able

[43] *Equality, Responsibility, and the Law*, above note 2, 51.

to do things that we could do with our self-respect left intact. It would not follow, of course, that the law should deny us our liberty to betray our friends, have simulated rather than real sex, or waste our talents. It would only follow that, when the law should leave us at liberty to do these things, that is not because we have a liberty interest in being able to do them.

6. Equality

So much for security and liberty. How about equality? It may seem remarkable that so far our discussion has not touched upon the idea. Equality, after all, is the *leitmotif* of Ripstein's book and has pride of place in its title. 'Reasonableness,' Ripstein even says at one point, 'is a description of the world from a particular perspective—the perspective of equality.'[44] So perhaps, to isolate exactly where Ripstein parts company with the open interpretation of the reasonableness standard in (J), we need to isolate an interpretation of (PJ) that would make it more *egalitarian* than (J).

One possible role for equality in (PJ) we can put on one side right away. Ripstein is not one of those who think that people have a distinct interest in equality in addition to their other interests. He does not mean to add 'equality' to the list after 'liberty' and 'security'. Those who believe that people have a distinct interest in equality are those who believe that the fact that A treats B in a certain way is a reason for A to treat C in that same way.[45] If A misjudges the rational importance to be attached to B's interests and therefore treats B worse (or better) than he was justified in doing, then according to this egalitarian doctrine A now has a reason to give C a similarly bad (or similarly good) deal. That new reason may tip the balance in such a way that A is now justified in doing to C what he was (*ex hypothesi*) unjustified in doing to B (and would often by the same token have been unjustified in doing to C, were it not for the additional consideration of equality). In other words, the standard for the proper treatment of each person

[44] *Equality, Responsibility, and the Law*, above note 2, 199.

[45] The best discussion I know of this kind of egalitarianism is Derek Parfit, 'Equality and Priority' in Andrew Mason (ed), *Ideals of Equality* (Oxford 1998).

comes to be dictated, in part, by the actual treatment meted out to other people, even though it was not itself proper treatment.

This egalitarian doctrine, if it were Ripstein's doctrine, would have interesting ramifications for the (PJ) injunction to have 'appropriate regard for both [one's own] interests and the interests of others'. For whether one is reasonable in one's treatment of other people would now depend, at least in part, on how one treats *oneself*. If one were too reckless or too cautious in respect of one's own life and limb, for example, then this would help to justify one in being similarly reckless or similarly cautious (as the case may be) with the life and limb of others. In some passages in which he stresses 'reciprocity' as an element of reasonableness Ripstein may seem to be flirting with this (as I think, immoral) doctrine.[46] But when it closes in on him he adeptly resists its charms. On encountering George Fletcher's one time view that in the law of negligence 'security [is] protected only in cases where risk imposition is nonreciprocal', he objects that 'driving at high speed might threaten security without violating reciprocity, provided that people all expose each other to the same unreasonable risk'.[47] If this counts—and I think it does—as Ripstein's repudiation of the thesis that A's bad behaviour towards B helps to justify B's similarly bad behaviour towards A, then presumably it counts *a fortiori* as his rejection of the doctrine that B's bad behaviour towards *B* (i.e. B's mistreatment of herself) helps to justify B's similarly bad behaviour towards A. I say *a fortiori* because the opposite conclusion would also be hard to square with Ripstein's repeated insistence that 'neither party may unilaterally dictate the terms of interaction'[48] as well as his claim that 'the reasonableness standard is not a concession to the defendant's particular limitations'.[49] It would also be impossible to square with the common law, which sets the standard of care that we each owe to each other in the law of negligence without any regard to the actual degree of care

[46] See e.g. *Equality, Responsibility, and the Law*, above note 2, 7.

[47] Ibid, 55, criticizing George Fletcher's 'Fairness and Utility in Tort Theory', *Harvard Law Review* 85 (1972), 537. Ripstein's criticism is a version of what Parfit calls 'the Levelling Down Objection' to egalitarianism: 'Equality and Priority', above note 45, 10.

[48] *Equality, Responsibility, and the Law*, above note 2, 188 and 194.

[49] Ibid, 193.

that we each happen to bestow upon ourselves (or for that matter upon third parties). The common law, in other words, does not hold that people have a distinct interest in equality that can tip the balance of their other interests. And nor, despite the prominence of the word 'equality' in his book's title and text, does Ripstein.

So to make the reasonable person's 'appropriate regard for . . . interests' more egalitarian, in the sense in which Ripstein is after, we clearly need to focus not on the list of interests to which she has regard, but the way in which she regards them. Should we perhaps read 'appropriate' in (PJ) to mean 'equal'? Possibly this is what Ripstein has in mind when he says that 'reasonableness is tied to the idea of equality'.[50] Possibly this is where he thinks that the 'distinctive' reasonableness standard in (PJ) parts company with the open interpretation of the reasonableness standard in (J). But if he thinks this he is mistaken. The substitution of 'equal' for 'appropriate' in (PJ) is either redundant or at odds with the law (and remember that (PJ) is supposed to interpret the law).

The substitution is redundant, to start with, if 'equal' simply means 'unbiased'. If someone is biased in the weight he gives to reasons then he does not give them their correct weight. He treats some reasons as defeated by countervailing reasons when in fact they are not, and others as undefeated when in fact they are. This being so, the open interpretation of the reasonableness standard in (J) already automatically includes a ruling against bias and adding such a ruling to (PJ) does nothing to show how (PJ) is meant to be distinguished from (J). Sometimes one has the impression that what worries Ripstein most is simply the prospect of self-centred people taking too many goodies (liberty, security, money, pleasure, etc.) for themselves at the expense of others—in other words leaning too much towards the pursuit of their own interests. One may well worry about this. But one need not invoke a 'distinctive conception of normative justification' to believe that when people take too much of something for themselves (whatever it may be), they take more of that thing than they are justified in taking. That really does go without saying. What could 'too much' mean here but 'more than is justified'? Of course this is not to deny that we still need to know how much

[50] Ibid, 7.

counts as 'too much' in a given case. But so long as 'equal' just means 'unbiased', a reference to equality doesn't help us to answer this question, for we can only know at what point we start giving too much weight to our own interests relative to those of others when we already know what weight is the correct weight to give to the various interests at stake—or in other words, when we answer the question raised by (J) of which reasons are undefeated. And when we answer this question we also answer the question of what would count as being unbiased. Beyond merely putting the latter question centre stage, the (PJ) standard, with 'appropriate' interpreted as 'equal', and 'equal' in turn interpreted as 'unbiased', still adds nothing to (J).

But here is a more textually credible way of reading all Ripstein's talk of equality. 'By supposing that all have the same interests . . . ', he writes at one point, 'the fault system treats parties as equals.'[51] So when he claims that the reasonable person standard in law is an egalitarian standard, does Ripstein perhaps mean only that it serves as a *levelled* standard, a standard that suppresses variations among different people's different interests in the way that it settles conflicts between them? Perhaps the proposal that I should give equal consideration to your interests means that your special (and in that sense 'unequal') interest in your fingers, as a concert pianist, is irrelevant to how much care I should take in my dealings with your fingers. Perhaps, according to Ripstein, I should treat your interest in your fingers as if it were merely the regular, non-concert-pianist interest.[52] Admittedly this proposal will strike a chord with anyone who is familiar with the tort of negligence at common law. The explanation of this resonance does not lie, however, in the fact that the tort of negligence is defined in terms of reasonableness. It lies elsewhere. In part, it lies in the complex two-stage way in which reasonableness figures in the tort's definition. Recall that the law of negligence asks us to *take reasonable precautions* to avoid all and only those (legally salient) injuries to others *that we can reasonably foresee*. What one can reasonably foresee depends on the ordinary standards of evidence

[51] Ibid, 50.

[52] Meaning the interest of a hairdresser? A master butcher? A tapdancer? A philosopher? Is there such a thing as a 'regular' interest in fingers?

and induction that apply to epistemic justification more generally. Barring the special circumstance in which I can justifiably infer that you are a concert pianist, the law of negligence does not give the fact that you are a concert pianist any significance at all. Not a reduced significance in proportion to the tiny glimmers of evidence that you are a concert pianist, notice, but no significance at all. But what if there is plenty of evidence, and I *can* justifiably infer that you are a concert pianist? Then the debilitation of your piano-playing abilities by the damaging of your fingers becomes a reasonably foreseeable eventuality. The measure of care I should take when I am dealing with your fingers—i.e. the measure of reasonable care—is correspondingly adjusted, at that point, for your special interest in your fingers. From now on I must be more careful with your fingers than I must be with some other people's fingers. Moreover, the requirement is not merely that I add a dash of extra care reflecting the extent to which it seems likely that you are a concert pianist. Now that we have passed the threshold of reasonable foreseeability, I must add extra care commensurate with your actually being a concert pianist, if that is what you really are.[53] Ripstein is mistaken if he thinks that the reasonableness standard allows for no such adjustment. In the law of negligence the second invocation of reasonableness not only allows for such adjustment but forces it upon the first.

What is true, of course, is that legal standards designed to govern many different interactions of many different people inevitably do make levelling assumptions about those people's interests. As Aristotle puts it, 'the law takes the usual case',[54] with the consequence that in *un*usual cases (e.g. those involving people whose livelihoods depend on their fingers never being harmed) legal rules tend to support rulings that would (apart from the broader rational case for having and using such levelling rules) be rationally indefensible. Clearly laws invoking the reasonableness standard share this built-in tendency to level everyone towards the usual case. But *pace* Ripstein they do not share that tendency *because* of their invocation of the reasonableness standard. On the contrary: they share it *in spite* of their invocation of the reasonableness standard. As H L A Hart famously explained, the resort

[53] *Paris* v *Stepney Borough Council* [1951] AC 367.

[54] NE 1137^{b}16.

to a reasonableness standard is actually one of the law's clever devices to reopen a bit of space for ordinary moral reasoning in a rule that would otherwise be apt to level it away.[55] The standard creates pockets of relatively fresh air in which lawyers and judges are free to argue on the facts of the actual, as opposed to the usual, case, and hence to adjust for special circumstances (including the parties' special interests). Why, after all, is the tort of negligence defined (indeed *doubly* defined) in terms of reasonableness? Mainly because the tort was forged to do yeoman service in coping with the many new conflicts of interest that arise in a modern society with increased mobility of capital and labour and a growing pace of technological change. The tort is shaped by the quest for maximum flexibility in coping with novel variations in people's circumstances, including novel variations in their interests. That not all such variations are accommodated—that the tort of negligence still does level people's interests to some extent—reflects the fact that the tort of negligence is not merely the tort of failing to be reasonable, *full stop*, as Ripstein occasionally seems to present it. Rather, it is the extremely convoluted tort of failing to take (reasonable) precautions to avoid all and only those legally salient injuries to others that we can (reasonably) foresee. I put the references to reasonableness in parentheses here to remind us just how much of the tort's definition remains even in their absence, and also to help confirm that their main job is to mitigate, not to compound, the law's tendency to level everyone to the 'usual' case. Without the first 'reasonable', in particular, wouldn't my fingers always necessarily count for exactly what a concert pianist's fingers would count for? And wouldn't that make the tort *more* egalitarian in the 'levelling' sense? In which case it comes close to inverting the truth to think that 'reasonableness is tied to the idea of equality' in that sense of 'equality'.

This despatches any thought we might have of reading 'appropriate regard' in (PJ) as 'equal regard'. That being so, I can think of only one further way to interpret Ripstein's repeated invocations of equality. Possibly when he says that 'reasonableness is a description of the world from . . . the perspective of equality', he does not mean that to be reasonable each of us must take the perspective of

[55] H L A Hart, *The Concept of Law* (2nd ed., Oxford 1994), 132–3.

equality in our dealings with others. Possibly he only means that the reasonableness standard *itself* takes that perspective. Possibly, in other words, Ripstein's talk of equality is just a shorthand reference to what I earlier called the 'non-partisan' character of Rawlsian public justification. Recall the Rawlsian view rehearsed above and apparently endorsed by Ripstein: Public justification, unlike its 'private' counterpart, is not aligned with a particular conception of the good, be it sound or mistaken. But recall also the key Rawlsian proviso: Not just *any* mistaken conception of the good is put on an equal footing with its sound counterparts, for it must also be a *reasonable* conception of the good to enjoy protection against official discrimination based on its unsoundness. It follows from this proviso that in order to determine what counts as an official being non-partisan in the relevant sense, one must first determine what counts as reasonableness on the part of those being judged by the official. That being so, one cannot also expect to determine what counts as reasonableness on the part of those being judged by the official by asking what would count as the official's being non-partisan. If we are to know what counts as reasonableness, in other words, it is no good telling us that it is the standard that would be applied by someone judging the agent 'from the perspective of equality', where this means 'without discriminating between reasonable people'. We do not know what would count as discriminating between reasonable people unless we already know, by some other means, who counts as a reasonable person in the relevant sense. Read in this way, Ripstein's invocations of equality would neither be redundant nor at odds with the law, but (assuming they are meant to help reveal what counts as reasonableness) they *would* be conclusory. They would restate, rather than resolving, the mystery that concerns us here.

7. Against aggregation

Ripstein's invocations of equality are at several points juxtaposed with rejections of an approach to justification that he calls 'aggregation'.[56] For example:

[56] He calls it aggregation at its first mention, viz. at *Equality, Responsibility, and the Law*, above note 2, 6.

> Rather than trying to balance ... interests *across* persons—supposing, in some way, that one person's gain can make up for another's loss—the fault system [in the common law of torts] balances them *within* representative persons.[57]
>
> My account of distributive justice ... employs the strategy of balancing ... interests against one another by weighing them within the representative reasonable person, rather than across persons.[58]

One wonders whether these remarks might point to a special way of counting interests beyond those encountered already, that would suffice to give (PJ) some special substance of its own?

Ripstein's remarks may bring to mind, first of all, Rawls' famous objection to trade-offs of one person's interests against another's. The basic utilitarian error, said Rawls, was that of 'extending to society the principle of choice for one man'.[59] With these words began the contemporary philosophical quest for a way of thinking about the many-person case which doesn't simply treat the many people in question as if they were one person. Is Ripstein joining that quest? It looks as though he is. But it is hard to fathom what rival way of approaching the many-person case he thinks he has found. How can it be a mistake to think about the many-person case on the model of the one-person case, and yet somehow not a mistake to turn the many-person case imaginatively *into* a one-person case by conjuring up an imaginary representative person who will act as the impartial repository of many people's interests? How does this procedure differ, exactly, from an *aggregation* of those many people's interests? How does Ripstein's reasonable person differ, in particular, from 'the impartial sympathetic spectator', whose presence in argument Rawls identifies as symptomatic of the basic utilitarian error he is diagnosing?[60] Personally I think that Rawls misdiagnosed the basic utilitarian error and thereby led a whole generation of political theorists to prescribe bizarrely misguided cures, many of which only served to aggravate the real malaise. So far as I can see the real malaise afflicting utilitarians (or at any rate afflicting those utilitarians that Rawls had in mind) was their amazing oversimplification of the one-person case. They didn't even begin to grasp what interests people

[57] Ibid, 50.
[58] Ibid, 266.
[59] *A Theory of Justice*, above note 39, 27.
[60] Ibid.

really have, let alone what further reasons for action people have that do not correspond to anyone's interests. If they had got near the truth on these matters, then their next move—that of assimilating the many-person case to the one-person case—would not have seemed anywhere near so questionable, and Rawls' criticisms of that move would never have had much plausibility. But all this is beside the point right now. Right now, the point is that Ripstein seems to endorse Rawls' diagnosis of the utilitarian error in one breath, but in the next breath seems to join the utilitarians in what he just diagnosed as their error.

This makes one wonder whether Ripstein really has a different problem in mind under the heading of 'aggregation'. Indeed his initial objection under that heading is to the idea 'that one person's *liberty* might have to give way to another's *security*'.[61] Is it possible that the real objection he has in mind is not to trade-offs between different people, but to trade-offs between different *interests* (e.g. between liberty interests and security interests), be they the interests of different people or of one and the same person? Is he borrowing a different anti-utilitarian bazooka from the Rawlsian armoury, namely the doctrine of *lexical priority*, according to which liberty is not to be sacrificed for anything apart from more liberty, be it one's own liberty or the liberty of another?[62] Is the point that, for the purposes of (PJ), only liberty-interests can override liberty-interests? No, this can't be the point either, for Ripstein again promptly embraces what he calls '[a]nother approach' to '*striking the balance* between liberty and security' (i.e. trading them off), namely by doing so 'within a representative person'.[63] So again we are back to the question of what the 'other approach' is. Ripstein's answer? Only that

> this approach expresses an idea of equality, for it aims to protect people equally from each other, by supposing all to have the same interests in both liberty and security.[64]

But this explanation, which is all that we have left of the anti-aggregation remarks, seems to have nothing whatever to do with

[61] Ibid, 6, emphases added. [62] Ibid, 52–6.

[63] *Equality, Responsibility, and the Law*, above note 2, 6, emphasis again added.

[64] Ibid, 6–7.

the acceptability of trade-offs among interests, either among the different interests of one person or among different people's interests. It is simply the proposal, already encountered under heading (5) above, that people's interests need to be *levelled* for the purposes of conducting such trade-offs. In other words, we are back to the case of the concert pianist and his special interest in his fingers. We know already that, at common law, the reasonableness standard does not eliminate the justificatory significance of such special interests, so that whatever its moral appeal (to me, very little), this way of pinning down the reasonable person fails as a credible account of what the law is getting at. But even if this levelling of different people's interests for the purposes of public justification were to emerge morally and legally triumphant, it is hard to see why that would count as a triumph against the *aggregation* of interests. It would not affect in any way the possibility that 'one person's liberty might have to give way to another's security' and would positively affirm the broader proposition 'that one person's gain can make up for another's loss', where 'make up for' signifies rational defeat. So Ripstein's hostility to aggregation, whatever it signifies, gives us no extra ideas for driving a wedge between (J) and (PJ) beyond those already compassed, unsuccessfully, under heading (5).

At a couple of points I thought Ripstein was going to let his anxieties about aggregation lead him down a different, and in my view more profitable, route. I thought he was going to contrast the justification or excuse of one's wrongs *tout court* (as it were, their *aggregate* justification or excuse) with the justification or excuse of one's wrongs *relative to the person wronged*. Ripstein cites approvingly, and indeed as an important influence on his own thinking, Ernest Weinrib's important work on the moral logic of the law of torts.[65] Yet in Ripstein's approach the most important feature of Weinrib's position appears to be played down. Weinrib stresses the fact that in the private law courts, unlike other courts, the justice that is to be done by the court is only justice *inter partes*. The justifiability or otherwise of the defendant's actions, precautions, decisions, beliefs, etc., is to be assessed relative to the

[65] Ibid, 53 n5, citing Ernest Weinrib's *The Idea of Private Law* (Cambridge, Mass 1995).

plaintiff's interests, not relative to human interests at large, the public interest, etc. In connection with this proposal one may think, in particular, of those taxing and widely discussed examples in which a defendant acts in self-defence against, or is provoked to attack, an innocent third party. The third party, say, is an uncomprehending weapon of the real attacker (e.g. has been wired up to explosives without realizing it) or has been set up by the provoker as a decoy target for the defendant's rage. There is something to be said for the view that the law of torts ought to take a different view of such cases from that taken by the criminal law. Arguably the wronging of the innocent victim by the defendant in such a case should be open to justification or excuse (as the case may be) in the criminal courts. And yet arguably there should be no equivalent defence to a tort action.[66] What had the plaintiff done, she may well ask, to warrant this kind of hostile treatment at the hands of the defendant? In the circumstances in which neither of them is morally culpable, but the plaintiff was passive (a stooge, an instrument) and the defendant was active (reacted to the attack, responded to the provocation), why should the plaintiff, of the two of them, be the one to bear the loss?

Ripstein would doubtless approve the general tenor of this question. But he does not seem attracted to a Weinrib-style answer that isolates the conflict of interests *inter partes* from the wider conflicts of interests involved:

> Parties engaged in potentially risky activities must show reasonable care for those who might be injured by those activities, not simply for the persons who turn out to be so injured. The abstraction of defining the standard of care in terms of the category of plaintiffs rather than the actual plaintiff follows directly from the requirement of treating the parties as equals. Each is required to show appropriate regard for the interests of others. Although fairness between the parties is the central issue in apportioning the risk, the relation between the parties is itself a microcosm of the more general relationship of equality in which we are all supposed to stand.[67]

[66] This is one interpretation of the famous decision in *Vincent* v *Lake Erie Transportation Co* 124 NW 221 (1910), holding that D's behaviour was justified all-told, but not justified *vis-à-vis* P.

[67] Ripstein, *Equality, Responsibility, and the Law*, above note 2, 52.

I am not sure that I concede Ripstein's interpretation of the common law on this point.[68] But never mind that. What matters is that there is an interesting issue here about the extent to which the common law is prepared to aggregate *everyone*'s interests in the law of torts, as opposed to just the interests *of the parties*. This issue is Weinrib's pet issue and one might have expected Ripstein ('much of [whose] account of the structure of negligence law follows ... Weinrib's') to pursue it. But it does not take long to work out why Ripstein instead lets the issue rest with the slightly equivocal and sketchy remarks just quoted. After all, Weinrib's line of thought raises the possibility that what is a reasonable reaction for the purposes of the criminal law is not always a reasonable reaction for the purpose of the law of torts, and *vice versa*. It raises the possibility, in other words, that the two areas of law do not always use the same substantive standard of justification, that they do not always balance the very same sets of reasons to determine which reasons are defeated and which undefeated, that some types of reasons are systematically excluded from the balance of reasons for the special purposes of the law of torts even though not for the different special purposes of the criminal law (and for all we know, *vice versa* too). If that were so, it would not be the best possible news for Ripstein's project. For it would tend to lend credibility to the open interpretation of the reasonableness standard, the interpretation which leaves entirely open, *pace* Ripstein, the substantive question of what will count as a justification in any given context. In other words, to the extent that (PJ) does add substance to (J)—and remember that we have still not

[68] If only A is injured and D took all reasonable precautions not to injure A, is it really the case that D nevertheless committed the tort of negligence towards A thanks to the fact that there were others *like* A in respect of whom D did not take all reasonable precautions? I think not. What is true is that the *duty of care* that is violated in committing the tort of negligence is a duty owed to all, including those identifiable only as members of a class of people, who might foreseeably be injured by D: *Haley* v *London Electricity Board* [1965] AC 778. But violating the duty of care is not yet committing the tort. The tort is committed only when one violates the further, narrower duty not to injure P *by* failing to take reasonable care not to injure P. One violates *this* duty only in respect of those whom one actually injures, and only if one actually fails to take reasonable care *vis-à-vis* those injured people *personally*.

worked out what substance it adds—Weinrib's line of thought, if legally vindicated, tends to favour (J).

8. No responsibility without judgment

Here, as you can probably tell, I have finally run out of ideas for interpreting Ripstein's claim that the law's reasonable person standard 'expresses a distinctive conception of normative justification'. The net result is that I have found no fully satisfactory answer in *Equality, Responsibility and the Law* to the question of what is supposed to make Ripstein's version of the reasonableness standard distinctive, of how it is supposed to differ from the open interpretation of the reasonableness standard that I always signed up to in the past. I have not solved the mystery of Ripstein's reasonable person. My failure to solve this mystery makes me wonder whether I have misunderstood Ripstein's objectives. From his introductory chapter, I understood him to be interested first and foremost in 'show[ing] that political morality, the morality governing the exercise of force, has its own standards of responsibility [e.g. of justification and excuse] that may well be out of place in other moral contexts'.[69] This objective clearly sets him against (J), and therein lay the origin of the mystery I have been trying to solve. But towards the end of the book, as his attention shifts to problems of social justice, I see that Ripstein begins to have a different enemy in his sights. His primary concern at this point is to destabilize what I will call the *anti-judgmental* doctrines of responsibility that find favour with some contemporary theorists of justice, such as Ronald Dworkin[70] and G A Cohen.[71] These doctrines could hardly be further removed from the doctrine that finds expression in (J).

Anti-judgmental doctrines of responsibility would have it that people bear adverse normative consequences in respect of their actions or choices or beliefs, etc. irrespective of whether those actions or choices or beliefs etc. are wrong, unjustified, mistaken,

[69] *Equality, Responsibility, and the Law*, above note 2, 5.

[70] Ronald Dworkin, 'What is Equality? Part 2: Equality of Resources', *Philosophy & Public Affairs* 10 (1981), 293.

[71] G A Cohen, 'On the Currency of Egalitarian Justice', *Ethics* 99 (1989), 906.

base, shallow, etc. Looking (as Ripstein puts it) 'to the formal features of individual choices, rather than their content',[72] they sign up to more or less sophisticated versions of the common saying that 'people should take the consequences of their actions'. This common saying is seriously unhappy. It reflects the widespread collapse, especially tempting to rampant right-wing individualists, of two entirely separate moral precepts. One is the timeless precept that wrongdoing carries adverse normative consequences. Acting wrongly gives birth to new obligations to apologize or compensate or make restitution or atone, and liabilities to be reproached or punished or shown mercy, etc. Some of these adverse normative consequences may depend on the absence of justification or excuse, while others need not. But all depend on one's action being wrongful. Notice, therefore, that this precept is only remotely connected with another according to which people have the power to change their normative positions (for better or worse) by choosing to do so. They may assume voluntary obligations by promising, vowing, agreeing, undertaking, etc. Obviously, once they have assumed such voluntary obligations, they have a longer list of wrongs that they might commit, and hence there are more possible occasions for them to be subject to adverse normative consequences such as duties to compensate or liabilities to be punished. The saying that 'people are responsible for their actions' tends, however, to collapse these two precepts. It tends to confuse the adverse normative consequences that people face when they fail to perform their obligations (whether voluntarily or non-voluntarily acquired) with the normative changes that people subject themselves to when they voluntarily take on new obligations. Put loosely, every action is seen as tantamount to a voluntary undertaking to pay the price of performing it. Never mind that I made no such undertaking. I am deemed to do so. Never mind that my action was not wrongful. That is beside the point. It is my action and, right or wrong, its costs are mine to bear. Non-judgmental doctrines of responsibility such as those espoused by Dworkin and Cohen elevate this popular conflation to the status of a philosophical position, by refining it attractively at the margins. They deem

[72] *Equality, Responsibility, and the Law*, above note 2, 268.

people to have agreed to meet the costs of their informed choices (Cohen) or the costs of the decisions and actions of theirs which reflect them rather than their predicaments (Dworkin). But in spite of the attractive refinements at the margins, these doctrines still subject people to adverse normative consequences of their actions—usually by holding them to have forfeited a right to continuing public support in respect of any additional costs that these actions bring with them—irrespective of the wrongfulness or the unjustifiability of the actions.

Ripstein rightly lambasts this anti-judgmentalism both as a cultural trend and as a philosophical position. He rightly holds out for the view that law and politics must know right from wrong, must support those who behave well and set itself against those who behave badly. In the positions taken by both Dworkin and Cohen he rightly detects more than a hint of that familiar lazy scepticism according to which any way of life is as good as any other, so that the inhabitants of that way of life should bear costs (or more broadly suffer consequences) that reflect the relative expensiveness of what they do but not its relative quality. He rightly sees that this is a close relative of the old and deep mistake of those who know the price of everything and the value of nothing. He also rightly sees that Rawls' position avoids this mistake. Rawls, after all, has no objection to public discrimination among people's pursuits and ways of life according to the reasonableness criterion (where a reasonable pursuit or way of life is understood as one that is believed by its participants, with justification, to be justified). So in opposition to the anti-judgmentalists, Rawls has no objection to a regime in which adverse normative consequences attach to unreasonableness (in the same sense) that do not attach to reasonableness.

Ripstein sees here a doctrine, one that grasps value as well as price, that can justify the law's pervasive reliance on the standard of the reasonable person. Even though he does not borrow Rawls' own criterion of the reasonableness of a person's pursuits and ways of life—a function of the reasonableness of her moral beliefs—he borrows much of its spirit. That is why, as we saw, he attempts to identify the elusive reasonable person in terms of various broadly Rawlsian doctrines, namely: (1) a focus on human interests rather than reasons for action more generally; (2) an emphasis on probabilistic modes of decision under uncertainty reflecting a broadly but not exclusively consequentialist view of human interests; (3) a willingness to grant people their justified but false beliefs in determining the justifiability of their actions; (4) reliance on a limited currency of 'primary goods' in terms of which to commensurate people's diverse ultimate interests; (5) belief in a distinctively egalitarian way of attending to people's interests; and (6) belief in some distinctively non-aggregative way of comparing and trading-off interests among people. In the course of experimenting with these doctrines—doctrines of widely varying worth—Ripstein offers countless fascinating arguments and insights. Indeed, among the many works of political and legal philosophy written under the pervasive influence of Rawls' *A Theory of Justice*, Ripstein's book is, in my view, one of the very few that genuinely advance its vision.[73] Nevertheless the book carries over from *A Theory of Justice* the basic problem that always haunted Rawls, and came to a head in the convoluted eponymous thesis of *Political Liberalism*.[74]

The problem was that Rawls was only ever willing to go half way in his rejection of the anti-judgmentalist doctrine. He always fought shy of the straightforward view—call it judgmentalist if you like—that all valid reasons (for action, belief, attitude, emotion, appreciation, etc.) are in principle available as public reasons, in principle fully admissible, for whatever they are worth and wherever they are pertinent, in public argument and public reasoning and public judgment.[75] Thus he devoted endless—in my view fruitless—philosophical energy to trying to keep his distance

[73] In fact I would pick out only one other of comparable importance, namely Will Kymlicka's *Liberalism, Community, and Culture* (Oxford 1989).

[74] John Rawls, *Political Liberalism* (New York 1993). I am not suggesting, of course, that Ripstein endorses the revised positions that Rawls takes in *Political Liberalism*. Like Kymlicka (previous note), he may well ally himself more closely with the spirit of *A Theory of Justice*. See *Equality, Responsibility, and the Law*, above note 2, 12.

[75] Although naturally sometimes different public fora are the proper habitats of different reasons. The various doctrines of the separation of powers (federal v provincial, executive v legislative v judicial, judge v jury, civil court v criminal court, etc.) serve to allocate public reasoning bureaucratically in such a way that not all officials are authorized to make use of all valid reasons all the time.

from so-called 'comprehensive' (I would rather say 'open') doctrines such as (J). The sad conclusion that *Equality, Responsibility and the Law* forces on us, for all its many cheering moments, is that even the cleverest and most inspired of Rawls' philosophical followers has no prospect of ever bringing this particular lifelong ambition to fruition.

9

THE MANY FACES OF THE REASONABLE PERSON

1. Introducing the reasonable person

The reasonable person (once known as the 'reasonable man') is the longest-established of 'the select group of personalities who inhabit our legal village and are available to be called upon when a problem arises that needs to be solved objectively'.[1] These days, partly because of his runaway success as the common law's helpmate, he has neighbours as diverse as the ordinary prudent man of business,[2] the officious bystander,[3] the reasonable juror properly directed, and the fair-minded and informed observer.[4] All of these colourful characters, and many others besides,[5] provide important standard-setting services to the law. But none more so than the village's most venerable resident.

In the minds of many, he is most closely associated with the law of torts, particularly the law of negligence, where he made his inaugural contribution (it is widely claimed) in 1837.[6] For the purpose of tort liability, it was soon possible to say:

> Negligence is the omission to do something which a reasonable man, guided upon those considerations which ordinarily regulate the conduct of human affairs, would do, or doing something which a ... reasonable man would not do.[7]

The law of torts continues to call on the reasonable person for this and numerous other tasks. It is he, for example, whose moral

[1] *Helow* v *Advocate General* [2008] 1 WLR 2416 at 2417–18 per Lord Hope.

[2] *Speight* v *Gaunt* (1883) LR 9 App Cas 1 at 19–20 per Lord Blackburn.

[3] *Shirlaw* v *Southern Foundries* [1939] 2 KB 206 at 227 per MacKinnon LJ.

[4] *Webb* v *The Queen* (1994) 181 CLR 41 at 52 per Mason CJ and McHugh J.

[5] For news of a recent arrival from the EU ('the reasonably well-informed and normally diligent tenderer') see *Healthcare at Home Ltd* v *The Common Services Agency* [2014] UKSC 49.

[6] *Vaughan* v *Menlove* (1837) 132 ER 490 (CP).

[7] *Blyth* v *Birmingham Waterworks* (1856) 11 Ex 781 per Alderson B at 784.

Torts and Other Wrongs. John Gardner, Oxford University Press (2019). © John Gardner
DOI: 10.1093/oso/9780198852940.003.0009

views determine which statements are defamatory (would they lower the plaintiff in the estimation of the reasonable person?)[8] and which losses are too remote to be recoverable (are they losses of a type that the reasonable person would not have foreseen?)[9] His services are also in heavy demand across many other areas of law, including (to name just a few) the law of contract (where he helps to set standards for both the formation[10] and interpretation[11] of contracts), administrative law (where, in the guise of the 'reasonable public authority', he sets the so-called *Wednesbury* standard for judicial review of administrative action),[12] the law of trusts (where he is the arbiter of dishonesty among those assisting a breach of trust),[13] and in criminal law (where he has played a central role in the shaping of various defences).[14] His place in English criminal law enjoyed notable legislative recognition in 1957, when the judges were told, in effect, to stop meddling with his role as a standard-setter in provocation cases:

> Where on a charge of murder there is evidence on which the jury can find that the person charged was provoked ... to lose his self-control, the question whether the provocation was enough to make a reasonable man do as he did shall be left to be determined by the jury; and in determining that question the jury shall take into account everything both done and said according to the effect which, in their opinion, it would have on a reasonable man.[15]

Since then, the reasonable person has made close to 50 further appearances in primary legislation in the United Kingdom, helping

[8] *Astaire* v *Campling* [1966] 1 WLR 34 at 41 per Diplock LJ.

[9] *Hughes* v *Lord Advocate* [1963] AC 837 at 85–6 per Lord Guest.

[10] *Smith* v *Hughes* (1871) LR 6 QB 597 at 607 per Blackburn J.

[11] *Investors Compensation Scheme Ltd* v *West Bromwich Building Society* [1998] 1 WLR 896 at 912–13 per Lord Hoffmann.

[12] *Associated Provincial Picture Houses Ltd* v *Wednesbury Corporation* [1948] 1 KB 223 at 230 per Lord Greene MR.

[13] *Twinsectra Ltd* v *Yardley* [2002] 2 AC 164 at 174 per Lord Hutton.

[14] Self-defence: *Attorney-General for Northern Ireland's Reference (No. 1 of 1975)* [1977] AC 105 at 138 per Lord Diplock. Necessity: *In re F* [1990] 2 AC 1 at 75 per Lord Goff. Arrest: *O'Hara* v *Chief Constable of the Royal Ulster Constabulary* [1997] AC 286 at 298 per Lord Hope. Duress: *R* v *Graham* [1982] 1 WLR 294 at 300 per Lord Lane CJ.

[15] Homicide Act 1957 s3.

the law out with topics as diverse as alcohol sales,[16] patents,[17] sunbeds,[18] asset-freezing,[19] and stalking.[20]

Because the reasonable person is used to set standards in so many corners of the law, it is natural to think that the standards he sets must be legal ones. In this essay I seek to convince you otherwise. The services of the reasonable person are in such heavy demand in the law, I will suggest, precisely because he sets extra-legal standards, and indeed extra-legal standards of a notably versatile kind. That, at any rate, is his basic task. Having given him that task, however, the law is often tempted to rein him in, to circumscribe in various ways the free play of his judgment. That is what happened in a big way with the law of provocation in England before 1957,[21] finally triggering the above-quoted legislative attempt to put a stop to it. But it happens in smaller and subtler ways all the time. There is an inevitable pressure, a pressure from the ideal of the rule of law, for courts to construct legal standards out of extra-legal ones. Yet the law cannot do its work in a sufficiently sensitive way without regular reliance on extra-legal standards. This is a creative tension at the heart of legal life, and one that it is the ultimate aim of this essay to explore, with the reasonable person as our guide.

2. The reasonable person as the justified person

The reasonable person, I have argued before, can also be thought of as the justified person.[22] This might seem like a strange suggestion. Do persons call for justification? In their entireties, perhaps not. But in various aspects or dimensions, yes. They call for justification, for instance, in what they do, in what they believe,

[16] Licensing Act 1964 s169A (as amended).

[17] Patents Act 1977 s60.

[18] Public Health etc. (Scotland) Act 2008 s95; Sunbeds Act (Northern Ireland) 2011 s1.

[19] Anti-terrorism, Crime and Security Act 2001 s5.

[20] Protection of Freedoms Act 2012 s111.

[21] 'The [pre-1957] courts ... built up a quite detailed picture of the reasonable man and his reactions in various circumstances.' J C Smith and Brian Hogan, *Criminal Law* (London 1965), 210.

[22] See 'The Mysterious Case of the Reasonable Person', now chapter 8 of this book.

in how they are disposed, in what they aim at, and (at least sometimes) in how they feel. We may debate, of course, exactly what calls for justification where persons are concerned. My point is that the reasonable person is someone who is justified wherever justification is called for. Inasmuch as his actions call for justification, he is justified in his actions. Inasmuch as his decisions call for justification, he is justified in his decisions. Likewise with his intentions, his beliefs, his emotions, his goals, his attitudes, his desires—you name it. According to a general account of justification that I have defended elsewhere, this means that the reasonable person's actions, decisions, intentions, beliefs, emotions, and so on (you name it), are taken, formed, held, or experienced (as the case may be) for undefeated reasons—for reasons that are neither outweighed nor excluded from consideration by countervailing reasons.[23]

So the reasonable person's task in the law, if you like, is the sound resolution of whatever rational conflict the law may throw at him. This makes him a sitting target for send-ups like this:

> While any given example of his behaviour must command admiration, when taken in the mass his acts create a very different impression. He is one who invariably looks where he is going, and is careful to examine the immediate foreground before he executes a leap or a bound; . . . who believes no gossip, nor repeats it, without firm basis for believing it to be true; . . . who never from one year's end to another makes an excessive demand upon his wife, his neighbours, his servants, his ox, or his ass; . . . who in the way of business looks only for that narrow margin of profit which twelve men such as himself would reckon to be 'fair' . . . ; who uses nothing except in moderation, and even while he flogs his child is meditating only on the golden mean. Devoid, in short, of any human weakness, with not one single saving vice, sans prejudice, procrastination, ill-nature, avarice, and absence of mind, . . . this excellent but odious character stands like a monument in our Courts of Justice, vainly appealing to his fellow citizens to order their lives after his own example.[24]

[23] John Gardner, 'Justifications and Reasons' in Andrew Simester and A T H Smith (eds), *Harm and Culpability* (Oxford 1996), reprinted as ch 5 of John Gardner, *Offences and Defences* (Oxford 2007).

[24] *Fardell* v *Potts* per Cocklecarrot J in A P Herbert, *Uncommon Law* (London 1934). The case is, of course, a figment of Herbert's imagination.

And for polemics like this:

> Will the reasonable person please stand up, and get out of this courtroom! The common law is obsessed with reasonable people. These people are pinnacles of virtue—courteous, placid, gentle, timely, careful, perceptive—in short, complete figments of our imagination. Yet they are permitted to perform a hideous function within the criminal law. Although no one is really like them, they set the standard for judging our frailties. If we do not match their glorious perfection, we are cast into the shadow of ignominy and damnation. It is time to say: Off with their heads![25]

These passages make for good comedy but bad critique. It is a mistake to think of the reasonable person as justified 'taken in the mass', meaning in every aspect or dimension at once. He performs only one standard-setting task at a time. When he is setting one standard for the law, he may—and sometimes must—be falling short in others. For example, the reasonable person's fear in the face of grave threats, recognized in the criminal law of duress, is justified fear. But in many cases of duress recognized in the criminal law, this justified fear merely excuses the actions that are performed in the thrall of it.[26] It does not justify them. When he submits to threats in such 'excuse' cases, the reasonable person is held by the law to be performing unjustified actions from a justified emotion. If his actions were justified, he would not need and could not intelligibly have an excuse for them. So here the reasonable person clearly is not, and is not treated by the law as being, justified in every which way at once. This makes it misleading to say that he is 'devoid of any human weakness' or that he is an epitome of 'glorious perfection'. He may be free of vice, but he is decidedly not free of shortcomings. He is not exempt from the universal human predicament. Like the rest of us, he often goes wrong in one way as the inevitable price of going right in another way. This is how it is possible to say, and is often said on behalf of

[25] R Sharon Byrd, 'On Getting the Reasonable Person Out of the Courtroom', *Ohio State Journal of Criminal Law* 2 (2004), 571.

[26] See Jeremy Horder, *Provocation and Responsibility* (Oxford 1992), 166–74. The theme is further developed in John Gardner, 'The Gist of Excuses', *Buffalo Criminal Law Review* 1 (1997), 575 (reprinted as ch 6 of Gardner, *Offences and Defences*, above note 23).

the law, that 'the reasonable person is capable of making mistakes and errors of judgment, of being selfish, of being afraid'.[27] He is always capable, depending on the particular standard-setting role that the law entrusts to him, of making reasonable (justified) mistakes and errors of judgment; of having a reasonable (justified) concern with his own interests; and of experiencing reasonable (justified) fear.

This meets one possible objection to thinking of the reasonable person as the justified person: the objection that this would make him incoherently perfect. A second objection, possibly brought to mind by how I have just disposed of the first, points out that the standard of the reasonable person is often used by the law to allow a measure of latitude in action, belief, emotion, decision, etc. This measure of latitude may be thought incompatible with understanding the reasonable person as the justified person. Surely one can be reasonable without actually being right? So, for example, under the *Wednesbury* test for judicial review of administrative action, the court grants a quashing order only if 'no reasonable authority, acting within the four corners of [its] jurisdiction' could have decided as the defendant authority did.[28] The point of this test, many agree, is to confine judicial overruling of administrative decisions to extreme cases, otherwise allowing wide latitude for authorities to arrive at their own decisions. The court is not to substitute its judgment for the authority's concerning the 'merits' of the decision, but only to review it for unreasonableness. How is this compatible with thinking of the 'no reasonable authority' test as making a demand for justification? Here's how. The thought is simply that decisions by authorities may be justified even if they are not the ones that the reviewing court would have preferred. This may be true even if the different decision that would have been preferred by the reviewing court would also have been justified. The point is not to give the authority latitude to err, to act without justification, but only to

[27] Fowler Harper, Fleming James Jr, and Oscar S Gray, *The Law of Torts*, volume 3 (2nd ed, Boston 1986), 389. For like remarks see e.g. *A C Billings & Sons Ltd* v *Riden* [1958] AC 240 at 255 per Lord Reid, and *Sharp* v *Highland And Islands Fire Board* [2005] SLT 855 at 861 per Lord Macphail.

[28] *Associated Provincial Picture Houses Ltd* v *Wednesbury Corporation* [1948] 1 KB 223 at 233 per Lord Greene MR.

give it latitude to follow, at its discretion, one justified path rather than another. Putting the point more technically, the point is not to allow the authority to act for a defeated reason—now *that* would be unreasonable!—but to allow it the widest possible latitude to determine for itself which of several undefeated reasons to act for.[29]

Since his outlook under the *Wednesbury* test is consistent with the view that there are many justified paths to choose from, you may think that the reasonable person cannot possibly be a Benthamite, or more generally a utilitarian, or more generally any kind of rational determinist. Benthamite standards, inasmuch as they routinely (aspire to) narrow rationally eligible options down to one, are presumably standards that the reasonable person cannot embody.[30] But that is the wrong conclusion to draw. The reasonable person does not embody, nor does he fail to accommodate, any particular account of which reasons there are, or of how and when they come to be defeated or undefeated by each other. He does not stand for one justificatory standard rather than another, or for one type of justificatory standard rather than another. He is neither value-pluralist nor value-monist, neither consequentialist nor nonconsequentialist, neither actualist nor probabilist, neither Kantian nor Benthamite. He does not stand for 'public justification',[31] 'impartial justification',[32] 'reasonable justification',[33] or

[29] The courts often say that the *Wednesbury* test gives extra latitude to public authorities, going beyond what an ordinary reasonableness test would give. See e.g. *Council of Civil Service Unions* v *Minister for the Civil Service* [1985] AC 374 at 410 per Lord Diplock. But in what way? It seems that such remarks mainly serve to emphasize that the courts should be very reluctant to find a decision unjustified under the *Wednesbury* standard. This does not alter the fact that 'reasonable' means 'justified', and that what is being applied is therefore a standard of justification for the decision.

[30] Compare George Fletcher, 'The Right and the Reasonable', *Harvard Law Review* 98 (1984), 949 at 980: 'The reasonable[ness standard] ... urges us in the direction of a pluralistic legal order.'

[31] Peter Benson, 'The Idea of a Public Basis of Justification for Contract', *Osgoode Hall Law Journal* 33 (1995), 273.

[32] W M Sibley, 'The Rational Versus the Reasonable', *Philosophical Review* 62 (1953), 554.

[33] Gerald Gaus, 'The Rational, the Reasonable, and Justification', *Journal of Political Philosophy* 3 (1995), 234. (Clearly 'reasonable justification' could be a harmless pleonasm—but that is not what it is for Gaus.)

indeed any other 'distinctive conception of . . . justification.'[34] He stands only for justification *tout court*. So when George Fletcher famously juxtaposes the 'paradigm of reasonableness' with the 'paradigm of reciprocity' in the law relating to the tort of negligence,[35] he misrepresents the standard-setting task of the reasonable person in this part of the law, and indeed in the law generally. Inasmuch as considerations of reciprocity bear on what qualifies as justified care-taking (or risk-taking) in the law, they also bear on what qualifies as reasonable care-taking (or risk-taking) in the law. Reciprocity is a possible factor in our approach to assessing reasonableness, not a rival to reasonableness. Whatever reasons are held to count towards justification, and however they are held to count, the task of the reasonable person is to count them. This is both the genius and the peril of his use in the law.

3. Passing the buck from law to not-law

Why peril? Because on this 'open' interpretation (as I have called it elsewhere)[36] the reasonable person can serve mistaken views about what qualifies as a justification no less readily than he can serve sound views. He can accommodate prejudice, bias, superstition, and gullibility to the extent that he is landed, as he so easily is, with the prejudice, bias, superstition, and gullibility of those who use him for standard-setting. Not for nothing have I persisted here with the law's habit of making him a 'he'. As Mayo Moran explains, it is thanks to his role in the law of torts that

> boys are often exonerated in situations that they knew to be dangerous on the basis that they reasonably yielded to temptation. In contrast, however, the claims of playing girls are routinely rejected even when the girl's behaviour does not seem nearly as dangerous as that of her male counterpart. . . . The possibility of exonerating the playing girl on the ground that she was—like her male counterpart—tempted into a situation of danger rarely seems to occur to courts even as an option.[37]

[34] Arthur Ripstein, *Equality, Responsibility, and the Law* (Cambridge 1999), 8.

[35] George Fletcher, 'Fairness and Utility in Tort Theory', *Harvard Law Review* 85 (1972), 537 at 540ff.

[36] In 'The Mysterious Case of the Reasonable Person', ch 8.

[37] Mayo Moran, *Rethinking the Reasonable Person* (Oxford 2003), 101–2.

This is only one of a wealth of examples, well-documented by Moran, of ways in which our reasonable person, put to concrete use by the courts, has helped to reinforce or uphold stereotypes. One might object, indeed, that renaming him 'the reasonable person' instead of 'the reasonable man' was in some respects a retrograde step, one that, in Elizabeth Handley's words

> merely serves to mask the maleness of the standard—to turn an explicit male norm into an implicit male norm. This possibility is particularly serious if the picture of a 'person' in the judge's mind is one of a man, which is very likely when the judge is a man and when our society in any event treats maleness as the standard or normal state for a human being and femaleness as a variation, an aberration.[38]

Moran and Handsley are emphasizing different problems that the law's reliance on the reasonable person poses for women. Sometimes women are mistakenly judged by male standards, or judged by mistaken male standards (Handsley). But sometimes they are not allowed to rely on the same standards that are used to give extra latitude to their male counterparts (Moran). Women lose out either way. There we see the dangerous versatility—even plasticity—of the reasonable person.

This already gives us reason to be a little cautious about Handsley's formulation. If the reasonable person often ends up giving effect to a male standard of justification that is not because he sets a male standard of justification. It is because he sets no particular standard of justification. He exists to allow the law to pass the buck, to help itself *pro tempore* to standards of justification that are not themselves set by the law, and which therefore are only as good as the standards of justification used by the person or people to whom the buck is passed. This point is often expressed in legal exegesis by saying that the question of what a reasonable person would have thought or done or said or decided (etc.) is a question of fact, not a question of law.[39]

[38] Elizabeth Handsley, 'The Reasonable Man: Two Case Studies', *Sister in Law* 1 (1996), 58 at 61.

[39] Examples: *Glasgow Corporation* v *Muir* [1943] AC 448 at 463 per Lord Wright; *R* v *McCarthy* [1954] 2 QB 105 at 112 per Lord Goddard CJ; *Qualcast (Wolverhampton) Ltd* v *Haynes* [1959] AC 743 at 757–8 per Lord Somervell and at 759 per Lord Denning; *Attorney-General for Northern Ireland's Reference (No. 1 of 1975)* [1977] AC 105 at 137 per Lord Diplock.

This distinction is notoriously troublesome.[40] For present purposes it is enough to note one important consequence of its use. A ruling which is arrived at 'on the facts' is to that extent not subject to legal generalization. Even when the ruling is by a higher court, and hence capable of altering the law, the reasons for it include some reasons that are not thereby adopted into the law for re-use in later cases. Yet even the legally unadopted reasons may, as Moran and Handsley emphasize, have involved generalizations. In fact they must have done: there are no reasons without generalizations, and that is true for bad reasons as much as good ones.[41] So once the question of what a reasonable person would have thought or done or said or decided (etc.) is classified as a question of fact, the generalizations made in the name of the reasonable person are not legal generalizations. They do not enter the law. They are used by the law to avoid the need for a legal generalization to be made. And that, so far as the law is concerned, is the genius of the reasonable person as all-purpose standard-setter. He is also an all-purpose buck-passer.

There is an account of the boundary between law and not-law, sometimes known as 'incorporationism', which refuses to allow that the law can pull off this buck-passing trick. The trick is doomed to fail, it is said, on conceptual grounds. According to the incorporationist, the law of any legal system consists of all the standards (reasons, rules, principles, etc.) that the system's law-applying institutions are bound by the law of their system to apply, never mind where the standards hail from.[42] So to the

[40] For a valuable attempt to unpack it, see Timothy Endicott, 'Questions of Law', *Law Quarterly Review* 114 (1998), 292.

[41] 'If a consideration which succeeds in one place fails in another, there will be an explanation of why it fails.' Jonathan Dancy, *Moral Reasons* (Oxford 1993), 24. Dancy's ensuing example reveals that he would say the same about relevance as he says about success. I cite Dancy here because his allegiance to 'moral particularism' might lead one to think he would reject the proposition in the text above, but in the relevant interpretation he embraces it. See Brad Hooker and Margaret Little (eds), *Moral Particularism* (Oxford 2000), especially the essays by Hooker, Crisp, Raz, and Dancy himself.

[42] Defences of incorporationism include: Philip Soper, 'Legal Theory and the Obligation of a Judge: The Hart/Dworkin Dispute', *Michigan Law Review* 75 (1977), 473; David Lyons, 'Moral Aspects of Legal Theory', *Midwest Studies in Philosophy* 7 (1982), 223; Jules Coleman, 'Negative and Positive Positivism', *Journal of Legal Studies* 11 (1982), 139; Wil Waluchow, *Inclusive Legal Positivism* (Oxford

extent that the English-law rules governing interjurisdictional conflicts of laws require English courts to give legal effect to rules of French law, those rules of French law are also rules of English law. And to the extent that the English-law rules governing the making of contracts require English courts to give legal effect to rules included in the contract by its parties, those rules included in the contract are rules of English law too. By the same token, to the extent that the English-law rules governing the standard of care for the tort of negligence or the judicial review of administrative action require English courts to give legal effect to 'considerations which ordinarily regulate the conduct of human affairs'[43]—meaning whichever standards apply apart from the legal rule that is currently being applied—then those standards must also, thanks to their incorporation, be part of the law currently being applied. They apply outside the law but once the courts are bound by law to apply them, they are unavoidably legal standards too. There is nowhere to pass the buck to.

The objections to incorporationism are many, and different objections apply in respect of different sets of standards supposedly incorporated into the law. In connection with the standards set by the reasonable person, the following objection strikes me as decisive.[44] It is part of the nature of law that law purports to make a difference to how we should otherwise conduct ourselves: to our actions or at least to how we reason towards action. Law purports to settle matters that would otherwise be unsettled, or to give us ways of settling matters that we would otherwise not have, or at least to influence us when we are unsettled. But when the law directs us to rely for some purpose only on 'considerations which ordinarily regulate the conduct of human affairs' it purports to leave us, for that purpose of that law, in just the same position we

1994); and (in a more hedged form) Matthew Kramer, 'How Moral Principles Can Enter Into the Law', *Legal Theory* 6 (2000), 83.

[43] Recall that this is the phrase used by Alderson B to explain the reasonable person standard in *Blyth* v *Birmingham Waterworks*, above note 7.

[44] It is based on the one advanced by Joseph Raz in 'Authority, Law, and Morality', *The Monist* 68 (1985), 295 and developed in his 'Incorporation by Law', *Legal Theory* 10 (2004), 1; also by Scott Shapiro in 'On Hart's Way Out', *Legal Theory*, 4 (1998), 469, and (in a vaguer way) by Ronald Dworkin in his *Justice in Robes* (Cambridge, Mass 2006), 238.

would be in if that law had not existed. It says to its addressee: 'In the following respect, do (decide, think, etc.) what you should do (decide, think, etc.) anyway, what you should do (decide, think, etc.) even if this law did not exist.' In saying this the law admittedly has a legal effect. It is the effect of neutralizing its own legal effect so far as the relevant action (decision, thought, etc.) is concerned. It is, if you like, a legally deregulatory legal effect. It is possible, but misleading, to describe such deregulation as a kind of regulation. Likewise it is possible, but misleading, to describe the law's passing of an issue outside the law for authoritative determination as a kind of authoritative determination of the issue by law. One can get away with such a misleading description mainly because of whom the issue is passed to. The issue is passed away from the law to some legal official (e.g. a magistrate or jury) acting, on behalf of the law, as its authoritative 'finder of fact'. The legally imposed duty of standard-setting remains within the legal institution and this makes it tempting to think of it as the setting of a legal standard, i.e. as an instance of incorporation into law of extra-legal standards. But it is not an instance of legal incorporation. It is an instance of legal buck-passing.

I hasten to add, for fear of giving succour to an error in the opposite direction, that there nothing to stop the finder of fact to whom the buck is passed making her determination with an eye to other law (meaning law other than the reasonable-person-invoking law that she is currently helping to apply). There is nothing to stop it but there is also nothing to require it. She may take the view that the 'considerations which ordinarily regulate the conduct of human affairs' on the matter in question include considerations owed to the law. She may, for example, take the view that the reasonable person as he figures in the law of tortious negligence normally draws the line at what the criminal law would regard as speeding, or what the law of contract would regard as breach of contract, or what another part of the law of torts would regard as trespass. The point is only that, inasmuch as she is charged with simply applying the 'considerations which ordinarily regulate the conduct of human affairs', the law does not specify which of those considerations may be owed to the law or how, in her assessment, the legally derived considerations, if any, are to be counted.[45] So it is true that the zone of the reasonable person may not turn out to be exactly a law-free zone. But it is a legally deregulated zone in the sense that the law leaves it to be determined as a question of fact, not a question of law, how the law (meaning other law apart from the law which is currently being applied) is to be counted inside that zone.

4. The case for passing the buck

Why would the law want to pass the buck like this from 'law' to 'fact', or in other words from legal standards of justification to 'ordinary' standards of justification? Why is it a selling-point of the reasonable person, in the eyes of the law, that he can be used to make this happen? An obvious factor is that passing the buck like this from 'law' to 'fact' mitigates the awesome responsibility, for judges, of having to set legal standards that are fit for re-use in future cases. Lurking behind this obvious factor is an explanation of what makes the relevant judicial responsibility so awesome, an explanation that also helps to make a moral case for some buck-passing. The moral case is sketched by Aristotle.[46]

Rules that exist to help us conform to other reasons cannot but be overinclusive or underinclusive relative to the reasons that they exist to help us conform to—relative (in other words) to the 'underlying' considerations on which we should act if we did not have the rule. Up to a point, the value of having the rule warrants our sticking to it even at the price of departures from what we would be justified in doing without it. But only up to a point. Sometimes we reach the point at which it would be better not to go along with the rule. The advantage that we gain from having the rule as a guide in what Aristotle calls the 'usual' cases is not enough to compensate for the extent to which it now tips us away from what we would otherwise (apart from the rule) be justified in doing. Yet tailoring the rule to eliminate this will only reduce the valuable help that it gives elsewhere.

This presents a special problem for the law, as Aristotle observes, for the simple reason that one cannot make law without

[45] For a good example see *Grealis* v *Opuni* [2004] RTR 7.

[46] NE 1137^{b}10ff.

making rules. Even when judges make law on a case-by-case basis, as they do in common law systems, they cannot do it otherwise than by developing rules on a case-by-case basis. These include statutory rules, which, although originating in legislation, are developed by successive judicial interpretations. They also include rules that originated with the judges themselves. The process of judicial development itself mitigates the problem of underinclusiveness, as compared with legislative alternatives. The whole point is that, by the case-law route, rules can gradually be extended to new cases. But all too often, however cautiously she extends the rule beyond what previous judges established, a judge veers across into overinclusiveness (perhaps in a different dimension from the dimension in which she was being cautious).

What then? Are we stuck with the overinclusiveness for future cases? The common law includes devices that allow judges to mitigate the overinclusiveness of rules they inherit from past cases, even when those rules bind them under the doctrine of precedent. Later judges may, for instance, help themselves to 'distinguishing' (narrowing the rule in a past case in a way that would still allow the older case to be decided the same way) and they may resort to 'equity' (a further body of legal rules which license discretionary departures, within limits, from mandatory legal rules). But these devices still wed the judge to further rules, which are themselves, by their nature as rules, infected with the problems of overinclusiveness and underinclusiveness that they are designed to solve. Sometimes so many and such varied underlying reasons are at stake that no rule can do justice to them, even when supported by extra rules for modifying the rule. Any attempt to marshal them into a rule will yield a rule that is either excessively underinclusive or excessively overinclusive (or both, but in different dimensions). Then it is tempting for the law to resort to a more radical solution.

One more radical solution is to build into a legal rule (which would otherwise be excessively overinclusive or underinclusive) a legally deregulated zone in which the many and varied underlying reasons are to be confronted by the decision-maker in their ordinary form, and applied direct, unmediated by law. Now there is, if you like, a non-rule embedded in the rule. Step forward the reasonable person, provider of just such a non-rule, setter of no particular standard of justification except whatever the finder of fact takes to be the ordinary standard of justification that would apply to the situation apart from the law. It is the reasonable person's main task to take the edge off the rule, by passing at least some aspects of its application back to what I called the 'underlying considerations' that it exists to serve.

5. A more problematic case for passing the buck

The above explanation of the appeal of the reasonable person as a standard-setter for law coexists with, but somewhat in tension with, another. Understandably, officials of the law are often keen for the law to be in tune with the thinking of ordinary folk. They fear, and not without cause, that by the gradual accretion of rules modifying rules modifying rules, etc., law has a built-in tendency to become abstruse and byzantine. This tendency makes it harder for non-lawyers both to follow the law and to accept it as legitimate. One way to mitigate this problem is to imbue the law, where non-lawyers have to do business with it, with the thinking of the ordinary member of the public, the so-called 'Man on the Clapham Omnibus'.[47] The reasonable person has sometimes done double-service as the Man on the Clapham Omnibus, or the average Joe.[48] This double-service gives rise to some important tensions for a conscientious person who is working in the law as a finder of fact. For such a person might not accept that the average Joe is as reasonable as all that.

Suppose that a juror in a criminal trial (say, a rape trial) is asked to determine whether a reasonable person in the situation of the defendant at the time of the alleged offence would have believed what the defendant believed (say, that the complainant was consenting to sex). The juror may take that to mean that she should assess whether the defendant's belief was justified, using whatever she (the juror) regards as the proper standard for justified belief. But suppose the question is put to her again, and now she

[47] *McQuire* v *Western Mornings News Co Ltd* (1903) 2 KB 100 per Collins MR at 109, attributing the characterization to Lord Bowen (without citation).

[48] The classic authority for such double-service is *Hall* v *Brooklands Auto-Racing Club* [1933] 1 KB 205 per Greer LJ at 224.

is asked whether an ordinary person in the position of the defendant would have believed what the defendant believed. Asked this, the juror may think that she should no longer be interested in whether the defendant's belief was justified, but instead in whether it is the kind of belief, justified or otherwise, that would be held by an average person in the defendant's position. She may indeed think—in a kind of mixture of the two approaches—that she should ask herself what beliefs average people would regard, whether justifiably or not, as justified beliefs for someone in the defendant's position to hold. According to our second explanation of why the reasonable person standard is in such high demand in the law, this is just what she should be thinking. She should be thinking about keeping the law in touch with the standards of the general public. But according to our first explanation it is not what she should be thinking. Instead she should be concentrating on what would actually be a justified belief. That way she will do her bit to avoid an underinclusive or an overinclusive rule about who counts as a rapist, never mind what other folk think.

There is a range of cases, to be sure, in which this dilemma is mitigated, in which it would be in order for our juror to treat as justified what is socially regarded as justified. This is the class of cases in which what is at stake is the optimal co-ordination of some area of social life, including perhaps sexual relations. Often, apart from any particular social milieu, there is more than one justified rule for dealing with the same situation. We can imagine that one possible rule for sexual consent (the formality rule) says: an immediate interest in having sex with someone has to be communicated in words; a pre-sex conversation is called for. Another (the spontaneity rule) says: immediate sexual interest is aptly communicated in non-verbal ways, such as enthusiastic undressing, so long as it is not verbally countermanded. Each rule has its pros and cons. Perhaps, abstracting from any particular social milieu, neither beats the other outright. Perhaps what is important, when we reach such an impasse, is not which rule prevails in any given place and time, but that one and only one of the rules does, so that people's sex lives develop with common expectations of how much is to be spoken and how much is to be left unspoken. The law might itself choose between the rules, as it might equally concerning the choice between different possible criteria of death, between different ways of electing MPs, between different ages at which alcohol can be bought, between different rules of statutory interpretation,[49] and between different ways of distinguishing tax avoidance from tax evasion.

Solving such co-ordination problems is clearly a key task for the law. But co-ordination problems may also sometimes be solved by social rules, for example by widely accepted tenets of etiquette and taste. In some societies the formality rule for sex may seem comical; but evidently not in all.[50] Possibly in some societies the formality rule is already the applicable social rule for sexual relations. In others the spontaneity rule may prevail. Let's suppose, for the sake of argument, that each rule is capable of co-ordinating well. When a social rule already co-ordinates well, the law may be hesitant to create a legal rule, which would inevitably draw different lines and might fail to gain social traction. Creating a legal rule in such a situation might even make co-ordination worse, by creating uncertainty over which of the two rules to use. Yet the law may want to give recognition to the social rule in various ways and for various purposes. For instance, it may want to take advantage of a successful social rule about the communication of sexual consent in setting the scope of certain sexual offences. One way to do so is via the device of the reasonable person, understood now as a regular person in the population who is conversant with the relevant social rule. The legal question of whether there was consent to certain sexual activity may then resolve into the following question for our imaginary juror: Would a reasonable person in the position of the accused have understood the complainant to be consenting? In more spontaneity-prizing populations, our imaginary juror may well imagine someone who uses the spontaneity rule; in more formality-prizing populations, she may well imagine someone who uses the formality rule instead. Either way the juror is applying the ordinary social rule, the one

[49] For a way of seeing this as a co-ordination problem, see my *Law as a Leap of Faith* (Oxford 2012), 43–5.

[50] For discussion of real-life attempts to institutionalize the formality rule, see Alan Soble, 'Antioch's "Sexual Offense Policy": A Philosophical Exploration', *Journal of Social Philosophy* 28 (1997), 22, and Eva Feder Kittay, 'Ah! My Foolish Heart: A Reply to Alan Soble's "Antioch's 'Sexual Offense Policy': A Philosophical Exploration" ', *Journal of Social Philosophy* 28 (1997), 153.

that is *ex hypothesi* co-ordinating well. She is thinking of the reasonable person as an ordinary person, and *ex hypothesi* that is (all else being equal) the right way for her to think in this kind of co-ordination problem.

You may be appalled by this supposed example of a co-ordination problem—the formality rule versus the spontaneity rule for sexual consent. You may say that the spontaneity rule is a convenient one for ordinary Joes but a burden for ordinary Jills—hence decisively unjust. Or you may say that the formality rule is a helpful protection in property dealings but a terrible passion-killer for sex lives—hence decisively stupid. You may regard these considerations as settling the matter of what the rule should be, in matters of sexual consent, for all times and all places. It suits my argument if you do. That was why I chose the example. It helps us to see that, for our imaginary juror, the co-ordination argument is no panacea. Using this argument, the reasonable person can be identified with the average person only for limited purposes and to a limited extent. If the case before her takes her outside those limits, to a point at which the problem is no longer a co-ordination problem, our imaginary juror's dilemma—is she being asked to consider what the average Joe round these parts would believe? or what a genuinely reasonable person would believe?—promptly resurfaces.

Romantic notions about the jury, according to which the jury is there to represent the person on the street, may help to conceal the dilemma from her. But what does 'represent' mean here? Should the juror masquerade as what she imagines to be the person on the street, substituting what she imagines to be that person's views on sexual matters for her own? Or should she just think for herself about how to behave in sexual matters, on the footing that, since she is serving on a jury, she must already be such a person and does not need to mimic one? The word 'ordinary' and its cognates can also be used, in a similar way, to conceal the dilemma. When asked to apply 'those considerations which ordinarily regulate the conduct of human affairs' does 'ordinarily' mean 'apart from this law' (as I used it in my earlier characterizations of the reasonable person) or does it mean 'typically' (as one might use it in characterizing the Man on the Clapham Omnibus)? Learned Hand J famously ruled in favour of the former interpretation. He wrote:

[I]n most cases reasonable prudence is in fact common prudence; but strictly it is never its measure.... Courts must in the end say what is required; there are precautions so imperative that even their universal disregard will not excuse their omission.[51]

Or as the point is put more boldly in a leading torts textbook:

General and approved practice may fall below the standard of the reasonable man, and if so, it is not a good defence.[52]

These remarks seem to me to respect the most basic role of the reasonable person in the law. They are consonant with the open interpretation. The reasonable person embodies no particular standard of justification, not even a socially prevailing standard. But there is no denying the appeal, for the law, of fudging the issue, conflating the reasonable with the socially acceptable. Sometimes, as we just saw, it may even be good to fudge it.

6. The reasonable person reined in by the law

By this and a range of other canny moves, the law may end up containing the reasonable person, recasting him so that (depending on the legal context) he stands for a particular standard of justification, or a particular approach to justification, rather than for justification *simpliciter*. That this can be done in so many ways, and so subtly, is another reason why the reasonable person is in such heavy legal demand. He exists to create legally deregulated zones in the law. Yet, with a bit of tweaking, he can also help, as needed, to put a little bit of law back in. Let me outline a few ways in which this is commonly achieved.

(a) Customary standards. We just noted the law's subtle blending of the reasonable person, understood as no particular standard of justification (and hence as whatever standard is supplied by the law's finder of fact), with the 'Man on the Clapham Omnibus' understood as a standard of justification pegged to prevailing social norms. When the law leans towards the latter, we should no longer think of the space occupied by the reasonable person as a

[51] *The TJ Hooper* 60 F 2d 737 (1932) at 740.

[52] W V H Rogers, *Winfield and Jolowicz on Tort* (15th ed, London 1998), 53.

zone wholly unregulated by law. The law now regulates the general approach that the fact-finder is supposed to take to the question of justification. She is supposed to determine, not whether a certain action, belief, decision, etc. was justified, but whether people, or some people, would in her judgment think it was justified (or would act, believe, decide as if it were).

Should we go so far as to think of such a customary standard as a legal standard of justification? Is our question of fact (what would a reasonable person do/think/feel/etc. in a situation such as this?) now being converted back into a question of law? I already suggested in the previous section that the answer is no. Customary law is certainly possible, but this is not an example of it.[53] This is an example of the law passing the buck to customary standards, standards that the law takes to apply apart from itself, and to which is merely instructing its authoritative fact-finders to give legal effect. Admittedly, if they refuse to follow that instruction they are erring in law. On the other hand, if they follow the instruction but in doing so make mistakes about what the relevant customary standards are, their errors are not of law but of fact.[54] At this point we are once again confronted with the 'incorporationist' thesis, the truth of which would make this distinction impossible to draw. But we know it can be drawn, because it is often drawn by the law itself.

It is drawn most conspicuously when the law helps itself to the customary standards of a specific trade or profession, such as plumbing or medicine. To determine what those standards are, expert evidence is called, and the finder of fact is supposed to consider this evidence in the same way as she considers other types of expert evidence, thereby determining for the purpose of the case

[53] See John Gardner, *Law as a Leap of Faith*, above note 49, 65–6.

[54] *Hunter* v *Hanley* [1955] SLT 213; *Bolam* v *Friern Hospital Management Committee* [1957] 1 WLR 582. Some fact-finders (e.g. magistrates) are open to judicial review, where they are subject to the *Wednesbury* reasonableness test (above note 28) in respect of their own determinations of reasonableness. The effect of *Wednesbury* is to convert some (wild) errors of fact back into errors of law. If 'no reasonable [fact-finder], acting within the four corners of [her] jurisdiction' could have found something reasonable, then the reviewing court neatly concludes that the fact-finder who found it reasonable was not acting within the four corners of her jurisdiction, and was thus in legal error.

before her the content and force of the relevant custom.[55] Like other determinations on the basis of evidence, that determination does not thereby enter the law. It is not available for reapplication in later cases, in which expert evidence on the same point must therefore be taken anew.[56]

True, expert evidence is rarely used to establish what the Man on the Clapham Omnibus would think, do, say, etc. But this is not because the question is taken to be one of law. It is because it is taken to be a question of fact belonging to common knowledge.[57] For that reason we should view the 'Man on the Clapham Omnibus' (and 'the Man on the Bondi Tram' and the like) as a modest legal circumscription, not a total legal recolonization, of the legally deregulated zone that is constituted by the law's invocation of the reasonable person.

(b) Specialized standards. We just noted the law's recognition of standards that are specific to particular trades or professions or (more generally) roles. Sometimes these roles are assigned to the reasonable person, who then becomes temporarily the reasonable civil engineer or the reasonable neurosurgeon or the reasonable hairdresser or (to recall examples already noted) the reasonable public authority or the reasonable juror. This prompts yet another interpretation of the word 'ordinary' and its cognates when used in connection with the reasonable person.[58] First, we might say, there is the ordinary reasonable person, designed to set standards for us all to be judged by in our nonspecialist pursuits. Then there are various more or less enhanced reasonable persons, designed to set standards for more or less specialized pursuits calling for more or less specialized competences. As this suggests, the enhanced reasonable persons

55 *Bolitho* v *City and Hackney Health Authority* [1997] 3 WLR 1151, where Lord Browne Wilkinson also helpfully endorses (at 243) the Learned Hand point about the relevance, but ultimate defeasibility, of professional standards.

56 Compare *Attorney General of New Zealand* v *Ortiz* [1984] AC 1 per Lord Brightman at 45 ('A question of foreign law is a question of fact upon which the trial judge requires the assistance of evidence') with *R* v *Wicks* [1998] AC 92 per Lord Nicholls at 105 ('The issue raised [by a jurisdictional challenge to bye-laws] is a question of law, on which evidence is not required.')

57 See *R* v *Turner* [1975] QB 834 per Lawton LJ at 841.

58 See Timothy Macklem and John Gardner, 'Provocation and Pluralism', *Modern Law Review* 64 (2001), 815.

normally exist to set *higher* standards of justification so far as the relevant specialized pursuits are concerned. In matters pertaining to electricity, for example, it is harder to live up to the standards of the reasonable electrician than it is to live up to the standards of the reasonable person in his ordinary 'vanilla' guise. It is harder, likewise, to live up to the standards of the 'reasonably competent carpenter':

> No doubt some kinds of work involve such highly specialized skill and knowledge, and create such serious dangers if not properly done, that an ordinary occupier owing a duty of care to others in regard to the safety of premises would fail in that duty if he undertook such work himself instead of employing experts to do it for him.... But the work here in question was not of that order. It was a trifling domestic replacement well within the competence of a householder accustomed to doing small carpentering jobs about his home, and of a kind which must be done every day by hundreds of householders up and down the country. Accordingly, we think that the defendant did nothing unreasonable in undertaking the work himself. But it behoved him, if he was to discharge his duty of care to persons such as the plaintiff, to do the work with reasonable care and skill, and we think the degree of care and skill required of him must be measured ... by reference to the degree of care and skill which a reasonably competent carpenter might be expected to apply to the work in question.[59]

The words 'must be measured' here mark, it seems to me, a modest legal circumscription of the reasonable person standard as applicable to cases such as this. Which cases are 'such as this'? The ones covered by the legal rule in this case. As so often with case law, it is not very clear what that legal rule is. Nevertheless it is tolerably clear that there is one. Its effect is to require, as a matter of law, that the reasonable person sometimes be recast by the trier of fact as the reasonably competent carpenter.

In enhancing the reasonable person like this, the law often goes further than regulating the occasions on which more specialist standards are to be used. It also regulates how the more specialist standards applicable to given roles are to be established. Often, it requires attention to be paid to the prevailing customs of the members of a particular trade or profession, which takes us back

[59] *Wells* v *Cooper* [1958] 2 QB 265 per Jenkins LJ at 271.

to our discussion under the previous sub-heading. But the law need not refer to any specialist customs. It can draw standards from many other sources. Sometimes it requires attention to be paid to other legal rules. So, for example, any driver of a vehicle in England (even a novice learner driver) is held by the law of negligence to the driving standards of a reasonable qualified driver of that vehicle, and those driving standards include those set by legislation, such as those concerning the condition of the vehicle.[60] Meanwhile a 'reasonable authority properly directing itself' is a public authority that is properly directing itself according to the body of law that defines its role, a body of law which thereby (explicitly or implicitly) circumscribes the range of considerations that it is legally proper for the authority to count in arriving at its decisions. These two examples together form an interesting contrast. In the case of the driver, the standard of justification is made tougher mainly by adding extra considerations (statutory rules of the road) that would not be applicable outside the driving context. In the case of the public authority the standard of justification is made tougher mainly by removing the option of relying on certain considerations that would be relevant to the decision if it were not being made by a public authority. The distinction sounds sharper than it is. Nevertheless it shows how many subtly different techniques the law has at its disposal for adding role-specific enhancements, and hence legal tweaks, to the all-purpose reasonable person.

(c) Personalizing the impersonal. One aspect of the all-purpose or 'vanilla' reasonable person that garners a lot of attention from lawyers is the so-called 'objective' character of any standard that he sets.[61] Recall that he is 'available to be called upon when a problem arises that needs to be solved objectively'.[62] Since 'objective' is a word that performs a lot of different philosophical and legal services, I will instead speak of the standards set by the reasonable person as 'impersonal.' They are impersonal in that they do not bend to the varying personal characteristics of those

[60] *Nettleship* v *Weston* [1971] 2 QB 691.

[61] Recent examples: *In re B (A Child)* [2013] 1 WLR 1911 per Baroness Hale at 1965; *Hayes* v *Willoughby* [2013] 1 WLR 935 per Lord Sumption at 943.

[62] *Helow* v *Advocate General*, above note 1.

who are judged by them. One reason why I have not so far been emphasizing the impersonal character of the standards set by the reasonable person is that it could not be otherwise. All standards for persons are impersonal standards. It is part of the nature of a standard for us that we are judged by it, not it by us.

Nevertheless the law is often tempted to make allowances, in how the reasonable person is envisaged by the finder of fact, for particular incapacities of particular defendants, when these are conceived as exculpatory or sympathetic. As this formulation suggests, the device of a partly 'personalized' reasonable person, by contrast with the role-specification device treated under the previous sub-heading, is most often used to reduce the standards of justification that particular people are held to. Having said that, it is sometimes hard to work out which device the law is helping itself to. Sometimes, for example, the law converts the reasonable person into the reasonable child (or the reasonable ten-year-old, or the reasonable teenager, etc.) for the purpose of judging a child's actions (or beliefs, attitudes, etc.).[63] Our expectations of children are of course different from our expectations of adults. But what does this mean? Does it mean that being a child is a role that comes with its own specialized standards of justification, like that of electrician, public authority, or car-driver? Or does it mean that children, although we might wish that they would live up to adult standards of justification, are often incapable of doing so, and therefore get a special dispensation in the form of a limited personalization of the reasonable person, now endowed with a measure of childishness? On the former view, when a child is too much like an adult in her responses, we may be disappointed, wishing that she would be more child-like. We may ask ourselves: 'Whatever happened to the innocence of childhood?' On the latter view we are more likely to think: 'Just as well she's got an old head on young shoulders!' Doubtless we tend to have both thoughts and probably there are elements of both thoughts in how the law accommodates children in its invocations of the reasonable person.

[63] For example, *Mullin* v *Richards* [1998] 1 WLR 1304; *R* v *Bowen* [1997] 1 WLR 372.

Attempts to personalize the reasonable person to mitigate his impersonal harshness often get into logical trouble. Some people, or some people at some times, are incapable of being reasonable. They suffer from severe mental illness, or are in the grip of hallucinogenic drugs, or have worked themselves up into a wild state. If the law attempts to endow the reasonable person with these personal characteristics in the name of compassion, then it ends up demanding that people be judged by the standard of an unreasonable reasonable person, which makes no sense.[64] The recent history of the law of provocation, in England, has been a history of exactly such logical trouble. Recall that, in assessing the availability of a provocation defence to murder, the post-1957 law required juries to 'take into account everything both done and said according to the effect which, in their opinion, it would have on a reasonable man'.[65] This provision, recall, was designed to put paid to a heavy encrustation of legal technicality that had built up over many years, in which the law went so far as to list particular things that reasonable men would and would not do in response to particular provocations.[66] Everything about the reasonable man was supposed to be returned by the 1957 Act to its deregulated condition, in which the jury, as fact-finder, would count everything in the situation simply for what it is worth, without further legal direction. But this new era did not last. A new layer of encrustation emerged, in which legal distinctions were increasingly drawn between features of the defendant that should, and those that should not, be attributed to the reasonable person for the purpose of evaluating the defendant's responses.[67] Before too long we were faced with the strange prospects of the reasonable schizophrenic, the reasonable obsessive, and the reasonable psychopath. These prospects put the courts increasingly at odds.[68]

[64] Russell Christopher, 'Justification: Self-Defense' in Joshua Dressler (ed), *The Encyclopedia of Crime and Justice Volume 2* (2nd ed, New York 2002), 900.

[65] Homicide Act 1957 s3, above note 15.

[66] For example, *Holmes* v *Director of Public Prosecutions* [1946] AC 588.

[67] *Director of Public Prosecutions* v *Camplin* [1978] AC 705; *R* v *Newell* (1980) 71 CrAppR 331; *R* v *Ahluwalia* [1993] 96 CrAppR 133; *R* v *Morhall* [1996] AC 90; *R* v *Humphreys* [1995] 4 All ER 1008; and many more.

[68] *Luc Thiet Thuan* v *R* [1996] 3 WLR 45; *R* v *Smith* [2001] 1 AC 146; *Attorney General for Jersey* v *Holley* [2005] 2 AC 580; *R* v *James* [2006] QB 588. For discussion, see (e.g.) Alan Norrie, 'The Structure of Provocation', *Current Legal Problems*

Further statutory reforms were prompted.[69] Whether they will add a more edifying chapter to the long story of confused and confusing attempts to personalize the impersonal remains to be seen.

(d) Setting rational priorities. Not all impersonal standards of justification invite us simply to 'take account of everything both done and said' in an undifferentiated way. In many situations, as already noted, there are many ways of being reasonable, and some are associated with one trait of character, some with another. People with different traits of character finding themselves in such situations would play up different reasons for acting (believing, feeling, deciding, etc.), and correspondingly play down others, all without veering into unreasonableness. One final way to add legal specificity to the reasonable person as standard-setter, then, is to attribute particular character traits (or the absence of particular character traits) to him by law, rather than letting the finder of fact settle which character traits he has. This still leaves the finder of fact deciding what, from within the horizons of a person with that character trait, counts as an important consideration, and what the effect is of such an importance-boost on which reasons are defeated, and which undefeated, in conflicts. So this tends to be a relatively gentle legal incursion into the fact-finder's deliberative space. We might say that it merely alters the emphasis.

Sometimes the relevant emphasis is already built in to the question that the reasonable person helps the law to frame. If we are thinking about how much pressure the reasonable person would be able to resist before participating in a crime, we are probably already thinking of the reasonable person as the person of reasonable fortitude. If we are thinking about how many taunts or insults a reasonable person would be able to tolerate before fighting back, we are probably already thinking of the reasonable person as a

(2001), 307; John Gardner and Timothy Macklem, 'Compassion Without Respect? Nine Fallacies in *R* v *Smith*', *Criminal Law Review* [2001], 623; Richard Holton and Stephen Shute, 'Self-Control in the Modern Provocation Defence', *Oxford Journal of Legal Studies* 27 (2007), 49.

[69] Coroners and Justice Act 2009 s56.

person of reasonable self-restraint. But in other cases the relevant emphasis, the character trait we are interested in, seems more debatable. Recall Learned Hand J's remark on the role of custom in determining reasonableness in the law of negligence.[70] He framed the question of what counts as 'reasonable care' in the law of negligence as a question of what precautions would be taken by a reasonably *prudent* person. We might object to this sneaky addition. We might say that the person we should be asked to emulate in the law of tortious negligence is, say, the reasonably considerate person or the reasonably fair-minded person. The suggestion is not, I hasten to add, that the law should license anyone to be imprudently considerate or imprudently fair-minded. That would clearly be unreasonable. It would be a case of being considerate or fair-minded to a fault. The suggestion is only that, within the range of the reasonable, there is sometimes scope for a little less prudence in the name of a little more consideration, or a little less prudence in the name of a little more fair-mindedness.

One might wonder, then, which character trait the law should choose to put centre stage in the law of tortious negligence. One possibility would be: different character traits in different areas of the law of negligence. Another possibility would be: no character trait before any other. The law should just invoke the vanilla, undifferentiated reasonable person as its standard-setter and let the finder of fact determine which virtue of the reasonable person is to predominate in which situation. I am inclined to think that in the English law of negligence, this is indeed the chosen solution, so that Learned Hand J's 'person of reasonable prudence' has no special part to play there.

You can see that some of the legal-village-inhabiting characters that I described at the outset as the reasonable person's 'neighbours' are variations, along these lines, on the reasonable person himself. They are family. The 'informed and fair-minded observer' is a reasonable person, but with scrupulous fair-mindedness as his most conspicuous trait, and hence with reasons of fairness as his highest priorities in the event of rational conflict. Meanwhile, the 'ordinary prudent man of business' is marked by not one but two

[70] Text at note 51 above.

special features that distinguish him from the vanilla reasonable person. He is prudent above all. He is also in a specialized role, as a business person. So his prudence distinguishes itself, one supposes, in respect of matters more specialist than those in respect of which Learned Hand J's reasonable person is marked out as prudent for the purpose of negligence law at large. The ordinary prudent man of business is particularly prudent when it comes to investments, or financial risks, one supposes, but perhaps no more than ordinarily prudent in giving haircuts, riding bicycles, or laying bricks.

One might wonder where, in this legal village, we can find the special standard of loyalty found in the law of fiduciary relationships, as famously explained by Chief Justice Cardozo:

> A trustee is held to something stricter than the morals of the market place. Not honesty alone, but the punctilio of an honor the most sensitive, is then the standard of behavior. As to this there has developed a tradition that is unbending and inveterate. Uncompromising rigidity has been the attitude of courts of equity when petitioned to undermine the rule of undivided loyalty by the 'disintegrating erosion' of particular exceptions .... Only thus has the level of conduct for fiduciaries been kept at a level higher than that trodden by the crowd. It will not consciously be lowered by any judgment of this court.[71]

Is the person of 'undivided loyalty' supposed also to be the person of reasonable loyalty? Clearly the law thinks him justified (hence reasonable) in what he does. He is held up as setting the proper standard of behaviour for the role of trustee. But interestingly he is not described as a 'reasonably loyal trustee' or the like. Two consistent explanations suggest themselves. One is that, when appended to virtue-names like 'loyalty', the qualification 'reasonable' allows a measure of excusatory latitude. That is what we get with 'reasonable fortitude' and 'reasonable self-restraint' in the criminal law. To be reasonably virtuous, we might think, it is sufficient but not necessary to perform justified actions, so long as one performs unjustified actions only on the strength of justified beliefs and justified emotions and the like. We may want to deny

[71] *Meinhard* v *Salmon* 249 NY 458 (1928) at 464.

any such excusatory latitude to trustees. A second explanation is that the role of trustee (unlike that of parent, businessperson, observer, physician, etc.) has no law-independent existence. There is no measure of a 'reasonably loyal trustee' until the law says just how much loyalty is expected of a trustee. So here, we might conclude, there is little or no scope for the law setting trustee standards to pass the buck to 'those considerations which ordinarily [i.e. apart from this very law] regulate the conduct of human affairs'. That being so, as we now know, the reasonable person and his familiars would not be the right choice to do the standard-setting. They would be reined in to the point of having little or no work left to do.

7. The reasonable person v the rule of law

What makes the various above-described ways of reining in the reasonable person attractive to the law? Different devices for reining in the reasonable person have different attractions and are typically used, as we have noted, for different purposes. Yet the law also has its reasons for reining in the reasonable person full stop, by any device it can find. They relate to the ideal of the rule of law (also known as the ideal of legality).

Perhaps most simply, the reasonable person (unconstrained by law) can be portrayed as the enemy of legal certainty. We spoke of the zone that the reasonable person occupies as legally deregulated. One could also call it a zone of legally licensed adjudicative discretion, or (more pejoratively) adjudicative arbitrariness. Anyone wanting to know in advance which way the courts may rule on her case is thrown back on ordinary practical reasoning—and with a nasty twist in the tale. It is not merely that she has to rely, as she might if there were no law at all in the vicinity, on identifying and counting 'those considerations which ordinarily regulate the conduct of human affairs'. No. Because there is law in the vicinity, and because she stands to end up on the wrong side of a legal ruling premised on that law if she makes the wrong move, she now has to work out how someone else, a finder of fact appointed by the law, will identify and count 'those considerations which ordinarily regulate the conduct of human affairs'.

And it may be even worse than that. Possibly she has to work out how someone else, a finder of fact appointed by the law, will think that the person on the street (or the Man on the Clapham Omnibus, the Man on the Bondi Tram, etc.) would identify and count 'those considerations which ordinarily regulate the conduct of human affairs'. The law gives our imaginary end-user no guidance on these matters. Who knows whether she will end up falling on the wrong side or the right side of the relevant legal ruling?

Lawyers, by professional training, are extremely sensitive to such deficits of certainty for the ordinary end-user of the law, and are routinely drawn into attempting to provide further guidance. Indeed it is part of the professional duty of the judge to provide it. She takes an oath, or otherwise commits herself, to doing justice according to law.[72] This is frequently misheard or misread as a commitment to apply already existing law and do no more. That is clearly not what any judge commits herself to doing. Clearly, like an arbitrator, she commits herself to doing justice. The 'according to law' bit is there to set constraints, often quite heavy constraints, on how she is to go about doing it. Some of the constraints are specific to particular legal systems and to particular judicial roles in them. They depend on whether, for example, the judge in question is endowed by the law with a power to distinguish, or a power to overrule. But other constraints are built into the very idea of serving as a judge in a court of law, such that, if any adjudicator were not subject to them, that fact would immediately cast doubt on whether she was acting as a judge in a court of law. One such general constraint is that, unlike an arbitrator, a judge is not entitled to confine her decisions to the particular facts of the cases in front of her, in such a way that her decision supposedly has no implications for how other cases before her or other judges are to be decided. It is a violation of the rule of law—and therefore of the

[72] *Secretary of State for the Home Department* v MB [2008] 1 AC 440 per Baroness Hale at 485. For further discussion of the oath and the duty it captures, see Gardner, *Law as a Leap of Faith*, above note 49, chs 7 and 10. In particular, these chapters explain why a duty to do justice according to law cannot be interpreted as simply a duty to apply the law.

main professional duty of the judge—for a judge to divorce the rule from the ruling in a case before her, either by establishing what the relevant legal rule is (or will henceforth be) while declining to apply it to the particular case before her,[73] or by deciding the case while denying that there is (or will henceforth be) a relevant legal rule to apply.[74]

Resort to the reasonable person as a standard-setter does not strictly speaking qualify as a violation under either heading. The reasonable person is only present in the case thanks to a legal rule that invites the reasonable person in, and the judge applies that rule. Yet the rule in question enables the judge to avoid deciding the case according to law alone. It allows her to pass the buck to the finder of fact, who is invited to use extra-legal standards to bridge the gap from legal rule to legal ruling. That finder of fact may indeed be the judge herself, doubling up her roles. When that is so she is legally licensed to carve up the issues in the case so that she gets to decide some of them free of the need, in doing so, to leave law behind that can be reapplied in later cases.

One may think that, although it does not violate the letter, this violates the spirit of the commitment by which a judge must do justice according to law. Not surprisingly, judges fret about where to draw the lines on this front. They worry about how much of the legal rule can properly be handed over for the finder of fact to determine its application to the present case free from the 'according to law' constraint.[75] Judges know that they would not be doing their duty if they determined that the whole legal rule, in every case, was simply (addressed to end-users of the law) 'do whatever the reasonable person would do' or (addressed to fact-finders in court) 'decide as the reasonable person would decide'. Either of these rules, stated more candidly, says to the judge: pass the buck on every question in the case (except the question of

[73] This includes what is sometimes called 'prospective overruling'. For a good judicial critique, see *In re Spectrum Plus Ltd* [2005] 2 AC 680.

[74] The temptation to do this is great, but ultimately does not triumph in *In re A (children)* [2001] Fam 147 (a 'very unique' case, says Ward LJ as he struggles with the point at 205).

[75] For clear expressions of such worries, see the cases listed in note 68 above.

whether this buck-passing rule applies) to the finder of fact. Such a rule would leave such a vast legal vacuum as to yield a clear abdication of judicial responsibility.[76] But short of such a vast legal vacuum, how much legal vacuum within any given legal rule is consistent with the fulfilling of the same judicial responsibility? Not surprisingly, on this score, judges are hesitant, conflicted, and inconstant. They are often drawn into containing the legal vacuum that they create by giving various nuggets of legal guidance concerning the milieu, the role, the capacities, and the moral character of the reasonable person. They are persistently tempted partly to re-regulate their own deregulated zones. That is what primarily explains the many faces of the reasonable person as we find him in the law.

8. Coda: unfinished business with 'incorporationism'?

In section 3, I mentioned an argument against 'incorporationism' which (I said) struck me as decisive. But I did not make the argument. I only mentioned it. So you may say that the remainder of the chapter rested on an anti-incorporationist way of thinking about law which went undefended. That, however, is not quite true. The chapter as a whole constituted the defence. How so? Well, the widespread use by the law of standards such as that of the reasonable person is often presented as the most decisive consideration in support of incorporationism. As a student of the workings of law in general, my aim here was mainly to show that the widespread use of such standards by the law is explicable, right down to the details, without making incorporationist assumptions. I showed this to be so by *exhibiting* that it is so: by explaining many of the details without making incorporationist assumptions. It happened that my explanation was shot through with English legal doctrine, especially with an English-law view of the distinction between questions of law and questions of fact,

[76] If the rule is rolled out to all cases, there is indeed no legal system. The legal vacuum is then not merely vast but total. Recall the discussion of 'scorer's discretion' in H L A Hart, *The Concept of Law* (Oxford 1961), 138–41.

and of that distinction's importance. But that parochial aspect of my explanation hardly matters. If the reasonable person can be ever-present in English law without incorporationism being true, then the mere fact that the reasonable person (or any relevantly similar standard) is ever-present in a legal system—in any legal system—provides no support for incorporationism. A different argument for incorporationism is needed. I have yet to discover any different argument for incorporationism.

10

PUBLIC INTEREST AND PUBLIC POLICY IN PRIVATE LAW

1. The public interest in justice

It was Ronald Dworkin who sparked the contemporary fashion, among lawyers and legal theorists, for contrasting 'arguments of principle' with 'arguments of policy'. Dworkin did not regard the two categories of argument as jointly exhaustive, even in the special setting of the courtroom.[1] But he did regard them as mutually exclusive. 'Arguments of policy,' he wrote,

> try to show that the community as a whole would be better off, on the whole, if a particular program were pursued. They are, in that special sense, goal-based arguments. Arguments of principle claim, on the contrary, that particular programs must be carried out or abandoned because of their impact on particular people, even if the community as a whole is in some way worse off as a consequence. Arguments of principle are right-based.[2]

The distinction is clearly precarious. Couldn't the protection of particular people against the negative impact on them of (other) policies aptly be described, even in Dworkin's 'special sense' of the word, as a policy of the law or a policy of the courts? Couldn't such protection be defended on the basis that the 'community as a whole would be better off' if the rights of its members were respected, upheld, enforced, etc.? Judges often do make arguments of that very form. Dworkin himself quotes an example from a speech by Lord Edmund-Davies:

> The disclosure [in legal proceedings, to others who are party to the proceedings] of all evidence relevant to the trial of an issue being at all times a matter of considerable public interest, the question to be determined is

[1] He thought that the arguments of lawyers and judges rely on 'policies, principles, and other sorts of standards': Ronald Dworkin, 'The Model of Rules I' in his *Taking Rights Seriously* (London 1977), 14 at 22.

[2] Dworkin, 'Introduction' in his *A Matter of Principle* (Oxford 1985), 1 at 2–3.

Torts and Other Wrongs. John Gardner, Oxford University Press (2019). © John Gardner
DOI: 10.1093/oso/9780198852940.003.0010

whether it is clearly demonstrated that in the particular case the public interest would nevertheless be better served by excluding evidence [from disclosure] despite its relevance. If, on balance, the matter is left in doubt, disclosure should be ordered.[3]

As Dworkin says, we should probably 'understand the reference to the public's interest in [disclosure] to refer to its interest in justice being done, not to its interest in the [disclosure] itself'.[4] But even with that tweak, worries Dworkin, Lord Edmund-Davies leads us astray. Whether he is talking about 'the public's interest in disclosure or in justice', says Dworkin, his Lordship's

[r]eferences to the public's interest ... make sense only as disguised and misleading references to individual rights, that is, as references to the level of accuracy that litigants are entitled to have *as against* the public interest in, for example, the flow of information to useful public agencies or newspapers.[5]

This objection, however, is overstated. If we make Dworkin's suggested tweak, and read Lord Edmund-Davies as talking about the public interest in justice being done, then there is a way of making sense of what his Lordship is saying that does not leave his references to the public interest as 'disguised and misleading' references to something else. Maybe his Lordship does not regard it as reason enough for a court to intervene on the side of a particular person that by doing so the court would avoid or mitigate an injustice against that person. Not all injustices, he is supposing, are automatically eligible to be avoided or mitigated with the support of the law. The support of the law in dealing with personal injustices that one faces is a kind of social assistance—a public sponsorship of one's cause—that is itself up for allocation. Since it is up for allocation there are inevitably questions about the

[3] *D* v *National Society for the Prevention of Cruelty to Children* [1978] AC 171 at 245, quoted by Dworkin in 'Principle, Policy, Procedure' in Dworkin, *A Matter of Principle*, above note 2, 72 at 94. (For clarity: The defendants in *D* v *NSPCC* argued that they would receive fewer reports of cruelty to children from members of the public if the identity of an informant were required to be disclosed in litigation to parents suspected of cruelty.)

[4] Ibid, 95. I have substituted Lord Edmund-Davies' word 'disclosure' for Dworkin's word 'information'. Elsewhere, Dworkin sticks to 'disclosure'.

[5] Ibid, emphasis in original.

justice of such support. It could be unjust for the law to protect one person against injustice, most obviously, if doing so comes at the price that the law will leave other people unprotected, or less protected, against injustices. And that price is always potentially payable. The support of the law for protection against injustices is inevitably a scarce resource. So there is always the question of whether avoiding or remedying this particular injustice against this particular person would be the *most* just use of the law. That, we can imagine, is where the 'public interest' mentioned by Lord Edmund-Davies comes in. He means the interest that we all share in having a legal system that justly allocates its inevitably selective attention to injustices.

Why is the support of the law for protection against injustices inevitably scarce, and hence inevitably selective? Most obviously, the supply of court time, judicial expertise, and legal representation is not infinitely elastic. You may say that this is the wrong kind of argument. You can't put a price on justice, you may say, meaning that the resources available for justice to be done should be limitless. A Minister of Justice who says 'we have to ration resort to the courts somehow' is presenting a bad policy choice as if it were an inevitability. I have resisted this 'no price on justice' view elsewhere,[6] and I will come back to it at the end of this essay. Meanwhile it is enough to note that, for as long as others hold the purse strings, judges, police officers, prosecutors, private litigants, regulators, lawyers, bar associations, legal aid agencies, and nonprofit advocacy groups are all working under conditions of scarcity in which not every injustice, not even every injustice that is brought to their attention, can be attended to. Prioritization among injustices is inevitable.

There is also an argument to the same conclusion that does not depend on shortage of resources. Legal doctrine cannot by its very nature be infinitely sensitive. Being composed of general rules that are made by finite beings, the law is destined to deliver, at best, an approximation of justice. As Aristotle says,

> all law is universal but about some things it is not possible to make a universal statement which shall be correct. In those cases, then, in which it

[6] In my *Law as a Leap of Faith* (Oxford 2012), ch 10.

is necessary to speak universally, but not possible to do so correctly, the law takes the usual case, though it is not ignorant of the possibility of error. And it is none the less correct; for the error is not in the law nor in the legislator but in the nature of the thing.[7]

Aristotle finds hope in 'the equitable, a correction of law where it is defective owing to its universality'.[8] But, as Aristotle makes clear, not all issues that come before all courts can be left open to equitable resolution in this sense. For then there would be no legal system. Instead there would only be what H L A Hart called 'scorer's discretion', an unruly succession of *ad hoc* arbitrations.[9] It follows that some injustice is an inevitable price of justice being done according to law. Imagine that the court dealing with litigant P's case develops the law by interpreting it in such a way as to remedy an injustice against P. It has the power to develop the law in this way, for it is the Supreme Court. Now imagine that litigant Q's case, to which the law as developed in P's case applies, comes before the Small Claims Court. This court, let's suppose, lacks the power to develop or to depart ('equitably') from the law as developed in P's case. Given the law as developed in P's case, justice cannot be done according to law by the court in Q's case. An injustice therefore goes legally unchecked. Appeal courts might of course be available to put this injustice right. Eventually the Supreme Court may get to deal even with Q's case. But then once again it has to develop the law if it is to do justice according to law. Now it has to develop the law in such a way that the law developed to deal with P's case does not apply to Q's case, or at least in such a way that the law developed to deal with P's case could after all have been developed or departed from by the Small Claims Court in Q's case. Either way, much the same problem recurs soon enough in R's case. The improved rule crafted to do justice in Q's case does not do justice in R's case, and R too needs to appeal, perhaps to the Supreme Court, to secure the necessary modification. And so on. At any given moment, the doing of justice by the law cannot but be selectively bestowed. For every just cause that is taken up by the law, there are other just causes that are concomitantly thwarted for the time

[7] NE 1137^{b}12–19. [8] 1137^{b}26–7.

[9] H L A Hart, *The Concept of Law* (Oxford 1961), 139.

being by the law, casualties of the unavoidable approximateness of legal rules.

Dworkin famously baulked at this last thesis. He resisted the picture of law as made up of rules that need to be iteratively modified or departed from to cope with their approximateness. The law, he thought, is a body of principles as well as, or as opposed to, a body of rules.[10] Principles are less approximate. They already bend in the direction of what Aristotle called 'the equitable' without needing a court or other authority to do the bending. Whatever one thinks of this Dworkinian gambit—personally I am among the unpersuaded[11]—it did not stop Dworkin from acknowledging another source of scarcity in the doing of legal justice, which for us will qualify as the third source. Number one, recall, was the shortage of resources in the judicial system. Number two was the inevitable approximateness of legal rules as tools for doing justice. Number three, meanwhile, is a problem about justice itself.

Dworkin noticed that in many cases that come before the courts, both sides have some justice on their side. To do justice on the side of the plaintiff or prosecution, the court must lend the imprimatur of the law to an injustice (one hopes that it is a lesser injustice) against the defendant. The court must condone violation of one sound allocative principle in order to insist upon conformity to another. Dworkin put the point in terms of competing 'abstract rights' that call for concretization in order to resolve the conflict between them. And, perhaps surprisingly, he had no objection to the idea that (what he calls) arguments of policy may figure in the concretization of abstract rights and hence the resolution of conflicts between them. Thus:

> B may say ... that no one can have a right to be protected against nuisance if the cost of that protection to the economic health of the community would be very great, and he may then add that since his factory employs most members of the community's working population, the cost of that protection for A would be plainly too high. Suppose the legislature is persuaded by this argument, and refuses to enact the statute

[10] See Dworkin, 'The Model of Rules II' in *Taking Rights Seriously*, above note 1, where he began to chip away at the 'rules' part.

[11] See my *Law as a Leap of Faith*, above note 6, 85–8.

A wants on that account. There might now be [a] temptation to say that the legislature's decision was a matter of policy rather than principle, but that would nevertheless be a mistake. The question before the legislature is still the question of whether, all things considered, A has the right he claims. If the legislature is persuaded that the answer to that question depends upon some calculation of consequences [for the community as a whole], that does not change the nature of the question it is trying to answer.[12]

Dworkin may be right that the *decision* here is, in his terms, one of principle. Likewise the *question*. Yet the *argument* remains, in his terms, one of policy.[13] That arguments of policy may be used to answer questions of principle, and hence to yield decisions of principle, is one Dworkinian surprise. We will come back to it later.[14] The Dworkinian surprise that concerns us first is that such arguments are *needed*. That they are needed goes to show that, even for Dworkin, the law's protection against injustice is a scarce commodity. How so? Because even for Dworkin some argument needs to be made to determine which of two rival causes, each of which is admittedly a just cause, is going to enjoy the support of the law. It is not enough to establish that without the law's support someone will be or remain a victim of injustice. The law's support must be defended on the footing that not all injustices can be tackled by the law. Officials of the law must determine (justly) which injustices the law is to tackle.

It is important not to conflate the two Dworkinian surprises. That the support of the law is scarce and cannot possibly be lent to every victim of injustice does not entail that policy arguments, in Dworkin's sense, are the only way of settling which injustices the law is to tackle. That the support of the law is scarce and cannot possibly be lent to every victim of injustice entails only this much: that the question of whether the law's support is justly allocated is not settled merely by pointing to the fact that someone will suffer an injustice if the law does not lend her its

[12] Dworkin, 'A Reply to Critics' in *Taking Rights Seriously*, above note 1, 291 at 296. See also 'Hard Cases' in the same volume, 81 at 99–100 and 'Principle, Policy, Procedure', above note 3, at 95–6.

[13] Notwithstanding his verbal legislation to the contrary: Dworkin, 'A Reply to Critics', above note 12, at 297.

[14] In section 5.

support. In section 2 we'll return to the possibility that policy arguments might help to settle the question of whether the law's support is justly allocated. But even if policy arguments never help to settle that question, we have already learnt enough to know that the just allocation of the law's support is nevertheless always (in Lord Edmund-Davies' words) 'a matter of considerable public interest'. You might imagine that private law litigation, of the kind in which his Lordship was officiating when he used these words, would be an exception. In private law litigation, you might have thought, the only justice to be done is justice *inter partes*. But every time justice is done *inter partes*, a public good—the legal system itself—is put at the special disposal of the parties. The parties are not the only ones affected by that special disposal. First, we are all affected by the depletion of inevitably scarce legal resources, the deployment of judges and lawyers and so on. Second, we are all affected by the way in which the law is developed to support the doing of justice as between these two litigants. Recall Aristotle's point that courts of law do not do justice *simpliciter*. They do justice according to law, meaning with the inevitable approximation of man-made rules. For every P for whom the legal rule does justice, there are bound to be Qs and Rs for whom it does the opposite.

How are we *all* affected by any of this? You may say that the Qs and Rs are but further private litigants. Even if each of them has a considerable interest in the legal rules that are crafted to support P in getting justice done, it doesn't follow that there is a considerable *public* interest in those rules. And yet plainly there is such an interest. The rules of private law do not exist only for litigants. They exist to facilitate and guide us all in our everyday social interactions. The legal system is a public good inasmuch as it brings the benefits of such facilitation and guidance inexcludably (even if differentially) to the lives of all. A just legal system is in that respect like clean air or an unspoilt view. Clean air benefits those with respiratory problems more than it benefits those with none. An unspoilt view benefits those whose homes face towards it more than it benefits those who merely see it in passing from the train or car. Yet while the air is still breathable by all and the view is still visible from publicly accessible spaces, the good remains a public one. Likewise with the legal system. Limited resourcing may mean that many are excluded from bringing their complaints of injustice before the courts. Yet they are not thereby excluded from the application of the rules under and by which the courts do justice in respect of such complaints. In spite of everything, outlawry has not yet been re-established.[15] That is why the justice of legal rules, including the justice of the legal rules governing access to and procedures before the courts, cannot be other than a matter of considerable public interest.[16] They affect us all. That, in turn, supplies the beginnings of one powerful argument in favour of increasing the opportunities (and hence resources) for people at large to bring their miscellaneous complaints of injustice before the courts: the legal system is more likely to be justly maintained, and in particular justly maintained as a public good, if all sorts of people somewhat randomly draw the courts' attention to all sorts of injustices. The randomness is one way of mitigating the problem of 'regulatory capture', in which those who are supposed to be held answerable to the rules effectively dominate the administration of them.[17]

2. From public interest to public policy

I warned against conflating the two Dworkinian surprises. That the support of the law is scarce and cannot possibly be lent to every victim of injustice means that there is a public interest in the administration of justice, even in private law cases. Yet it does not follow that arguments of policy, in Dworkin's sense, should be used to settle which injustices the law is to tackle, let alone be relied upon in tackling them. For it might be argued that the

[15] On outlawry, see John Gardner, 'The Twilight of Legality', *Australasian Journal of Legal Philosophy* 43 (2018), 1.

[16] Here I confine myself to claiming that a just legal system is a contingently public good, in the sense explained by Joseph Raz in *The Morality of Freedom* (Oxford 1986), 198–9. It could be that the view from the road will be blocked by new houses, that air for breathing will be distributed as a private commodity, and that some people will be banished into outlawry. Those are the contingencies which make the publicness of each good contingent. Arguably a just legal system is also an inherently public good in Raz's sense, but it would be unnecessarily digressive to develop the argument here.

[17] I developed this argument, and others to the same conclusion, in my book *From Personal Life to Private Law* (Oxford 2018), ch 6.

public interest in the administration of justice is best served by a self-denying way of administering justice in the courts that is oblivious to precisely such arguments of policy.

Notice that this argument—that that the public interest in the administration of justice is best served by judicial obliviousness to arguments of policy—is *itself* an argument of policy in Dworkin's sense. It points to the consequences, for the wider community, of judges being oblivious to the consequences, for the wider community, of what they do. Here is a remark by Lord Scarman that brings out the point in conveniently Dworkinian terms:

> If principle inexorably requires a decision which entails a degree of policy risk, the court's function is to adjudicate according to principle, leaving policy curtailment to the judgment of Parliament. Here lies the true role of the two law-making institutions in our constitution. By concentrating on principle the judges can keep the common law alive, flexible and consistent, and can keep the legal system clear of policy problems which neither they, nor the forensic process which it is their duty to operate, are equipped to resolve. If principle leads to results which are thought to be socially unacceptable, Parliament can legislate to draw a line or map out a new path.[18]

If judges should avoid arguments of policy, you might wonder, what is Lord Scarman doing resorting to just such an argument in favour of judges avoiding arguments of policy? If he is not 'equipped to resolve policy problems', how come he is mysteriously equipped to resolve the policy problem of how to 'keep the common law alive'? One reaction might be to follow Neil MacCormick, who 'contest[ed] the reasonableness of Dworkin's stipulative definition of "policy" '.[19] Maybe the problem of how to keep the common law alive, or more generally of how to serve the public interest in the administration of justice, should not be regarded as a policy problem in the relevant sense. True, it is a policy problem in Dworkin's special sense, but why not simply liberate Lord Scarman from that sense in favour of a better sense? That will not be my way forward. I propose to stick, for present purposes, with Dworkin's sense of the word 'policy'. Instead let me rescue Lord Scarman, at least temporarily, by the simple

[18] *McLoughlin* v *O'Brian* [1983] 1 AC 410 at 430.

[19] Neil MacCormick, *Legal Reasoning and Legal Theory* (Oxford 1978), 262.

expedient of leaving second-order policy arguments out of contention. Second-order policy arguments are arguments, like Lord Scarman's, that speak for or against (further) resort to policy arguments. I can leave them out of contention because in what follows I will be focusing on objections to judicial resort to policy arguments that are specific to their use in deciding *issues of private law*. By their nature, second-order policy arguments are used to decide issues of constitutional law, or at any rate issues in that part of public law that regulates the uses of judicial *versus* legislative authority. True, Lord Scarman's issue about 'the true role of the two law-making institutions in our constitution' came up in a private law case. But that does not mean that it is a private law issue.

Reading this may prompt you to worry about the robustness of the public law/private law distinction. And so you should. But a robust public law/private law distinction is presupposed by those who think along the following lines, and we should allow them their distinction *arguendo* in order to assess their thinking. That is because, if their thinking is right, that will itself lend the requisite robustness to the public law/private law distinction:

> The court's task [in tackling issues of private law] is to specify what the relationship of doer and sufferer requires in the context of a particular dispute. Because private law adjudication involves justifications that pertain only to the relationship between the parties as doer and sufferer of the same harm, a court cannot impose on the relationship an independent policy of its own choosing. Rather, a court intervenes at the instance of the wronged party to undo the unjust harm.... So understood, private law adjudication works justice between the parties without legislating to promote the general welfare.

The implicit contrast here is with a public law in which 'the legal authorities of the state select their favored goals and inscribe them into a schedule of collectively approved aims'. These are Ernest Weinrib's formulations.[20] They are, however, echoed or endorsed in work by Arthur Ripstein, Rob Stevens, and others.[21] All grant

[20] Ernest Weinrib, *The Idea of Private Law* (Harvard 1995), first passage at 144, second at 7.

[21] Arthur Ripstein, *Private Wrongs* (Harvard 2016), 4–6; Rob Stevens, *Torts and Rights* (Oxford 2007), 326; Allan Beever, 'Corrective Justice and Personal Responsibility in Tort Law', *Oxford Journal of Legal Studies* 28 (2008), 475 esp at 497–500. Similar, but with no 'policy' talk: Richard Wright, 'Right, Justice, and

Dworkin's view of what counts as a policy argument, namely an argument that 'that the community as a whole would be better off' if a certain ruling were made. And all follow Weinrib in regarding judicial resort to such arguments as inimical to doing justice *inter partes*, which is, they think, the only proper task for courts when dealing with private law issues.

We already know of one way in which this Weinribian thesis needs to be tamed. Remember Aristotle's remarks quoted in section 1. Courts of law, unlike arbitrators, do not exist to do justice in unadulterated form, whether *inter partes* or otherwise. Courts exist to do justice according to law. That does not mean, as Dworkin famously thought that it must,[22] that courts only get to apply existing law. As Lord Scarman observes, the courts too are 'law-making institutions'. The 'according to law' restriction, rather, bears on *how* the courts get to make law. Unlike a legislature, a court gets to make law only by applying it to a particular set of facts or, as Weinrib puts it, 'in the context of a particular dispute'. Yet, whether a court is applying existing law or making new law in the process of applying it, it is constrained to decide any case that comes before it by applying one or more legal rules to the facts of that case. That means that courts do not have the option of deciding the case before them in isolation from all other cases. Whatever rules courts may rely upon to decide the case are, in their nature as rules, potentially applicable in an indeterminate number of future cases. So, *pace* Weinrib, it is decidedly not the case that courts dealing with private law issues can be content with 'justifications that pertain only to the relationship between the parties' in the particular case before them. Inevitably the same justifications to which the court appeals in connection with this relationship pertain equally to all other possible relationships that are legally alike, i.e. that fall under the same legal rule or rules on which the court relies in deciding this case. As Aristotle taught us, a legal rule that does justice in the present case, being inevitably

Tort Law' in David Owen (ed), *Philosophical Foundations of Tort Law* (Oxford 1995), 159 esp at 167–8.

[22] Dworkin, 'Hard Cases', above note 12, 85: 'not some new duty created in court'.

an approximation, always threatens to do injustice when applied in later cases.

Inasmuch as a court has the legal power to make law simply by applying it, then, it has a responsibility to a population of potential law-users far wider than the pool of litigants before it right now. It has a responsibility to maintain the law in good shape for all of us, i.e. as a public good. It cannot do so without attending to at least some of the consequences of its proposed decision for the wider community. Minimally, a responsible court cannot but attend to what Bernard Rudden called the 'juridical consequences' of its proposed decision across the range of future cases, litigated or otherwise, that might be caught by whatever legal rules it proposes to leave behind.[23] Since all judges know that it is impossible to anticipate the entire range of cases that might be caught by whatever legal rules they leave behind, the existence of this responsibility may well dispose them to use such law-making powers as they have only sparingly and cautiously, making only the smallest legal adjustments needed to do justice in the case before them, lest by embarking on more ambitious adventures in law reform they leave behind them a larger legacy of injustice, and in particular—in private law—a larger legacy of injustice *inter partes*. They trust that the smaller the steps they take, the less they gamble with other law users' futures. Hence what Weinrib himself labels 'the specifically judicial function of casuistically developing the law'.[24]

You may be tempted to say that 'juridical consequences' are not consequences in the sense that matters for the identification of a policy argument. That being so, Weinrib's thesis does not need to be tamed to accommodate them. Something like this seems to be Neil MacCormick's line. He agrees that

> to declare a particular right (*jus dicere*) is necessarily, in the role of an impartial judge, to declare it as available in every like case. Hence, as a person of prudence and forethought any judge must look across the range of possible situations which will have to be covered by this ruling in point of right. Such consideration of a range of possible cases cannot

[23] Bernard Rudden, 'Consequences', *Juridical Review* 24 (1979), 193 at 197.

[24] Ernest Weinrib, *Corrective Justice* (Oxford 2012), 72.

but be necessary to adequate assessment of the acceptability of the decision entertained in the present case.[25]

MacCormick takes this attention to juridical consequences (which he says are 'logical implications') to be quite different from 'conjectural . . . forecasts about the likely impact of novel rules or rulings on the way people will conduct themselves'.[26] About judicial resort to the latter he is considerably less sanguine. Is this not simply the Weinribian position spelt out in more detail? Is Weinrib's objection to policy arguments not mainly targeted at judicial reliance on the anticipated behavioural consequences, as opposed to the merely juridical consequences, of private-law decisions? It is hard to say. In the passage quoted above, Weinrib contrasts 'work[ing] justice between the parties' and 'legislating to promote the general welfare'.[27] Every judicial option being discussed by MacCormick falls into the space between these two poles, space which Weinrib leaves entirely uncharted. Although thinking beyond how to do justice between the parties, MacCormick's judges are also, quite clearly, not legislating, and they are clearly keeping well away from anything so grand as 'the general welfare'. MacCormick's judges are interested primarily in future injustices that might be wrought by the law as they propose to leave it, and MacCormick's question is whether they should limit themselves to worrying about the injustices that the law they are applying would wreak if only it were to be given perfect effect, or whether they should also worry about the likelihood that, thanks to their application of the law, injustices are actually going to be done, for example, because of perverse incentives or misinterpretations.

Combining MacCormick's distinction between juridical and behavioural consequences with Weinrib's polarization of the possibilities, we can now see at least four distinct controversies that might be described (without departing from the Dworkinian characterization of a policy argument) as controversies over whether judges should resort to policy arguments when adjudicating issues of private law.

[25] Neil MacCormick, 'On Legal Decisions and Their Consequences: From Dewey to Dworkin', *NYU Law Review* 58 (1983), 239 at 251.

[26] Ibid, 252.

[27] See text at note 20 above.

(a) Should a judge in a private law case attend only to the position in which her proposed decision will leave the particular parties litigating before her, or should she also attend to the position in which it will leave others to come in their wake?

(b) Does 'the position' to which the private law judge should attend in (a) include only the legal position in which it will leave people (i.e. the decision's 'juridical consequences') or does it also include the decision's empirical effects on actual behaviour?

(c) When, under (b), a private law judge attends to either the juridical or empirical consequences of her proposed decision or both, is the appropriate standard of evaluation for her to use in doing so that of 'promoting the general welfare', or indeed that of promoting anyone's welfare?

(d) Whatever standard a private law judge should use for evaluating the consequences of her proposed decision under (c), should she reason like a legislator in bringing her evaluations to bear on whatever decision she makes?

3. On behavioural and juridical consequences

I have already supplied my own answers to questions (a) and (d). On question (a): judges in courts of law are not arbitrators. They are there to do justice according to law, which means by the application of legal rules. Often, in their attempts to do justice according to law, they leave modified legal rules behind for later users to contend with. It would be an abdication of responsibility for them not to attend to the predicament in which those later users are left by those modified rules. It will not always be possible for later users to have further modifications made to do justice their cases by returning to the courts; nor should they lightly be expected to attempt it. The impact of the law upon them should so far as possible be anticipated in the way that the law has already been developed before it affects them. And that means anticipated by the courts in developing the law.

On the other side of the same coin we find my answer to question (d). Just as judges in courts of law are not arbitrators, so they are not legislators. They are there to do justice according to law, which means by the application of legal rules. Except when they issue practice directions to regulate their own adjudicative processes, judges—unlike legislators—do not get to reform the law merely because it needs reforming. They get to reform the law only inasmuch as the problems created by the existing law are at issue between the parties to the case, and only inasmuch as the law can be reformed in the course of applying it to the facts of the case, and only inasmuch as the improvement can be defended by means of an argument (a 'legal argument') in which other legal rules serve as operative premises, and only inasmuch as the change can be made consistently with the binding decisions of higher courts in earlier cases, and subject to various other constraints.[28] Such constraints—the details of them vary between different systems and traditions—differentiate the work of a court from that of a legislature irrespective of whether the court resorts to arguments of policy. How can it be irrespective of whether the court resorts to arguments of policy? An argument of policy (in Dworkin's sense) can qualify as a legal argument so long as the legal rules on which the court relies invite or require the court to attend to the consequences of their decision for the wider community. And many do. It is that very fact about the state of the law, or more precisely the state of private law, that so concerns Weinrib *et al*.[29] They deprecate the tendency for courts to say: 'this is where private law itself confronts us with a policy question'. They say that this is no way for a private law issue to be adjudicated.

How about question (b)? I tend to share MacCormick's view that, in the main, judges should avoid 'conjectural … forecasts about the likely impact of novel rules or rulings on the way people will conduct themselves'. My reason is Lord Scarman's reason: neither judges, nor the forensic process which it is their duty to operate, are particularly well-equipped to make such forecasts. Judges do not have on-demand access to the legions of civil servants and subject matter specialists whose principal job is to investigate (for legislators, government departments, regulators, etc.) the likely behavioural impact of novel rules or rulings. In a way this is a corollary of the very nature of law: any subject matter

[28] For more detail, see my *Law as a Leap of Faith*, above note 6, ch 7.

[29] See notably Allan Beever and Charles Rickett, 'Interpretive Legal Theory and the Academic Lawyer', *Modern Law Review* 68 (2005), 320 at 328.

can come up at any time in any case before the courts. A case that seems to be about squabbling neighbours can turn out to be about electrical regulations or the care of chickens or tree surgery or the nature of music. The counterpart of a civil servant in a courtroom is a lawyer, a specialist in the law and hence inevitably called upon to be (otherwise) a subject matter dilettante. Yes, she knows about contracts, but contracts can be about anything from cosmetics to cohabitation to cryogenics. Yes, she knows about divorce, but the bones of contention between estranged spouses can be as various as home education, horticulture, and hedge funds. Why not create a dedicated corps of courthouse researchers and policy advisers, a forensic civil service, to assist judges with the behavioural consequences of their decisions in these and other areas? It might be done—and it is done in very limited ways with expert testimony and court-commissioned reports by psychiatrists, psychologists, social workers, probation officers, and so on—but implemented on a larger scale with retained officials it carries many risks, including risks to the independence of the judiciary and to the continued primacy of legal reasoning in the courts. And it would anyway be duplicative. We have professionally supported executives and legislatures to adjust the law for its behavioural consequences, including, where necessary, to correct problems in the law that come of judicial inadvertence to those same consequences. Recall Lord Scarman: 'If principle leads to results which are thought to be socially unacceptable, Parliament can legislate to draw a line or map out a new path.'[30]

The problem with all of this, however, is that inasmuch as it bears on the capacity of courts to anticipate and hence adjust for the behavioural consequences of their decisions, it seems to bear no less on their capacity to evaluate the juridical consequences. MacCormick writes as if the juridical consequences of a court's decision might somehow be evaluated independently of the likely further consequences that those juridical consequences would have if the decision were perfectly conformed to:

> In considering the juridical consequences of a ruling by way of its implications for hypothetical cases we discover whether a ruling commits

[30] From the passage quoted at note 18 above.

> us to treating as right deeds that subvert or fail of sufficient respect for the values at stake, or to treating as wrong forms of conduct which include no such subversion or failure. Either consequence is unacceptable because it wreaks injustice, that is, fails the proper virtue of legal institutions.[31]

Although 'values at stake' does not point away from the evaluation of legal rules and rulings by their likely consequences if they are perfectly conformed to, much of MacCormick's discussion suggests that the way to avoid 'subversion or failure [of respect]' for any given value in a legal rule or ruling is to 'uphold' the value in the rule or ruling. Roughly: if people (including other officials) were to conform perfectly to the rule or ruling, would *they* be respecting the value in question? Would it be, in that sense, a good rule or ruling to have, a better rule or ruling than we would otherwise have? But that is clearly not the only question. There is also the question of whether such improvement in people's respect for the relevant values as can be credited to the rule or ruling (assuming perfect conformity to it) is worth the cost, for those who are going to be subject to the rule or ruling, of adapting to it. The courts whose decisions have juridical consequences are, by definition, altering people's legal positions and therefore, still assuming perfect conformity with the law, messing around with people's lives. Limiting their attention to juridical consequences, then, in no way insulates the courts from making 'forecasts about the likely impact of novel rules or rulings on the way people will conduct themselves'. That remains true even if one thinks, with MacCormick, that upholding the value of *justice* is the paramount concern of the law. The question still arises: Is the justice that lies in conformity to the just rule or ruling worth the burdens, possibly injustices, that some people would have to bear in order to conform?

These considerations fortify the case for judges to use their law-making powers only minimally and with circumspection. That case, we can now see, is not limited to those occasions on which the courts resort to policy arguments to justify whatever changes they make in the law. It is more general. Even when a change

[31] 'On Legal Decisions and Their Consequences', above note 25, 256–7.

in the law is defended on what Dworkin would call 'principled' grounds, it has side-effects for at least some law-abiding people. Inasmuch as they are law-abiding, it necessarily changes their behaviour. That is the whole point of it. A responsible court cannot avoid asking whether the impact of those changes of behaviour on the lives of such people, and those around them, would be a price worth paying for the envisaged change in the law. And that question does not disappear merely because the courts abjure any inquiry into whether people really will conform to the changed law. Perhaps, to repeat, the courts should assume that people will be law-abiding, and leave it to other institutions to deal with any diminution in law-abidingness brought about by the legal change they have in mind. Still the courts must ask whether, on the assumption of law-abidingness, the legal change they have in mind would wreak more havoc in the lives of those touched by the change than could be justified by its *ex hypothesi* welcome juridical consequences. That the smallest legal change is the one that wreaks the least havoc is a possible judicial rule of thumb for minimizing 'conjectural ... forecasts about the likely impact of novel rules or rulings on the way [law-abiding] people will conduct themselves'. There is little here to alarm those, like me, who doubt whether judges are well-placed to make such forecasts. By and large they need not do so. But that does not mean that they have no responsibilities regarding the behavioural consequences of their decisions. Rather it means that by and large such responsibilities can be discharged indirectly, without making conjectural forecasts, by using something like the rule of thumb just mentioned.

Having said that, experienced lawyers and judges can surely be expected to have some distinctive professional insight into certain behavioural consequences of their work, such as consequences for comity among courts or among authorities more generally, or for the maintenance of the rule of law or some aspects of it. So we can see why Lord Scarman might have thought that, notwithstanding the inevitable dilettantism of legal work, second-order policy arguments of the kind that he allowed himself to make were not out of bounds to the courts. That, however, reminds us of a point we encountered before. Weinrib and his followers tell us that a *private-law specific* case exists against judicial resort to arguments of policy. None of the foregoing remarks about the relative paucity of judicial expertise in respect of behavioural consequences is private-law specific. They are all of more general application. Without their own civil service to assist, courts are surely no better placed to work out the behavioural consequences of granting *certiorari* against a housing authority or *habeas corpus* against the immigration service than they are to work out the behavioural consequences of granting specific performance of a contract to the plaintiff, or in granting a defendant's application to strike out a claim for repossession of his home. Indeed one might suspect—we would need empirical research to be sure—that judges would tend to wreak even more havoc in attempting to adjust for behavioural consequences in making the former (public law) orders than in making the latter (private law) orders. For if one lives in a rule-of-law regime, in which public bodies are relatively law-abiding, one might reasonably expect that a public-law order will attract more attention and yield more attempts at conformity by bodies other than the original body addressed by the order. Many of these attempts will have yet further consequences for the behaviour of others. Thus the behavioural consequences of making public-law orders might well be even harder to adjust for than those of making private-law orders. Here we have the beginnings of a second-order policy argument for the conclusion that *ceteris paribus* judges should be even more cautious in attending to the behavioural consequences of what they do in adjudicating issues of public law than they should be in adjudicating issues of private law. And that obviously turns the Weinrib view on its head. How are we to get it back on its feet?

4. The othering of the public

One possibility is that we are misunderstanding what Weinrib means by 'public law'. Possibly he does not mean to include, under that heading, the contribution of the courts to the law of the constitution, or their work in reviewing administrative decision-making for errors of law and abuses of power. Perhaps he is putting the whole of the common law, including the prerogative writs, on the 'private law' side. Or perhaps, even more ambitiously, he wants us to think of all adjudicative work as 'private law' work. What he says about 'public law' points in various competing directions. At one point he says that the private law/public law distinction is 'broadly reflect[ed]' in the adjudication/legislation distinction.[32] At another point, however, he puts 'administrative tribunals', as well as criminal prosecution, on the 'public law' side of the line.[33] We are not here to provide a detailed commentary on Weinrib's text. But such vagueness about the characteristics of public law is not unique to him. For those who deprecate the resort to arguments of policy in private law, public law often represents (if I may resort to some phenomenological jargon) the 'silenced other'. Of it little is spoken, and yet always something vaguely disreputable is known. Most often a kind of impurity or corruption is insinuated. Public law may have a few 'juridical aspects, expressible through norms of constitutional and administrative law' but it is 'the home of the political'. Private law, by contrast, is 'purely juridical', and hence, we glean, the real deal, law in its pristine form.[34]

It would be interesting to investigate further the cartoon foil that public law has become in this narrative, and the associated difficulty of drawing a non-conclusory contrast between it and private law. A more pressing task, however, is to expose the no less cartoonish representation of the goals of public policy that is often used to make those goals seem particularly alien to the work of private law courts. This is where we finally reach controversy (c) on my earlier list. Arguments of policy, we have followed Dworkin in saying, are 'goal-based' in the special sense that they 'try to show that the community as a whole would be better off' if a given programme were pursued or rule were adopted or decision were made, etc. That, as we know, is already a stipulative definition, using the word 'policy' in a 'special sense'.[35] But in Weinrib's hands, and in those of his followers, talk of 'policy' acquires a yet more specialized flavour. Making the community as a whole better off mutates into 'promoting the general welfare'. It sounds not much different until one appreciates that 'welfare' is

[32] *The Idea of Private Law*, above note 20, 8.

[33] Ibid, 48.

[34] Ibid, 211–13.

[35] MacCormick, *Legal Reasoning and Legal Theory*, above note 19, 262–4.

being used as a technical term. It is used in the sense in which it is used in 'welfare economics', a usage widely adopted by so-called 'economic analysts of law'. Their brand of 'welfarism', as I will call it, has at least the following three quirky commitments:

(i) Welfare is not what the etymology of the word leads one to expect. It is not literally acting well or doing well. My welfare does not lie in how I act. It lies in the state I am in, whether or not my actions contributed to my being in that state.

(ii) There is no possibility of my welfare being affected by the value of anything except to the extent that such value is reflected in my own valuations. My welfare improves (declines) just in virtue of my getting more (less) of what I value, or my getting something that I value more (less). (This leaves room for debate about what it takes to value something in the relevant sense. Many set a low threshold captured in the word 'preference'.)

(iii) Welfare is a master-value, or a master-currency of value, into which all other kinds of value that may exist are to be converted for some or all purposes, and at a minimum for the purpose of evaluating public policies. Public policies are sound if and only if they meet some specified welfare-improvement condition. Usually but not always the condition is welfare-maximization across a specified population. (This leaves room for debate about which is the right population to specify.)

Weinrib apparently cannot imagine a policy argument that is free of these narrow sectarian teachings. To his way of thinking, anyone who sees the law as an instrument of policy goals is condemned without further ado to see the law as 'a means of forwarding the community's aggregate welfare through a strategy of maximization'.[36] That, it seems, is the only policy goal that anyone could possibly have. There is no room for the idea that ensuring that justice is done, or ensuring that a certain kind of justice is done (corrective, *inter partes*, according to law, etc.), might be a freestanding policy goal, one that calls for attention

[36] *The Idea of Private Law*, above note 20, 48.

independently of, and sometimes vies for attention with, other freestanding policy goals, such as enabling sporting and artistic excellence, improving the balance of trade, tackling corruption, reducing homelessness, promoting competition, augmenting pension provision, improving public health, providing humanitarian aid, professionalizing the police, protecting people from domestic violence, or supporting valuable personal relationships. These cannot be freestanding policy goals, for each is intelligible only inasmuch as it can be cashed out in the currency of welfare, and thereby subsumed under the only freestanding policy goal that there is. No possibility, then, that 'social choice' (as it is sometimes called) might actually offer us a choice. There may be a choice of policies, of course, but there can be no choice of policy goals. Where policy goals are concerned, increased welfare is the only item on the menu. That is the story of policy evaluation as told by many economists, including economists of law. And for the most part it is the story conceded by Weinrib and his followers, who are content to let it go unchallenged, indeed seemingly to advocate on its behalf, so long as they can resist its intrusion into private law.

I say 'for the most part' because another story, perhaps only a subplot, sometimes intrudes. Whether or not policy goals are by their nature evaluable only in welfarist terms, they are by their nature 'collectively approved'. So now we must have, in some sense, a choice of policy goals: 'the legal authorities of the state select the favored goals'.[37] The two stories, one denying any choice of policy goals and the other offering just such a choice, can be reconciled in various ways. 'Social choice theory' responds to various uncertainty problems in determining the welfare-optimality of particular policies by considering possible mechanisms, such as voting systems, by which collective policy choices could be made, those mechanisms to be judged by their more general welfare-optimizing tendencies. Dworkin connects political choice to welfare-maximization in just this way. The electoral ballot is an (imperfect) way of counting the preferences, satisfaction of which is to be maximized according to 'the most influential background justification' for public policy 'in the Western

[37] Ibid, 7.

democracies', which is 'some form of utilitarianism', here understood as pursuit of 'the highest aggregate welfare'.[38] Perhaps Weinrib likewise imagines some convergence, even interdependence, of welfare-maximization as the one true policy goal and 'collectively approved' subsidiary policy goals that are 'select[ed]' via the political process. He says little to confirm or deny that this is the more complete picture that he has in mind. For, again, his only concern is to place private law outside the political process, meaning, for him, that policy evaluation, conceived in welfarist terms, has no part to play in it.

Is it true that modern politics in 'the Western democracies' is welfarist or 'at least in [some] informal way' utilitarian?[39] Maybe. If so, that would help to explain why our politics are currently in such deep trouble. The curiosity is not that Weinrib would wish to rescue private law from such a depressing end, but that he is so ready to consign public law, public policy, and indeed the rest of public life to the same fate. He casually throws them under the welfarist bus. To what end? After all, we do not need to show that private law is special to establish that judges in private law cases should not pursue *bad* policy goals, such as 'welfare-maximization'. That they are bad policy goals is already enough to show that nobody should pursue them, whether she be private law judge, member of parliament, government minister, civil servant, prosecutor, army officer, or voter. In testing the proposition that private law adjudication should be kept free of policy goals, we need instead to be confronted with examples of *good* policy goals that private law judges should not pursue. Weinrib and his followers offer few if any such examples. In particular they do not consider the freestanding policy goal, the one of which I have

[38] All but the final quoted words are from Dworkin, 'Do We Have a Right to Pornography?' in his *A Matter of Principle*, above note 2, 335 at 360; the final quotation is from 'Why Efficiency?' in the same volume, 267 at 274.

[39] Utilitarianism is a broad church and many of its most famous adherents are not welfarists. Bentham rejected tenet (ii). Mill rejected tenets (ii) and (iii). Possibly someone who also rejected (i) would no longer be recognizable as a utilitarian even in what Dworkin calls an 'informal way'. Yet she might still find space for herself in the wider consequentialist tradition, depending on various other aspects of her thinking. On the limits of this space, see Campbell Brown, 'Consequentialize This!', *Ethics* 121 (2011), 749.

made so much in this paper, of seeing to it that justice is done according to law.

Pursuing this policy goal differs, as I have said time and again, from merely doing justice (*inter partes* or otherwise). It requires judges to think ahead to other cases in which the law as they apply it (and thereby often develop it) could be reapplied. They have to think about the consequences, not just for the parties to the present case (will that cover the hospital bill? what's to become of the house? etc.) but for the wider community of law-users still to come, including those who might go to court (is it clear enough what they need to plead? will they face impossible burdens of proof? etc.) but also those who might not (will the law be asking too much of learner drivers? are we handing too much legal authority to doctors? etc.). And none of this, notice, is private-law specific. It is also applicable in criminal cases, judicial review cases, cases heard in 'administrative tribunals', etc. It is, to repeat yet again, the distinctive policy-evaluation responsibility that differentiates adjudication from arbitration.

Is this distinctive policy-evaluation responsibility much different, in respect of its distinctiveness, from those of other officials of government and law? From what I understand of the processes of government in 'the Western democracies', the answer is no. Head prosecutors, competition regulators, Ministers of Energy, chief medical officers, etc. all have their distinctive policy-evaluation responsibilities. Each of them ends up doing some things that might be described as 'cost-benefit analysis'. But by and large each has his or her own list of more or less specialized costs and benefits to take into account. A chief prosecutor does not factor into his decisions the benefit of the country's meeting its own power consumption needs, but by the same token a Minister of Energy does not factor in the reputational costs to the justice system of persisting with the prosecution of people who were facing grave moral dilemmas. You might be tempted to think that in such a parcelling out of deliberative labour, there must be a centralized 'cost-benefit' analysis of everything taken together, if only to allocate budgets to each policy portfolio (ministry, department, agency, etc.). But why? We have many processes to sort out these and similar problems about the co-ordination of policies. We have manifesto promises made at election time, parliamentary scrutiny of government programmes, cabinet and its committees, ministerial budgetary negotiations with the treasury, and so on. This is not to say that the processes we use to co-ordinate policies are immune from evaluation, or that they should be evaluated according to something other than their success in soundly co-ordinating sound policies. It is merely to say that the expression 'soundly co-ordinating sound policies' should not be interpreted to mean that we have just one overarching policy goal to which all the sound policies must be understood to be contributing, and in terms of which sound policy evaluation must (therefore?) always be conducted. If one reads it that way, it is not surprising that one is driven to place the courts outside the whole business of policy evaluation and hence to deprecate judicial resort to policy arguments. Not surprising, but still a mistake.

5. Legal instrumentalism

I have concentrated here, perhaps *ad nauseam*, on one way in which the courts cannot responsibly avoid counting the consequences of their decisions. They cannot responsibly avoid counting the consequences of their decisions, or at least some of the consequences of their decisions, for the decisions of future courts. When they count those consequences, I have suggested, they should do so in the currency of justice, more specifically the currency of justice done according to law. I have described the doing of justice according to law as a 'freestanding' policy goal, not to be subsumed into the pursuit of maximal welfare or any other supposed master-currency for evaluating policy.

You may take this to mean that, in my view, the doing of justice is intrinsically, rather than instrumentally, valuable. But that does not follow. And it is not true. As my other writings on private law amply bear out, I tend to think that norms of justice are mainly justified by the good consequences of having them and using them.[40] Here 'using them' means using them in a freestanding way. Hence my parenthetical quizzical 'therefore?' towards the end of the previous section. From the fact that norms

[40] For the most recent statement, see my *From Personal Life to Private Law*, above note 17, especially ch 6.

of justice are justified by the good consequences of having them and using them it does not follow that, in one's reasoning, one can freely replace the norms with the good consequences of having them and using them. In fact, precisely the opposite follows. If there are good consequences of having and using a certain norm, then, by not having or not using the norm, *ceteris paribus* one sacrifices those good consequences. That is how doing justice according to law can qualify as a freestanding policy goal even if there is no intrinsic value at all in justice being done. We'd better be seeking conformity with the norm, not seeking the good consequences of having it and using it, or else we'll miss the good consequences of having it and using it.

Does this make me what is sometimes known as a 'legal instrumentalist'? For the reasons laid out in section 3, not in the following sense, which is Weinrib's strictest sense:

> Instrumentalist theories view private law as a means of forwarding the community's aggregate welfare through a strategy of maximization often expressed in economic terms.[41]

How about in the following looser sense, also owed to Weinrib?

> An instrumentalist account understands private law as a means to something else.[42]

I am happy to be associated with legal instrumentalism in this looser sense, on the understanding that the 'something else' need not be 'the community's aggregate welfare' or anything similarly monopolistic. In fact, in that looser sense, I would like to sign up for recognition as a *triple* legal instrumentalist. That is because I endorse the following three loosely instrumentalist theses:

Legal instrumentalism 1: The decision of a court is (for the most part) justified by the good consequences of that decision for the doing of justice according to law (which includes but is not limited to the doing of justice in the case being decided).

Legal instrumentalism 2: Norms of justice (including those to which a court conforms in the doing of justice under *Legal*

[41] Weinrib, *The Idea of Private Law*, above note 20, 48.

[42] Ibid, 49.

instrumentalism 1) are (for the most part) justified by the good consequences of having them and using them.

Legal instrumentalism 3: A court should (for the most part) be pursuing the good consequences mentioned in *Legal instrumentalism 1* in the course of making its decision.

Yet none of this even slightly tempts me, and indeed nothing could induce me, to endorse the following thesis:

Legal instrumentalism 4: The courts should (for the most part) be pursuing the good consequences mentioned in *Legal instrumentalism 2* in the course of making their decisions, or at any rate they might as well do so for all the difference it makes.

Once we have the irrelevant distractions of welfarism cleared away, a sensible criticism of resort to policy arguments in judicial decisions is one that limits itself to rejecting *Legal instrumentalism 4*, and rejecting it on the ground that trying to look behind the doing of justice really can make a difference for the worse. That is the sensible criticism mounted by Lord Scarman and Neil MacCormick. Rejecting *Legal instrumentalism 1, 2*, and *3* into the bargain is overkill. It is overkill even if one thinks that justice according to law is always justice *inter partes* or (in Weinrib's favoured term) 'bipolar' justice.[43] For *Legal instrumentalism 1, 2*, and *3* can clearly accommodate such 'bipolarity' without difficulty. Just add '*inter partes*' after 'justice' in my formulation of *Legal Instrumentalism 1* and everything still flows.

Even Dworkin, often bewitched by his own principle–policy distinction, did not go as far as to abandon *Legal instrumentalism 1, 2*, and *3*. Remember what I billed as his second surprise? He had no objection to the idea that arguments of policy may figure in the case for or against norms of justice. They may be used to settle which injustices are justly tackled by the law. That is all that it takes to open the way to *Legal instrumentalism 2*. But it is still a very long way from there to *Legal instrumentalism 4*.

Dworkin's second surprise was one thing that I promised to come back to. Here is the other thing that I promised to come back to: the idea that justice is beyond price. Taken as a demand

[43] Ibid, 76.

for limitless funding for the judicial system, the idea is fantastical. Every pound or dollar assigned to the courts is a pound or dollar not assigned to healthcare, transport, housing, policing, etc. Even without the ideologically driven 'austerity capitalism' of the last decade, there will always be competition for resources, including for public funds. The Minister of Justice is there to fight for the judicial system in the competition. We may well decry the pathetic budgetary settlements achieved by Ministers of Justice in many countries in recent decades, leading to crumbling court buildings, demoralized judges, and many people without adequate legal representation. We may well protest at the false economies that brought us to this sorry state. But we do our protests no favours by claiming that the judicial system does not raise any question of cost. What we can reasonably say is that the *judges themselves* need to be insulated so far as possible from questions about the cost of their own judicial work, and about the cost of the work of lawyers, litigants, administrators, and others that is necessary for the performance of their work. For the overriding duty of the judges is to do justice according to law. In their own work, they often need to be able to proceed *as if* such justice were beyond price. Even though they all know that the truth is otherwise, it is best for them not to be distracted by that truth while working on the doing of justice.

That is the main point at which *Legal instrumentalism 3* shows its mettle. That the doing of justice according to law owes much of its value to its further consequences does not show, and does not even tend to suggest, that those who actually do justice according to law should be attending to those further consequences in the way proposed by *Legal instrumentalism 4*. It is quite enough work already for them to attend to the consequences of what they do for the doing of justice according to law. The wider value of that work is not best quantified and defended by those who are doing that work while they are doing it. There need to be others, such as Ministers of Justice working with specialist civil servants, as well as retired judges and other lawyers in the legislature, active professional associations, well-qualified legal scholars and researchers, campaigning groups, and so forth, who take that work off the shoulders of the judges in court. We might think that the judges themselves, in extrajudicial activities, could be added to the list. Yet that addition is fraught with danger. Conspicuous extrajudicial campaigning and politicking threatens to undermine the judges in their judicial work, both by distorting the way in which they look upon the cases that come before them and by undermining their reputation as dispassionate administrators of justice

In the political hurly-burly, the judges cannot do much to defend themselves. That helps to explain why the judicial system has become so severely under-resourced in many countries. It behoves the rest of us to expose and resist what, for the most part, the judges themselves must daily grin and bear. Most conspicuously, it behoves the government and the legislature to compensate, ideally at the level of constitutional practice, for the relative powerlessness of the judges in speaking up for the importance of their own work. If I may end with a parochial dig, we need there to be something like a Lord Chancellor with gravitas, clout, independence-of-mind, extensive legal expertise, and established commitment to the rule of law. We do not need there to be a *mere* Minister of Justice, some here-today, gone-tomorrow party-political hack who might equally have been Minister of Anything or Minister of Nothing.

11

BREACH OF CONTRACT AS A SPECIAL CASE OF TORT

1. What is the law of torts?

Here is a way of distinguishing the law of torts from other parts of the law, the same one that I set out in chapter 1. On this account the law of torts is a law of

(a) civil recourse
(b) for wrongs
(c) in which primarily corrective justice is attempted
(d) in a primarily reparative mode
(e) in response to claims for unliquidated sums
(f) where the duties breached are non-contractual.

Since chapter 1 was many pages ago, allow me now to repeat and augment some explanation of each of these criteria.

Criterion (a) serves to distinguish the law of torts from criminal law and public law. It means: the plaintiff has the legal power (on the filing of paperwork and typically the payment of a court fee or issue fee) to initiate and terminate court proceedings against any defendant of his or her choosing, without needing the permission of the court or of any other official to do so, and without needing to show good grounds for doing so. If a want of good grounds is to put an end to the proceedings, that must await an application by the defendant to the court to strike out the plaintiff's claim. If there is no such application, the plaintiff can insist on a full trial, and if the defendant still does not mount a good defence, even a groundless claim must succeed. The court's 'public' legal powers regarding the conduct of the proceedings are in these ways and some others subject to the litigants' exercise of their 'private' legal powers. There may of course be occasional curtailments of those private legal powers, for example, for a plaintiff with a record of vexatious litigation, or one who is held to be abusing the judicial

Torts and Other Wrongs. John Gardner, Oxford University Press (2019). © John Gardner
DOI: 10.1093/oso/9780198852940.003.0011

process by their conduct of the proceedings. But these tend to be narrow exceptions. In some legal systems the court may augment them with financial disincentives to plaintiff procrastination, for example, by landing the plaintiff with some of the defendant's extra legal costs.

This 'civil recourse' criterion,[1] criterion (a), might reasonably be used to differentiate 'private law' from the rest of the law. Within private law so differentiated, criterion (b) keeps the law of torts apart from the law of unjust enrichment and some parts of the law of trustee liability. In these parts of the law the basis of the plaintiff's claim is not wrongdoing but absence of right. When A receives property belonging to B by C's mistake, or receives C's property on trust for B's benefit, A has limited rights in respect of the property. But as Hohfeld taught us, it is not automatically the case that A is in breach of duty (i.e. commits a wrong) whenever he lacks a right.[2] There may have been nothing to alert A to the fact that C paid money into A's bank account, and A may, as yet, have done nothing with the money. So far, the money is just sitting there. Private law sometimes grants B or C a remedy against A in such a case, never mind that A has not so far done anything with the money, let alone done anything wrong, even in the eyes of the law. However A commits a tort only when his receipt from C turns into conversion (by his assuming control of the property received) or detinue (by his keeping the property received in the face of a demand for its return). In the law of torts, wrongdoing is of the essence; even actions that would not naturally be thought of as wrongful must be *cast as* or *treated as* wrongful to fit into the law of torts. Often, to be sure, there has already been detinue in an unjust enrichment lawsuit: A has wrongfully refused to return a mistaken payment to B or C when asked. The point is that in an unjust enrichment claim, unlike a tort claim, the wrongful refusal is irrelevant to the availability of the remedy.

[1] So named by John Goldberg and Ben Zipursky, writing together and apart. See notably Ben Zipursky, 'Civil Recourse, Not Corrective Justice', *Georgetown Law Journal* 91 (2003), 695.

[2] W N Hohfeld, 'Fundamental Legal Conceptions as Applied in Judicial Reasoning', *Yale Law Journal* 23 (1913), 30ff.

Criterion (c) creates a contrast between the law of torts and a conceivable branch of law—something like the early Roman law of delict, perhaps—in which there is a primarily retributive aim to civil recourse. Corrective justice means justice in the undoing, so far as possible, of some transaction that has already taken place. Retribution, although a reaction to a transaction that has already taken place, goes beyond the undoing of it. It lumbers the wrongdoer with extra deprivation or suffering beyond what is necessary to unravel the transaction. It is true that in some contemporary jurisdictions the law of torts licenses retribution in the form of an award of punitive damages. Such an award is, however, supplementary to an ordinary corrective award. First the court tries to put things back, so far as it can be done, into the order they would have been in had the tortious wrong not been committed. Only then does it ask whether some punitive award is also called for. As criterion (c) says, the law of torts *primarily* attempts corrective justice. It need not stop there.

Criterion (d) keeps the law of torts distinct from the law of equitable wrongs. Repair is the response to wrongdoing that has primacy at common law. It is the only remedy that one has a right to. The rest is in the discretion of the court. In equity one has no right to repair—in equity every remedy is discretionary—and moreover repair is not equity's first choice. Equity's first choice is disgorgement of profits. Disgorgement of profits is corrective, hence satisfying criterion (c). But it is not reparative because the aim is to eliminate the defendant's gains, not the plaintiff's losses, and the two need not match. I may profit from wrongful exploitation of your confidential information in a way in which you yourself would never have profited had I respected your confidences. *Ceteris paribus* my gains then exceed your losses. Equity, the enemy of undeserved rewards for wrongdoers, characteristically transfers my ill-gotten gains to you. True, the law of torts may occasionally do the same, but repair of losses nevertheless remains tort law's characteristic remedial response. As criterion (d) says, the mode of correction in tort law is *primarily* (but need not be exclusively) reparative.

Criterion (e) is needed to distinguish between the original proceedings to obtain an award of damages against the tortfeasor and subsequent proceedings for enforcement of the award as a judgment debt. More generally, criterion (e) means that proceedings for debt recovery are not tort proceedings. In tort proceedings, how much money is to be paid by the defendant to the plaintiff to cover the plaintiff's losses is one of the issues up for determination by the court. In an action for debt the amount owed may of course be disputed by the parties but the court does not ask what sum would cover the plaintiff's losses. It looks for a sum that has been determined prior to the proceedings by some other authoritative intervention, for example, by a judgment in prior proceedings or by a contract that fixes a price. Such a sum is known in private law as a 'liquidated' sum. Tort claims are, by contrast, claims for 'unliquidated' sums.

This brings us finally to criterion (f). Criterion (f) serves as a placeholder for some explanation of why breach of contract is not a tort even though it meets all of the other criteria, (a) to (e). Seeking such an explanation is the principal task of this essay.

2. Is a further criterion needed?

Although I have now done some work to elaborate criteria (a) to (e), you may say that I have not done nearly enough. Leaving many stones unturned, I have so far failed to show the need for criterion (f). The law of breach of contract, you may object, is already distinguishable from the law of torts by reference to one or more of the other five listed criteria, once they are more fully explained and understood. Accordingly, there is no need for an extra criterion (f) to distinguish breach of contract.

Some think that the law of breach of contract parts company with the law of torts as far back as criterion (b). Breach of contract is not wrongful. It is not a breach of duty. This view is often associated with Holmes, who famously wrote: 'The duty to keep a contract at common law means a prediction that you must pay damages if you do not keep it—and nothing else.'[3] There are numerous puzzles about this pronouncement. One of the most interesting concerns the meaning of 'must pay damages'. Is this too merely a prediction? Or is it, as it sounds, a formulation of

[3] O W Holmes, 'The Path of the Law', *Harvard Law Review* 10 (1897), 457 at 462.

a norm according to which the payment of damages is (or may lawfully be) required under certain conditions? Holmes tends to stick with the latter view; he does not go so far as to deny that 'consequences [are] attached to the act by law'. If he is right about this, the contract does create a duty. It is just that the duty is more complex than it may seem from the way in which the contract formulates it. At first sight, it may seem that I have a contractual duty to deliver the widgets to you on Tuesday. But on the Holmesian view of the law, it turns out that instead I have a contractual duty *to pay you damages if I do not deliver the widgets to you on Tuesday*, or perhaps (a different matter) a contractual duty *either to deliver the widgets to you on Tuesday or to pay you damages*.[4]

The effect of such Holmesian reinterpretations is not to undermine the idea that there is a legal duty to keep (perform) a contract. Rather, the effect is to alter what counts as performance of a contract in the eyes of the law. In the eyes of the law, on the Holmesian view, an implied term of every contract is that one may perform it by paying damages. There is very little in the common law of contract that supports this view, and much that tells against it. Be that as it may, however, the view helpfully disposes of the idea that breach of contract is not a breach of duty. Breach of contract is a breach of duty—thus wrongful in the eyes of the law—but, interpreted according to law, the contract is only breached when damages go unpaid.

A sophisticated development of the Holmesian view says that, while breaches of contract may often be wrongful, often they are not wrongful, because they are justified. Thus, even when a breach of contract is wrongful, it need not be wrongful in order to qualify as a breach of contract. Its wrongfulness is beside the point. This is often known as the 'efficient breach fallacy', because it is usually advanced by economistic types who suppose

[4] The second interpretation is suggested by Holmes' claim (ibid) to enjoy Lord Coke's support in advancing the first interpretation. Holmes says that, in *Bromage v Genning* (1616) 1 Rolle 368, Coke interpreted what was ostensibly a contract to grant a lease as a contract 'at [the landlord's] election either to lose the damages or to make the lease'. I do not read Coke as advancing any such interpretation of the contract, but be that as it may the interpretation is quite different from an interpretation according to which the landlord's only contractual duty is to pay damages if he doesn't grant the lease. Holmes does not seem to notice the difference.

that all and only efficient actions are justified (and what is more that economic efficiency is the only efficiency that counts).[5] Whatever we may think about the importance of efficiency, let alone economic efficiency, we may agree that breaches of contract are sometimes justified. The question is why that is supposed to count against the claim that breaches of contract are necessarily breaches of duty. Justified breach of duty is no oxymoron. It is indeed an everyday experience. Stopping to assist at the scene of a traffic accident, let's suppose, I missed my chance to visit you in hospital as I promised that I would. Even though I did the right thing overall, I still breached my duty to you. I still wronged you. While I was assisting at the scene of the accident, I should have had some compunction. What about my duty to you? In virtue of the breached duty, I now owe you an apology and a substitute visit today (unless the duty is retrospectively waived by you as the person to whom it is owed). The justification does not obliterate the duty nor therefore the wrongfulness in its breach.

Even if you warm to the Holmesian view and/or its working out in the efficient breach hypothesis, notice that it is hard to explain why either should be specific to the law of contract. Naturally enough, indeed, Holmes extends his reinterpretation to the law of torts: 'If you commit a tort, you are liable to pay a compensatory sum.'[6] That is the totality of your legal position as a tortfeasor, he thinks; no breach of duty, nothing literally 'tortious', need have been involved. And as for efficient breach, torts, like breaches of contract, may well be justified. That is the situation in *Vincent* v *Lake Erie Transportation Co*,[7] in which a ship's captain lashed his ship to V's jetty without V's permission, in order to save the ship and crew from a rising storm. Justified, says the court, but still an actionable trespass. Some are inclined to reanalyse the case as an unjust enrichment case, in which there is no trespass, and more generally no wrong, but simply a duty to

[5] Borrowing the title of Daniel Friedmann's excellent article, 'The Efficient Breach Fallacy', *The Journal of Legal Studies* 18 (1989), 1.

[6] Holmes, 'The Path of the Law', above note 3, 462.

[7] 124 NW 221 (1910).

pay for the use of the jetty.[8] That reanalysis shows the power that criterion (b) has among lawyers as one of the criteria for differentiating the law of torts. But like the efficient breach hypothesis, it trades on a misconception: it trades on the false assumption that if an action is justified, i.e. the right thing to do in the round, then it cannot be in breach of duty, i.e. wrongful. With that false assumption eliminated, we can see that criterion (b) differentiates the law of breach of contract and the law of torts *together* from (*inter alia*) the law of unjust enrichment. Or, if it fails to do so, it fails in a way which does not differentiate the law of torts from that of breaches of contract.

How about criterion (c)? Is the law of breach of contract primarily corrective? Leaving aside the question of what counts as performance (see above), you may say that the law of breach of contract is oriented towards obtaining performance no less than towards correcting non-performance. An award of damages may be corrective, but an order for specific performance surely is not, for if it is carried out the contract is performed and nothing needs to be corrected. This claim, however, confuses an order for specific performance that is made in anticipation of a breach (i.e. before the time for performance falls due) and an order for specific performance that is made as a remedy for breach (i.e. once the contract has already gone partly unperformed). If the contract has already gone partly unperformed, it is analytically too late for perfect or complete performance. The widgets were due on Tuesday but they did not show up. At this point an order for specific performance can only be an order to substitute a different performance for the one that *ex hypothesi* did not take place. Here, as with an award of damages, corrective justice is the aim of awarding specific performance.

Should we anyway be conceding that, in the law of breach of contract, there is an orientation towards performance that is not shared with the law of torts? No. Contracts are to be performed, no doubt. But torts are equally to be avoided. In the eyes of the law it is better not to commit a tort than to repair a tort, just as

[8] For excellent discussion see George C Christie, 'The Unwarranted Conclusions Drawn From *Vincent* v *Lake Erie Transportation Co*. Concerning the Defense of Necessity', *Issues in Legal Scholarship* 5 (2006), 1.

in the eyes of the law it is better to perform a contract than to repair a breach. On both sides, doing one's ('primary') duty in the first place is what the law would rather see. A common response is that, if this is so, orders for specific performance ought to be the law's first remedial choice.[9] That does not follow. There are many collateral objections (difficulty of supervision, challenges in securing interparty co-operation, etc.) to offering the order for specific performance as a default remedy, or a remedy as of right, in the law of contract, mirroring the many collateral objections to using injunctions as a default remedy, or a remedy as of right, in tort law. That the law prefers performance does not even tend to suggest that the law should routinely be *ordering* it in preference to the payment of damages (relatively easy to supervise, not much interparty co-operation needed, etc.)

This brings us to criterion (d) as a possible way of differentiating the law of breach of contract. In the law of torts, I claim, damages are reparative. No doubt that word could be used for contractual damages too. But doesn't that usage gloss over some very fundamental differences between the two? In contract we default to an 'expectation' measure of damages (putting P in the position that she ought by now to be in, according to the contract) whereas the tort measure is more like a 'reliance' measure (rolling things back to where they were before)? I am not sure that this characterization of the tort measure is in any way helpful.[10] But be that as it may what the two measures have in common is far more important than what divides them. In both branches of the law the aim of damages awards is to put P, so far as money can do it, in the same position as she would have been in had D's primary obligation been performed. Superficial differences in measurement should not distract us from the fact that this is reparation; it is at least (and I would also add: can be at most[11]) partial repair of the wrong.

[9] For the most thorough treatment of remedial priority, see Dori Kimel, *From Promise to Contract: Towards a Liberal Theory of Contract* (Oxford 2003), ch 4.

[10] Michael B Kelly, 'The Phantom Reliance Interest in Tort Damages', *San Diego Law Review* 38 (2001), 169.

[11] A theme of my book *From Personal Life to Private Law* (Oxford 2018), ch 4.

What of criterion (e), the unliquidated character of tort damages? Surely most, or at least many, breach of contract actions are for liquidated sums? That may be so, because the parties to contracts have scope to set figures for liquidated damages in their contracts in advance, thereby potentially turning their contractual causes of action into actions for debt. Notice, however, that this is a parasitic practice. It presupposes that the basic breach of contract action is an action for unliquidated damages. The parties simply make a pre-emptive liquidation at the point of contracting, to save trouble and expense later. There is a good deal of law regulating the ways and the extent to which this may be done, for example by contrasting the contractual provision for payment of liquidated sums with penalty clauses.[12] All of this law is set against the background that the law of damages for breach of contract meets criterion (e).

3. Filling out criterion (f)

So criterion (f) is surely needed, and our attention turns to giving it some content. At first sight it requires a positive characterization of contract in order to finish explaining what a tort is. But as I said it is a placeholder, so appearances may be deceptive. In spite of how it is formulated, condition (f) leaves open how the underlying contrast should be framed.

The classic suggestion is that contractual obligations, unlike obligations in the law of torts, are voluntary obligations. They are not imposed by law but undertaken by the parties to them, and given legal recognition. This is not a feature unique to contractual obligations. Obligations of confidence, for example, are also voluntary obligations. But these were sidelined already at criterion (d). They are neither obligations in tort nor in contract.

The classic suggestions meet with equally classic objections. Stated at their most general, the classic objections are these:

(1) Not all contractual obligations recognized by law are voluntary. Consider terms implied into contracts by law, sometimes

[12] For a recent development of the contrast in the law of England and Wales see *Cavendish Square Holding BV* v *Talal El Makdessi (El Makdessi)* [2015] UKSC 67.

inexcludably, never mind what the parties take themselves to be volunteering for. Or consider the law's 'objective' interpretation of some contractual terms, which land the parties with legally imposed contractual obligations often quite different from those that they volunteered to undertake.

(2) Conversely, not all tort-law obligations are not voluntary. Consider, for example, the tort of negligent misstatement derived from *Hedley Byrne* v *Heller*,[13] in which one has the option of not acquiring any obligation in the law of torts, simply by making no representations. Or consider the availability of disclaimers in the law of torts: very often one has the option of ruling out obligations that would otherwise be recognized by law. Does the optionality of such obligations not suffice to make them voluntary obligations in the contract-law sense?

Here is a simple response to objection (1). The classic suggestion is not that each term of a contract is a voluntary undertaking. The suggestion is that contracting is a way of voluntarily undertaking obligations, and that none of the (non-voluntary) obligations that one acquires when contracting are acquired except as the corollaries of some voluntary obligations that one acquires when contracting. Thus: no terms implied in law without other terms that are *not* implied in law; no objective interpretation except by one's voluntary subjection to that interpretation in virtue of the fact that one contracted; no contractual obligations at all without a contract.

Here, meanwhile, is a persuasive response to objection (2), a response first laid out by Joseph Raz.[14] 'Voluntary obligations' are obligations that one has because one undertook them, where the 'because' points to reasons in favour of one's having the obligation. These could be called 'affirmative reasons'. The class of voluntary obligations then excludes obligations where the only importance of the fact that one volunteered is negative, i.e. it only serves to meet an objection to the imposition of the liability. True, the

[13] [1964] AC 465.

[14] Joseph Raz, 'Promises in Morality and Law', *Harvard Law Review* 95 (1982), 916.

Hedley Byrne doctrine requires that one volunteered one's representation to the representee, but only to serve a negative role in the argument, i.e. to meet the independent rule-of-law objection that one should not incur liabilities in the law without having had an opportunity to avoid doing so. That one volunteered the representation does not point to any affirmative reason for the incurring of the liability.

These replies suffice to show that the classic way of contrasting contract-law obligations and tort-law obligations can survive important boundary skirmishes. That is not because the replies resolve all possible boundary skirmishes. There are never-ending borderline cases of everything and it is not the task of philosophy to resolve them all. Lawyers themselves have the job of resolving them, by proposing more or less arbitrary classificatory rules. I say 'more or less' here because it is reasonable to expect philosophers to be able to cast some light on the classificatory rules by showing that they are reasonably robust under pressure. What we should worry about are only distinctions that break down too rapidly. The classic distinction between voluntary and non-voluntary obligations does not.

4. Tort before contract

One may conclude: a voluntary obligation is a special case of an obligation. There are vanilla obligations and then there are voluntary ones. Tort-law obligations form the general class and contract-law obligations are a special class carved out of it. Breach of contract is then a special case of tort.

Notice that this is not merely a logical priority. It is a justificatory one too. There is something odd about being able to add to one's obligations (as well as subtract from them) by voluntary means. Why do one's obligations not answer comprehensively to reasons? To put it in other ways: Why would we have any other than the obligations that we ought to have, never mind what obligations we might wish we had? How are we able to break loose from reason by will, or supplement reason with will? There are many ideas in circulation. All of these ideas concede the primacy of reason and hence the oddity of voluntary obligation conceived as a supplement or departure from it. How is all this possible? The answer must surely take us to yet further reasons. There are reasons why we should—in addition to having the obligations that reasons would anyway give us—have the ability to create further obligations for ourselves. And yes: there is something to be said for our having the ability to add to our obligations, shaping our normative arrangements with others, forging commitments, developing relationships, sometimes even being able to dispense with now redundant obligations carried forward from an earlier time in our lives, or departing from default obligations that we would otherwise owe. There is room here for fully voluntary obligation, acquired by contract, promise, vow, or oath, as well as imposed by others thanks to our own consent. There is also room for obligation avoided by limitation or disclaimer. Nor should we forget the semi-voluntary acquisition of obligation, as in the case of friendship: no single act of the acquirer, or of another, constitutes the exercise of a normative power that changes the obligation of the acquirer. What makes it all possible is the desirability—a rational case—for our being able to change obligations by opting to do so. Even though particular obligations we acquire like this may be, so to speak, suboptimal in their own rights (perhaps, indeed, they must be so?), there is no such suboptimality in the system taken as a whole.

If all this be true, then justificatorily as well as logically, tort law obligations belong to the basic class. Contractual obligations can only be understood in contrast with them, as special cases.

5. An objection

Tort law obligations, it may be objected, are not really vanilla obligations. They are legally created obligations. Legally created obligations are a special class of obligations. Obligations in contracts are not legally created, so they are the general class. They are legally recognized once created by the parties.

A reply: True, contractual obligations are not legally created. They are only legally recognized, i.e. according to the law they would exist apart from the law and the law only tries to give legal effect to them. The law may of course give them a curious legal interpretation in the process, thereby crossing the line from legal recognition to legal creation. Then on top of that the law adds a few extras, 'implied by law'. Nevertheless it is true that the base type of contractual obligations are legally recognized obligations, not legally created ones.

Yet this is true equally of the law of torts. According to the law, many tort-law obligations would exist apart from the law and the law only tries to give effect to them. The law may of course give them a curious legal interpretation in the process, thereby crossing the line from legal recognition to legal creation. Then on top of that the law adds a few extras, 'implied by law'. Nevertheless it is true that the base type of tort-law obligations are legally recognized obligations, not legally created ones.

Thus our suggestion survives. The law of torts and the law of contract are alike in containing obligations that are legally created only on the back of an attempt at legal recognition of extra-legal obligations. Call this the class of legally shaped obligations. Within this class, tort law obligations are of the vanilla type. Contract-law obligations are of the special voluntary type.

6. The inverted economistic view

Economists interested in private law have often treated the law of contract as primary, and the law of torts as derivative. Tort rules simulate contractual terms where high transaction costs lead to a failure to contract. Such failure is also described as 'market failure'. The simulation of contract by tort is inevitably far from perfect. Tort strives artificially (and very fallibly) for a Pareto-optimality that comes naturally, so it is claimed, to contract.

Pareto-optimality is a property of allocations.[15] Allocations are Pareto-optimal when nobody's allocation can be improved without thereby worsening the allocation of another. Contractual allocations are taken to be naturally Pareto-optimal because, if only transaction costs were low enough, everyone would naturally make contracts to avoid a worsening of their own allocation. They would reallocate what they have to another only in return for receiving something that they value more, thereby securing a Pareto-improvement. Thanks to transaction costs, however, not everyone

[15] An excellent conspectus with a private law focus: Jules Coleman, 'Efficiency, Utility, and Wealth Maximization', *Hofstra Law Review* 8 (1980), 509.

gets to do this. Some end up involuntarily bearing the 'externalities' of the contracting activities of others. The law of torts exists to price such externalities so as to approximately reproduce the allocative effect of the contracts that those burdened with externalities would make, were it not for the cost of their contracting.

Although much simplified, this is the core case for the primacy of the law of contract over the law of torts, according to economists of private law. The best way to think of the law of contract is to think of it as augmenting, or supplementing, the law of torts. This does not entail that the best way to justify the law of contract is to justify it as an augmentation or supplementation of the law of torts. Possibly, as the economists think, the order of justification is the other way round. Allow me to end, however, by casting some indirect doubt on this economistic view by exposing some misconceptions that may sometimes help to contribute to its appeal.

Here are two misconceptions that may sometimes help to contribute to its appeal:

i. The law of contract is the rulebook, or one rulebook, of the marketplace. Failure to contract is 'market failure'. But why? Why is the availability of contract, institutionalized in the law of contract, not itself a market commodity? It is not clear why contract should be featherbedded by public support through law. Surely the law of contract is itself just one possible (non-market) solution to market failure?[16]

ii. Economists since Adam Smith have been more than happy to ride two ideological horses at once, one utilitarian and the other libertarian.[17] In contract law the two can be made to meet by presenting an unfettered freedom to contract as a recipe for utility-maximization. But are economists entitled to ride a libertarian horse if they see nothing in freedom but its utility?

[16] For further reflections see my polemic 'The Twilight of Legality', *Australasian Journal of Legal Philosophy* 43 (2018), 1.

[17] Coleman, 'Efficiency, Utility, and Wealth Maximization', above note 15, at 526.

NAME INDEX

SUBJECT INDEX